Landscapes, Rock-Art and the Dreaming

New Approaches to Anthropological Archaeology

Editor-in-Chief

Thomas E. Levy, Department of Anthropology, University of California, San Diego

Associate Editors

Guillermo Algaze, Department of Anthropology, University of California, San Diego
Paul S. Goldstein, Department of Anthropology, University of California, San Diego
Augustin F. C. Holl, Department of Anthropology, University of Michigan, Ann Arbor
Joyce Marcus, Department of Anthropology, University of Michigan, Ann Arbor

Anthropological Archaeology offers a methodologically refreshing approach to the study of cultural evolution. It recognizes the fundamental role that anthropology now plays in archaeology and also integrates the strengths of various research paradigms which characterize archaeology on the world scene today, including new or processual, post-processual, evolutionist, cognitive, symbolic, marxist and historical archaeologies. It does so by taking into account the cultural and, when possible, historical context of the material remains being studied. This involves the development of models concerning the formative role of cognition, symbolism, and ideology in human societies to explain the more material and economic dimensions of human culture that are the natural purview of archaeological data. It also involves an understanding of the cultural ecology of the societies being studied, and of the limitations and opportunities that the environment imposes on the evolution or devolution of human societies. Based on the assumption that cultures never develop in isolation, Anthropological Archaeology takes a regional approach to tackling fundamental issues concerning past cultural evolution anywhere in the world.

This new series welcomes proposals from 'intellectual foragers' whose interests combine field research with theoretical studies of issues of cultural evolution in the past and in the ethno-archaeological present. The series differs from much theoretical discourse in archaeology today in that it is dedicated to publishing work firmly grounded in archaeological fact, while also venturing to explore more speculative ideas about how cultures evolve and change.

Published titles in the series:

West Africa and the Atlantic Slave Trade: Archaeological Perspectives, edited by Christopher R. DeCorse

Early Urbanizations in the Levant: A Regional Narrative, Raphael Greenberg

Egypt and the Levant: Interrelations from the 4th through the Early 3rd Millennium B.C.E., edited by Edwin C. M. van den Brink and Thomas E. Levy

Forthcoming titles in the series:

Archaeology, Anthropology and Cult: The Sanctuary at Gilat, Israel, edited by David Alon and Thomas E. Levy

Landscapes, Rock-Art and the Dreaming

AN ARCHAEOLOGY OF PREUNDERSTANDING

Bruno David

Leicester University Press
London and New York

Leicester University Press
A Continuum imprint
The Tower Building, 11 York Road, London, SE1 7NX
370 Lexington Avenue, New York, NY 10017-6503

First published 2002

British Library Cataloguing-in-Publication Data
A catalogue record for this book is available from the British Library.

ISBN 0-7185-0243-4 (hardback)

Library of Congress Cataloging-in-Publication Data
Bruno, David, 1962–
    Landscapes, rock-art, and the Dreaming: an archaeology of preunderstanding/Bruno David.
      p.cm. — (New approaches to anthropological archaeology)
    Includes bibliographical references (p.) and index.
    ISBN 0–7185–0243–4 (alk. paper)
    1. Australian Aborigines—Antiquities. 2. Dreamtime (Australian Aboriginal mythology).
    3. Australian Aborigines—Ethnic identity. 4. Australian Aborigines—Public opinion.
    5. Public opinion—Europe. 6. Australia—Antiquities. I. Title. II. Series.

    GN666.B788 2002
    305.89′915—dc21   2001038629

Typeset by CentraServe Ltd, Saffron Waldon, Essex
Printed and bound in Great Britain by Bookcraft

Contents

List of Figures

List of Tables

Preface

It is easy to forget the basic assumptions that have given rise to popular notions. Nowhere is this more obvious than when an erroneous idea has become common wisdom, when in a given frame of understanding the 'mythic' and the 'real' silently merge. But there comes a time when our assumptions – our prejudices – having become ingrained in popular ethos, reveal their inadequacies and contradictions, and the house of cards crumbles of its own emptiness. It is then that we realize the time has come to surrender certain preconceptions, and call for a revision of even our most cherished ideas. It is one such story that this book explores.

In the West, the ethnographically known Dreaming of Aboriginal Australia has come to symbolize Aboriginality. It presents itself in Western thought as ahistorical, and as constitutive of an ancient and timeless Aboriginality. What, we may ask, has brought about this set of assumptions? Is it indigenous thought itself, or have Aboriginal beliefs – what we normally think of as philosophy, religion, science when we apply it to our own intellectual arena – been re-interpreted through pre-existing Western world-views, already deeply coloured by notions of progress, by evolutionary and hierarchical notions of primitiveness and stasis? With such questions in mind, what does archaeology tell us about patterns of change and continuity in Aboriginal pre-History? Do the historical 'facts' confirm our preconceptions, or do they challenge them? And if the two do not meet, where have our preconceptions come from? These are some of the questions about Western constructions of Aboriginality addressed in this book.

In a sense the idea for this book arose from a dilemma. The Australian Aboriginal social and cultural worlds have been much written about by social anthropologists the world over, and yet Aboriginal Australia's ancient past has to date largely been written about as the history of *objects* – stone tools, middens, rockshelters, cave paintings – as outcomes of ecological strategies and environmental adaptations. That these objects have been engaged by people, not simply as 'subsistence economies' but as entangled in systems of meaning and symbolic relations, is a topic of enquiry rich in promise yet largely untapped. From an archaeological perspective, I wanted to explore this potential, to write an Aboriginal history that was not just alternative, for alternative implies something away from the centre, but an Aboriginal history with people, as sentient and sensual beings living in a meaningful, engaged and engaging world, at its heart. To do this, I decided to tackle the socialness of things, alterity, identity and being. Nevertheless, the history that I write is written through a Western sociological lens, and in this sense represents in the first instance a commitment to Western authorship in dialogue with Aboriginal world-views, rather than a commitment to the experience of Aboriginal being. This is very much an etic rather than emic thesis.

My original intention was to attempt such a project by discussing Aboriginal lifeways in relation to the writings of various established philosophers who had written about the socialness of things – Martin Heidegger, Jacques Derrida and Hans-Georg Gadamer, in particular – as a way of unfolding the social and experiential embeddedness of objects and the social and experiential embeddedness of how objects are written about. People, as subjects, are not detached from their worlds (and therefore from the objects of engagement). Nor are the authors who write about them. One way of getting to a social history could therefore be by accessing the history of worldly engagement, and by addressing the hermeneutic process. I wished to point out that in both of these senses, the archaeology of things is, by definition, an archaeology of the social, of subjectivity, and of the sensual as much as it is objective.

However, I was not entirely satisfied with this initial direction, for I also did not want the book to be merely an exposition of ideas of famous philosophers and the implications of their views for a social, hermeneutic or phenomenological archaeology. Nor is this book *about* theory, although theory is explicitly used to guide my approach; it is about the history of Aboriginal cultures and Aboriginal being, and about how the West has come to see Aboriginal history, from an archaeological perspective. It is also a commentary on archaeological practice. I wanted to present the Australian Aboriginal past in a new way, and to question some of our preconceptions about this past along the way. It was not the ideas of philosophers that I wished to focus upon, but the Aboriginal past, and how this past has come to be understood in Western thought. In this I have been much influenced by the writings of one of my favourite archaeological authors, Richard Bradley, who says what he has to say, tapping into the writings of various non-archaeological writers where it helps his own story. This is the path that I, too, follow in this book (albeit in a way different from Bradley's), using the philosophical writings that have influenced my own thinking as a backdrop rather than as the centre. This is the direction I have come to take.

I have followed a number of conventions in the following pages. For one, I talk of the non-written past as 'pre-History' rather than 'prehistory'. I do this as an attempt to avoid the evolutionary loadedness of the notion of prehistory common to much early archaeological and popular writings on the subject. I here aim to nuance a distinction between ancestral 'hunters and gatherers' of 'the stone age' from modern peoples who hunt, forage and fish and who use stone tools – to signal some explicit conceptual distance between ancestral pasts and living indigenous peoples, for I argue in this book that it is precisely such notions that are often blurred or even denied in our language and literature.

I also sometimes refer to radiocarbon dates and sometimes to calibrated ages. Wherever radiocarbon dates are presented, they are listed as 'years BP'; calibrated ages are presented as 'years ago'. By convention, I also refer to the Common Era (CE) and Before the Common Era (BCE) instead of AD and BC, in reference to 'people of all faiths who utilise the traditional Western calendar' (Ehrman 2000, p. 8).

Much of the data and some of the ideas presented in Chapter 3 have previously been presented in Meredith Wilson and my paper entitled 'Re-reading the landscape: place and identity in NE Australia during the late Holocene', published in 1999 in the *Cambridge Archaeological Journal* 9 (2): 163–88. I thank the McDonald Institute for Archaeological Research, Cambridge University, for permission to re-work some of this material. Similarly, some of the data on Cape York rock-art (Chapter 9) was originally presented in *Archaeology in Oceania* 34 (3): 103–20.

I would also like to thank Mike Smith for letting me use some of his unpublished material in Chapter 4, and Josephine Flood for permission to write about material that we collected together from 1988 to 1991 on Wardaman rock-art (Chapter 5).

Many of the chapters of the book were written following detailed archaeological and ethnographic research. I particularly thank the Djungan community and the Kuku Djungan Aboriginal Corporation in Mareeba for permission to write about their heritage. Special thanks to Sam Wason and his family, and to the Grainer, Richards and Archer families. Thanks to Cliff Grogan, Lester Rosendale and the Lee Cheu family concerning Kuku Yalanji rock-art. In Wardaman country, particular thanks to the Raymond family, Bill Harney Snr and the Wardaman Aboriginal Corporation.

In Chillagoe, thanks particularly to William Johnson and Daphne Brumby. Many thanks to the Central Land Council in Alice Springs and to the numerous people who gave advice on Chapter 4; every effort has been made to ensure that the content is sensitive to restrictions traditionally applied to cultural information. As advised, I have also omitted all reference to the location of cultural places from this chapter.

Thanks also to Mrs Wilson and her family at Palmerville Station for permission to undertake fieldwork, and to Lana Little at Chillagoe for assistance. Much of the work presented in this book was undertaken and supported with assistance from Earthwatch between 1995 and 1997. Thanks to Earthwatch and the Earthcorps for their help. This book was begun while a Visiting Fellow at the Museum of Archaeology and Anthropology, University of Cambridge, in 1998. Many thanks to Chris and Anne Chippindale and the Museum staff.

Many people have commented on various parts of this book. Thanks to Luddy Andersson, Bain Attwood, Rachel Bekessy, John Bradley, Athol Chase, Chris Clarkson, Jackie Collins, Linda Daley, Tim Denham, Nic Dolby, Peter Dwyer, Nick Evans, Tim Flannery, Simon Haberle, Peter Hiscock, Rachel Hughes, Jane Jacobs, Rochelle Johnston, Peter Kershaw, Marcia Langton, Stephen Legg, Ian Lilley, Harry Lourandos, Jane Lydon, Ian McNiven, David Mercer, John Morton, Mike Morwood, Tim Murray, Oona Nicolson, Kevin O'Connor, Mariastella Pulvirenti, Bert Roberts, Paul Rogers, Mike Smith, Phil Smith, Sander van der Kaars, Sam Wason, and Meredith Wilson. Aboriginal Affairs Victoria (thanks to Rochelle Johnston), John Grindrod, Ian McNiven, Mike Morwood, Museum Victoria (thanks to Mary Morris), Paul Taçon, Graeme Walsh, Fiona Walsh and Peter Veth supplied photographs; they are individually acknowledged in the appropriate figure captions, and I am grateful to each. Thanks also to David Bush for making me aware of the words that preface Chapter 10; their origins are unknown. I would particularly like to thank Kevin Hart, Walter F. Veit and Jimmy Weiner for checking closely and commenting on my understandings of Derrida, Gadamer and Heidegger, and Lynette Russell who read the entire manuscript and made valuable critical comments throughout. I also thank Tom Levy, the Series Editor, and two anonymous referees for making valuable comments on an earlier draft. For reasons outlined above – in particular my wish to emphasize the authorship of archaeological writings rather than focus on their authority as a source of positivist historical canon – I have not followed every suggestion, but the referees' original questions and suggestions have enabled me to focus more sharply on various critical points. I am particularly grateful to Tom Levy and Janet Joyce, Editorial Director at Continuum, Susan Dunsmore for copyediting, and Valerie Hall, Sandra Margolies and the production team at Continuum for their support during the course of this project.

Many thanks also to the Department of Geography and Environmental Science, Monash University, for a wonderful collegiate environment in which to undertake the research presented here. Thanks to Bianca Roggenbucke, Jean Newey, Shane Revell, Gary Swinton and Maureen Upston for their help, and to Gary Swinton for drafting the figures. Thank you also to Bill Harney Snr and the Wardaman Aboriginal Corporation for permission to reproduce the cover photograph.

Bruno David
August 2001
Melbourne

To Lynette and Ian, Dylan Yawa and Fin, Françoise Passard

Many general statements about the aborigines rest on a narrow basis of exiguous facts, sometimes on no factual basis at all. That is especially true of statements about their religious life. More intensive regional study cannot alone correct the misunderstandings.

W. E. H. Stanner

1 Introduction

[T]heirs is today the world's oldest continuous culture, with easily the world's oldest continuous religion.

(Chambers 1999, p. 11)

I heard it in the streets. 'The Dreamtime, the oldest religion in the world'. And I read it in the newspapers. New Age bookshops carry titles that appeal to those who seek answers to the mysteries of life – answers they hope they might find in the Dreamtime's ancientness. Titles like *Dreamkeepers*, and *Voices of the First Day: Awakening in the Aboriginal Dreamtime* abound on the bookshelves, invoking an archaic yet strangely familiar call of pre-modern passions in a complex, modern world. Friends are attracted by its ancestral appeal, lured to its unfathomable timelessness. It is primordial, it seems pre-existent, it hails from the deep past yet exists in a fully modern society. The Dreamtime or Dreaming of Aboriginal Australia is well known yet little understood in popular culture; we are all aware of it, in one way or another. It calls on us as Aboriginal religion, as Aboriginal world-view. It also calls on us as something that has always been there, the hallmark of Aboriginal being. The Dreamtime is not so much ancient as timeless. But these are sentiments unvoiced, and leave no trace that they are born of an opposition to things we know better from our own history books, things temporal and emergent. The Dreaming is there as a signature of Aboriginal belief, a timeless artefact of a once isolated people, who dwelt on the 'other' side of the world. But like all things cultural, the Dreaming must have a history; it must have arisen out of human practice some time in the past. And if the Dreaming, as Aboriginal worldviews of recent, ethnographic times emerged through the course of history, there surely were times in the past when Aboriginal people thought differently about the world. What are we to make then of these notions of timelessness with which we in Western thought popularly imbue the ethnographically known Dreaming? These are the stories explored in this book.

When the first European settlers arrived in Australia in 1788, they encountered a land vastly different from their northern homelands. Eighteen years earlier, upon reaching Australia's eastern shores, Lieutenant James Cook (1968, p. 322) had written in his journal that, 'we see this country in the pure state of nature; the Industry of Man has had nothing to do with any part of it, and yet we find all such things as nature hath bestow'd upon it in a flourishing state'. Perceived as geographically isolated and virtually untouched by the movement of time, the 'Natives of New Holland' were seen as part of this natural vista, 'the most wretched People upon Earth . . . They live in Tranquility which is not disturbed by the Inequality of Condition' (idid., p. 323). Here was the noble savage of the dawn of time.

Following these early contacts, a small number of key concepts have gradually come to define Australian Aboriginality in European thought. Such concepts have served to frame a Western imaginary of what constitutes 'legitimate' Aboriginal culture: technologically, spears, boomerangs and stone tools; economically, 'nomadic' hunting and gathering; musically, didgeridoos and clap sticks; ritually, corroborees and dances; and spiritually, the Dreaming. I am not writing here about how Aboriginal people have shaped their own identities, but how understandings of Aboriginality have been shaped in the popular Western imagination.[1,2] Such thematic constructions have served to create a notion of geographical homogeneity and temporal stasis, even though some 250 Aboriginal language groups were present at the time of European invasion (the term 'Aborigine' has itself produced an ethos of homogeneity; see Attwood 1989; Russell in press). Such concepts have also served to reduce notions of Aboriginality to a 'people without history' (cf. Wolf 1997), despite an Aboriginal presence spanning more than 40,000 years. To be a nineteenth-century English woman or man conjures a very different image from one of the Neolithic. But a nineteenth-century CE and fifth-millennium BP Aboriginal person need hardly be differentiated in popular thought, being reduced to an assemblage of timeless constitutive themes abstracted from a more or less timeless ethnography. To see Aboriginal society in such terms is to deny its historical character, its ability to change; it is to construct a view of what it means to be Aboriginal around a display of material and metaphysical artefacts instead of communities of people rich in cultural experience, salience and social dynamism. Such popular constructions of Aboriginality are based on a set of beliefs from mid-twentieth-century literature that gave us the term 'The Timeless Land', traceable directly to the same worldviews that earlier gave rise to Cook's sentiments of a people in a 'pure state of nature'. Aboriginal people, culture and cosmology have been associated, falsely, with concepts of timelessness, a way of being beyond time, a people who may have a past but who remain without a history.

There is an aspect of this colonial construction of Aboriginality that I wish to visit in this book by bringing into focus the historical character of one key component of what is popularly understood to define and symbolize Aboriginality: the Dreaming, as we have come to know it from ethnography. The apparent timelessness of the Dreaming has long mystified European observers, conjuring images of an ancient people in harmony with their surroundings. The ahistoricity of the Dreaming of recent times is implicit in much popular writing – 'fictional' and 'non-fictional' – on Aboriginal Australia, a theme I explore in some detail in Chapter 6. In its Western formulation, the Dreaming is loaded with preconceptions that position Aboriginal people in a particular social and evolutionary standing in the public imagination, at once shaping and denying Aboriginal personhood. Such constructions of the Dreaming shape Western concepts of Aboriginality by establishing for all time the character of indigenous ontology. But they also impoverish, in that they have come to replace human sentiment, diversity, experience and being in the making of an ontologically convenient and sanitized Aboriginality.

I question such formulations in the following pages by suggesting that when viewed through Western historical modes of thought the ethnographically known Dreaming beliefs are not timeless, and that by persisting with this trope of historical timelessness, the dominant colonial reading of Aboriginality has denied 'the world's oldest religion' (see Chapter 6) historical movement. Were this prevalent, static dogma to be correct, Aboriginal being would be frozen in a system of beliefs that is at once ancient and beyond time. In questioning this stance, I explore from an archaeological perspective the scientific evidence for the Dreaming's historical becoming. My main thesis is that to Aboriginal people the Dreaming is timeless; to Westerners the Dreaming is also timeless. But the temporalities that imbue and inform these two notions of timelessness are different, embedded in vastly dissimilar preconceptions. Western understandings of the purported timelessness of the Dreaming of ethnographic times say more about us as empowered colonial observers than they do about indigenous ontologies. Australian Aboriginality need not have always been steeped in ethnographically documented Dreaming world-views to be legitimate and existent; nor need it always be the case for the future (contra Davis and Prescott 1992). It is not a timeless Dreaming frozen in nineteenth- to twentieth-century ethnography that forever identifies indigenous Australians, but themselves as culturally and historically engaged people. The Dreaming as we have come to understand it, I will argue, is a late ontological snapshot of an Aboriginal history of great depth and movement.

Preunderstanding

In its concern with the archaeology of a specific set of belief systems, this book contains two interwoven threads. The first confronts the antiquity of the ethnographically known Dreamings of Aboriginal Australia, methodologically an exercise towards an 'archaeology of mind' and towards an archaelogy of 'being-in-the-world', much heralded as one of the most troublesome of archaeological tasks. I approach this assignment via philosopher Hans-Georg Gadamer's (e.g. 1975, 1988) concept of 'preunderstanding', earlier drawn from Martin Heidegger's (1962) notion of 'Vorgriff' in *Being and Time*.[3] Preunderstanding concerns the initial conceptual conditions through which people interpret their world. It concerns a world whose presence – whose pre-sense – is already known through the historicity of one's own being. All things appear to us through the system of meanings already at work in the cultural framework from which we approach the world. Our knowledge of new things therefore only ever occurs through our pre-existing world-views, through what we already 'know' and experience as the truth of the world. In the words of Brice Wachterhauser:

> [People] always have inherited a way of looking at things around them long before they begin to modify that way of looking and understanding. Our lives become defined by these preunderstandings; in this sense, we are our preunderstandings and we do not simply have them in the way we have a coat or a pair of shoes. (1986a, p. 22)

Michael Stanford (1998, p. 192) similarly notes that, 'when we meet something unfamiliar . . . our first instinctive reaction is to try to make sense of it. This is to fit it into the context of the familiar. In this sense, experience is always "knowledge of the known"' (Gadamer 1985, p. 181).

Like his friend and teacher Martin Heidegger (e.g. 1962), Gadamer thus argues that interpretation is over-determined by a pre-understanding that shapes the truth of the world; understanding is not an act but a pre-judicial process that moulds one's identity as a cognitive and world-wise being through one's preunderstanding.[4] Preunderstandings are the culturally conditioned conceptual frameworks that guide interpretations of things; in Aboriginal Australia of recent times, the regionally varied Dreaming world-views. An archaeology of preunderstanding thus opens a window not only onto the attribution of meaning in the past, but also onto human identity. It is the archaeology of this condition that guides this book. As an example I consider the ethnographically known Dreaming of Aboriginal Australia, and how to investigate its long-term history through the archaeological record.

But there is a second thread that shapes this book. If all new things are interpreted in the light of what is already known, then what does this say about Western understandings of non-Western cultural practices, such as the Dreaming? Any attempt to understand things foreign – other ways of being, the unexperienced past, or doubly problematic, the past of others – is always undertaken through the analyst's own, already domesticated mind, making it difficult to know whether conclusions reflect the gazed Other or past, or the gazing present. 'Understanding always implies a preunderstanding which is in turn prefigured by the determinate tradition in which the interpreter lives and that shapes his prejudices', writes Gadamer (1988, p. 86). Understanding history always implies a 'fusion of horizons', an interlacing of past and present. This is critical to our roles as archaeologists – as commentators on the past, our own as that of other cultures – for it identifies the archaeological project as being equally about the present as about the past.

Gadamer's preunderstanding, therefore, concerns the cultural framework through which we interpret the world *in the (already known) present*. It articulates the hermeneutic nature of all knowledge; all understanding is historically positioned, and understanding this historical positioning always takes place in the present. In that our present understanding of things is effected through an historically positioned preunderstanding, all knowledge hermeneutically fuses the past and the present.

Preunderstanding is thus more than 'world-view' although, like world-view, it also encompasses all the patterns of behaviour that are taken for granted as part of a 'normal' way of life. Preunderstanding does *not* mean a specific evolutionary stage that precedes rational thinking and explanation, nor does it refer to a 'mythic' past. It rather presents a person or people's world-views as a hermeneutic process. A focus on the archaeology of Aboriginal preunderstanding(s) is not the same as a focus on the archaeology of Aboriginal world-views, for it brings to the fore the need for self-reflectivity. Reflecting on Western constructions of the historicity of the ethnographically known Dreaming is thus the second theme of this book.

Therefore, although it may be correct to say that preunderstanding guides interpretation and shapes one's experience of the world, to trace the archaeological visibility of Aboriginal preunderstandings requires a consideration of my own interpretative framework. These two components cannot be so easily separated, as the latter suffuses and is a pre-condition of the former – as author, my preunderstanding is constitutive and ontologically prior to the preunderstanding of the ethnographically known Dreaming that I will write about. Authorship is necessarily authoritative in that it is laden with the power of the author's words, a supposedly post-colonial Western archaeology of Aboriginal ontology begging self-reflectivity. I shall return to this point in Chapter 10.

The Dreaming as preunderstanding

When Europeans first arrived in Australia, the regionally varied Dreaming world-views were the preunderstandings through which indigenous knowledge in much, if not all, of mainland Australia and many of its offshore islands emerged. Aboriginal knowledge was always founded on a prior truth steeped in the Dreaming. There are many examples of this in the sociological and anthropological literature.

Here I cite three. The first two are from Wardaman country in Australia's Northern Territory, an Aboriginal group whose culture, Dreaming ontology, and land we will have the chance to re-visit many times during the course of this book. Francesca Merlan, a linguist and social anthropologist who has worked with the Wardaman since 1976, recounts the process by which Wardaman elders gave meaning to unfamiliar, newly refound rock-art[5] in their own traditional lands (Merlan 1989, pp. 18–19). She describes how a Wardaman elder interpreted large paintings at two rockshelters near the Yingalarri waterhole as Lightning Brothers, Dreaming beings better known from Delamere Station a few kilometres to the south. In 1988, however, Merlan made more detailed recordings of Dreaming stories and paintings from various parts of Wardaman country, and all other Wardaman elders argued that the Yingalarri paintings were not Lightning Brothers but *gulirrida* Peewees (Magpie Larks). Merlan (1989, p. 18) notes that for these elders *gulirrida* help define a particular patri-territory, including the sites of the Yingalarri area. The Lightning Brothers are not found at Yingalarri but in a patri-territory located to the south; 'The single informant's identification of the large figures here as Lightning Brothers is viewed by other Wardaman as tantamount to ignoring and collapsing important differences among Wardaman sub-areas.' The Yingalarri paintings were agreed to be *gulirrida* by reference to a Dreaming preunderstanding.

That same year, Merlan visited another rock-art site in Wardaman country, this time at Innesvale Station a few kilometres northwest of *gulirrida* country (Figure 1.1). The elders who accompanied her claimed to be unfamiliar with the site, although one elder soon remembered that he had been there many years before as a little boy. Merlan (ibid., pp. 18–19) notes that this area of Innesvale Station is part of a patri-territory associated with *menngen* White Cockatoo, *gunajarri* Marsupial Mouse, *jembe* Death Adder, and other Dreaming beings. It is not directly associated with *gulirrida*, and indeed there is another patri-group between *gulirrida* country and this part of Innesvale Station. Merlan (ibid.) recounts how the Wardaman elders came to understand the newly found paintings by reference to the Dreaming:

Figure 1.1 *Menngen*, White Cockatoos at Mennge-ya (after completion of excavations), Wardaman country, 1989

When we first arrived at the little-known Innesvale site, and people saw the large engraved figures, one man immediately identified them as peewees. Knowing that the moon dreaming site, associated with the peewee patri-group, was not far to the west, he seemed to be making the identification in terms of the convention that such major figures as the engravings would be identified with the same group as a near-by known major site . . . This began a confrontation of different possible interpretations, largely carried out in Wardaman but also in Jaminjung and Kriol, which shortly began to produce a limited set of possibilities and at least apparent consensus among some of the senior people present. The discussion went as follows.

First a suggestion was made by a man who is not a member of the cognatic grouping most closely associated with the Yingalarri area that the engraved figures were *gulirrida* 'peewees'. There was a pause, following which a woman patrifiliated to the intervening Innesvale area . . . launched a series of remarks to the effect that the peewees were not everywhere. Moreover, she claimed that the original senior informant referred to above had been wrong to say that the peewees were travelling dreamings in any case. The same woman suggested the engravings might be *guyarru* 'masked owl' . . . It then emerged that the suggestion regarding masked owl had come from another woman who was not able to be on the trip with us (as her husband was ill), but with whom there had been discussion before the trip, based on shared understanding of its general location, about the possible associations of the engraving site we were viewing. After some conversation, it was generally agreed that masked owl was actually located at a place called Wujarr, some distance from where we were and in another patri-country. This idea was then put aside, and three senior informants, one after another (including the woman, one of whose patri-dreamings is white cockatoo) suggested that the engravings were white cockatoo, and were linked to the nearest known major site at Wiynbarr waterhole a few kilometres away, which has white cockatoo as one of its major dreaming associations. The man who had first suggested *gulirrida* then suggested the site was called Mennge-ya 'at the white cockatoo'; and another senior woman, normally very reserved (the mother's father's brother's

daughter or genealogically and socially close 'mother' of the one associated with white cockatoo, but not familiar with this area of Wardaman country), volunteered the observation that she thought the suggestion of peewees was wrong, and that of white cockatoo was right. It was repeated several times then and throughout the day that the oldest man with us had actually been at this site years ago, and that its identification with white cockatoo was of long standing.

Despite great initial uncertainty, in each of these cases the identity of the newly observed paintings was negotiated by reference to existing knowledge, as preunderstanding.

Fred Myers observed a similar process of meaning attribution among the Pintupi, an Aboriginal group whose lands are located 675 km to the south of Wardaman country in central Australia:

One morning a group of men gathered near a white gum tree on the creek bank where they waited for two older men. A younger man had, as they put it ambiguously, 'found something'. But they did not know what it was. Because they had close relationships with the traditional owners of this area, the two elders were presumed to have special knowledge of local myth. On the one hand, the men were fearful about the consequences of the discovery, lest the owners of the country attack them with sorcery for disturbing a secret site. On the other hand, they wondered if the discovery were 'gold' or 'opal', value for which the owners might pay them.

When the older men arrived, the group went down to the creek and examined the discovery, an outcrop of some sedimentary crusty rock that had been exposed by erosion. The men chipped off a bit and examined the colors, then dug around the area to expose more of the rock. Although one man expressed his fear of sorcery for having desecrated a sacred site belonging to others, the enterprise continued. One of the two elders speculated confidently that this rock must be from the Kangaroo Dreaming with which the creek is associated. Knowing that two men in The Dreaming had speared a kangaroo at a point five miles east, he deduced that they must have gutted it here on the way back. No one had ever told him this, however. The Papunya people were ignorant of this fact, he said.

This Kangaroo Dreaming, the men

maintained, is important because it is associated with ceremonies in which men 'show special designs (*wamulu*) and make women and children go under a blanket'.[6] As the men continued digging, three of them looked to see if there was gold in the composite; for others, 'gold' was simply a metaphorical equivalent to the traditional value of sacred sites. Throughout the inquiry, the participants oscillated between assuring themselves that the owners of the country had told them not to be afraid if they found anything hereabouts and a hopefulness that they would be paid for 'finding' this thing.

Finally, examining the uneven distribution of colors in the composite, they decided it was the sloppy stomach contents of the gutted Dreaming kangaroo. The red elements in it, one man suggested, must be the vegetable fluff that had been colored with red ochre and stuck to the two men's bodies, since traveling with body decoration was common for many mythological figures . . .

Subsequently, little was made of the event, at least to my knowledge, but one man continued to talk of the find . . . By now, everyone was satisfied that the rock was the stomach contents of the gutted kangaroo who had been speared and must have been crawling along the creek trying to return to his *ngurra* [camp, country, place] near Yayai soakage. (Myers 1986, pp. 64–6)

These anecdotes illustrate how the Wardaman and the Pintupi recently attributed meaning to specific parts of their experienced landscapes by reference to an already meaningful world saturated with preunderstanding. The process is a general one, and applies to all cultures around the world, our own included. In the examples cited above, the interpretation of the rock-art or place was located in a certain view of the world that could be drawn upon to inform the interpreter's new observations. Some lines of evidence were corroborative: dominant figures in the Wardaman rock-art were of Dreaming significance; the land was also of the Dreaming; the identity of the art was to be found in the identity of the land and of the Dreaming events relating to place. But others were not: the paintings finally interpreted as White Cockatoos in Wardaman country resembled the well-known Lightning Brothers of Delamere Station, and so could potentially likewise have been interpreted in this way; previous items of rock-art were interpreted as Peewees nearby, but there was a geographical limit to Peewee country. In the end, the agreed interpretations were the ones that best fit the 'facts', as preunderstanding. Both Wardaman and Pintupi cosmology were seen to operate as preunderstanding negotiated through novel experiences and communication rather than as rigid and unchanging sets of knowledge. This is a defining characteristic of preunderstanding in general.

The meaningfulness of objects

Meaning is thus given to specific objects and ideas by reference to a world already rich in meaning. The signification of specific things and preunderstanding are negotiated in time as a result of the impact each has on the other, a point I return to in Chapter 5 when discussing the shifting nature of the sign in a network of signs via Jacques Derrida's concept of *différance*. This is the case with the construction of knowledge everywhere: identifying something as meaningful is not about inventing the meaningfulness of things from no-thing, but locating a new observation in an already present and meaningful interpretative framework. Indeed, I will argue in the course of this book that this is precisely what the West has done with Aboriginal notions of the Dreaming following its Western discovery, re-interpreting it – and therefore understanding it – in relation to a Western preunderstanding (thus necessarily appropriating or compromising it ontologically in the process). At the same time, material items such as cave paintings or rocks in the landscape are not merely passive *receptors* of meaning, modifying preunderstanding in their coming-into-existence. Through their meaningfulness, objects and ideas affect how we experience the past, present and future as sentient reference points of the world we know.

Because things are meaningful, people engage with their world in culturally patterned ways. Objects are engaged through historically and culturally ordered human behaviour, resulting in an ordered archaeological signature that is the mark of preunderstanding. There is a close relationship between Gadamer's preunderstanding and the popular sociological concept of *habitus*: preunderstanding informs, and is therefore a condition of Pierre

Bourdieu's (1977) *habitus*. It is because of this disposition of human behaviour that an archaeology of preunderstanding – and an archaeology of the ethnographically known Dreaming – are at all possible.

Objects, subjects and the engaged world

Because objects have a physical life that extends beyond the moment, they continuously shape preunderstanding, giving them a semblance of agency. Robin Boast (1997) and Julian Thomas (1993a) have commented on this, particularly in relation to the conventional treatment of objects as passive, and subjects as active agents. Meredith Wilson and I (David and Wilson 1999) have elsewhere noted that by treating material items as external objects, we, as subjects, become disassociated from our lived and experienced world; material things are denied a role in the construction of the world as experienced, and separated from our very identity and being. In this inadequate formulation, where by definition the passive object is conceived in contradistinction to the active subject, Boast notes that objects receive meaning and identity exclusively from the subject, but do not impart it. In this sense objects are 'out there', timeless receptors of meaning, while subjects define themselves in isolation. Human action and identity are distinct from their surroundings. To resolve these deficiencies, Boast proposes viewing the relationship between people and material things not in terms of subject–object, but rather as subject–subject. This is his solution to recognizing the influence of material culture on the way we *pre*ceive and relate to things as experience in and of the world.

Wilson and I (David and Wilson 1999) are also uneasy with the traditional view of objects as 'out there' when addressing our own existence. However, we take a different approach from that of Boast, in that were objects synonymous with subjects, they would be capable of surpassing the historical moment as agents. In Theodor Adorno's (1996, pp. 27–8) words, 'if the thought readily yielded to the object, if its attention were on the object, not on its category, the very objects would start talking under the lingering eye'. We argue instead that in addressing the world, as a whole or in part, people touch on *relations* between things when discussing the world of objects.

The way in which interpretation and understanding are mediated by preunderstanding is thus an expression of specific relations between the engaging object in an already meaningful world, and the interpreting subject. These relations are never fixed; they are continuously in a state of becoming. As human identity is constructed through engagement, so too is human identity in a continual state of change. As a result, both interpretation and preunderstanding are in constant states of flux, being redefined by the co-engagement of experiencing and communicating agents and objects through time. It is in the nature of such relations between people and their engaged material world that an archaeology of preunderstanding, 'mind' and human identity can take place.

An archaeology of world-views

Thus while one specific theme of this book concerns an archaeology of the Dreaming known from ethnography, there is also a more reclusive thread that explores some of the implications of culturally patterned objects, including rock-art, for an archaeology of preunderstanding. Rock-art is used to explore these themes as it is one of the most abundant, and most visual, of all archaeological remains. What I wish to show in the following pages is that Australian rock-art and other aspects of the cultural landscape can be used to investigate patterns of change and continuity in the way people engaged with their worlds, particularly as it relates to the Dreaming as known from recent times. As symbols located in preunderstanding, rock-art and other products of cultural behaviour are windows onto the past. Sometimes the Dreaming as we know it today will be implicated in the material products of past human behaviour in Australia; at other times it will not be. Whether or not the Dreaming that we know of from ethnography is implicated in more ancient times will depend on whether or not past behavioural conventions and their operative contexts are recognized to have been akin to those of recent times. My objective is not to *retrieve* the experience of past meaningful landscapes, but to track back in time the antiquity of the recent

Dreaming's ordered material expressions to identify its historical emergence. An archaeology of the Dreaming and an archaeology of preunderstanding therefore coalesce in an investigation of patterning in the world of engaged objects and experienced landscapes in Aboriginal Australia.

An archaeology of the Dreaming is undertaken in this book by reference to three of its material manifestations. In Chapter 3, I describe how the Djungan of northeastern Australia have used the Dreaming mountain of Ngarrabullgan during ethnohistoric times *because* of its Dreaming significance. Tracing back through time the antiquity of this use, I suggest an archaeologically identifiable antiquity for the mountain's ethnohistorically known Dreaming signification. In Chapter 4, I move to the arid core of central Australia, examining archaeologically the antiquity of ethnographically renowned ritual sites. In Chapter 5, I explore in some detail the antiquity of rock-art symbolism in Wardaman country, focusing on the art known to have represented various Dreaming beings or events at the time of their creation. My aim in each of these chapters is to identify when in the past the kinds of behaviours ethnographically known to have been associated with Dreaming world-views first emerged in the archaeological record.

I take my methodological lead from the view that knowledge of history is founded on a dialectic: history unfolds forward in time, while at the same time we trace the origins of what we know *back* in time. This dual movement guides my own project. By tracing archaeological signatures of ethnographically documented world-views back from a recent to a more distant past, the antiquity of specific archaeological details – and, by implication, of cultural expressions – can be traced. At the same time, tracking the emergence of new archaeological expressions from a distant to a more recent past enables us to position cultural traits in historical perspective. Rather than jumping from one historical period of time to another, the method involves a tracing of continuity so as to identify and highlight discontinuities.

The organization of this book follows this movement back and forward in time. I begin by describing the ethnographic Dreaming as preunderstanding in Chapter 2, identifying its archaeological expressions in selected parts of Australia in Chapters 3–5. In these chapters I move back in time from the ethno-archaeological known to the temporally distant unknown. I then attempt to shed further light on temporal trends by examining patterns of change and continuity in other aspects of the Australian archaeological record. This is done by considering cultural change, and the archaeological record, as a product of the forward motion of time (Chapters 7–9). Putting these two lines of evidence together, I conclude with discussions on the origins of the Dreaming as we know it today and on the hermeneutic nature of this understanding (Chapters 6 and 10).

Notes

1. Wally Caruana (1993) has written that there is a tendency in Western thought to view the world as forever changing, whereas Australian Aboriginal peoples have focused more on its immutable dimensions. He suggests that Western constructs of Aboriginality around notions of change serve to marginalize Aboriginal people's own understanding of the world as continuous and in equilibrium. However, I would note that Western constructions of an atemporal Aboriginality are based on a different set of premises from those that shape Aboriginal notions of continuity and equilibrium. It is one such Western premise that I address in this book; I do not question the legitimacy of Aboriginal constructions of reality.

2. Lynette Russell (in press) has written extensively on the literary construction of Aboriginality. The interested reader is directed to her work for further details on the subject.

3. The Catholic theologian, Karl Rahner, developed an intriguing account of *Vorgriff* by way of the experience of God. Similarly, the Lutheran pastor Rudolf Bultmann was also influenced by Heidegger. Bultmann used the term 'preunderstanding' to argue that the Scriptures needed to be de-mythologized by understanding the time and place of their writing – the network of signs of their writing. Bultmann was thus interested in interpreting the Scriptures by reference to hermeneutics – much like Gadamer, yet applied to different contexts (Mueller-Vollmer 1985).

4. John Caputo (1986, p. 432) notes that Heidegger's 'Dasein' is no more nor less than 'a being that always and already is possessed of an understanding of Being – and hence of its own Being, of the Being of others and the Being of things', that is, of preunderstanding.

5. Following Paul Taçon and Christopher Chippindale's (1998) lead, I hyphenate 'rock-art' to distinguish such practices from the Western artistic programme, which is closely tied to a market economy.

6. 'Go under a blanket' here means that women and children hide; this refers to making a public display of their not being able to witness particular sacred things or events, sacrosanct objects or happenings that men only can see, especially when boys are 'caught' for initiation.

Part I

The Present Past

2 The Dreaming

The 1890s are often said to have been a turning point in Australian history. These were the years of Australia's first great depression, following decades of economic boom. The Anglo-Boer War of 1899–1902 had begun in South Africa; for the first time Australian troops paraded in Melbourne and Sydney, and volunteer civilians from Australia fought in an overseas war. Tom Griffiths (1996a, 1996b) has written of the rise of popular enthusiasm for natural and Aboriginal history during the 1890s, and the emergence of Australia's own Heidelberg school of landscape artists (including Arthur Streeton and Tom Roberts). These were also the years that were soon to see Australia emerge as a nation, the eve of Federation (1 January 1901). There was a growing sense of national identity. With good reason, the last decade of the nineteenth century has been called 'the nervous nineties' by John Docker (1991), described as 'the ending of a childhood' by Brian Fitzpatrick (1946, cited in Griffiths 1996a), and heralded as 'a time of nationalistic visions' by Tom Griffiths (1996a, 1996b). The century was turning, and a way of life was being left behind.

In these defining years the face of Australian exploration also changed. No other expedition symbolizes this mood of change more than the Horn Expedition. On 8 March 1894, William Horn, a 53-year-old mining magnate and pastoralist from South Australia approached the South Australian Premier with a proposal for a scientific expedition to the MacDonnell Ranges in central Australia. William Horn would finance the expedition himself, not with profit but with scientific advances in mind.

Unlike previous expeditions, the aim of the Horn Expedition was not to find inland seas or mountain passes. Nor was it to discover rich mineral fields or green pastures. This was to be an expedition like no other; it was to be run by scientists in the pursuit of scientific knowledge. Until then scientific observation had always been incidental to the more urgent aims of discovery. In the words of Baldwin Spencer, editor of the official report, the campaign's aim was 'not to explore new country, but to examine as carefully as time permitted the country in and about the McDonnell Ranges' (Spencer 1896, p. 2). Until then, the objective of all Australian expeditions had been to discover and fill in 'blank spaces' on the map. Horn's expedition was to go to an area where at least six exploration parties had previously been (Jones 1996).

The expeditioners were assembled via unusual means. Seeking to engage the approval of the government, William Horn asked the Premier of South Australia to name two scientists and to encourage the Premiers of Victoria and New South Wales to send one each. John Mulvaney recounts the ensuing events:

> Government and university bureaucracy moved rapidly in those times of handwritten

letters . . . By early April the South Australian government had agreed to support Horn's proposal and the other two Premiers were so informed. On Thursday, 5 April the Victorian Premier wrote to the Chancellor of the University of Melbourne (the Victorian Chief Justice), who acknowledged receipt of that letter in his own hand on the same day. He had the matter placed on the council agenda for the following Monday, 9 April.

Presumably Horn had nominated his preferred team, because the South Australian Premier requested the release of Baldwin Spencer, Melbourne's biology professor. The council meeting agreed to release Spencer for twelve weeks and provided funds for a temporary replacement. By 28 April the Victorian Premier had been notified of this decision, approved it, and informed his South Australian counterpart.

The party, including Spencer, left Adelaide by a special train bound for Oodnadatta on 4 May, less than eight weeks since Horn's initial proposal. (1996, p. 4)

The expedition was large, even by the standards of the day: William Horn, expedition organizer and financier; Sir Edward Stirling, medical officer and anthropologist, and the most senior scientist on the expedition; Ralph Tate, geologist and botanist; Charles Winnecke, surveyor; Francis Belt (Horn's nephew) and G. A. Keartland, collectors and taxidermists; Alexander Watt, geologist and mineralogist; Baldwin Spencer, zoologist and photographer; C. E. Pritchard and W. Russell, prospectors requested by the government; and 'the usual camp men – a cook [C. Laycock], two white men [H. Edgar and R. Taylor] and two Afghans [Guzzie Balooch and Moosha Balooch] . . . and black "boys" [one of whom was called Harry] to serve as guides' (Spencer 1896, p. 2; Mulvaney 1996, pp. 5–6).

The expeditioners were to report on the natural history of the area and on the 'manners, customs and appearance of the aboriginals in their primitive state' (University of Melbourne Council Minute Book 1893–95, p. 147 and associated letters, cited in Mulvaney 1996, p. 4). This was to be the first expedition in Australian history where Aboriginal life formed a focus of attention. At that time the general belief was that Aboriginal people were a 'dying race'. To record information on Aboriginal peoples would be to collect a future

memento of what once had been. The Horn Expedition was to go to a known place, collect scientific materials and information, and return with specimens and photographs. As Philip Jones (1996, p. 19) has noted, 'In contrast to almost every other expedition of the century the Horn Expedition had no destination, except to return to its point of departure.'

In its geographical sense, this is precisely what happened. But in Australia's intellectual history, the Horn Expedition represents a point of no return. Not because of any discoveries hailed at the time, but largely through an unheralded observation with regards to the region's indigenous peoples, one that was to profoundly affect Western conceptions of Aboriginal people. But it was not Stirling, the anthropologist in the party that was responsible. It was Frank Gillen, the postmaster and Special Magistrate at Alice Springs, in correspondence with Baldwin Spencer, the expedition's zoologist. This was the beginning of a long partnership that was to help revolutionize anthropology in Australia and abroad.

When Spencer first set out with the Horn Expedition in 1894, little was known of Aboriginal Australia. Indeed, their position at the bottom of the social evolutionary rung was well established by European social commentators of the time. Spencer himself subsequently became an influential social evolutionist, retaining such views until his death in 1929, well after they had begun to lose popularity in the anthropological and popular imagination.

At the time of Spencer and Gillen's first meeting during the Horn Expedition – on 15 July 1894 – anthropologists fell more or less into two categories: the artefact collector or fieldworker based in the colonies; and the museum- or university-based armchair theoretician who patroned the collector almost exclusively from *his* lofty base in New York, Paris, Oxford or Cambridge (Morphy 1996a). Within 25 years of their first book (Spencer and Gillen 1899), this division would evaporate. After the Horn Expedition's publication, Spencer, the university professor and Gillen, the man on the ground, presented their Australian results in unison. As would also be the practice of their pioneering contemporaries Alfred Haddon (1855–1940) and W. H. R. Rivers (1864–1922), both of the University of Cambridge, anthropological theory and practice were fast becoming recognized as two sides of the same coin (Morphy 1996a). The Horn Expedition is a symbol of these changes.

It is in the course of these conceptual shifts that the Dreamtime emerged in Western thought. Although there is some debate when the word was first coined, it would appear to date from some time between 1894 – when Spencer and Gillen met during the Horn Expedition – and the appearance of the 1896 report (Morphy 1996a, 1996b; Wolfe 1991). Spencer attributes the term to Gillen. The first known reference is found in *Through Larapinta Land*, Spencer's narrative of the Horn Expedition:

> The blacks have a rather curious myth to account for the origin of the pillar [Chambers' Pillar, a prominent landform in central Australia; Figure 2.1]. They say that in what they call the Alcheringa (or as Mr. Gillen appropriately renders it the 'dream times'), a certain noted warrior journeyed to the east and killing with his big stone knife all the men, he seized the women and brought them back with him to his own country. Camping for the night on this spot he and the women were transformed into stone, and it is his

body which now forms the pillar, whilst the women were fashioned into the fantastic peaks grouped together to form what is now known as Castle Hill, a mile away to the north. (Spencer 1896, p. 50)

In a footnote on the same page, Spencer further acknowledges that he is 'indebted to Mr. F. J. Gillen for this information'. And again on page 111 of the same article, he writes:

> The morality of the black is not that of the white man, but his life so long as he remains uncontaminated by contact with the latter, is governed by rules of contact which have been recognised amongst his tribe from what they speak of as the 'alcheringa', which Mr. Gillen has aptly called the 'Dream times'.

Alcheringa is an Arrernte term that refers to a timeless age when the world was given its present order by the ancestral beings who animated the cosmos. It is during this age of creation that the earth was given form. There are many stories relating to this formative age. Here is one recorded by Spencer and Gillen themselves:

Figure 2.1 Members of the Horn Expedition at Chamber's Pillar, 23 May 1894 (*Source*: Baldwin Spencer. Morton and Mulvaney 1996, plate 24)

Standing up amongst a great stretch of sand-hills, in the angle of country enclosed by the Hugh River on the east and the Finke on the south-west, is a great column of sandstone rising from a broad pedestal, the total height of which is about 170 feet. The broader face of the column measures twenty-five yards, and the narrower fifteen. Together with other turret-shaped rocks close by, it forms a most conspicuous feature in the landscape, and can be seen from far away. It is called Chambers Pillar, or Idracowra, by the white men, this being a corruption of the native name *Iturka worra*, a term of contempt applied to a man who has connection with women of the wrong class or section.

Tradition says that in the Alchera, a powerful *Oknirrabale* [wise old man] came from the east. He had been circumcised, but not subincised [therefore he had not undertaken the full rituals of male adulthood], had run away after the operation of *Lartna* [circumcision ceremony], and, being very strong, had been able not only to defend himself, but also to force a number of women to go away with him. Among these women were included those who were *Allira* [his and his brothers' daughters], *Umba* [his sisters' daughters], *Mura* [his wives' and potential wives' mothers], *Uwinna* [father's sisters] and *Unkulla* [daughters of father's sisters]. He settled down amongst the sand-hills, and, when he died, the column arose to mark the spot; the turret hills representing the women. (Spencer and Gillen 1927, p. 350).

It was clear to Spencer and Gillen that local Aboriginal people had their own way of understanding the world and all that stood in it. Through Spencer's contacts in Australia and overseas (including Sir James Frazer at the University of Cambridge), coupled with an international thirst for first-hand information on what was then thought of as 'primitive' peoples, Aboriginal beliefs fast became known to the world at large. From 1896 on, Australian Aboriginal people were to be increasingly understood in relation to what came to be known as the Dreamtime or Dreaming, although it would be many years before these terms were to be widely used. Even Spencer and Gillen rarely used the words, especially in their early writings; as Morphy (1996a, 1996b) has noted, it is not used once in their first book *The Native Tribes of Central Australia* (Spencer and Gillen 1899).

Paradoxically, the eventual ready acceptance of the Dreaming in the popular and scientific imagination may have been aided by its implicit reference to a dreamy, misty psyche that social commentators of the day nostalgically associated with their own distant past (see Chapter 6). The Dreaming epitomized a primitive Other that was less concrete and modern than themselves, but to which they could nevertheless relate.[1]

Understanding the Dreaming

Our understanding of the Dreaming has come a long way since these early days, although it has taken many twists and turns in the anthropological literature since the late nineteenth century. Rather than retrace its history as a concept, I would like here to follow some of the Dreaming's dimensions as understood today. It is in its ability to direct human behaviour – and by implication the archaeologically recoverable material remains of Dreaming-mediated praxis – that the Dreaming's significance to this book will be realized.

W. H. R. Stanner, perhaps *the* non-Aboriginal commentator who has done more than any other to unfold the mysteries of the Dreaming, once wrote that there are two ways to speak of it:

1 To 'think black'. That is, to enter into the world of Aboriginal Australia by considering indigenous thought in relation to indigenous praxis; to experience the world of Aboriginal Australia by locating individual aspects of life in relation to others within indigenous thought.

2 To 'relate to things familiar in our own intellectual history. From this viewpoint, it is a cosmogony, an account of the begetting of the universe, a story about creation. It is also a cosmology, an account or theory of how what was created became an orderly system. To be more precise, it is a theory of how the universe became a moral system' (Stanner 1987 [1956], p. 228).

Throughout this chapter I will employ the second method so as to shed light on Aboriginal world-views by reference to our own Western constructions of the world. I paint with a broad brush in this chapter, reserving more detailed and regionally specific ethnographic presentations for the relatively focused concerns of later chapters.

The Dreamtime, or Dreaming, was probably (but not certainly) a pan-Australian cultural frame, although its specific structures and expressions in stories, songs and the like differ across space. It 'corresponds to absolute or whole reality, that which comprehends everything and is adequate to everything. It is the total referent of which anything else is a *relatum*' (Stanner 1989, p. 26). The Dreaming of various parts of Australia are preunderstandings of the world through which all interpretation is based. It is a positioning of existence, an ordering of being. In the words of social anthropologist Fred Myers (1986, p. 47), the Dreaming 'must be treated phenomenologically as a given condition of "what there is," an endowment of being and potential that defines for [indigenous Australians] the framework of human action'.

Before venturing into the world of the Dreaming, we must first consider our investigative scale. It could be said that the Dreaming is not one thing but many, for it varies from Aboriginal group to Aboriginal group. This is of course correct – Dreaming stories, rituals and other practices differ across space. In some parts of Australia 'great guardian-spirits', such as Baiame in southeast Australia, could be found (Stanner 1965a, p. 216). In others they could not. Nicolas Peterson (1972, p. 23) has written that among some Aboriginal groups, such as the Warlpiri, a person may recognize a conception totem that relates to a place belonging to a patrimoiety not of their own. Among other groups, such as the Murngin, this is not the case. However, a particularistic conception of the Dreaming is unsatisfactory when it comes to understanding Aboriginal Australia as a whole, for there are also commonalities that are found across much, if not all, of mainland Australia. Difference and similarity are two sides of the same coin, and all understanding relates to its corresponding scale of inquiry. An island-wide perspective requires an island-wide examination.

Many Australian indigenous cultures have a word that can be interpreted, figuratively or literally, as 'the Dreaming'. In Wardaman country in the Northern Territory it is *buwarraja*. In Arrernte it is *alcheringa*. *Alchera* means 'dream'; *-inga* is a suffix that means 'of': thus, *alcheringa*, 'of the dreams' (Morphy 1996b, p. 176). In Pintupi country it is *jukurrpa*. In Yir Yoront it is *larr-wolhlvm*, and so forth. When speaking in English or Kriol, the word 'Dreaming' is not used in all parts of Australia; others may be applied, such as 'Story' or 'Storytime' in north Queensland. But they are much the same thing. In each case, the local term refers to various things including (1) an ancestral period of creation; (2) the creative forces or 'ancestral' spirit-beings themselves; (3) the formative events of that age; (4) the logic and law of the creative period that continue into the living present; and (5) the codes imposed in the Dreaming onto the human world. In this light, Paddy Japaljarri Stewart has this to say about the Dreaming:

> This is the story about jukurrpa (Dreaming) in the old ways what they used to do and used to learn from their old grandfathers, grandmothers and grandparents and in the Dreamtime this is what they used to learn . . .
>
> When my father was alive this is what he taught me. He had taught me traditional ways like traditional designs in body or head of kangaroo Dreaming . . . and eagle Dreaming. He taught me how to sing song for the big ceremonies. People who are related to us in a close family they have to have the same sort of jukurrpa Dreaming, and to sing songs in the same way as we do our actions like dancing, and paintings and our body or shields or things, and this is what my father taught me. My Dreaming is the kangaroo Dreaming, the eagle Dreaming and budgerigar Dreaming so I have three kinds of Dreamings in my jukurrpa and I have to hang on to it. This is what my father taught me, and this is what I have to teach my sons, and my son has to teach his sons the same way my father taught me, and that's the way it will go on from grandparents to sons, and follow that jukurrpa. (1994, p. 305)

The Dreaming is creation, an understanding and explanation of the world and how it works, a moral code, law and lore. It relates to the creation of the world, to a timeless past when 'people' and 'animals' and all things animate and inanimate were more or less free to wander the cosmos and act, not having yet attained their defining features. But it is also a time when these defining features were obtained. I say 'more or less' free, for at the same time that the ancestral beings were free to act in any way possible, their actions were both defining of, and defined by, the characteristics of the things they would create. This is not a condition of linear time, whereby a preceding cause defines an outcome. Rather, the outcome simultaneously defines the original cause of the act. To give one story: the Koko Minni of north Queensland believed that the crow got its black plumage when two rainbirds became

> engaged in a wrestling match, and the elder one, finding himself beaten, began to lose his temper. The younger one, of course, was anxious to prolong the struggle. In order to separate them, their mother (a crow) covered herself with excrement, and rendering herself thus dark and offensive, soon frightened her sons into obedience. The crow has kept her colour. (Roth 1903, p. 14)

The crow is black because she covered herself with excrement because she is black . . .

The Dreaming is thus a condition when the present world emerged from the unformed. It is also where people's spirituality and worldly condition are defined by their links to the beings of the creative age. An individual whose Dreaming is Kangaroo is imbued with Kangarooness by virtue of his or her essential investment with the spirit being that *is* Kangaroo. A hill that may have been created in the Dreaming when the Kangaroo lay there and was transformed into that hill is integral to that person's being and identity. There is a mutual relationship here – even to say that the essence is not in the Kangaroo or in the person, but in the mutuality – each element helping to define the other. This is a mutuality mediated by the Dreaming ancestral beings from whom all existence emerges.

Unlike Christian thought, the Dreaming is based on a view of the cosmos as an interrelated network without subjects or objects. This is not a world 'out there'. It is rather an existence that is defined by the relationships of everything that is and that was. In this all-encompassing framework of understanding, the Dreaming encapsulates an experienced world that can be approached from various angles, as indeed it has been since the pioneering works of Spencer and Gillen and Carl Strehlow. The Dreaming at once gives birth to, directs, clarifies, legitimates, defines and explains a world of relationships, giving iden-

tity to the people who engage not just *with* but *in* the world.

There are different ways of considering the Dreaming. Each dimension is not autochtonous. It does not act on its own behalf, as if addressing a disparate part of reality. Rather, the Dreaming as a way of understanding existence represents a total perspective on reality, a perspective that is self-affirming and that is therefore locked from the inside. In discussing various dimensions of the Dreaming, therefore, the categories should not be seen as separate entities. Nor should they be seen as interacting parts. They are unified at an intimate level. The dimensions I use below – the Dreaming as religion, morality, law, geographical mapping, social mapping, time, ontology – are presented to organize discussion rather than to define and edify organic parts, and should not be seen as categoric properties of the Dreaming. Together they represent a single, unified perspective.

The Dreaming as religion

Western theoreticians of the late nineteenth and early twentieth centuries, seeing the world's cultures as ranked hierarchically from primitive (Australian Aborigines) to advanced (Europeans), saw the Dreaming as a confirmation of the non-religious nature of Aboriginal life. Perhaps the most influential thinker of this mould was Sir James Frazer (e.g. 1933), who claimed that 'among the aborigines of Australia . . . magic is universally practised, whereas religion in the sense of propitiation or conciliation of the higher powers seems to be nearly unknown' (1933, p. 55). Not only was magic considered by Frazer as areligious, but it formed the first of three evolutionary stages: magic, religion, science. Through his direct communications with Baldwin Spencer – himself a renowned social evolutionist – Frazer was very much aware of the *alcheringa* or Dreaming; in 1927 Spencer and Gillen dedicated *The Arunta* to 'our master Sir James Frazer. This record of a stone age people is offered in gratitude and admiration' (Spencer and Gillen 1927, p. v), and Frazer (1938) wrote the Preface to the second edition of *The Native Tribes of Central Australia*. But it would not be long before Frazer's evolutionary ideas were to be rejected, and Aboriginal thought, as expressed in the Dreaming, was to be widely appreciated as a religious system of beliefs in its own right.

Paradoxically, some of the earliest published discussions of the Dreaming were as religion, or rather as sets of religious beliefs (although Spencer in particular tended to avoid the term 'religion', lest Australian Aborigines were implicated to rank more highly in Frazer's evolutionary ladder). Pastor Carl Strehlow (1871–1922), a Lutheran missionary first stationed at Bathesda Mission near Cooper's Creek and then at Finke River Mission at Hermannsburg, and Andrew Lang (1844–1912), the influential Oxford University-based Scottish writer on myth, ritual and totemism, even suggested that the Arrernte and neighbouring groups recognized supreme beings or High Gods (thereby being predestined to the Christian god the missionaries were espousing) (see also Veit 1991, 1994, 2001). This was a characterization of indigenous thought considered to be preposterous by many of their contemporaries, Spencer and Gillen included (see in particular Appendix D of Spencer and Gillen's (1927) *The Arunta*).

By 1965, Stanner was able to write that:

> [if] the word 'religion' means, as its probable etymology suggests, two dispositions in man – to ponder on the foundations of human life in history, and to unite or reconcile oneself with the design incorporated in those foundations – then the Aborigines were a very religious-minded people. (Stanner 1965a, p. 213)

Religious understanding began to be seen as a means of objectifying the subjective experience of life by attributing meaning to things through reference to a larger whole. It also began to be seen as an alignment of the way things are with the way they should be (without necessarily defining a 'complete' world of alternative possibilities). In this sense, there could be no consideration of Aboriginal religion without reference to the Dreaming.

In its religious dimension the Dreaming came to be understood as a philosophy that explained existence and the creation of the world, people included. It addressed an ever-present past when 'people', 'animals' and all things had not yet attained their defining features, in the process explaining the concreteness of the present. The Dreaming relates to a time when the present world emerged from the unformed through the action of life-sustaining forces which, allegorically, tended to take on human characteristics (e.g. the Arrernte story that explains the origin of Chambers' Pillar, as recounted by Spencer and Gillen and cited above). In this sense, the Dreaming traces both our own, human origins, and that of the world that sustains us.

Stanner has noted that:

> If Aboriginal culture had an architectonic idea I would say that it was a belief that all living people, clan by clan, or lineage by lineage, were linked patrilineally with ancestral beings by inherent and imperishable bonds through territories and totems which were either the handiwork or parts of the continuing being of the ancestors themselves. This belief was held in faith, not as an 'official truth' or dogma, but as part of a body of patent truth about the universe that no one in his right mind would have thought of trying to bring to the bar of proof. The faith was self-authenticating. (1998 [1976], p. 1)

By modern standards Stanner's universal reference to patrilineality seems outmoded, as shown by the existence of matrilineal systems of descent in some parts of Australia. But when we substitute 'by descent' for the word 'patrilineally', Stanner's overall statement rings true.

The Dreaming is told in stories, songs, paintings and the like. Stanner (1987 [1956]) has noted that Dreaming tales may relate great marvels, the original institution of things in the cosmos, or a present social order that already operated in the Dreaming. Dreaming stories are a recounting of, and accounting for, origins and the way things are – hence the use of the English words 'Story' or 'Storytime' rather than 'Dreaming' in some parts of Aboriginal Australia. Their recounting represents both human *engagement with* the Dreaming and *performance of* the Dreaming. Engagement not only because all things are already connected with the life essences that gave birth to the world during a past creative era, but also because in their propensity as life essences, Dreaming beings continue to give presence to the world. To exist is thus to engage both with and in. And story telling is performance of the Dreaming because in the telling comes the re-presentation, the articulation of a pre-existing order to an awaiting social audience. The archaeological implications of this performative quality will be further explored in Chapter 4.

The Dreaming's performative and engaging qualities are articulated wherever there are people whose lives are guided and given meaning by it, for every action is steeped in a preunderstanding that *is* the Dreaming. But two aspects require singling out, for one is highly visible, and the other has served as a major force in anthropological thought (at times misguidedly): ritual and totemism. Both will reappear in later chapters, and therefore require discussion. Both have also been influential in understanding the Dreaming as we know it today. Each exposes a different perspective on the Dreaming's religious dimension. More to the point, each has significance for the way Aboriginal people related to place in the recent past. As a result, the Dreaming's ritualistic and totemic dispositions have left behind distinctive archaeological traces, the nature of which will be explored in Chapters 3–5.

Ritual

If ritual is defined as a prescribed act 'with a high degree of formality' (Barfield 1997, p. 410), then Aboriginal religion can be said to be highly ritualistic. In its engaging sense, each ritual is an act of faith in the Dreaming itself, while in its performative sense it is a duplication (with or without modification) of a preexisting conviction (per-formative). But ritual activity does not pervade every aspect of the Dreaming; nor are ritualistic practices the same everywhere.

Ritual involves bodily engagement targeting the confirmation of a specific belief or system of beliefs set in an ontological framework. A. P. Elkin (1964, p. 195) has suggested that Aboriginal rituals in general can be broken down into three types: historical, initiation, and increase. Historical rites re-enact the events of the ancestral heroes of the Dreaming, and in the process bring to life the formative act. These are formal, structured enactments observing well-known social orders: women and men, initiated and uninitiated, members of particular moieties, clans or lineages each play their structured parts. During such rituals, songs are sung, bodies are decorated, and paraphernalia are used while their Dreaming significance may be explained to the newly initiated. In this sense, it can be said that all rites are historical in substance.

Initiation rites involve a social transformation of the self, an individual's crossing in a communal world. Initiation rites operate in a world of cosmological order and hierarchy, for they activate the crossing of increasingly elevated levels of knowledge, social standing and spiritual achievement; they are stages in socialization (Stanner 1965a, p. 219). Both this order and its hierarchy were founded and continue to be perpetuated through the Dreaming. As Stanner (1965a, p. 219) has noted, 'the canon of the rites was invariable: to subdue refractory unfinished personalities to a purpose held to be sacred and timeless. They put on the body, mentality, and social personality of initiates ineffaceable signs designating stages in the socialisation' of people.

Initiation rites invariably involved physical challenges and ordeals: among men circumcision and subincision in parts of western and northern Australia; the plucking of facial and bodily hairs in parts of Victoria; among men and women tooth evulsion in many parts of Australia; cicatrization across much of the continent; and the fastening of arm bands in some parts of Western Australia (Elkin 1964). Each aspect of the ritual was a pre-requisite to obtaining cumulatively higher-order levels of secret–sacred knowledge of the Dreaming, as it relates to the mysteries of the world. Each helped to confirm and further one's preunderstanding of the way things are, and how they have become so.

So-called 'increase' rites involved formalized activities calling directly on the Dreaming ancestral forces to maintain, and sometimes to enhance, the 'natural' world's fecundity. Elkin writes:

> Just as there are spirit-centres for human beings, so there are for natural species. Some heroes not only left human spirits at known places, but, in addition, made other sites, equally well known, to be the centres from which the life, or the spirits, of particular natural species would go forth and so cause the latter to increase in the normal manner. If the hero were connected, for example, with the kangaroo, having it for his totem and possibly being able to adopt its form, he might have performed ceremonies for the increase of kangaroo at one place and left a great stone not only to mark the site, but also as a store-

house of kangaroo life or spirits; another place on his journey might have been sanctified and made efficacious by the loss of some of his blood or part of his body, or by his body being transformed into stone. Such a site is henceforth sacred. It is a channel from the creative and eternal dream-time. The creative power is brought into operation and causes the increase, for example, in this case, of kangaroos, by the care bestowed on, and the rituals performed at, the site. (1964, p. 222)

Every rite is by definition social, for each is an enactment of belief operationalized in a social order, by socially organized actors. In Australia, rites are given direction and meaning through the Dreaming, for it is in the Dreaming that the social order is legitimated and that social changes are seen to operate, in the process memorializing the events of the Dreaming.

Rites hold a special place in religious thought, for it is here that people act out their religious beliefs in a formal and more or less public way: 'each ritual occasion vivified in the minds of celebrants the first instituting of the culture, deepened the sense of continuity with men's beginnings, and reaffirmed the structures of existence' (Stanner 1989, p. 153). It is in ritual also that the sacred paraphernalia are engaged. They are for these reasons what Stanner has called the high points of religion.

Totemism

That anything can be written about Aboriginal religion and the Dreaming without commencing and ending with totemism is very much a sign of the times. Not so long ago many would have said that the Dreaming *is* totemism in its ultimate form.

The term totemism was coined from the Ojibway (Native American) word *ote* (possessive *otem*) by J. F. McLennan in 1869 to refer to 'the worship of plants and animals' (Stanner 1965a, p. 223). However, like 'magic' it soon came to stand for the lowest rungs of religious thought, an evolutionary precursor to a belief in high gods. In both of these capacities – in its definition as relating to the worship of plants and animals and in its evolutionary overtones – totemism has been a major stumbling block to understanding Aboriginal religious thought and religious organization. Where it remains useful – and it is in this capacity that I restrict

my discussions – is in its conceptualization of the 'natural' world as a structured system, and in its linkage of people's essences within this inherent structure. Totems are in this sense what Stanner (ibid., p. 226) has called an 'existent' – 'an entity, an event, or a condition' – to which people are essentially linked; the very condition of a person's existence relies on an already present existent.

Across mainland Australia people are linked to the 'natural' world through the creative events of the Dreaming that brought all things into earthly existence. The Dreaming also gave birth to the clans, the lineages, the social order now found in the world. By giving rise to order it naturalized the social and socialized the natural. This was achieved by various means, each of which linked people to the 'natural'. A person may have a particular affinity with, say, Kangaroo by virtue of his or her conception or birth place, descent, or a specific event that took place before, during or after their birth. These links between people and the 'natural' world, the 'plants and animals', have implications for what a person can and cannot do in the course of their life, including speech, marriage, residence, ritual roles, and the like. It is these links between people and the 'natural' that have traditionally been discussed as totemic by anthropologists. Today, what links people with the 'natural' world tend not to be considered as 'totemic' but as 'Dreamings', avoiding the former term's historical implications.

For these reasons Stanner (1965a, p. 225) proposed considering *totems* rather than *totemism* when discussing Aboriginal thought. Unlike Elkin (1964), who had earlier thought of totemism as the key to understanding Aboriginal religion and the Dreaming, Stanner suggested that rather than identifying types of totems, a more fruitful approach may be to distinguish between a totem's mode of acquisition. He identified four such modes: in dream; conception; augury; and descent and affiliation. In part because of the multiplicity of modes of acquisition, an individual is linked to more than one totem, or, as it is now more commonly referred to, more than one Dreaming. Each such link would bring with it its own behavioural codes. In the words of Stanner (1965a, p. 226), a totem is thus simply

> a sign of unity between things or persons *unified by something else* . . . The 'something

else' is one or more of a possibly vast set of significations of that totem . . . One of the most common is the symbolic complex 'one flesh – one spirit – one country – one Dreaming'.

In this unity, codes of conduct are imposed, bringing into play the Dreaming's moral load.

The Dreaming as morality

While Stanner contemplated the place of good and bad in the Dreaming, he remained puzzled about its moral message until the end (e.g. Stanner 1965a, pp. 217–18). He was confronted with a dilemma: while the Dreaming was a moral tale, it was not itself moral (see also Morphy 1998). The Dreaming beings appeared to operate under the same moral order that blanketed the world of the living, and yet they often transgressed it. In some cases, the message was clear: good and bad were established and communicated with appropriate social responses. One story from the Adnyamathanha of the Flinders Ranges (South Australia) serves here as an example:

A long time ago there was an old women who was staying with her daughter who was about to have a baby. Ever since she had become pregnant, the daughter had been suffering from headaches.

One day when the daughter's husband was off hunting, the daughter once again complained about pains in the head. The mother didn't like it, and picked up a stick and hit her daughter on the back of the neck, killing her.

The old woman hid the body in the camp. Later in the day, the husband came home from hunting. The mother met him before he came into the camp where her daughter was lying, and said: 'You can't come to the camp, because your wife is going to have the baby now. Then tomorrow we're going to move on to another camp.' So he went off to get wood.

The next day the man's mother-in-law moved to the next camp, carrying the dead woman, who by now was stiff. The man came and asked where his wife was, and the old woman told him she was at *Virdnirvirdni-nurrunha* which means 'the woman is stiff'.

The woman and her son-in-law agreed that the next day they would travel only a very short distance. The husband went out hunting again while they were moving, and

when he came back, asked where his wife was today. The mother said she was camped at *Yungga-umburrumburri* which means 'body puffed up', and he could not see her. The old lady went into the *widlya* [shelter] and imitated the crying of a baby so the husband would not be suspicious.

The man returned to his camp. He was thinking to himself that he had never heard the name of that place before. The next day when he asked where his wife was today, the woman told him that she was camped at *Thungga-pudupudu* which means 'the body is putrid'.

The man became suspicious because he couldn't hear the baby crying, nor could he hear his wife talking. When the old woman went to the creek to get water, he went into the *widlya* and had a look. There he found his dead wife. His mother-in-law saw him walk away from the camp.

He took his boomerang and killed the old woman, then made a song about it.

After that he dug a grave and buried his wife. Then he put the body of his mother-in-law into the last *widlya* that she had made at *Thungga-pudupudu*, and walked away. (Turnbridge 1988, pp. 128–9)

But sometimes the story ends in a way that seems to go against the moral grain. Among the Wardaman of the Northern Territory, for example, there is a story that has the wrongdoer (by indigenous law) victorious (Figure 2.2) (David *et al.* 1994, p. 245):

Yiwarlarlay is the home of the Lightning Brothers, Yagjagbula and Jabirringgi . . . The former is young and handsome, whereas Jabirringgi is older and rather unattractive. Ganayanda is married to Jabirringgi. Every day, one of the two brothers goes hunting, bringing back the day's catch to Yiwarlarlay. One day, as Jabirringgi returns from the hunt, he hears his brother [having intercourse] with Ganayanda in a secluded fissure in the rock. In anger, he throws a spear at Yagjagbula, who evades it. The two brothers take up positions on the surrounding plains, whence a fight erupts, creating the lightning in the skies. The frogs come up from the south, as does the rain, who watch the brothers fight. Eventually, Yagjagbula wins the fight by knocking Jabirringgi's head-dress off with his boomerang.

Figure 2.2 Ganayanda, Yagjagbula, and Jabirringgi, Yiwarlarlay, Wardaman country

Searching religious thought for a moral code applicable to everyday life is avowing the relevance of a higher order to our earthly existence. As a 'moral universe', the Dreaming 'has not only mythic but also continuing human implications' (Berndt 1998 [1979], p. 29); it is in this that the moral significance of the Dreaming is found. The lesson involves not simply judging each human action as good or bad. More importantly, it positions people as being responsible for ensuring maintenance of the moral code through ritual observances of one kind or another. As Ronald Berndt has aptly written:

> Mythic beings, like human beings, can choose one course of action in contrast to another. The choice they make has consequences for themselves and for others, but does not necessarily commit them irrevocably. However, one consequence of the mythic action for human beings . . . is ritual advantage. It results in the introduction of ritual which, supposedly, would not have come about without a wrong act taking place. Out of bad, comes something good. In the myth itself, no moral judgement is made: it is simply that this is the course of events which brings about ritual benefits – 'this is how it came about' . . .
>
> If and when they [the mythic beings] 'do wrong', or 'go wrong', it is within the context of an already-shaped destiny. (ibid., pp. 30–2)

The Dreaming explains the way things are by reference to how they became. But it is in the world of the living that people must meet their moral responsibilities established in the Dreaming. In this sense it stands as law, to many *the* primary fabric of the Dreaming.

The Dreaming as law

The Dreaming identifies a timeless past when the law was set forth into the world. Through the actions of the Dreaming beings, the living were handed down a cosmological order which, by its appearance, became the law of the land. In defining an individual's spiritual being, the Dreaming defined her or his relationship to other people, to the 'spirits', and to the land. These connections carried responsibilities for everyday behaviour, as well as ritual roles for more formalized events.

Each Aboriginal group recognized its own law, in that the Dreaming differed from place to place. Such laws had behavioural implications carrying across all aspects of life: kinship networks had to be recognized; people were required to behave in circumscribed ways towards particular individuals; specific languages were to be used in given contexts of talk; the land was to be 'looked after' in particular ways; ritual performances needed to be fulfilled. In this sense, the Dreaming formalizes the conditions by which people should live as social and territorial beings; when the law is transgressed, appropriate means of redress are called for.

By now it should be clear that both people's and the land's identities were intricately bound through the Dreaming both as lore and law. Law is the sum of indigenous behavioural codes sanctioned – operationalized and legitimated – in and by the Dreaming. The Dreaming conceptually signs the land by giving it a cosmogonic history and structuring laws which date back to a beginning and that are passed down from generation to generation. The ancestral beings founded all things existent, including the law as it applies to the world of the living: food taboos, ritual obligations, avoidance rules, marriage regulations. But as evident in the behaviour of the ancestral Dreaming beings, the possibility of transgression was also present from the beginning. The Dreaming beings created the land as it is experienced by people, a landscape at once of personal sense and of geographical and socio-political design.

The Dreaming as geographical mapping

The people's law is the law of the land. In pursuing a social order constructed in the Dreaming, Aboriginal people also pursue a territorial understanding possessing its own economic and political regulations. Social order and the land's identity are not separate for, as already noted, people and land are inextricably linked. Francesca Merlan (1989, pp. 4–9) captures this point well when discussing relationships between people and between people and place in Wardaman country in Australia's Northern Territory:

> The Wardaman use the word *laglan* 'country, place, site' (also camp) to refer to tracts of country and places within them to which they claim attachment, as in the phrase

nganinggin laglan 'my country'. Each such country is composed of many different sites, at least some principal ones of which are associated with estate-linked *buwarraja*, that is, creator figures or 'dreamings' which are saliently or exclusively identified with that particular country. An example is the association of *girribug* 'pheasant coucal' with a particular country . . . of which the Willeroo homestead and some neighbouring places are focal sites. In addition to these estate-linked and bounded dreamings, through each country there pass at least some mythological paths of other, long-range dreamings, many of which . . . happen to come from the west and northwest . . . Thus each country, or 'estate' (see Maddock 1982) is defined by a particular constellation of far-travelled and more local dreamings and sites.

Individuals are related to places by virtue of their own relationship to the various Dreamings that identify the land. It is through the Dreaming that place is conceived and understood, and it is by reference to the Dreaming as law that what can and cannot happen at a place is determined. The Dreaming stories are in this sense both a way of understanding the nature and history of a particular region and a singular aspect of the landscape. It is a way of giving geographical space meaning, of mapping the experienced world. In *Dingo Makes Us Human*, Deborah Bird Rose (1992) writes of places as 'strings', or webs of connections that link places to each other by reference to the Dreaming events that give them meaning. Places are threaded into the Dreaming as the organizational logic of the world in which people dwell. In this sense, the landscape is not so much a stage upon which people live out their everyday existence as an intricate part of their very existence. Through the Dreaming, place is engaged. The world as known is constructed in a process of dwelling, a point we shall come back to in the next chapter.

The Dreaming as social mapping

Let us recall Deborah Bird Rose's concept of the landscape as a network of 'strings' linking each place into a whole (1992, p. 53): 'Dreaming strings fix country and people, demarcating human and geographical identity.' The Dreaming relates people to the order of the cosmos. People and all things were intimately inter-connected and social identification was closely tied to the world order. Through the Dreaming, the human order was not isolated from the rest of existence. Gender relations, alliances, the distribution of languages, kin structures and the rules that govern each are conceptually mapped by the Dreaming, giving each a mien of natural order. The conception of an ordered 'natural' world could through a Dreaming world-view be substituted for an ordered 'cultural' world and territorial mosaic, the distinction between each being redundant.

The Dreaming as time

In 1956 Stanner wrote that there were two major problems with the term 'Dreamtime'. The first was an insinuated misty dreaminess, as the word implies. Dreams tended to be interpreted as a direct connection with the activity and energy of the life-giving and life-sustaining essences of the Dreaming; an animation of the Dreaming forces. But the Dreaming was more than this. A dream may pertain to the Dreaming, but it is a revelation momentary and short. It is a revelation *in* time. The Dreaming is the entire, timeless logic of existence through which all things are understood, dreams included. The second problem was thus a preoccupation with a creative time, a 'golden age' gone by. The difficulty was well recognized by Stanner: the Dreaming is not just of the past, for Dream-time is motionless (while at the same time imbued with change, and paradoxically therefore with movement). The Dreaming beings did not depart the world at the end of a past creative era. They metamorphosed into the earth and the stars and the sky and all things known; the Dreaming operates in earthly life itself. In peopling the world – in filling a primeval void that never existed temporally, for there is nothing before the Dreaming – the Dreaming ensured that it would only become accessible by reference to the worldly filling it created. It is as if the Dreaming emptied itself in creating the human world. In its cosmogonic role – as explanation of how the world came to be – the Dreaming transformed itself into the world of the living. The law continues to direct existence; land continues to breathe life; people continue to engage; the vitality of the creative forces does not cease. Life unfolds, and the world remains pregnant with both life and meaning. All things continue to stamp the world with the mark of the Dreaming. The Dreaming is of the past as it is of the present and of the future.

Stanner's (e.g. 1965a; 1998 [1976]) answer to this dilemma was to coin the term 'The Dreaming' with capital T and capital D. He further qualified his use of the term by referring not to a 'dream-time' but to an 'everywhen'. Place, not time, took precedence, the same worldly place in which people now walked and dwelt.

Marcia Langton (in press) nicely describes how the Dreaming encapsulates experiences of time. Using an apt analogy, she notes how we, in Western society, see in the night sky a gallery of stars, lights that emanate from large balls of fire millions of light years away. In this sense, when we see the stars we see more than lights; our preunderstanding and experience of astronomical–cosmological time are expressed and reaffirmed in the spatial and temporal emanations that we behold. So it is with the Dreaming. Langton notes that in Aboriginal Australia, people are co-defined with their ancestral spirits and clan lands; the land's identity is inscribed in a sensual recognition of ancestral belongings. This involves a temporal as well as a spatial recognition. As with the analogy of the night sky in Western thought, in Aboriginal Australia the land's identity emanates from the ancestral Dreaming beings who give shape and meaning to the world. Following the philosophical writings of Emmanuel Lévinas (e.g. 1987), Langton notes that the living Aboriginal person gains her or his inalienable (Dreaming) identity from the ancestors, creating a temporal continuity with originating but ever-present Dreaming beings. In this sense, preunderstanding is a condition of worldly engagement experienced as dimensions of time and place; the Dreaming imbues life with particular experiences of time.

The Dreaming as ontology and experience

This discussion on the Dreaming commenced with Spencer and Gillen first coining the term around 1896. Subsequently, various dimensions of the concept were considered. We are now back at a consideration of the Dreaming not as religion, time or mapping, but as the conceptual framework of a world that is experienced by Aboriginal people. This is the Dreaming a world-view, an ontological frame-

work through which people position themselves in the world and the world in themselves. It is an explanation of the world and of all reality, Stanner's 'total referent'.

It was, again, Stanner (1987 [1956], p. 227) who first expounded the notion that the Dreaming should be considered as ontology rather than in its more narrow sense as religion (for recent discussions of the Dreaming as ontology, see Myers (1986), Rose (1992) and Swain (1993)):

> The truth of it seems to be that man, society and nature, and past, present and future, are at one together within a unitary system of such a kind that its ontology cannot illumine minds too much under the influence of humanism, rationalism and science. One cannot easily, in the mobility of modern life and thought, grasp the vast intuitions of stability and permanence, and of life and man, at the heart of aboriginal ontology.

Stanner saw the Dreaming as a philosophy and conduit of life, reaching three conclusions about what the Dreaming and its tellings in stories, songs and the like signify:

1 A kind of commentary on reality – 'a poetic key to Reality'.
2 'A "key" to Truth', a vast catalogue of what is known about the world.
3 A 'key' or 'guide to the norms of conduct, and a prediction' of how people will err (Stanner 1987 [1956], pp. 227–9). In this sense, they are a charter of and for action.

Unlike Emile Durkheim (1858–1917), the French sociologist who, by stressing the importance of religious belief in social solidarity and collective consciousness pondered the operation of Aboriginal society in religion, Stanner saw the operation of a world-view in society. It is in the Dreaming that all Aboriginal behaviour operated, guiding and explaining human actions.

Discussion

The landscape of Aboriginal Australia resonates with significance and meaning as it resonates with the powers of the spirit beings of the Dreaming. The landscape is shaped by the Dreaming; it is a timeless spectacle of the Dreaming's creative performance. A waterhole may be a fertile source of life from whence spirit essences emerge out of the depths of the earth, imbuing the living with pregnancy. A tree may be the source of taipans or death adders or rock pythons, a brush or tap against its branches a release of its fecund energies. Such places are powerful and latent, dangerous and life-giving; not always can they be travelled through by people, lest the power of the source overwhelm. But they are dwelt in nonetheless – the world is experienced not *through* the Dreaming but *as* the Dreaming. It resists fictionalization, successfully explaining and guiding human behaviour and the workings of the world at large. The Dreaming is a cosmology rooted in earthly reality and made concrete by bodily engagement in a world that is the product of the Dreaming. It frames human behaviour; it has ideological and material presence.

As guiding principles, perceptions of the world and all that is present in it have implications for the way people order their material world. In this sense the Dreaming signifies containment in both its senses: it *holds* all that is meaningful, in that everything is, by the fact of its very existence, understood in relation to it. And all interpretation is *restricted* by a preunderstanding founded in the Dreaming.

Take for instance a church and an abattoir. A world-view devoid of spiritual existence, if there ever was such a thing, would not recognize the existence of sacred places within its own sphere of sanction. And it is difficult to conceive of abattoirs in a world where the life of animals is divine and where the divine is not to be harmed. In both cases, the material world is ontologically ordered as a result of human engagement. Where there is cognition, there is structure. And where there is organizational structure, there is the trace of cognitive participation. This, of course, is the stuff of archaeological inquiry.

In this chapter I have written at some length about the Dreaming in general terms. I have given examples of specific Dreaming expressions from various parts of Australia without examining in any detail the Dreaming beliefs and material expressions of any one Aboriginal group. I have also suggested that, as preunderstanding, the Dreaming is a compass that directs one's interpretation of the world, and one's actions within it. But I have made no reference as to *how* this preunderstanding

has affected the material world. Nor have I made any reference to its archaeological visibility. What I attempt, in the following chapters, is such an endeavour. More to the point, I isolate behavioural characteristics of specific Dreaming beliefs and practices, and trace the antiquity of those material expressions archaeologically. To get to an archaeology of the Dreaming of ethnographic times (as ontology that informed recent human behaviour) – to trace its antiquity – I focus on three of its material expressions: (1) regional behaviour as traced by virtue of a *place*'s Dreaming significance; (2) *ritual* behaviour as it relates to historically documented Dreaming beliefs; and (3) *symbolic* behaviour as it relates to the land as marked, through rock-art, by recent Dreaming beliefs. These fields of inquiry form the subject of the next three chapters.

Note

1. Patrick Wolfe (1991) has argued that the Dreaming is a Western linguistic construction. But his thesis is very different to the one I suggest here. I am suggesting that one reason why the concept of the Dreaming caught on in Western thought was because of the social evolutionary perceptions of the time. The very word 'Dreamtime' suggested a more dreamy past than the Western, 'civilized' concrete present, but I am not questioning the legitimacy of the *concept* signified behind the word as a signifier of indigenous thought. Wolfe not only suggests that the *word* 'Dreaming' or 'Dreamtime' was constructed in the English language by non-Aboriginal people, but what we have come to know as the indigenous *concept* behind it also. Wolfe makes no reference to Aboriginal ontology and yet gives no credence to the Aboriginal reality of what is expressed in the English words 'the Dreaming', suggesting that the entire concept captured by the term is a colonial fabrication. The core of his argument is that the Dreaming, as a signifying word, is a Western concept, and therefore what is signified by it is also Western. But all nouns capture the world as categories: in giving Aboriginal ontology a name, by definition a process of categorization takes place. By the very process of linguistic expression – and in our case, by communicating in English – the speaker transforms an experience of the world into its linguistic representation, which is not the same thing as the

experience itself. Denying the existence of what one tries to express and categorize through language (whether or not it is because an acceptable word cannot be found) *because* it is expressed in language is throwing the baby out with the bathwater.

If post-colonialism is a rumination of the colonial process, I would suggest Wolfe's own construction of a colonially constructed Dreaming is itself a colonial construction as much as a post-colonial critique. Howard Morphy (1996b) has offered an excellent response to Wolfe's arguments to which I direct the interested reader.

3 Placing the Dreaming: The Archaeology of a Sacred Mountain

When Europeans first arrived in Australia, the Dreaming informed Aboriginal people about the world. The landscapes in which people carried out their everyday lives possessed an order guided by regionally varied Dreaming-based preunderstandings. As human behaviour is always emplaced, *place* was imbued with a spatial order informed by the Dreaming. In the Dreamings of ethnographic times we thus see the reasons for life's spatial order, an orderliness that signals conceptualized, signified and experienced place. Such spatial patterning can be investigated archaeologically, giving us a way of tracing its historical becoming. It is the archaeological signature of the way place has been constructed in the Dreaming of ethnographic times that is addressed in this chapter.

Before venturing into an archaeology of the Dreaming's spatial dimensions, let me explore the socialness of 'place', and its often much confounded 'space'. The theoretical position that animates this chapter will emerge in the process. Such theoretical positioning charts how the archaeological record can be read, opening new doors into the past. It is in the second part of this chapter that I follow this path by addressing an archaeology of the ethnographically known Dreaming through its spatial dimensions.

Place and space

The concepts of 'space' and 'place' have a long history in Western philosophy, dating back at least to the classical Athenian writings of the mid-first millennium BCE (see Casey (1998) for a masterful exposition on the history of these concepts). In contrast to the early Greek writers, such as Plato, who wrote of abstract, latent *space*, or Aristotle, who wrote of *place* as the location of everything held,[1] in Aboriginal thought it is the Dreaming that both shapes and contains. In its cosmogonic dimensions, the Dreaming gives rise to a world of places that locate the ancestral beings precisely at the moment of their engagement in the world they are creating. The Dreaming reveals place by the creative events that are already in place. This is non-linear, timeless place, recounted by emplaced storytellers. The Dreaming gives sensibility to engaged place, inscribing it with cultural topography. In this sense the Dreaming is more than the movement from an empty void to a created world spatially contained in infinite Euclidean space. It is the emplacement of place itself.

The where of the Dreaming is thus not void, as non-existent space. Even in the space that precedes the world's Dreaming creation, the Dreaming beings are already emplaced; or more correctly, place is already in the process of emergence. Simply, there is no space, or place, that precedes the Dreaming. One example from the Adnyamathanha of the Flinders Ranges in South Australia:

> A long time ago there was a big snake called Akurra who lived up in the ranges. He was thirsty, so he went down to Lake Frome for a

drink. He drank a lot of salt water at the lake. In fact, he drank the lake dry.

Akurra drank so much salt water that his belly became bloated and he became heavy. As he lumbered up towards his home in the ranges, his belly carved out a great gorge. He also made lots of waterholes where he camped in the gorge as he climbed back up into the hills. The first of these waterholes was Akurrula Awi.

He kept on coming up, gouging out the gorge, until he came to Nuldanuldanha. He camped here and made another big water-hole. From here he went on to Valivalinha, and made another waterhole. After that the next important waterhole that he made was Adlyu Vundhu Awi.

From here he went up into Mainwater Pound. He kept on climbing up the creek until he arrived at Yaki Awi, and there he stopped. This is where he came to stay for the rest of his life, and he is still there today.

He often comes up out of the waterhole at Yaki and makes rumbling noises in his belly. You can hear that big rumbling noise from a long way away. (Tunbridge 1988, p. 6)

The space of the Dreaming is timeless; it is constructed in a Dream-time not temporal but formative, unfolding out of time. Akurra the giant snake travels not in nothingness but in dimensional and directional space. The story is filled with pre-existing spatial references: Akurra travels from one place to another, in the process giving each its defining features and bringing it into existence. He 'lived *up* in the ranges'; 'went *down* to Lake Frome', drinking so much that his belly became *enlarged*. Akurra 'lumbered *towards* his home *in* the ranges' and 'camped *in* the gorge' that he created as he 'climbed back *up into* the hills'. And he 'kept on coming', camping here and there. This is a world not unformed but already formed while forming.[2] Unlike Plato and Aristotle, the Dreaming speaks of space and place not as essential or containing, but as emergent. Place *is* the world, the lake, the hill, neither held nor holding but existent as it becomes. Place is moved in, but it is never on the outside, for the outside unfolds as place in its conception. There is no abstract space in the Dreaming, for all space is the place of the Dreaming. Whereas Plato's formulation denies the possibility of an archaeology of space – space being pre-given, and thus outside the

target of inquiry because it is ultimately outside human engagement – the Dreaming presents space as always occupied, engaged and examinable.

An archaeology of place

Joseph Grange has written that without place

> there would be neither language, nor action nor being as they have come to consciousness through time. There would be no 'where' within which history could take place. 'Where' is never there, a region over against us, isolated and objective. 'Where' is always part of us and we part of it. It mingles with our being, so much so that place and human being are enmeshed, forming a fabric that is particular, concrete and dense. (1985, p. 71)

As Henri Lefebvre (1991, p. 8) has noted, 'spatial practice consists in a projection onto a (spatial) field of all aspects, elements and moments of social practice'. It is this social projection, replete with preunderstanding, that is touched upon in an archaeology of place. In the process, we touch on patterns of change and stability in the *experience* of place and in the construction of personal being and social identity.

James Weiner (1991, p. 31) has also noted that 'Our intentions and concerns structure the world; . . . Lived space is constituted as the graphic record of such intentional conscious-ness over time.' Our intentions and concerns are historically and culturally positioned in systems of meaning and grounded in place, and knowledge and experience of the world are the coming into being of meaningful space. Because of its meaningfulness place has authority, and it is by reference to such authority that comes understanding. Places can be 'understood as centres of meaning, or focuses of intention and purpose' (Relph 1976, p. 22, cited in Weiner 1991, p. 31). Place is the mean-ingfully constituted loci of experience medi-ated by historically founded preunderstanding.

The capacity of preunderstanding to shape space is what gives it its archaeological poten-tial. In that the Dreaming defines all places, place has structure – place *is* structure – a structure that can be investigated empirically. I am referring here to an archaeology of place not as defined by Binfordian paradigmatics, but to an archaeology of place aimed at accessing the preunderstanding that crafts it.[3]

The social production of place

Place is occupied in human engagement, and therefore the use of space is from the outset social. The theme of place shaped by, and shaping of, social relations, receives what may be its most influential direction in the work of Michel Foucault, who writes of place as institutionalized and given substance by the operation of social relations. This is operation in two senses, *activating* place in its worldly presence and surgically *dissecting* space in the process of engagement. Each aspect of this dual act concerns the power of place, a power that leaves an archaeological mark.[4] I explore this concept of the power of place further in the following pages, for this powerfulness articulates how preunderstanding structures place in social engagement.

The power of place

Place is socially engaged in the everyday workings of society. This is power as a condition of place – by virtue of the social construction and constriction that guides human action and reproduces behaviour in a social space, place emerges as empowered, as a force that influences how we live in a constructed world. At the same time, place is also a condition of power – social power is always emplaced. Power, writes Michel Foucault (1997a, p. 169), 'is the fact that it is a strategic relation which has been stabilised through institutions'. Lived space to Foucault is controlled by social structures, and institutional space is what controlling social practices operate in. Because places are always constructed in strategic social relations – in social order – it can be said to be constituted not *by* relations of power, but *in* relations of power (Foucault 1997b, p. 290).

Foucault focuses much of his writings on delimited spaces such as asylums and prisons. These are categoric places whose existence is made possible by the social construction of *classes* of people with a particular relationship to the rest of society. For example, asylums and prisons are places where particular kinds of individuals deemed unfit for social engagement, 'social delinquents', are isolated for the 'good' of society. The principle of place as co-constructed with classes of people and classes of behaviour applies to all places, as spaces defined in social engagement. Hospitals, churches, schools, paths, village greens and gardens are all prescribed behavioural spaces. There is no neutrality in place. All place is observed, constructed, engaged space.

All places are thus already 'here', present in preunderstanding but in a constant state of (re)definition through engagement. It is through our familiarity of – through relationships with – places that we delineate the world. In this sense place is valorized space. One creek may be fished, another may not; a mountain mined while another 'preserved' for socio-political reasons often far removed from their relative 'economic' potential. 'Economy' also enters this world of meaning, for demand, production and socio-political power are all subject to emplaced social and cultural circumstances, and economy is mediated by preunderstanding. The experienced landscape continuously unfolds in space and time as relationships with surroundings are built on, discovered, negotiated, unveiled.

It is thus not just an outside world that we map in geographical space, but rather *territory*, as already owned, contextualized and continuously renegotiated space. History is positioned to address not so much the nature and dynamics of outside realities, but of people's relationships with their surroundings as fields of experience. History, like geography, is about tracing landscapes of engagement.

The Panopticon

Perhaps the best example of the social construction of place is the Panopticon. It is the 'best' because it is also the most obvious in its extremity.

Jeremy Bentham (1748–1832) was a British philosopher and legal reformer, the founder of Utilitarianism. He believed that the usefulness of any law was in its ability to generate social harmony and happiness (social good). One way to ensure this end was to isolate felons in a prison designed for unseen surveillance: his Panopticon penitentiary of 1791.

The plans for the Panopticon were drawn. It was to be a semi-circular building with the prisoners' cells around the perimeter and observation galleries in the centre. The prisoners would be seen by the centralized inspectors, but the inspectors could not be seen by the prisoners. Obedience and social discipline were the aims. This would be achieved by the uncertainty of whether or not one was being observed.

In its pure form the Panopticon was never built, but in a sense it was already present in a panoptic society. It gave institutional and architectural presence to the late eighteenth and early nineteenth centuries' 'age of machines'; it was, claims David Lyon (1994, p. 63), a product of its day: 'the Panopticon epitomised the kind of "social physics" so popular with the *philosophes* of his day. It neatly translated the clockwork image of being human seen in La Mettrie's *L'Homme Machine* into an architectural reality.'

The Panopticon was for Foucault the ideal example of social discipline in the modern world:

> Whereas in earlier times the failure of social control would result in punishment that was public and brutal, modernity introduced clean and rational forms of social control and punishment. The unruly crowd is rendered manageable; no plots of escape from prison, no danger of contagion if they are sick, no mutual violence if they are mad, no chatter if schoolchildren, and no disorders or coalitions if workers. The crowd is replaced by a 'collection of separated individualities'. As Foucault (1977, p. 201) says, Bentham made 'visibility a trap'. (Lyon 1994, pp. 65–6)

For Foucault the Panopticon served

> to induce in the inmate a state of conscious and permanent visibility that assures the automatic functioning of power. So to arrange things that the surveillance is permanent in its effects, even if it is discontinuous in its action; that the perfection of power should tend to render its actual exercise unnecessary; that this architectural apparatus should be a machine for creating and sustaining a power relation independent of the person who exercises it; in short, that the inmates should be caught up in a power situation of which they themselves are the bearers. (1977, p. 201)

Lyon (1994, p. 66) notes that a 'disciplinary threshold' was crossed in the Panopticon: 'Older, more costly, and more violent forms of power fell into disuse and were superseded by "a subtle, calculated technology of subjection".'

The Panopticon represents an architectural space configured by a panoptic preunderstanding. What gives the Panopticon its power are not the walls, cells or observation tower. It is not even the uniformed officers that survey the scene. It is the social condition that led to its conception and formal presentation in the first place, and in which it was to operate. It is the categorization of illness, deviance, normality, the differentiation and allotment of appropriate behaviour and behavioural space. The Panopticon was built in social consciousness as an appropriate place for deviants, their surveillance and treatment. The condition that gave rise to the Panopticon was a panoptic preunderstanding, a panoptic sense of place, society, alterity and self. The Panopticon alerts us to the possibility of a *spatial history* as a way of accessing preunderstanding.

At first appearance the Panopticon may seem inappropriate for a general discussion of place as socially constructed. After all, the Panopticon is bounded by walls and conceived to contain and constrain social deviance and deviants. It represents a particular kind of built space that is differentiated, physically demarcated, and separated from the rest of social space. In addressing the Dreaming, are we not interested in the 'natural' environment, a concern qualitatively different from the artificial construction that is the Panopticon?

In one sense, the Panopticon and so-called 'natural' places are one and the same, as both are known, signified and experienced in social engagement. Both are defined in contemporary social relations; both are constructed in the public imagination. Like the Panopticon, 'natural' places reveal themselves as social space.

We could discuss the social construction of place by reference to Christian churches or Islamic mosques; abattoirs or vegetarian wholefood shops; birthing clinics or cemeteries; Trafalgar Square or the Bastille (see Smith 1999); the Mississippi River or the Amazon; the Andes, the Himalayas or the Alps. In each case, place is imbued with a meaning that expresses (and in the process impresses) social and cultural values.

Veronica Strang (1997) has thus written about how differing cultural values underpin Aboriginal people's and white cattle farmers' relationships with land in and around the Aboriginal township of Kowanyama in northwest Queensland. 'Uncommon ground' – one land, two landscapes – is her term for this process of giving meaning to the world we experience in the process of social dwelling:

> Social processes are also processes of interaction with the environment as a whole, which provides the medium through which values are created and expressed. The landscape is a crucial part of this medium, and the development of an effective relationship with the natural environment depends on the location of certain values in the land. (Strang 1997, p. 176)

Such values are informed by preunderstanding. As preunderstanding changes, so do our relationships with places. The way we use and relate to places – the way we live in the landscape – also change, along with their material manifestations. Although the concepts are separate, the way we signify and use place are inter-connected, in that to signify, and to use, are to identify. In the rest of this chapter, I discuss the archaeology of one particular signified place, the Djungan Dreaming mountain of Ngarrabullgan, through this understanding. I argue that Ngarrabullgan's Dreaming significance has shaped its human engagement during ethnographic times, a shaping that has left behind a particular material trace that can be archaeologically investigated. My aim is to identify when the mountain's Dreaming perspective emerged in the depths of history. I begin with the ethnographic present, for it is from here that the mountain's Dreaming significance is recognized and defined. It is by reference to these recent times that the Dreaming's archaeological signature – and a spatial history of the Dreaming – can be traced back in time.

Placing the Dreaming: an archaeology of Ngarrabullgan

Ngarrabullgan is an imposing, cliff-lined sandstone and conglomerate mountain located some 100 km northwest of Cairns in northeastern Australia. It is 18 km long, 6.5 km wide and surrounded by 200–400 m cliffs along most of its periphery (Figure 3.1). The top of the mesa is amply vegetated by distinctive, endemic grass-tree-dominated woodlands.[5] In contrast, the area immediately around the mountain, and extending for tens of kilometres in all directions, consists of volcanic and metamorphic sediments. The vegetation off the mountain is more open, sclerophyll woodlands.[6] The fauna on top are also different to those found off the mountain, with very few terrestrial mammals occurring on the mountain – only two individuals of a single species have ever been sighted after years of faunal surveys. This has been the case at least since the late Pleistocene. Permanent waterholes are relatively common on the mountain, and can occasionally be found interspersed along creeks and rivers near its base. Ngarrabullgan is, therefore, a well-demarcated geological, botanical and zoological 'island' in a terrestrial landscape.

Ethnohistory

When Westerners first visited the region in the late 1800s, Ngarrabullgan was – as it continues to be today – at the geographical and spiritual heart of Djungan Aboriginal country, which extends from the Mitchell River in the north, Baker's Blue in the east, the Hann Tableland in the southeast, the Featherbed Ranges in the south, and Elizabeth Creek in the west. Norman Tindale (1974, p. 167) noted that Djungan country covered some 3400 km²; at 50 km², Ngarrabullgan is only a small part of their territory. Surrounding Djungan country is a network of other landed language groups: Wagara[7] to the west and northwest, Kuku Minni and Kuku Yalanji to the northwest, north and northeast, Muluridji to the north, Mbabaram to the east and southeast, and Wagaman to the south and southwest.[8] Peter Sutton has written that such Aboriginal languages mark

> the lands whose owners under Aboriginal customary law were given particular languages during the mythic foundation of the world, the Dreaming, and it plots those land/language associations. It is a general rule in Aboriginal Australia that languages are held to have originated when Dreamings (Ancestral Beings, totemic heroes) invested the land with meaning and with human beings. (1991, p. 50)

Figure 3.1 Ngarrabullgan (Mt Mulligan), cliffs, northern end

Djungan country thus represents the lands whose owners under customary law were given the Djungan language during the creative acts of the Dreaming. The people who trace their ancestry as Djungan hold exclusive primary indigenous associations with both the land and the language.

Little is known of Djungan socio-cultural practices for the early European contact period. Lauriston Sharp (1939, pp. 439–49) noted that during the early parts of the twentieth century, the Djungan were organized around named patrilineal moieties – a two-fold social division recognizing descent through the father – 'associated with strongly developed totemic patterns . . . and by clearly defined local patrilineal clans responsible for the practice of a totemic

ancestor cult'. The moieties (commonly known as 'skins') consisted of *Raku* and *Walar*, *Mirki* and *Muranggan*. These were each divided into two sections (also known as 'skins'), *Kupandji*, *Worpu*, *Djilandji* and *Karpandji*. According to Sharp (1939), the *Kupandji* and *Karpandji* sections were of the *Raku/Walar* moiety, and *Worpu* and *Djilandji* were of the *Mirki/Muranggan* moiety. Members of one moiety could not marry other individuals of that moiety: groups were exogamous (Mathews 1898, p. 251; 1899, p. 110; Roth 1897, p. 68; 1910, p. 100).

R. H. Mathews (1898, p. 251) also noted that there were totems attached to each group, and that 'the children take the name of the complementary section in the division to which their mother belongs':

Personal names are derived from one or more of the multiple clan totems or in many instances from the place names of particular clan countries.

> . . . the land is divided up into unnamed clan domains which include a number of individual named countries. The several countries constituting a clan domain need not be contiguous . . . Each individual member of the clan is associated with a few of these countries, which become the person's 'homeland' . . . and which may provide him with a personal name. (Sharp 1939, p. 443)

In this way, each person belonged to a specific, named section, which recognized descent through strict lines according to indigenous law; and these sections in turn belonged to one of two named moieties. These were territorial affiliations that linked people to the land via the ancestral beings of the Dreaming. Like Mathews, Sharp (1939, p. 443) also wrote that 'the patrilineal totemic clan is an important element in the social structure . . . The clans normally have multiple totems'; 'each of the moieties has its own peculiar totems and . . . there is a strict tabu against any person killing, eating, or in any way harming the chief of these moiety totems'. The moiety name *Raku* refers to a local, small, nocturnal bird which Sharp could not identify, but which he noted was 'characterised by its regular metallic call' (1939, p. 269). He also observed that *Mirki* refers to 'the night owl or mopoke. These birds and their eggs, although not good eating anyway, are tabu . . . where they are the moiety totems.' *Walar*, a small yellow bee, is a supplementary totem, as is *Muranggan*, a larger black bee. However, 'there are no totemic tabus on the use of the honeys produced by these bees' (Sharp 1939, p. 443). Sharp also wrote that:

> Annually or at less frequent intervals . . . a member of one moiety kills the bird totem of the opposite moiety and publicly desecrates and exposes the body. There then follows a ceremonial mock combat between the males of each moiety, in which harmless reed spears are ordinarily used. Occasionally, however, the sacrilege may be considered more seriously; recently among the Wakura [Wagara, a neighbouring group which recognized a similar totemic lore] a *Raku* man who

had killed *mirki* was speared through the leg by *Mirki* men.

> According to a myth . . . the two moiety birds, as anthropomorphic mythical ancestors, were the original inhabitants of the country. Eventually, when other ancestors had come into the land, *Mirki* was attacked, surrounded by grass fires, and even though he took refuge in a hollow tree, as *mirki* does not, he had to change into a bird to escape. This action led all the other ancestors to change into the various bird, animal, and other forms they have now, and thus brought to a close the mythical ancestral period at the beginning of time [the Dreaming]. (ibid.)

Djungan elder Sam Wason presently stresses that *mirki*, the night owl, is the sacred bird of Ngarrabullgan. This probably indicates that the mountain was unequally associated with each of the two moieties (and in particular the territorial responsibility of the *Mirki* moiety), although there is no explicit knowledge of Ngarrabullgan's clan or moiety affiliations today.

The 'devils' of Ngarrabullgan

In 1926 Francis Richards, a long-time European resident of the area, wrote of the mountain's local Dreaming significance:

> These natives were highly superstitious and had an intense fear of devils. There were four of these –
>
> (1)   The Beerroo, who lived anywhere.
> (2)   The Eekoo (or mountain devil), who lived on Mount Mulligan [the European name for Ngarrabullgan].
> (3, 4) Mooramully, Barmboo – Water devils inhabiting waterholes.

Most sickness was attributed to the agency of these devils, the blame generally falling on the Beerroo or the Eekoo. These devils were able to throw hooks, stones, or pieces of wood into the body without leaving a mark. The Eekoo's home was a lake on Mount Mulligan (Lake Koongirra), and natives were very afraid to go near this lake or into its waters; though the Rhoonyoo (or witch doctor), being a companion of the Eekoo, could enter the water without fear. The Eekoo was generally held responsible for any sickness when on the mountain. The natives have an interesting legend to account for the origin of

Mount Mulligan and its lake. The mountain, which was built by the wallabies on the advice of the eaglehawk, was originally a huge pile of stones. A swamp pheasant built its nest on the mountain and hatched its young. The Eekoo came along and killed the nestlings. The pheasants in their anger thereupon started a bush fire to burn the Eekoo, and so great was this conflagration that it melted the stones and so formed the towering cliffs of Mount Mulligan. To save his life the Eekoo created the lake and took refuge in its waters; and so the lake became his home. Although the lake is the home of the Eekoo, strictly speaking he is not a water devil but wanders about anywhere on the mountain.

The Mooramully and Barmboo lived in the waterholes, and were responsible for deaths by drowning or sickness coming on shortly after a swim. All these natives were excellent swimmers. If a native were caught in quicksands he declared that the Mooramully had pulled him under. The booming noise made by ripples against a washed-out bank was the voice of the Barmboo. The Mooramully was an important spirit, since he not only initiated the Rhoonyoo or witch doctor, but also kept him supplied with knowledge and worked for him. When the rainbow came out, this was the Barmboo himself. If it shone on a native (other than the Rhoonyoo) he would die. (Richards 1926, pp. 256–7)

Today, the Djungan elders stress Eekoo's and Mooramully's presence on the mountain, and a need to keep these spirits informed of one's approach and actions whenever on the mountain (Mooramully is also present in waterholes off the mountain). What emerges from both the early historical literature and from present-day attitudes is that Ngarrabullgan was and is a place cautiously approached by Djungan individuals, as the mountain is the home of potentially dangerous spirit-beings. When we visited the mountain in the 1990s to undertake archaeological surveys and excavations, the members of the Djungan community who accompanied us repeatedly discussed the spirits of the mountain, particularly Eekoo. Night-time discussions invariably revolved around the spirits and what could be done to keep them away from camp sites.

Not surprisingly, archaeological evidence of past human occupation on the mountain is sparse, and rather different from that in surrounding areas. Systematic archaeological surveys have been undertaken on and around Ngarrabullgan between 1991 and 1997. During this time, numerous transects and quadrats were walked by research teams for any evidence of past human activity. Each artefact encountered was recorded, giving insights into the social construction and use of place (see David *et al.* 1998 for details of research methodology).

Only a single culturally modified tree – evidence of economic activities such as the extraction of honey or possums, or of the production of tools or weapons (e.g. spear tips, shields, containers) – has been found on the mountain, whereas such trees are common at its base. In the area around the mountain we located 95 stone artefact scatters, while on the mountain only 31 were recorded, despite more intensive surveys on top. When the differences in the size of the two surveyed areas are taken into account, we find that for every square kilometre off the mountain there is an average of 63 sites. On the mountain sites are more sparsely distributed, at an average of nine sites per square kilometre. The size of these sites also differs, depending on whether they are located on or off the mountain: on average, sites off the mountain possess nearly nine times as many stone artefacts as those on the mountain.[9] Viewed in a different way, stone artefact densities on the mountain average 19 artefacts per square kilometre; off the mountain they average 1046 artefacts.

The types of rock-art found on and off the mountain are also different. Most of the rock-art on the mountain consists of hand stencils, whereas off the mountain it consists of paintings (David 1998). Many of the rock-shelters capable of being occupied on the mountain show a lack of surface evidence of cultural activity (e.g. ash, stone artefacts, rock-art); those off the mountain invariably do. Clearly, while there is some evidence of visitation on the mountain, it is of a different order to that off the mountain. Taking the ethnographic information into account, the archaeological differentiation of the mountain from surrounding areas makes sense, given Ngarrabullgan's special Dreaming significance as the home of dangerous 'devils', rendering habitation on the mountain during ethno-graphic times potentially hazardous and therefore less likely.

In order to address the antiquity of this dual archaeological signature between the mountain and areas around it, a programme of excavation was initiated. The logic for this research was based on the idea that if the archaeological signature of recent times relates to recent Aboriginal relations with place, then we may be able to trace back through time the emergence of the mountain's Eekoo-mediated Dreaming significance, as an apt example of spatial history. With this aim in mind, systematic archaeological excavations were undertaken both on and off the mountain. Ten rockshelters with evidence of surface cultural materials were identified on the mountain, and 21 off the mountain (surveys for rockshelters have been very limited off, but extensive on, the mountain). All the sites on the mountain were test-excavated, plus one shelter that showed no surface signs of human occupation (Waterhole Cave), as well as a sample of five rockshelters from the basal cliff face and nearby areas, the furthest being 1 km from the mountain. To determine the regional meaningfulness of the cultural trends, the results were also compared with excavations in caves and rockshelters more than 50 km from the mountain, in the Chillagoe, Mitchell-Palmer and Laura regions to the west and northwest. The results of these investigations are summarized below.

The ancient past

Archaeological research in Djungan country began in 1991. We now know that people have been in the region for more than 35,000 years, with particularly intensive occupation after c. 5400 years BP (Bird et al. 1999; David 1993). However, until now research has concentrated – as indeed it has almost everywhere in Australia – on origins and on the first appearance of new cultural traits, including aspects of lithic technology, food production, settlement patterns, and artistic conventions. The *cessation* of cultural practices has been paid little attention; evidence for patterns of site abandonment has rarely been considered in Australian archaeology (but see Hiscock 1986; O'Connor et al. 1993). It is this issue that I wish to focus on here.

The sites

Sixteen rockshelters have been excavated (Figure 3.2). Eleven are situated on top of the mountain (Painted Ell, Tunnel Shelter, Bush Peg Shelter, Hand Shelter, Fig Tree Shelter, Nonda Rock, Grass Tree Shelter, Gorge Creek Shelter, Quinine Bush Shelter, Ngarrabullgan Cave, Waterhole Cave); three are immediately at the base of its cliffs (Kookaburra Rock, Courtyard Rock, Dragonfly Hollow); one is on a small, isolated cliff detached and immediately to the west of the mountain (Lookout Shelter); and one is located on the surrounding undulating plains 1 km to the north of the mountain (Initiation Cave). All bar Waterhole Cave contain cultural materials.

Except for Ngarrabullgan Cave, cultural materials in the excavated sites on the mountain are restricted to stone artefacts, charcoal, burnt or fire-cracked stones, pieces of ochre (some use-worn), and rock-art. The absence of bone and other food remains is startling, particularly given the large number of sites sampled. This absence cannot be explained as a result of mechanical or chemical break-down; rockshelters off the mountain but located within the same geological unit as those found on the mountain all possess animal remains, in some cases in great abundance. Further, the mountain top possesses shallow sediments; the rockshelters are no exception. This is because of a general lack of wind-blown or alluvial sediments reaching the plateau, topographically a regional high point, from surrounding areas. Consequently, cultural materials deposited on the ground surface may remain exposed for considerable periods of time. It is only with the onset of human occupation that sediment accumulation becomes apparent in most rockshelters, and there tends to be a direct correlation between sedimentation rates and artefact deposition rates, indicating possible measures of intensity of site use over the long term. In many cases, sedimentation is rapid over brief periods associated with individual occupational events, largely but not entirely the result of hearth-induced concentrations of ash. Most rockshelters are relatively well stratified, albeit shallow.

Ngarrabullgan Cave[10] is by far the largest cave or rockshelter yet recorded on the mountain (Figure 3.3). Today, the ground surface is littered with charcoal from past campfires,

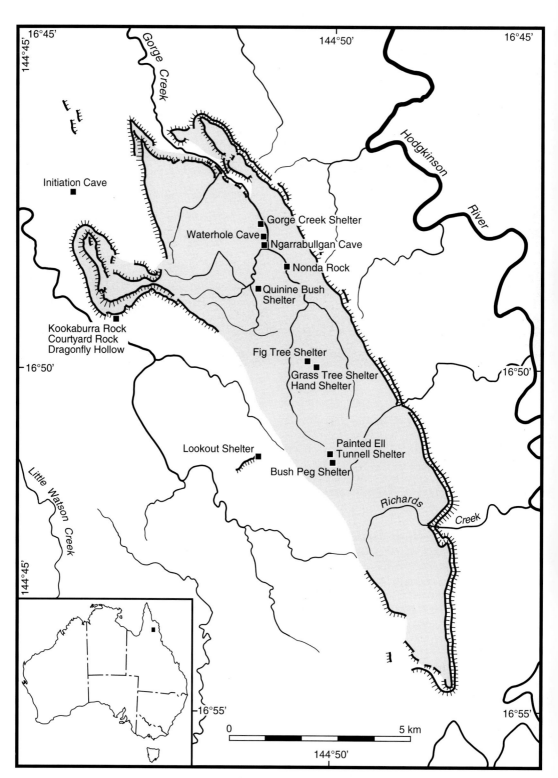

Figure 3.2   Locations of excavated rockshelters, Ngarrabullgan

Figure 3.3 Ngarrabullgan Cave

although their individual configurations cannot be delimited as the charcoal merges from one fireplace to another.

At Ngarrabullgan Cave a series of occupational events beginning shortly before 35,000 years BP, and possibly continuing until around 32,000 years BP (Bird *et al.* 1999; David 1993), are evident. The site was then abandoned until *c.* 5400 years BP, after which it became frequently used until *c.* 900 years BP (*c.* 1000–1200 CE). A single radiocarbon date has been obtained for the last *c.* 730 years (calibrated age), despite dating more than 50 excavated charcoal samples (most being AMS dates on single pieces of charcoal).

Sixteen samples of charcoal were also randomly collected from the present cave floor (Figure 3.4). All of this charcoal came from the surface; no charcoal buried in the consolidated matrix was extracted, as the aim was to date the latest occupational events, not the older buried deposits. No scree deposits lead into the cave, and the rocky surface immediately outside the site does not allow large trees to grow. We can therefore assume that the large pieces of charcoal are the result of human firing activity within this large cave.

Of the sixteen radiocarbon-dated samples, only one revealed a determination from the last *c.* 650 years[11] (calibrated ages), reminiscent of the similar pattern revealed from the excavation (Table 3.1). The implication is that while the mid to late Holocene period witnessed considerable occupation, site abandonment was under way by the beginning of the second millennium CE, and virtually complete by the end of the thirteenth century CE. Was this abandonment an isolated case, a change in the incorporation of a particular cave in a more or less stable regional settlement system? Or rather, does this historical circumstance represent broader alterations in systems of land use? This issue requires consideration of the timing of abandonment at the other excavated sites.

There is evidence of human occupation from the other excavated rockshelters at Ngarrabullgan dating back at least 26,000 years BP, with a number of sites showing traces of use beginning during the late Pleistocene or early

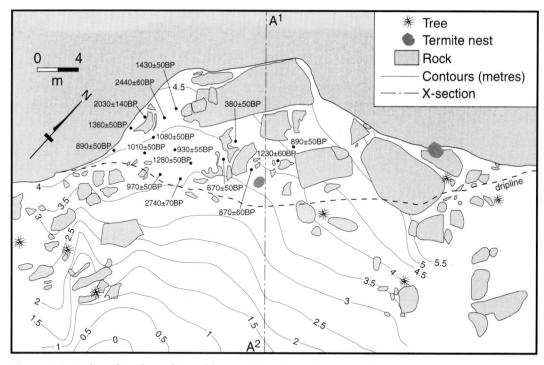

Figure 3.4 Radiocarbon dates obtained from surface charcoal, Ngarrabullgan Cave

Table 3.1 Radiocarbon determinations and calibrated ages (following OxCal Program v.3.0) (at 95.4% confidence level), Ngarrabullgan Cave surface results.[12]

Radiocarbon date (years BP)	Calibrated age (in calender years CE or BCE)	Laboratory no.
380 ± 50	1430–1640 CE	Wk 5792
670 ± 50	1260–1400 CE	Wk 5780
870 ± 60	1030–1260 CE	Wk 5789
890 ± 50	1020–1240 CE	Wk 5783
890 ± 50	1020–1240 CE	Wk 5794
930 ± 55	1010–1220 CE	OZB 086
970 ± 50	970–1190 CE	Wk 5787
1010 ± 50	890–1160 CE	Wk 5786
1080 ± 50	820–1030 CE	Wk 5784
1230 ± 60	660–950 CE	Wk 5790
1280 ± 50	650–880 CE	Wk 5785
1360 ± 50	590–780 CE	Wk 5788
1430 ± 50	530–680 CE	Wk 5781
2030 ± 140	400 BCE–250 CE	Wk 5793
2440 ± 60	770–400 BCE	Wk 5791
2740 ± 70	1060–800 BCE	Wk 5782

Source: after Stuiver and Kra 1986.

Figure 3.5 Hand Shelter (excavation in progress)

Holocene (Tunnel Shelter, Grass Tree Shelter, Quinine Bush Shelter, Nonda Rock). These sites were more or less continuously re-used (at an archaeological timescale) until final abandonment during the late Holocene. Human occupation in the other five sites on the mountain (Figure 3.5), and in the five excavated rockshelters near its base, began at various times after around 5000 years BP (see David and Wilson 1999 for details of each site). Again, human occupation appears to have been recurrent until the sites were finally abandoned. In all sites, with the possible exception of Bush Peg Shelter, this final abandonment took place by 1400 CE (Table 3.2) (cf. David and Wilson 1999).

Ngarrabullgan in regional context

Although use and occupation of the Ngarrabullgan plateau by people were common throughout much of the Holocene, extending back into the late Pleistocene, by around 1400 CE – and probably as early as 1300 CE – rockshelters on top of the mountain largely ceased to be used. This pattern is apparent both at Ngarrabullgan Cave – the largest cave known on the mountain – where campfire use almost entirely stopped by this time and in the timing of abandonment of all the other known rockshelters on or immediately adjacent to the mountain. Could it be that the occupational trends evident for Ngarrabullgan are one expression of a broader demographic trend, a reflection of declining local populations alone? Is site abandonment around 1300–1400 CE, some 600 years before the advent of Europeans, a broader phenomenon that applies to the occupation of caves and rockshelters in all parts of northeastern Australia, rather than specifically to the onset of a new signification of Ngarrabullgan?

To address these questions, let us consider the timing of site abandonment in all excavated caves and rockshelters from other parts of northeastern Australia where such data are available. Information on the timing of final abandonment of sites within 200 km of Ngarrabullgan is currently available for rockshelters from three regions, the Laura sandstones, and the Mitchell-Palmer and Chillagoe limestone outcrops (Figure 3.6).

Table 3.2 Radiocarbon dates and calibrated ages (following OxCal Program v.3.0) representing timing of abandonment of rockshelters (calibrated ages at 95.4% confidence level).

Site	Radiocarbon date (years BP)	Calibrated age (in calender years CE or BCE)	Laboratory no.
Bush Peg Shelter	420 ± 50	1410–1530; 1550–1640 CE	Wk 6191
Nonda Rock	650 ± 50	1270–1400 CE	Wk 6190
Hand Shelter	667 ± 33	1270–1320; 1340–1400 CE	Wk 5864 + Wk 5865
Tunnel Shelter	710 ± 50	1220–1320; 1340–1400 CE	Wk 6185
Painted Ell	780 ± 80	1030–1310; 1350–1390 CE	Wk 6183
Courtyard Rock	810 ± 80	1020–1290 CE	OZB 778
Gorge Creek Shelter	910 ± 40	1030–1210 CE	OZD 878
Grass Tree Shelter	690 ± 50 to 1050 ± 50	1240–1400 to 880–1050; 1090–1120 CE	Wk 6186 Wk 6187
Quinine Bush Shelter	1150 ± 50	770–1000 CE	Wk 6188
Lookout Shelter	1600 ± 45	340–560 CE	OZB 801
Kookaburra Rock	1630 ± 80	230–600 CE	OZB 781
Initiation Cave	2410 ± 50	770–390 BCE	Wk 6026
Dragonfly Hollow	3000 ± 80	1430–1010 BCE	OZC 068
Fig Tree Shelter	older than 560 ± 50	older than 1290–1440 CE	Wk 6189

Laura

The Laura sandstones are found 100 km to the north of Ngarrabullgan. They consist of a 300 km-long, arcing belt of dissected weathered sandstones and conglomerates containing thousands of rockshelters, many of which carry rock-art and evidence of past habitation. Excavations at Early Man Rockshelter, Sandy Creek 1 and 2, Yam Camp, Magnificent Gallery, Giant Horse, Hann River 1, Red Horse, Red Bluff 1 and Mushroom Rock (Morwood and Hobbs 1995; Morwood and L'Oste-Brown 1995a; Rosenfeld *et al.* 1981) have concentrated on the timing of earliest occupation and cultural changes through time, largely bypassing the question and potential significance of patterning in final site abandonment. However, some data on the latter are at hand, in the form of near-surface radiocarbon determinations, the presence of items of material culture from post-European contact times, and/or depictions of recent (post-European contact) material items or fauna in the rock-art.

At Early Man Rockshelter, Sandy Creek 2 and Red Horse (Morwood and L'Oste-Brown 1995b; Morwood *et al.* 1995; Rosenfeld *et al.* 1981) glass artefacts testify to the use of the shelters after the arrival of Europeans around the 1870s. At Giant Horse, paintings of European motifs (including horses) imply site use since that time (Morwood 1995a). At Magnificent Gallery, Mike Morwood and Silvano Jung (1995, pp. 97–9) note that

> the most recent period of use involved an exponential increase in rates of artefact deposition which peaked immediately before European contact . . . Aboriginal use of Magnificent Gallery began about 15,000 years ago, and probably continued to early in the European contact period (i.e. AD 1875).

At Red Bluff 1, 'in the European contact period' the site 'is reported to have been a summer campsite' (Morwood 1995b, p. 131). Unfortunately, however, no temporal data are at hand to determine the timing of final abandonment at the other sites. In short, at Laura evidence for final site abandonment is available from six sites. In each case, occupation is apparent until the arrival of Europeans late in the nineteenth century.

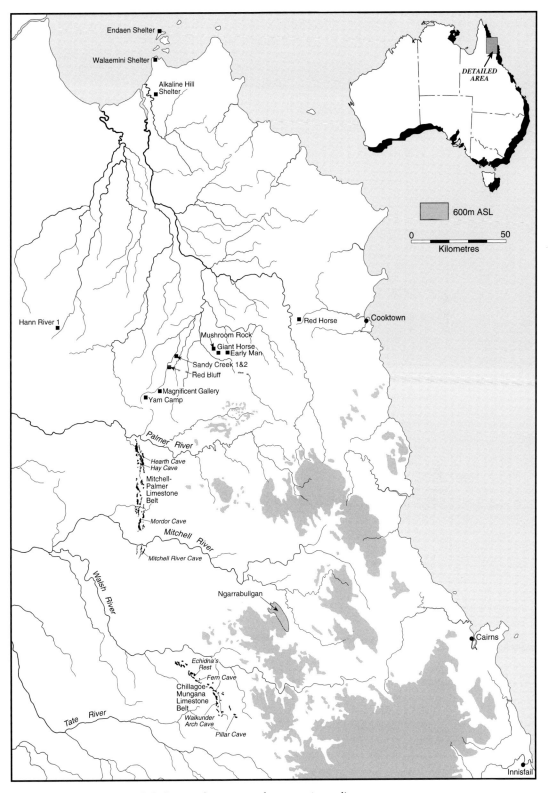

Figure 3.6 Excavated rockshelters and caves, northeastern Australia

Figure 3.7   Cave-riddled limestone outcrop near Rookwood

Mitchell-Palmer

The Mitchell-Palmer limestone belt is a 60 km-long, 5 km-wide belt of Upper Silurian to Lower Devonian karst towers (430–390 million years old), located some 60 km northwest of Ngarrabullgan. The limestone towers often exceed 1 km in length and 500 m in width, jutting more than 100 m above the surrounding plains. These are impressive rock formations possessing regionally distinctive soils and vegetation communities. Many shallow rockshelters and deep caves occur near the junction of the karst towers and their surrounding pediments. Some of the caves extend for many hundreds of metres into the rock, usually in pitch-black conditions but sometimes illuminated by roof collapses creating sky-lit chambers. No evidence of human presence has yet been found in the deep caves. However, evidence of Aboriginal occupation in rockshelters as well as in sunlit cave entrances is abundant. One of the most common and readily observable indications of past human presence is the rock-art.

Just south of the Mitchell River, the Mitchell-Palmer limestone dips below the ground surface, only to re-appear 35 km to the south, near Rookwood (Figure 3.7). This southernmost extension is known as the Chillagoe limestone belt. It formed at the same time as the Mitchell-Palmer limestones, and both sections are recognized as local extensions of a single geological unit, the Chillagoe Formation.

Temporal data on final abandonment are available from two excavated caves from the Mitchell-Palmer limestone belt. At Hay Cave (Figure 3.8), occupation began around 30,000 years BP, with final abandonment taking place 350 ± 55 years BP (calibrated age = 1440–1650 CE, possibly extending into the post-contact period). At Mordor Cave, cave paintings include the depiction of a pig, indicating site use during the post-European contact period (David and Chant 1995).

Chillagoe

Five caves have been excavated from the Chillagoe limestones some 50 km southwest of Ngarrabullgan. The antiquity of final site abandonment has been dated in two of these.

Figure 3.8 Excavation in progress, Hay Cave

At Echidna's Rest, site use began at an unknown time before 3000 years BP and continued into the last 200 years (and likely into the European contact period) (David 1990). At Fern Cave, occupation began around 30,000 years BP, and continued until the end of the Pleistocene at some as-yet undetermined time between $17,200 \pm 100$ years BP and $10,200 \pm 210$ years BP. Fern Cave is located near a large, permanent spring. Occupation at this site during the height of the last glacial maximum, and shortly thereafter during a period of time characterized by marked aridity, has elsewhere been explained by this unusual environmental context (David and Lourandos 1997).

Conclusion

Rockshelter use at Ngarrabullgan ceased almost entirely after the fourteenth century CE, a temporal trend not matched in neighbouring regions. This is well illustrated by the observation that in nine of the ten excavated sites for which information on final abandonment is available in places away from the mountain, occupation is manifest until or near the early European contact period, between 100 and 200 years ago (the exception is Fern Cave). This contrasts with the case at Ngarrabullgan, where no such evidence is apparent.

Similarly, 34 radiocarbon dates relating to the final period of abandonment of caves and rockshelters have been obtained from regions including and surrounding Ngarrabullgan. Thirty-two of these come from Ngarrabullgan (the other two are from Hay Cave in the Mitchell-Palmer, and Fern Cave near Chillagoe). Yet, the most recent of all radiocarbon determinations – the one closest to, and statistically overlapping with, the timing of European invasion – comes from Hay Cave some 80 km away. Furthermore, none of the excavated sites from Ngarrabullgan show any trace of items of material culture from the European contact period. This is in marked contrast to caves and rockshelters in surrounding areas, such as Chillagoe, Laura and the Mitchell-Palmer, where glass artefacts and rock paintings of animals introduced by Europeans are common. While caves and rockshelters on, and immediately around, Ngarrabullgan were systematically abandoned by the fourteenth century CE, other places further away continued to be inhabited until the advent of European invaders. What happened at Ngarrabullgan that led to this situation? What are the implications of this scenario for the way people related with and signified place in northeastern Australia during the late Holocene?

First, abandonment around 600 years ago at Ngarrabullgan was systematic: it involved a near-total cessation of hearth construction and site use at Ngarrabullgan Cave – the largest known rockshelter on the mountain (and situated near a permanent waterhole, a generally uncommon environmental setting in this seasonally dry landscape) – as well as the cessation of use of the smaller sites strewn across the mountain-top and at its base. That is, changes in both individual site and regional land use are implicated. Of course, no open sites have yet been excavated and such a programme would now be desirable, but such sites are uncommon on the mountain, and in no instance would they appear to constitute more than fleeting visits. European objects such as flaked glass have not been recorded from any site on or near the mountain, and yet many have been found in surrounding areas.

Should we view, then, the abandonment of Ngarrabullgan by *c.* 600 years ago as a simple human response to changes in resource availability, to a depauperization of economic resources on the mountain? This is unlikely, for three main reasons:

1 Pre-European site abandonment on the mountain is matched by a similar trend in rockshelters off, but adjacent to, the mountain (Lookout Shelter, Dragonfly Hollow, Kookaburra Rock, Courtyard Rock and Initiation Cave).
2 Permanent sources of freshwater (lakes, waterholes) are more abundant on than off the mountain.
3 Pollen work from a core on the mountain does not indicate any major environmental changes coincident in time with the period of site abandonment. The largest permanent water source on the mountain – Lake Koongirra – has held freshwater for at least 6000 years (Butler 1998).

Whatever its ultimate cause(s), abandonment by the fourteenth century CE appears to have been mediated by the onset of a new system of signification that rendered the mountain inappropriate for habitation. This, in essence, matches the mountain's Dreaming significance as recorded by Europeans early in the twentieth century, and reported by present-day Djungan elders. If human behaviour is grounded in relations with place, and if the world is engaged through its meaningfulness, then the archaeological changes documented above suggest that during the early stages of the second millennium CE experience of place and country had changed dramatically in what is now known as Ngarrabullgan.

Why the change in people–land relations around the fourteenth century CE I do not know. One implication, however, is that it involved a change in systems of meaning relating to place. The archaeological changes suggest that Ngarrabullgan attained new cultural significance. If the recently documented Dreaming belief system – which today gives Ngarrabullgan meaning – emerged in its modern form only during the later stages of the Holocene, a connotation is that it is not only Aboriginal symbolic, artistic or socio-economic systems that can be shown to have changed, but more fundamentally the framework of preunderstanding that informed engagement and through which experience of life was ordered. The archaeological changes documented at Ngarrabullgan and surrounding areas, coupled with the ethnographic record, imply the emergence of a new way of relating with place some 600 years ago, akin to the Dreaming as recorded ethnographically.

Ngarrabullgan thus offers an opportunity to investigate the dynamics of people's ethnographically known Dreaming engagement with place in this part of north Queensland back into the late Holocene. As expressed through abandonment, we may say that Ngarrabullgan presents evidence of a process of re-definition, the re-domestication of a landscape. And as part of a spatial story involving a relationship between people and place, Ngarrabullgan and its immediate vicinity 'constitute[s] part of a domain of social negotiations' (Tilley 1993, p. 55). The Ngarrabullgan archaeological trends imply a systemic change in the way people related to and perceived their world around 600 years ago: there was a re-definition of place, and therefore a perceptual shift. I suggest that it was around that time that the ethnographically documented system of signification which gave the mountain meaning in the recent past first approached its modern form. The emergence of Ngarrabullgan's modern Dreaming significance took shape not deep in antiquity, but likely hundreds rather than many thousands of years ago.

Notes

1. In Plato's (*c.* 428–348 BCE) *Timaeus*, we read of *chora*, a pre-existing space in which all of reality is created (de Botton 1999). It is there, already present at the moment of creation. It pre-exists not as nothingness – as void – but as latent space. This is cosmogonic space originating before all origins. It is space without beginning, space as pre-existence. In his *Physics*, Aristotle (384–322 BCE) is not so much interested in the (non)origins of space as in the placeness of all things (Aristotle 1983). Everything is found in place. Place becomes a container in which things are located, and all action occurs in place. This is dimensional space, a vessel that contains or surrounds and an immovable presence that bounds the contained. To Aristotle, place holds primacy, for all things exist only in their emplacement. But if place is primacy, what of the creative energies of the Dreaming?

2. It could be argued that the translation of indigenous stories into English has created a dependence on particular tenses not necessarily present in the original language; this translation creates new temporal contradictions. In such a view the apparently contradictory temporality expressed in the Tunbridge and other Dreaming stories could be taken as a function of translation rather than of indigenous thought. However, I would argue instead that the non-linear temporality expressed in the English language translation expresses the non-linear temporality of the preunderstanding that gave rise to the indigenous Dreaming stories. The apparent temporal 'contradictions' are only contradictions when viewed from a linear Western temporality, not when seen through non-linear time as expressed in a Dreaming preunderstanding (cf. Benterrak *et al.* 1984; Muecke 1992).

3. Binford's (1982) 'archaeology of place' was concerned with site patterning, both within a place and between atomized places. He was concerned not with an archaeology of preunderstanding as accessible through an archaeology of place, but with an archaeology of adaptive strategies:

> I am interested in sites, the fixed places in the topography where man may periodically pause and carry out actions. I am concerned with site patterning both in the frequency with which occupations occur at different places, and in the processes which generate associations among archaeological materials at sites. Site patterning in both within-place and between-place contexts is a property of the archaeological record. The accuracy with which we are able to give meaning to the record is dependent upon our understanding of the processes which operated in the past to bring into being the observed patterning . . .
>
> The processes which cause site patterning are long-term repetitive patterns in the 'positioning' of adaptive systems in geographic space. Site patterning derives from repetition, or lack thereof, in the spatial positioning of systems. It is suggested that the factors which condition the positioning of systems may be somewhat different from the factors which condition the internal operation of a system. In fact, humans may reposition their adaptive strategies in a landscape, a tactic which may generate variability in the archaeological record while serving to foster stability within the ongoing system. (Binford 1982, p. 6)

Unlike Binford, I take my directing cue not from adaptation, but from the concept of place as articulating social power.

4. Knowledge, and the preunderstanding that comes with it, are by nature hegemonic, and in this sense are inherently powerful. As human behaviour is always emplaced and informed by preunderstanding, place is itself hegemonic. Lefebvre (1991, p. 6) writes of the power of hegemony:

> A particular 'theoretical practice' produces a *mental space* which is apparently, but only apparently, extra-ideological. In an inevitably circular manner, this mental space then becomes the locus of a 'theoretical practice' which is separated from social practice and which sets itself up as the axis, pivot or central reference point of Knowledge. The established 'culture' reaps a double benefit from this manoeuvre: in the first place, the impression is given that truth is tolerated, or even promoted, by that 'culture'; secondly, a multitude of small events occur within this

mental space which can be exploited for useful or polemical ends.

Hegemony operates on and in social practice. All world-views are inherently hegemonic, including the Dreaming. More to the point, hegemony is found in preunderstanding, and the hegemony of social practice is ultimately found in *habitus*.

5. The dominant taxa on the mountain are Myrtaceae (including *Eucalyptus*, *Melaleuca* and *Callistemon*), Proteaceae (*Grevillea*, *Persoonia* and *Hakea*), *Xanthorrhoea johnsonii* and grasses (*Poaceae*).

6. Plant communities off the mountain are generally dominated by ironbark (*Eucalyptus crebra*) and ironwood (*Erythrophleum chlorostachys*) in the upper storeys, and kangaroo grass (*Themeda triandra*) and various spear grasses (*Aristida* spp.) in the lower. Stands of ti-tree (predominantly *Melaleuca viridiflora*) occur in patches (Butler 1998).

7. Most language names here follow the spellings of the Institute of Aboriginal and Torres Strait Islander Studies in Canberra. Where they do not, it is either by request of local indigenous groups, or because of established, alternative linguistic conventions.

8. When Europeans first arrived in Australia, some 250 Aboriginal languages were spoken across the continent; each was as distinct from another as French is to English. In addition, each language possessed various dialects, making Australia a diverse linguistic bloc. Djungan and neighbouring languages are but one of a group of historically related languages that cover about 80 per cent of Australia. Together, this geographically widespread language family has been called 'Pama-Nyungan' by linguists, the word for 'person' being *pama* or *bama* in northeastern Australia, and *nyungan* in the southwest. The languages of the Non-Pama-Nyungan group occur mostly in central-north or northwestern Australia. Various linguistic characteristics separate these two language groups. One example is the tendency for Non-Pama-Nyungan languages to pack a very large amount of information – even a whole sentence – into a single verb form, such as *punnungamkawunkumawinhatdangathanintha* in Murrinh-Patha, a Non-Pama-Nyungan word that means 'they few already ran away from them two males' (Walsh 1991, pp. 39–40). Pama-Nyungan words do not behave like this, smaller amounts of information being loaded into many different words (Walsh 1991).

9. The largest artefact scatter on top of the mountain possesses fifteen stone artefacts; off the mountain the largest site possesses 402 artefacts. On the mountain, average artefact numbers are two per site, while off the mountain they average seventeen per site.

10. Ngarrabullgan Cave is a large sandstone shelter, 47 m wide by 14 m deep and with a floor area covering 268 m^2. Ceiling height is a maximum 6 m near the dripline.

11. This sample, dated to 380 ± 50 years BP (Wk 5792), was located *c.* 4 m from a radiocarbon date of 350 ± 65 years BP (OZB 192) for excavated materials, and may relate to the same occupational event.

12. Some researchers 'correct' all southern hemisphere radiocarbon dates by subtracting 40 years prior to calibration (cf. Vogel *et al.* 1993). However, the validity of this offset is disputed by many radiocarbon experts. Following the latest advice from Mike Barbetti of the NWG Macintosh Centre for Quaternary Dating in Sydney (personal communication 1999), I have not offset in this way any of the radiocarbon dates presented in this book. In either case, the general chronologies discussed here would not be affected.

4 Performing the Dreaming: Ritual in the Arid Zone

The Oxford English Dictionary and *The Dictionary of Anthropology* (Barfield 1997, pp. 410–12) each list two definitions of ritual, one specific and one general. In its narrow sense, rituals are described as 'prescribed, formal acts that take place in the context of religious worship' (ibid., p. 410), such as the Christian mass. In its more general sense, ritual is defined as:

> any activity with a high degree of formality and a nonutilitarian purpose. This usage includes not only clearly religious activities, but also such events as festivals, parades, initiations, games, and greetings. In its broadest sense, ritual may refer not to any particular kind of event but to the expressive aspect of all human activity. To the extent that it conveys messages about the social and cultural status of individuals, any human action has a ritual dimension. In this sense, even such mundane acts as planting fields and processing foods share a ritual aspect with sacrifice and the mass. (ibid.)

Or as the *Oxford English Dictionary* puts it, in its most extended and trivial sense ritual concerns action occurring as a result of 'social convention or habit'.

According to this broadest definition, ritual is therefore how we do or communicate things socially through cultural codes. Ritual is repetitive behaviour in the sense that it involves normative action. All culturally patterned behaviour is ritualistic – leaving the house at a pre-allocated time in the morning to get to work, catching the bus rather than walking, or walking rather than catching the bus. The distinction between work-time and home-time, the social schedule that temporalizes this division, and the gendered tasks that operate it, are socially codified and in this capacity frame our actions as ritual. Socially routinized actions are in this sense conflated with ritual actions by virtue of their social codification and normative expectation: how behaviour is socially structured has become a ritual order. Many, but not all, anthropologists use ritual in this broadest sense.

I use ritual in a less inclusive sense. Social codification may be a necessary condition of ritual, but it is not, in the sense adopted in this book, a sufficient condition. Rituals are more than ways of doing things – they are more than *habitus* as socially circumscribed behavioural styles, and more than routine as repeated behaviour. Pierre Bourdieu (1977, p. 218) coined the term *habitus* 'to set aside the common conception of habit as a mechanical assembly or preformed programme'. It refers to 'a system of lasting, transposable dispositions which, integrating past experiences, functions at every moment as a *matrix of perceptions, appreciations, and actions*' (ibid., pp. 82–3). *Habitus* is behaviour 'Objectively "regulated" and "regular" without being in any way the product of obedience to rules'; it can be 'collectively orchestrated without being the product of the organizing action of a conductor' (Bourdieu 1980, p. 53). It informs the social actor, and social order is a condition of *habitus* (ibid., pp. 53, 291). People engage with their material world through *habitus* informed by a preunderstanding of the world. *Habitus* is the bodily engagement of preunderstanding. But *habitus* is not ritual.

While rituals are informed by preunderstanding, they are also active performances – intentional, somatically (involving the body) choreographed actions whose purposes are beyond themselves. Rituals employ formal social codes to call upon an outcome. Because these codes are informed by preunderstanding, ritual can be thought of as a somatic codification of preunderstanding. Ritual, in the sense used in this book, is a social act that involves codified performance by a socially defined actor or set of actors. In its performative dimension, ritual implies a conscious awareness of the act, and intentional action *for* something.

Rituals are explicitly meaningful acts. They cannot be reduced to social habit (in the sense of routine), play (cf. Keesing 1991) or theatre (contra Richard Schechner, e.g. 1987, and to a lesser degree Victor Turner, e.g. 1987). Ritual action is aimed at achieving an outcome that is beyond its own execution, a purpose beyond itself, although there is no guarantee that the effect will match the original anticipation. Dancing around a fire is only ritualistic if it has an intended purpose beyond the dance, if the dance calls upon an intended outcome. Rituals emerge from a normative view of the world and are called upon whenever the world as known requires animation or re-animation through performance. Ritual, therefore, animates and affirms social values already present in preunderstanding. In social performance, ritual sentimentalizes preunderstanding. In this sense it also helps shape future social sentiment and personal identity.[1]

Rituals are thus distinctive kinds of social acts that are informed by, but not synonymous with *habitus* and preunderstanding. They are also more particular than the routines of Max Weber and Anthony Giddens, who were more concerned with the deep social and psychological causality of normative behaviour than with ritual as a means of causing a worldly effect. Weber (e.g. 1958) saw the world as occupied by people who attach meaning to things, including their own feats. Those meanings take hold of people, directing individuals

to behave in patterned ways. We may call these patterned ways social routines. Similarly for Giddens (1995, p. 150), 'The continuity of daily life is not a "directly motivated" phenomenon, but assured in the routinisation of practices', a routinization governed by tradition. There is 'ontological security' when social life is patterned and self-replicating, because innovation and uncertainty are threatening. For Giddens (e.g. 1995), as for Erving Goffman (e.g. 1959) before him, social routines are thus a way of dealing with psychological anxiety. They are a social 'presentation of the self', effecting social reproduction in the process.

Like Giddens' routines, rituals as used in this book express a world order and bring into effect its operation. But a ritual action is a particular kind of performative routine undertaken with a delayed outcome in mind. Rituals are thus frameworks for actions that are (1) socially mediated; (2) codified; (3) performed; (4) aimed at achieving something; and (5) consciously engaged. This combination of sociality, codification and somatic performance gives ritual behaviour a high archaeological visibility. It is this propensity that makes ritual performances of the Dreaming of ethnography particularly amenable to archaeological investigation.

Dreaming rituals and the totemic landscape in central Australia

In this chapter I investigate the archaeology of Dreaming rituals from one part of Australia only, the Arrernte[2] lands of the arid centre. My reason for this geographical focus is simple: it is only here that the archaeology of ritual places has been systematically attempted by Australian archaeologists.

The anthropologist Nicolas Peterson (1972) has noted that understanding Aboriginal relationships to place across all of Australia during the ethnographic period requires consideration of totemic classification. Totems relate people to place through the Ancestral beings and creative events of the Dreaming, and totemic affiliations are maintained and celebrated in ritual performances. Peterson (1972, p. 13) follows Meyer Fortes's (1967, p. 6) definition of totemism, as 'beliefs and practices in which relations of a special kind between persons and designated groups of persons, on the one hand, and natural species of animals and plants or artificial objects, on the other, are postulated'. Totems, he argues – as Baldwin Spencer and Frank Gillen (e.g. 1899) similarly implied before him – were in the first instance attached to localities. It is by virtue of this emplacement that people gained their own totemic affiliations (Peterson 1972). Because people were conceived in place, were born in particular patri- or matri-estates, and died in place, they were from birth affiliated with emplaced Dreaming beings. From the outset, people were born into a socially meaningful, ordered world by virtue of a Dreaming preunderstanding of the where of their existence, an existence recognized through totemic affiliation. Spencer and Gillen discuss these totemic relationships with reference to the Arrernte and neighbouring groups:

> Every individual in the tribe is born into some totem – that is, he or she belongs to a group of persons each one of whom bears the name of, and is especially associated with, some natural object. The latter is usually an animal or plant; but in addition to those of living things, there are also such totem names as wind, sun, water or cloud – in fact there is scarcely an object, animate or inanimate, to be found in the country occupied by the natives which does not give its name to some totemic group of individuals.
>   . . . Every prominent feature in the landscape of the Arunta country, whether it be a solitary mulga tree on a stony plain, a water-hole, a low ridge or a high mountain peak, is associated in tradition with some *Knanja* or totem group . . . the same local association with totemic groups holds good for the whole of the large area occupied by the Arunta people. (1927, pp. 67, 88)

Every Arrernte individual belongs to a particular patriclan and recognizes the totems of this patriclan. Patriclans are of primary importance, although totemic affiliations attained via other means are also recognized, entailing a range of responsibilities and behaviours in ritual and in everyday practice. Totemic membership, for example, involves ownership of particular symbols and dances, some of great secrecy and others of public standing. They also require formal celebration and ritual maintenance. During these rituals, the creative events of the Dreaming are commemorated, and their ongoing significance for the living is ritually fed in a visual show of solidarity and spiritual guidance. These rituals address the Dreaming's significance in place, for, as already noted, totemic identity relates to the deeds of the Dreaming beings as it relates to specific parts of the landscape. For example, the Kangaroo totem emerges not in no-where land, but through the emplaced actions of the ancestral Kangaroo in the Dreaming. It is in specific places that the Kangaroo's fecundity is carried into the world of the living during the Dreaming. In Kangaroo country, the Kangaroo's essence is passed down from generation to generation through conception, descent, adoption and other means. Again, to cite Spencer and Gillen, as an example of this relationship between people, place and totem:

> The members of each totem claim to have the power of increasing the number of the animal or plant, and in this respect the tradition connected with Undiara, the great centre of the kangaroo totem . . . is of especial interest. In the Alchera [*sic*, read Alcheringa, or Dreaming] . . . a special kangaroo was killed by kangaroo men and its body brought to Undiara and deposited in the cave close by the water-hole. The rock ledge arose to mark the spot, and into this entered its spirit part and also the spirit parts of many other kangaroo animals (not men) who came subsequently and, as the natives say, went down into the earth here. The rock is, in fact, the *Knanja* stone of the kangaroo animals, and to them this particular rock has just the same relationship as the water-hole close by has to the men. The one is full of *Kurunas*[3] of kangaroo animals, just as the other is full of those of men and women.
>   . . . Every animal such as a kangaroo is supposed to have a *Kuruna* or spirit part, just like a human being has. As a *Kuruna* it has no legs or arms or head, but goes into its mother and grows into a kangaroo or rat or wild dog, as the case may be. An emu *Kuruna* goes into an emu, who lays an egg containing the little emu *Kuruna*, which is very small and cannot at first be seen, but it grows into an emu inside the shell and hatches out from this just like a little kangaroo or human baby grows inside its mother's *ekura*, or baby bag, and hatches out. (1927, pp. 84–5)

Through ritual, the Kuruna were celebrated and their reality confirmed. More correctly, through ritual the worldly existence of the spiritual was celebrated, and the future safeguarded. The very possibility of this relationship was formally recognized, and the ontological framework for its continuity confirmed. Through ritual roles and ritual participation, during ethnographic times relations between people, place and the Dreaming were maintained, giving individuals and groups social and experiential emplacement.

The archaeology of Dreaming rituals: Mike Smith and the antiquity of the totemic landscape

Because some Dreaming beliefs known from ethnography involve specific ritual behaviours in specific places, it is possible to investigate their antiquity through an archaeological investigation of ritual remains. In principle this is a fairly straightforward exercise: identify a ritual place, list the ritual's material manifestations, and trace its origins back in time through archaeological investigation. However, such archaeological research has been rare in Australia. Only one researcher has ever undertaken such systematic research with ritual and the totemic landscape in mind: Mike Smith, then of the University of New England. Appropriately, given the history of the Dreaming in anthropological thought, Smith's research has focused on the antiquity of Arrernte and neighbouring systems of land use and, more recently, on the central Australian totemic landscape.

In 1988, Mike Smith presented his doctoral research on the archaeology of central Australia. In this work, the results of which were published in a string of papers (e.g. 1986c, 1993, 1996), he investigated patterns of change and continuity in the use of specific ethnographically known Dreaming ritual places in central Australia (Figure 4.1).

Figure 4.1 Public ceremony danced by Luritja men at Tempe Downs, June 1894 (*Source*: Baldwin Spencer. Morton and Mulvaney 1996, plate 12)

Although his research was not then explicitly addressing the totemic landscape, his excavation results were well suited to such concerns. At some of Smith's excavated sites, various types of rituals and the Dreaming beliefs that informed them had earlier been documented by Spencer and Gillen (1899, 1927) and Theodor Strehlow (1971). Recognizing this potential, Smith (1996; Smith *et al.* 1998) recently reviewed his own doctoral results to address the antiquity of central Australia's totemic landscape. In the following pages I explore the results of Smith's excavations in relation to late nineteenth- and early twentieth-century ethnographic sources, for together they enable us to systematically consider the antiquity of central Australian Dreaming rituals known from ethnography. Where permitted by Arrernte elders, for some of the stories and associated rituals are highly restricted, I present the Dreaming stories relating to each site in some detail, for they will give a sense of how the landscape and rituals have been culturally shaped.

Therreyererte and the Native Cat Dreaming

At the time of Spencer and Gillen's visit to Alice Springs in 1896, the *tjilpa* (Spencer and Gillen's 'Achilpa'), or Native Cat (*Dasyurus geoffroii*) totem group was clearly important to the Arrernte (Spencer and Gillen 1927). Therreyererte is a major totemic centre associated with the wandering Native Cat ancestors (Spencer and Gillen's 'Therierita'; see also Strehlow's (1971, p. 550) 'Therereta'). The site is located in eastern Arrernte country, but has significance to other groups as well, for it is but one place in a long chain of linked Native Cat centres stretching some 2500 km across the centre of the continent.

The *tjilpa* tradition concerns the travels of the ancestral Native Cats from near Spencer's Gulf in the south to Australia's northern coast. During these travels, the ancestors left behind the spirits of Native Cats, rituals specific to each totemic centre (including initiation rites in some places), and other sacred traditions (Smith 1988, pp. 274–5). I recount here in some detail Spencer and Gillen's (1927, pp. 355–90) account of the *tjilpa* Dreaming story, for it is in this story that Therreyererte's Dreaming significance is found.

The Native Cat tradition revolves around Numbakulla, a supreme ancestor whose name means 'always existing' or 'out of nothing' (Spencer and Gillen 1927, pp. 355–6). It is Numbakulla who gave rise to every individual's spirit, to the totemic rituals, sacred objects and places, and to the totems themselves. In fact, it is Numbakulla that gave rise to everything associated with the Dreaming:

> He arose 'out of nothing' at a place called Lamburkna, far away to the south, in the country now occupied by the Dieri tribe. He was the great original *Inkata Alchera Numbakulla* [head man of the totemic traditions of the Dreaming]. From Lamburkna he started out and travelled far away to the north over country now occupied by the Dieri, Urabunna, Wonkgongaru, Luritcha, Arunta and Ilpirra tribes. East and west he wandered to the furthest points of the Macdonnell, Strangways and all the central ranges; northwards his travels extended to a camp later on visited by the *Inkata Achilpa kupitcha* [head man of a totemic party of the Native Cat Dreaming], beyond what is now called Tennant Creek, on the Wauchope River, between the former and Powell Creek. (Spencer and Gillen 1927, p. 356)

During his Dreaming travels, Numbakulla created the totemic centres for the various Dreamings, giving sacred rituals to each place:

> At every such place he put his foot down, saying, *Nana, Knanja Achilpa, Erlia, Arura,* etc.; here is wild cat, emu, kangaroo, etc., Knanja [totem]. Then he drew and left on some rock or ground surface what is called a *Churinga ilpintira* – that is, a special design or mark associated with the totem of that locality. Each of these designs now forms the distinctive mark or *Ilkinia* of the Knanja of that place.
>
> While traversing the country he not only created mountains, rivers, flats and sand-hills, but also brought into existence all kinds of animals and plants. After returning to what is called his *Tmara maraknirra* (a very great camp), at Lamburkna, he first of all made a cave or storehouse in a rock, in which, later on, to secrete the Churinga [the sacred objects], of which, as yet, there were none. Storehouses such as this one are scattered all over the country. Every Knanja has a certain number associated with it. (ibid., p. 356)

Numbakulla began making the storehouse for the sacred objects at Lamburkna, his great camp, painting the sacred rock drawings and planting the sacred pole of the Native Cat totem in and near the cave. Once the storehouse was made, he made the Churinga, or sacred totemic object, into which the spirit of the Native Cat was placed. The Churinga was placed on top of the sacred rock painting inside the cave, and the spirit emerged, giving rise to the first Native Cat person. This was the original head of the Native Cat totem group.

Numbakulla then made the local totem centres and many Churinga sacred objects representing the various totems, each Churinga possessing a Kuruna spirit. These spirits emerged from the Churingas, giving birth to the head person of each totem group. All the original Churingas also contained very many secondary Churingas, each containing a Kuruna spirit. Numbakulla sent the great head of the Native Cat totem across the land to place the original Churinga of each totem at the centres that he had previously made. It is these places that are now recognized as the totemic centres of Arrernte country, latent with the life powers of the totemic beings with which they are associated.

The original Churingas of each totem had two parts: one male, one female. Originally tied together, the two parts held the spirits of men and women. In their emergence from the Churingas, men and women were born.

Numbakulla also emplaced the totemic rituals:

> Numbakulla showed everything to the *Inkata Achilpa maraknirra* [the great Native Cat ancestral head]. He taught him how to perform ceremonies connected with the various Knanjas, just as they are carried out at the present day. They are spoken of collectively as *Nalungwa*, and are now shown to the younger men as they pass through the various grades of initiation, first during the ceremony of circumcision or *Lartna*, then during that of subincision or *Ariltakuma*, and lastly, during the much more lengthy, important and final Engwura [this is the name of the long sequence of totemic rituals] ceremony, after which the younger men are admitted to the status of *Urliara*, or fully initiated member of the tribe. These ceremonies are concerned especially with the doings of the Alchera ancestors.

> Numbakulla, as said, explained everything to the *Inkata Achilpa maraknirra* ... everything used in all ceremonies, and gave him final instructions in regard to all matters concerned with the founding of the Knanjas. Before he went away he painted his Kauwa-auwa [sacred pole, now used in the Engwura rituals] all over with blood to assist him in climbing, and said to the *Inkata maraknirra* [great totemic head], *Unta Engwura Kauaua kurka atchikka* – you use a small Kauaua [sacred pole of lesser nature than the *Kauwa-auwa*] at Engwura [totemic ceremonies]. He also said, *Unta tmara Lamburkna Knanja*; Lamburkna is your Knanja [totem] camp: *Churinga talkara indulla-irrakura ingwana*; the Talkara [sacred object] is your *Churinga indulla-irrakura* [the sacred object from which each person's spirit comes]; *Knanga Achilpa*, Achilpa [Native Cat] is your Knanja [totem]: *illa moinja*, take care of it: *Ambilia-ekura tera ingwana*, the two *Ambilia-ekura* [sacred objects used during rituals] are yours; *Ambilia-ekura kuruna injaira oknirra*, a very large number of Kuruna [spirits] are in the *Ambilia-ekura; unta oruka Mbanbiuma*, you by and by (make) *Mbanbiuma* [ritual to maintain in the world the thing represented by the totem]. Finally he said to the *Inkata Achilpa maraknirra, unta Churinga, niinda, Pertalchera* – your Churinga, one, (is in the) *Pertalchera* [storehouse of the sacred object]: *illina allpurijigga tmara nukwa eritjikka*, we two will go up to see my camp. Telling the Inkata to follow him, he began to climb up the tall Kauwa-auwa, and reached the crosspiece, but the blood had made it too slippery for the Inkata, who slid down, so Numbakulla went on alone, drew the pole up after him and he was never seen again. (Spencer and Gillen 1927, pp. 359–60)

The *Inkata Achilpa maraknirra* travelled across the land with the Churinga of the various totems, placing them in the future totemic centres. From these Churinga emanated the human spirits, and in this way the entire landscape became animated with people of the various totems.

From the main camp at Lamburkna, the *Inkata Achilpa maraknirra* threw a special totemic object of the Native Cat totem to Wairidija, in Dieri country to the south of Arrernte country. This sacred object contained a spirit from which emanated a great Native Cat headman, who returned to Lamburkna. Here the *Inkata Achilpa maraknirra* gave him two sacred pouches teeming with the Kuruna spirits of Native Cat totemic beings, to be used in the Engwura rituals. The *Inkata Achilpa maraknirra* then taught the headman everything that he had learned from Numbakulla, sending him back to Wairidija. From here he took out a pair of sacred objects from one of the pouches, giving rise to a minor Native Cat headman and to a woman called Illapurinja. In his turn, the minor headman was taught everything that the great headman had learnt from the *Inkata Achilpa maraknirra* (including how to make Churinga sacred objects). He was also given the two sacred pouches containing the Kuruna spirits of Native Cat individuals. Illapurinja and the minor headman then travelled across the country, seeding the country with Native Cat Churingas, each containing the Kuruna of a Native Cat person. First they went north, then west and northwest, until they reached Arrernte country. At some of the camps, Engwura rituals were performed, culminating in the taking of sacred objects, and in the process Kuruna spirits, from the pouches. During these rituals, ancestral pairs of men and women were sent forth to found the totemic centres that now criss-cross the country. Together, the minor headman and Illapurinja thus founded the Native Cat totem group, although the Kuruna spirits of each and every member of the Native Cat totem had previously been created by Numbakulla, as was the case for the other totem groups (ibid., pp. 360–4).

Illapurinja and the minor headman then moved on, the headman carrying the sacred pouches and Illapurinja a sacred pole, wrapped beyond recognition. During their travels they stopped at various places. As they rested, the headman lay his head on the sacred pouches. On two separate occasions, a Kuruna spirit entered Illapurinja, upon which two special men called Tmalpunga and a woman, Lungarina, were born into the world. On both occasions, numerous Kuruna spirits also entered Illapurinja, and eventually Lungarina also, giving birth to very many men. The only two women in the world were Illapurinja and Lungarina.

The party travelled on, making a series of camps along the way. In these camps were deposited the sacred pouches and the sacred objects, arranged two by two. At each camp, the headman selected various Churinga sacred objects, each with its own Kuruna spirit – male or female – giving rise to men and women emplaced in the various totemic camps. Some of the men were called Twanyirrika. Following directions from the headman, the two Tmalpunga and all the other men were circumcised by the Twanyirrika. On this event, the first Engwura ritual was held, at a place prepared in a way that had been pre-ordained by Numbakulla.

The last set of events of the ritual cycle was the *Mbanbiuma*, the ceremony designed to maintain the numbers of the totemic animal, plant, and so forth. The *Mbanbiuma* represents the so-called 'increase' ceremony of early anthropological writings, but in this particular instance its bearing was the reproduction of people. The headman then sent to each totemic centre one or more pairs of men and women, each with pairs of Churinga. Each man and woman had with them a partner of the correct kin affiliation, thus activating also the kinship system that was to be followed in life.

In addition to people emerging from the Kurunas present in the Churinga that were held in the sacred pouches, the headman also organized for children to be born from Churingas that were to be made by the elders of the various totemic groups. The headman imbued some of the trees with Kuruna spirits, so that eventually the elders would know which wood should be cut to make the sacred objects that held a person's spirit.

Moving on, the headman, the women Illapurinja and Lungarinia, and the special men Tmalpunga and Twanyirrika (of whom there were two of each) set up camps across the land. Along the west side of Lake Eyre, the Engwura rituals were again undertaken. They kept moving on, at each place making sacred caves to store sacred objects. Just before entering Arrernte country, a last Engwura ritual was undertaken, but here everything did not go quite right. As the Twanyirrika men circumcised the other men, one of the latter was injured in the process. The Twanyirrika men were chased by all the other Native Cat men, escaping to the original ritual place, where they died. The headman continued his journey northwards into Arrernte country, creating the camping places that people were to live in thereafter.

First the headman divided his party into two groups, one going eastwards with a wise old man carrying one of the sacred pouches, the other going northwards under his own leadership. In their travels, the two parties performed already established Engwura rituals in named places. They also learned new rituals that became incorporated into the Engwura ritual series, such as subincision and fire rites. Eventually the headman, by now an old Native Cat man, died, nostalgic for his totemic home at Lamburkna. Where he died a boulder sprang, facing towards Lamburkna. The other members of the parties kept going, one group eventually reaching Therreyererte, where the Native Cat subincision and Engwura rituals were performed (Spencer and Gillen 1927, pp. 355–90).

The Native Cat rituals of Therreyererte

At Therreyererte the Native Cat rituals continued to be performed into the twentieth century, as witnessed and documented by various individuals, Spencer and Gillen included. As Smith notes, Therreyererte is a totemic centre, a strategic point along the ancestral Native Cat totemic route. He writes:

> Due to its totemic importance Therreyererte was the site of large ceremonial gatherings involving several hundred people ... The ceremonies were held after summer rain when the plant foods, especially seeds, were judged to be ready. Water for the camp was available at these times from several rock-holes in the gorge although none of these are permanent. Several hundred people are drawn in to the ceremonies including Wongkonguru, Southern Arrernte, Alyawara, eastern Arrernte, and Central Arrernte. The use of waters and plant foods at Therreyererte and in the surrounding area was carefully restricted before one of these occasions. But even with this husbanding of resources it is said to have been necessary for the majority of women and children to camp some distance away from the site, as far as 15 km, and to supply food daily to the men camped at Therreyererte. (1988, p. 274)

This set of circumstances makes an archaeological investigation of Therreyererte's ethnographically known Dreaming status particularly appealing. Use of the site during recent times appears to have been limited to ritual activity focusing on the Native Cat totem (ibid., p. 275),

restricting the chance that excavated cultural materials will relate to other activities not associated with such rituals. Keeping in mind the dangers of approaching sacred objects and places – throughout Australia, individuals who accidentally or knowingly ventured too close to such places were often killed, as has been amply reported by early commentators such as William Lloyd Warner (1958) and Mervyn Meggitt (1962) (see Nicolas Peterson (1972) for specific listings of such killings) – it is unlikely that occupation at Therreyererte represented visits outside the ritual realm. Furthermore, in its regular ritual re-use Therreyererte promises good archaeological visibility. A lack of permanent water sources at the site further militates against the chances of its use as an everyday camping ground.

Dick Kimber and Mike Smith (1987) have published a description of one of the last large Engwura Dreaming rituals to be held at Therreyererte; the following description of this ceremony is based on their observations. They describe the coming together of people from the north, east, south and west. The travellers are from various language groups: the Alyawara from the northeast, the Wongkonguru from the south, the central and eastern Arrernte. Each group had been summoned to participate by the Arrernte Native Cat totemic elders. Great travellers were dispatched with message sticks informing the recipients when the Therreyererte ritual was to take place. As the visitors approached Therreyererte, sometimes from more than 500 km away, they established many camps, patch-burning the landscape along the way. The Arrernte themselves waited eagerly for their arrival, establishing their own base camps more than 20 km away from the ritual site, so as to ensure that sufficient food resources would last – kangaroos, bandicoots, grass seeds and the like – for the ritual gathering. Many people would converge, and in this arid zone food and water could be quickly depleted. Because of this, ritual gatherings needed to be well planned to coincide with the early rains, a time when waterholes filled and young shoots sprung up following the controlled burnings of the landscape that attracted grazing kangaroos ('firestick farming', cf. Jones (1969)).

The Therreyererte rituals were aimed at instructing young initiates in the law of the

Dreaming, as passed down by the elders. While Therreyererte's was a sacred ritual event, many 'profane' social activities were also undertaken. Friends and kin relations would meet, often for the first time in many years. Objects would be exchanged and marriages held. This was a time of rejoicing and a time to settle disputes. Many of the visitors brought gaming objects: in the case documented by Dick Kimber and Mike Smith (1987), the Wongkongurru men of the Carpet Snake totem brought *kultjera* throwing clubs in anticipation of great games.

The various peoples of central Australia were socially linked, even those who had never previously met. Sometimes these links were through marriage, sometimes through totemic affiliation, sometimes through other means such as adoption. During ethnographic times people were always linked through the eight-class kinship system – a method of reckoning kin affiliation first ordained by the Dreaming ancestors who laid down the law – enabling every individual to locate themselves socially in relation to any and every other individual. The names for each class varied from language group to language group. In Australia the eight-class system is peculiar to the peoples of the risky arid and semi-arid regions, a feature that led Aram Yengoyan (1976) to suggest that they enabled people to construct widespread social networks which could be called upon during times of economic hardship or uncertainty (such as droughts).

Kimber and Smith (1987, p. 229) have noted that the participants of Therreyererte's Native Cat rituals consisted of 'localised land owning group[s] of fifty to one hundred people'. As the various groups got nearer to the site, messengers were sent by the elders to request they not approach too close to the totemic centre. Camps were established next to secondary water sources, for Therreyererte itself would not be occupied until all visitors had arrived. Eventually,

> When all the groups were within one or two days' walk from the site, the senior men raised a great pall of black smoke by lighting a highly resinous variety of spinifex. All groups then began moving towards the ceremonial ground. First to arrive, nearly a day ahead, was the local group, whose members then waited and watched the smokes of the approaching visitors. It was apparent that the people from the west would arrive next, so two young men were sent to act as lookouts from a low hill. The rest waited quietly as the excitement mounted. The senior men arranged several false alarms about the arrival, raising expectations even higher. Then suddenly the two young men appeared at a run and the ceremonial leaders issued commands. The women and children knelt in a huddled group, faces to the ground. Fifteen metres away the men stood in ranks, most of them unarmed, a few senior men with spears and woomeras [spear throwers] but held in the non-combat position, and all with their backs to the approaching group. Fairly at first, then louder, came a deep chant:

> Wah! Wah! Wah!

> Feet were pounding in time as the men from the west came at a stamping run towards the site owners. The chanting and the stamping grew louder. Now the local group was totally vulnerable – men unarmed and apparently unaware of the approach, women and children unprotected. The leaders of the western group reached the meeting place. They threw green branches on the women and children then, still chanting and stamping, passed between the waiting men and women. The rest of their tightly knit group repeated these actions, in their turn becoming entirely vulnerable. But the waiting ranks of men joined them and, in the chant of released tension and friendly excitement, ran some hundred metres from the women and children before turning and streaming back again. By now the women and children of the western group were beginning to arrive and people joined in animated discussion. After a short interval, the local group provided food and water and the western people walked to a clump of mulga, where for generations past they had made their camps. (Kimber and Smith, 1987, p. 231)

Soon the visitors from all the different countries had arrived. With some 400 individuals in camp, goods were ceremoniously exchanged. People from the northeast had brought *pituri*, the native narcotic that grew 450 km away; stone artefacts from well-known quarries came from 550 km to the northwest; from up to 300 km to the north came redbean necklaces; boomerangs came from as far away as 500 km to the south (Kimber and Smith 1987, p. 231).

After the first round of gift exchanges, the dancing began. Women from the Dancing Women Dreaming celebrated their own Dreaming stories. Women, men and children all engaged in various ceremonies, re-enacting the events whose origins lay in the Dreaming itself.

Throughout the ritual, seed foods were gathered by the women, daily brought back into camp at the entrance to the gorge. Seed foods made the ritual gatherings possible, for they were a staple food source that enabled large gatherings to be sustained (see Chapter 8). The members of the various totemic groups that gathered at Therreyererte relied heavily on it for the duration of the ritual. The heavy grinding stones were its physical manifestations, their raw material source being in the nearby hills. Game was also collected or hunted, the small game by women and men, the large animals by men. Maintenance ceremonies were practised to ensure the survival and reproduction of species. 'The men cleared bushes away from heaps of stone which were then restacked or realigned, and key stones were rubbed to free the seed food essence', write Kimber and Smith (1987, p. 235); 'the women's ceremony involved digging at a pit site to retrieve, handle and sing over their sacred stones before burying them again'.

Eventually all attention focused on two events. The first was a precursor to secret–sacred men's rituals. It dealt specifically with the Dreaming and human history of Therreyererte. As secret and sacred events, these rituals could not be attended by all (secret–sacred aspects cannot be recounted here). Some stages in the ritual cycle were open to both sexes, initiated and uninitiated alike. But as the ritual progressed, their secrecy and sacredness increased. Generally, men assisted women in their rituals, and vice versa. As the secrecy grew, the rituals became increasingly exclusive.

Among the most sacred were the rituals relating to initiation and to the teaching of Dreaming truths by the elders. During these events, attendance was highly restricted. The rituals commemorated the ancestral Dreaming activities, with direct reference to the ancestral spirit beings that were always present in the landscape. Therreyererte, as a focal totemic place in the Native Cat creation story, was loaded with power, both as a source of human fertility and of dangerous law-giving, life-ordering principles.

The second ritual event to take place at Therreyererte was more open, celebrating specific events such as 'a successful emu hunt or an amusing incident in camp' (Kimber and Smith 1987, p. 232). The range of stories told and celebrated was broad.

Late on the first day, the men filed up the gorge at Therreyererte, regrouping at a rock platform some distance from the main camp. 'No woman or child could pass beyond the entrance to the gorge', write Kimber and Smith (ibid., pp. 232–3). 'No man, not even the most senior ritual leader, dared visit the rockholes alone, for the Native Cat, sire of the Dreaming was too powerful, too ruthless in his vengeance if errors of judgement in protocol or ritual occurred.'

Men of various totemic affiliations – Wedge-Tailed Eagle, Emu, Dingo – participated in the Native Cat rituals. As site managers they had an important role to play, for it is they who assisted the Native Cat men, the owners of the site, during the course of the ritual, making sure that proper protocols were observed.

Eventually the group of men were called into a natural amphitheatre, where the elders sang the songs of the Dreaming, and the younger men joined in and listened, learning in the process. They then visited the nearby rock-art sites, the art symbolically depicting the Dreaming beings and events under celebration.

During the course of the rituals at Therreyererte, sacred objects were made or retrieved from their storage places. These were restricted items – headdresses, sacred stone or wooden objects, paints – whose powers were required for successful ritual performances. The painted designs were themselves of the Dreaming, depicting the various totemic affiliations. Some two weeks were spent at the Native Cat sacred site, during which time the elders led and instructed the younger men. After each set of ritual performances, the elders led the younger men back to their camps near the gorge entrance.

The Therreyererte ritual meeting ended suddenly when the women told the elders that the food supply was running out. The rituals were rapidly wrapped up, and decisions were made about future events. On that last day:

Less than an hour after the women's arrival at the Native Cat camp with the usual daily seed foods and small game, everyone had gone. Only old campfires, flattened branches on mulga trees that had been used to improve the shade, spinifex tussock windbreaks, a few bones and pieces of hide, the grinding stones, and human footprints remained. In a few weeks only the stone artefacts would be left – and the Dreaming. (ibid., p. 236)

The archaeology of Therreyererte

Aboriginal people have been in central Australia since at least 32,400 ± 500 years BP, as is evident by excavations at Puritjarra (Smith *et al.* 1998). This leaves us with a considerable span of time through which to trace back the kinds of ritual activity known from ethnography at Therreyererte.

Mike Smith's (1988, 1989, 1993, 1996; Smith *et al.* 1998) research has been reported in various published and unpublished manuscripts, but it has never been used to explore the historical emergence of the ethnographically known Dreaming. I draw on this work with this aim in mind.

During ethnographic times, human occupation during the Therreyererte Native Cat Dreaming rituals took place at the entrance of the gorge in which secret–sacred rites were held by the elders and younger men. The camps involved large numbers of people undertaking everyday activities – food preparation, cooking, tool manufacture and curation, painting, exchange, sleeping. As Kimber and Smith (1987) have noted, over the long term the only archaeological traces of the rituals are likely to be the stone artefacts and the hearths. It is therefore an investigation of the antiquity of hearth and lithic deposition that archaeological research should turn to when questioning the antiquity of site use at Therreyererte.

Smith's excavations are well suited to such investigations. Excavations were undertaken along the flats where camps associated with the Native Cat rituals were noted during ethnographic times. Stone artefacts were scattered throughout the area prior to excavation, evidence of the recent use of the site. Surface grindstones featured in the hundreds, further evidence that occupation was relatively intensive when the site was used.

Following systematic augering across the site to determine the nature of sub-surface deposits, Smith excavated in an area that proved to be densest in stone artefacts.[4] By Smith's estimates, initial occupation at Therreyererte probably began around 3000 years BP (calibrated to around 1400–1000 BCE) (Smith 1988, p. 279). Around the fourteenth century CE, the site witnessed a four-fold increase in sedimentation rates.[5] Such an increase has been attributed by Smith to the onset of intensive human activity in the surrounding landscape, with firestick farming increasing colluvial erosion upslope and sediment deposition in the lower elevations in the vicinity of the camps. Here, then, are the first signs of the antiquity of the human use of Therreyererte, beginning during the first half of the second millennium BCE, with a major increase around 600 to 700 years ago.

Rates of charcoal, stone artefact and animal bone deposition reveal similar, and indeed more pronounced, trends than is apparent from sedimentation rates alone. Charcoal rates – reflecting a combination of landscape firing (firestick farming) and campfires increased ten-fold from layer 2 to layer 1. A total of 6962 flaked stone artefacts were excavated. Deposition rates increased thirty- to forty-fold some 600 to 700 years ago, from 280 to 10,765 stone artefacts per thousand years. Bone rates, represented mainly by kangaroo and wallaby remains, also increased some thirty-fold at this time, from 73 to 2237 grams per thousand years. The change-over from the lower layer 2 to the upper layer 1 is sudden. Some of the stone artefacts come from a considerable distance away, in the case of chalcedony at least 35 km distant. The potential sources of most raw materials, however, are widespread, so it has not been possible to precisely trace past geographical links archaeologically.

A total of 54 grindstones or grindstone fragments were excavated, showing a similar trend to the other cultural items. All but a single piece were recovered from layer 1. The implication is that camping activity based largely, if not entirely, on the procurement of seed staples dates to the last 600 to 700 years. Similarly, ochre was only found in layer 1, except for 0.8g (of a total of 20.2g) from the very surface of layer 2. Ochre fragments were found in every excavation unit of layer 1.

Each of the depositional rates investigated

– sediments, charcoal, flaked stone artefacts, bone, ochre, grinding stones – reveals comparable temporal trends, implying a major increase in intensities of human site use around 600 to 700 years ago. All cultural materials were found *in situ*, showing no evidence of re-deposition such as in the form of water-rolling, lag deposits or truncation. Based on the archaeological evidence for increased levels of food procurement (as evidenced by both the bones and the grinding stones), tool use and manufacture (flaked stone artefacts), the establishment of camp fires and firing of the landscape (charcoal and sedimentation rates), and artistic activity (ochre), Smith (1988) argued for the onset of new relations to place 600 to 700 years ago. The commencement of intensive camping activity at Therreyererte at this time is even further emphasized when it is realized that evidence for seed grinding only then attains a clear archaeological presence. Given that rituals such as those observed ethnographically at Therreyererte cannot take place without appropriate, large-scale food supplies – such as are met by seed staples, which are ground on grinding stones – the implication is a lack of ritual meetings of the type recorded ethnographically at this site before the fourteenth century CE. This interpretation is consistent with the temporal patterning of ochre deposition rates, and by implication painting activity. The archaeological evidence implies that while people occasionally camped at Therreyererte shortly before 1000 BCE, initial occupation was fleeting, and appears not to have involved large-scale gatherings. This all suddenly changed during the fourteenth century CE, when the initial signs of intensive camping first appear. Like Smith (1988), I conclude that the first signs of Therreyererte's Native Cat totemic significance, as expressed in ritual activity, emerges in the archaeological record late in history, likely some 600 to 700 years ago.

Kweyunpe

The Therreyererte results are interesting, but they represent only one site in a geographically expansive totemic landscape. Fortunately, results of archaeological investigations at other totemic sites are available, enabling a better evaluation of the Therreyererte patterns.

Kweyunpe is a totemic site in Arrernte

country. In 1896, during the course of the Horn Expedition, Spencer and Gillen (1899, pp. 314–16) recorded the Dreaming story as it relates to Kweyunpe (Spencer and Gillen's 'Quiurnpa'). Theodor Strehlow (1971, p. 379) also makes brief reference to the site, which he writes of as Kujunba in his *Songs of Central Australia*.

The rituals of Kweyunpe

The sacred Quabara ritual was attended at Kweyunpe only by men (Spencer and Gillen 1899, pp. 288–94, 316). For six weeks the ceremonies continued. Individuals of various totemic affiliations participated and, in addition to the local totemic affiliation, other totems and ancestral totemic beings and events were also celebrated (ibid., pp. 288–94, 312–14). The details of these totemic affiliations and associated rituals are restricted and cannot be further discussed here.

The archaeology of Kweyunpe

Kweyunpe does not appear to have been a general camping ground. It does not possess any permanent water source, and was probably visited during ethnographic times only in relation to ritual activity celebrating the site's totemic affiliation, although it is possible that it was used for general camping after rains. In these characteristics, Kweyunpe is reminiscent of Therreyererte (Smith 1988, p. 249).

Kweyunpe is also located in Australia's arid centre. Archaeological investigations in a series of small rockshelters located in a small valley between a low ridge and the Mt Ertwa Range were undertaken by L. Kyle Napton and E. A. Greathouse (1985) in 1980, and by Mike Smith two years later. This is a part of Kweyunpe containing evidence of past camping activity both within the shelters and on the surrounding slopes and flats; the two rockshelters excavated by Napton and Greathouse were discussed by Spencer and Gillen in 1899 (caption to Figure 92). These two sites, identified by Smith (1988, p. 250) as Kweyunpe 1 and 2, are formed by the rock outcrop that is depicted in Spencer and Gillen's (1899) Figure 92. Some 2 km away, on flats near two other small rockshelters, is further evidence of past human activity in the form of stone artefact scatters. It is one of these that Mike Smith excavated in 1982 as Kweyunpe 6.

Kweyunpe 1. Kweyunpe 1 is a small sand-stone rockshelter located towards the northern end of an exposed sandstone outcrop, the same outcrop that also houses the other two exca-vated sites, Kweyunpe 2 and 6. Kweyunpe 1 immediately fronts the narrow but open valley, the flats of which can easily be accessed down a very gentle slope.[6]

Archaeological excavations at Kweyunpe 1 revealed four major stratigraphic units. The two lowermost units contained massive sand-stone rocks and possibly bedrock extending down to 1.3 m below the present ground sur-face. A few cultural materials were found towards the top, gradually decreasing to a com-plete absence in the lowest levels. Above these layers came a series of sandy layers that pos-sessed much charcoal and that were rich in stone artefacts. A radiocarbon date of 265 ± 75 years BP was obtained for near the interface between the underlying rocky layer and the culturally rich overlying sands. Of the 4552 stone artefacts excavated, the majority came from above the radiocarbon date (we are not told the exact proportion, and the raw num-bers are not listed). Ochre – likely evidence of painting activity – was also recovered, together with twelve grinding stones and mullers only from the upper units above the radiocarbon date.

There is, therefore, little evidence for human occupation at Kweyunpe 1 before approximately 300 years ago, and it is probable that the few cultural materials in the underly-ing sandy and rocky units – that is, the material pre-dating the seventeenth century CE – have filtered down the deposit from above.

Kweyunpe 2. Kweyunpe 2 is located some 3 m above the valley floor, 200 m from Kwe-yunpe 1. The area sheltered under the over-hang is 22 m long and 4.5 m wide.[7] Following archaeological excavations, cultural materials were found to be most abundant among the top sediments, decreasing significantly with depth. The stratigraphy was similar to that of Kweyunpe 1, indicating likely comparable dep-ositional histories.

A radiocarbon determination was obtained from near the base of cultural materials, revealing a date of 320 ± 55 years BP. Of the

10,905 stone artefacts recovered, four were of top or bottom grinding stones, indicating that seed grinding took place at the site. As was the case at Kweyunpe 1, there is no indication that human activity preceded the middle of the second millennium CE.

Kweyunpe 6. Kweyunpe 6 is a small rockshel-ter, again facing the valley, measuring 11 m long by 4 m wide.[8] Smith (1988, p. 256) exca-vated at Kweyunpe 6 and dated the begin-ning of intensive human occupation to 590 ± 80 years BP.[9] By extrapolation from the depth-age curve, he cautiously proposed the commencement of human occupation some-time around 2000 years BP, although this age is an estimate that should be treated as broadly indicative rather than precise. Most of the cul-tural materials, including the charcoal, stone artefacts and animal bone remains came from layers 1 and 2; that is, from units dating after around 1400 years BP by reference to the depth-age curve. It is also during this time that all of the ochre (total = 21.2g), as well as the only definite seed grinding stone, were deposited. Smith (ibid., p. 266) concludes that densities of cultural materials increased approximately three-fold after approximately 1400 years BP, and judging 'from the stone artefacts the new pattern of site use was stable once established', although 'some reorganisa-tion of activities did occur' around 600 years ago.

Together, the three excavations at Kwe-yunpe imply use of the area only during the late Holocene, with patterns of occupation consistent with those recorded during ethno-graphic times dating only to the last 1400 years or so. Intensities of human activity at Kwe-yunpe increased through time, as evidenced by the occupation of an increasing number of rockshelters through the last 1400 years. There is no archaeological evidence of ritual activity, such as recorded by Spencer and Gillen in relation to the totemic landscape, prior to about 1400 years ago.

Keringke and the Kangaroo Dreaming

Keringke is a Kangaroo totemic centre in east-ern Arrernte country. Strehlow (1971, p. 377) noted that this is a site where maintenance ('increase') ceremonies were undertaken, involving members of the Kangaroo totemic group. Kangaroos are an important source of meat food in much of Australia, and central Australia is no exception. However, as Strehlow (ibid., p. 305) notes 'it is a curious fact that in many parts of the Aranda area there seem to have existed extremely few *dramatic* performances in which the Kangaroo ancestors were brought before the eyes of novices and initiates'. According to Strehlow (ibid., p. 306), most of the Kangaroo ceremonies were maintenance rituals. Often such rituals were restricted to men of the Kangaroo totem, and whose conception totemic place was located in the general vicinity of the ritual event. The only other individuals attending such rituals were the brothers, fathers or father's fathers whose own Kangaroo totemic centres could be found nearby. However, nearby camping sites included other family members, and meetings for Kangaroo rituals could in this way result in the congregation of large numbers of people. Géza Róheim (e.g. 1945) further noted that such rituals represented the ceremonies where the totemic animal was made or created. During the rituals, the actions of the Dreaming ancestors were repeated via formalized acts, ground drawings and reference to sacred paraphernalia (including Churingas).

Theodor Strehlow (1971, p. 307) claims to have been one of the very few non-indigenous Australians to have witnessed a Kangaroo maintenance ceremony, first at Alice Springs in 1933, and then at Jay Creek in 1950 (the second ritual of which he filmed). I cite Strehlow's first-hand account directly:

> The . . . kangaroo (*rara*) increase ceremonies were invariably opened by the staging of . . . a semi-sacred act that could be witnessed by the women of this district from a distance of some thirty yards away. The [act] used to be performed late on one afternoon and again very early on the following morning. It was not itself an increase ceremony, but was regarded as the indispensable prelude to the kangaroo increase ceremonies. After the . . . act had been staged twice, the kangaroo totemites could proceed immediately to their utnitjia rites . . . Then began the utnitjia ceremonies themselves. A ground-painting was put down . . . close to the rocks in the mulga flat which represented [the various] kangaroo ancestors who had come from . . . kangaroo centres and passed to their last rest here.

When the second semi-sacred act was staged, the spectators were summoned to a kangaroo wallowing area, which was said to represent the place from which the ancestral Kangaroo had emerged onto the world. The small depressed area was lined with the blood of Kangaroo totemites, and covered with down feathers which were said to represent the 'kangaroo fat from which all the remaining kangaroo ancestors had sprung into life' (Strehlow 1971, p. 308). At the centre of the depression a hole was dug and decorated with blood and down. Into the hole was placed a sacred Kangaroo totemic object.

Strehlow continues:

> When the spectators, who had quietly been invited to come, arrived at the ground-painting, they found . . . the chief of the kangaroo totemic clan, who had been decorated to represent the [Kangaroo] ancestor, reclining on his right elbow, with his head bowed low upon his right shoulder, some ten yards away from the white [kangaroo wallow depression], in an attitude of heavy sleep. His back was turned upon the ground-painting. He wore the red [sacred object] on his head; two long white down-stripes had been added to it for the occasion. No raiankama call broke the silence, and there was no ceremonial . . . dance. Near the ground-painting, on the side away from the sleeping [Kangaroo ancestor], sat Urteraninja, the oldest man present of this kangaroo clan. He took up a red-ochred shield, and with its back smote the ground slowly, so that its beating sounded like the striking of a great clock in the stillness of the night. Slowly life appeared to come into the kangaroo ancestor. He stirred a little, raised his head, lowered it again, moved gently, shook himself, raised his body off his elbow, and finally turned around and faced the [depression]. While Urteraninja kept on beating the ground slowly with the shield, the Krantji chorus chanted very softly the [kangaroo wallow depression] verse . . .
>
> [The Kangaroo ancestor] now put down both his hands on the ground and pulled his body forward, squatting on his toes and imitating the slow actions of a grazing kangaroo. Halfway to the [depression] he rested, as though but half-awake. It took him several minutes of leisurely progress to reach the ground-painting. All his movements were slow and stately. When he had reached the edge of the [depression], he knelt down, put

both hands upon it, bent down slowly till his chin almost touched it, and blew upon it suddenly; or rather, he 'sneezed' upon it in the manner characteristic of the kangaroo's 'sneeze'. This was repeated several times. Finally, he put down both hands on either side of the central hole, and 'sneezed' into this hole itself. He then drew away a little, fell over on his right elbow, and once more assumed his original sleeping attitude, his back turned upon the [depression]. Ekunjambarinja, the only man present who belonged to the kangaroo totem by reincarnation [that is, he was the only Kangaroo man of the place in which the ritual was being performed], now leapt up, placed his hands on [the Kangaroo ancestor's] shoulder, and removed the [sacred object] from the latter's head. The beating of the shield ceased; and the act was over. (ibid., pp. 308–9)

After two days further ritual events were performed, involving the use of the same kangaroo wallow depression and various decorated sacred objects. Again, the performances replicated ancestral events and called upon the Kangaroo's fecundity, various ancestral Kangaroos being the focus of attention. The rituals lasted some 16 days, during which time many performers were involved (ibid., pp. 307–13).

The above observations were not made in relation to Keringke, but during a Kangaroo 'increase' ritual elsewhere in Arrernte country. They give, however, some indication as to the general nature of such rituals. Smith has more generally noted that:

> Large groups of people are said to have gathered [at Keringke] periodically to perform the Kangaroo ceremonies. Men could camp with their families on the sandy flat at the mouth of the gully. The non-public sections of the ceremonies centred on a small, ephemeral rockhole a short distance up the gully, and in the hills beyond. (1988, p. 270)

The archaeology of Keringke

The open site of Keringke is found around a temporary rockhole linked by a gully to a 300 m by 500 m wide basin. Archaeological research was undertaken at Keringke (Kurringa, Kurringke) by Eugene Stockton (1971, pp. 55–60) in 1969. Over 100 grinding stones and large numbers of flaked stone artefacts were scattered over a broad distance around a

temporary waterhole. Also present was a cluster of some 50 rock engravings. Two excavations – 3 m² in total – were undertaken within the basin, at locations where stone artefact densities appeared to be at their densest and sampling different parts of the site. Flaked stone artefacts were recovered from all excavation units, although they petered out at the base. The smaller of the two trenches showed evidence of post-depositional disturbance, so Stockton relied mostly on the main trench for temporal trends.

Seed-grinding stones were restricted to the upper half of the main excavation, while ochre was found throughout. Animal bones, interpreted as food remains by Stockton (ibid., p. 60), were recovered from all but the basal excavation unit in the main trench. A radiocarbon date of 920 ± 130 years BP (ANU 426) was obtained for a near-basal level representing the beginning of human occupation. This means that this part of Keringke was probably first used sometime between 1009 and 1239 CE (calibrated ages, 95.4 per cent probability). There is no known archaeological evidence at Keringke for the ethnographically documented Kangaroo 'increase' rituals before this time.

Urre and the Grass Seed Dreaming

According to Smith (1988, p. 236), the open site of Urre is a totemic centre for the important grass seed food staple, *Eragrostis eriopoda*. Maintenance rituals were reportedly performed here, but few details of the site's Dreaming significance are available. Strehlow (1971) identifies the place as Wora on his map of central Australia, but does not discuss its Dreaming significance.

The archaeology of Urre

Like Therreyererte, Kweyunpe and Keringke, Urre is also located in arid central Australia. It contains complex rock outcrops, a large claypan, and some 2 km away a temporary waterhole. During ethnographic times, this waterhole was the site of major camping.

Mike Smith (1988, pp. 236–43) dug a series of auger holes across, and excavated a single 1×1 m test pit towards the centre of, the camping ground near the waterhole in 1985. He notes that while this is not a permanent waterhole, it is regionally important because of a general lack of water in the area. Grinding stones and other evidence of camping activity are spread across a considerable area. Rock-art and other signs of camping activity occur about 1 km away. The latter include stone artefact types dating to the late Holocene.

Urre contains two major stratigraphic units, a lowermost red clayey sand grading to a compact grey sand above it. Stone artefacts were recovered from the upper parts of the lowermost layer, layer 2, and layer 1 above it. A single radiocarbon date of 980 ± 80 years BP was obtained from the interface between layers 1 and 2; by extrapolation from the depth-age curve, an age of around 3600 years BP is implied for the commencement of human occupation (Smith 1988, pp. 237–40).

Densities of stone artefacts and charcoal peak during layer 1, with a ten-fold increase after *c.* 980 years BP. Artefacts made on the foreign red chert occur through much of layer 1, implying the arrival of objects from some distance away at various times during the last thousand years or so. Grinding stones, a prerequisite to large group congregations in this region, only appear in the top half of layer 1. Animal bones were only recovered from layer 1, although the degree to which this is due to taphonomic bias is uncertain (ibid., pp. 240–3).

These results imply that people have probably been visiting and camping at Urre since around 3600 years BP, but that it was not until 1000–1200 CE that intensive camping activity began. Such intensive camping was associated during ethnographic times with the Grass Seed maintenance rituals. Prior to 1000–1200 CE, there is no evidence at Urre for the types and intensities of camping activities associated with the Grass Seed maintenance rituals documented by Strehlow.

Discussion

In this chapter I have touched upon aspects of ethnographically documented Arrernte Dreaming rituals and the logic that frames them. I have also attempted to trace these back in time via archaeological research. In doing so, it is not just the history of rituals that I have addressed, but that of the entire system of preunderstanding that informed those rituals. Formal, periodically repeated ritual events represent a codification of social and ontological conditions: ritual is embedded in the preunderstanding that gives rise to it. In the examples considered in this chapter – Native Cat at Therreyererte, Kangaroo at Keringke, Kweyunpe, and Grass Seed at Urre – rituals were borne of the Dreaming beliefs that informed them. The preunderstanding that framed ritual behaviour was enacted and reproduced in the ritual performances. In this capacity – in the activation of a world-view through the codification of social rhythms – people externalize and objectify preunderstanding. In that ritual articulates preunderstanding, both ritual and preunderstanding become self-serving and self-reproducing, each helping realize itself and the other.

Ritual is therefore never just a mechanical production of the Dreaming. It is also a social and symbolic construction of an entire world order experienced and legitimated through codified performance, in that to perform is to give substance to the truth of one's being. In ritual the knowing subject projects her or his preunderstanding of all reality into the world, transforming abstract existence into worldly experience. Through formalized actions – through an institutionalization of solidarity in the performance of preunderstanding – people shape their landscapes as fields of experience.

Nicolas Peterson (1972), Joël Bonnemaison (1995) and Bernard Moizo (1998) have noted that ritual also bears a territorial imperative. Through ritual we look after our own existence in the world. This is an existence in social place. It is not the outcome that is commemorated in ritual – but *the ownership of process.* Christian rituals, such as Easter or Christmas, do not merely or meekly celebrate a past event such as the crucifixion or the birth of Christ, but the personal ownership of a process of identification with those events and their spiritual outcomes. In this sense, we celebrate our own existence as ontological beings through rituals; in ritual we celebrate the social construction of meaning.

And so it is with the Dreaming known from ethnography. The rituals documented above reflect upon a world constructed in the Dreaming. The Dreaming emplaced existence, and the totemic affiliations are sanctuaries in which people reside – more, it is the only where in which people could reside. Without the ancestral beings there would be no place, for there would be no created world. In their affiliation with totemically emplaced beings, people are rightfully emplaced. In such affiliations they also possess the laws of the land, handed down since the time of creation by the ancestral beings. It is through those Dreaming laws that social life is structured and regulated, not as behaviour free-floating in abstract space, but situated in a regulated world. In the process, social and territorial structures are legitimated and set forth onto the world. In the words of Bonnemaison (1995, cited in Moizo 1998, p. 669):

> le territoire commence avec le rite. Il est même le plus immédiat des rites, on le sent d'autant mieux qu'il est physique, par exemple lorsqu'on marche à pied – d'où le sens des pèlerinages qui vont vers des sanctuaires (laïcs ou religieux) (Territory begins with ritual. It is even prior to ritual, in that territory appears in its very physicalness, expressed even when we walk, as in a pilgrimage towards a sanctuary [sacred or profane].)

To trace the antiquity of ethnographically known Dreaming rituals is thus larger than the ritual itself. It is a mapping of ontology, in the sense that it concerns the way people perceive (come to know) their own reality; it is a mapping of a special kind of territorial behaviour. Rituals give a sense of place, a sense of territory. It is the Dreaming beings that created the world as a structured place to be occupied by *categories* of people (as rightful owners of knowledge about the world as differentiated space). The ritual cycles are a celebration and social reproduction of the emplacement of people as categorically totemic beings.

The number of known totemic ritual places that have been archaeologically investigated are few, and they all come from the arid core of Australia. But at a broad temporal scale, an internally consistent trend is emerging for site and regional land use in this region, beginning with the Pleistocene occupation of the occasional site, followed by the initial establishment of large numbers of sites during the late Holocene, beginning around 3600 years BP (more will be made of this general trend in Chapter 7). Evidence of human occupation throughout this time is, however, always of low intensity. Some time between 1400 and 600 years ago we are faced with the first signs of intensive human activity. Systematic seed grinding begins – as evidenced by the first appearance of seed-grinding stones at Therreyererte, Kweyunpe, Keringke and Urre, and in large numbers at that – a point I shall return to in Chapter 8. At this time also ochre first regularly appears in the sites discussed here. Sedimentation rates and stone artefact, animal food and charcoal deposition rates increase significantly, implying major increases in intensities of site use. It is to this period, to the last 1400 years (and especially to the last 1000 years), that we can trace back in time the first archaeological signs of the ritual events that Spencer and Gillen, Strehlow and others documented towards the end of the nineteenth and the beginning of the twentieth centuries. As was the case at Ngarrabullgan, the Dreaming beliefs documented ethnographically cannot be traced any deeper into antiquity, implying the emergence of a new way of performing belief, perceiving the world and relating to place late in the course of pre-History.

Notes

1. These themes create obvious passageways into the social thoughts of both Durkheim and Radcliffe-Brown. I resist elaborating on Durkheim's writings on social consciousness and Radcliffe-Brown's on the social construction of ritual structures as these have been amply discussed by many others (see for example, Morphy 1998; Swain 1985).
2. Various spellings of 'Arrernte' have appeared in the literature over the years, including Arunta and Arunda, among many. In this chapter I use the currently accepted 'Arrernte' except where I am citing original works that have employed other conventions.
3. 'The spirit of every individual' (Spencer and Gillen 1927, p. 620).
4. A 1×1 m² pit (Pit Z90) was systematically excavated so as to quantify stone and sediment deposition rates in that part of the site that contained the densest quantities of subsurface artefacts. Coupled with the results of the auger holes, a broad spatial sequence was identified for the site as a whole (Smith 1988).

   Smith reports the presence of two stratigraphic units, an upper, 30–60 cm thick brown silty sand, and an underlying sandstone rubble intermixed with brown silty sand. The excavation reached a depth of 1.4 m before bedrock was encountered. In addition, a thin, sterile red sandy deposit represents aeolian sands deposited over the site since its use ceased sometime during the first half of the twentieth century. There was a total lack of European materials in the excavation, implying that human activity ceased not long after the arrival of Europeans.

Human occupation at Therreyererte began shortly before a radiocarbon determination of 1830 ± 110 years BP (SUA 2519), during deposition of the lowermost stratigraphic unit. The change-over from layer 2 to layer 1 took place shortly before a radiocarbon date of 400 ± 50 years BP (SUA 2520), probably equivalent to around 570 years BP (Smith's estimate), or sometime during the fourteenth century CE when calibrated to the tree-ring curve.

5. From a mean of 23 mm per thousand years during layer 2 to 90 mm per thousand years during layer 1.

6. Because of slope directions and other taphonomic indicators, Napton and Greathouse believed that sedimentation at the site was likely to have been relatively fast and erosion unlikely, promising the likely preservation of past occupational materials.

Kweyunpe 1 rockshelter possesses some 60 m² of sheltered floor space (an area 16 m long by 4 m wide). Three juxtaposed 1 × 1 m squares were excavated, forming a trench entirely contained within the dripline. Both Kweyunpe 1 and 2 were excavated in arbitrary 10 cm excavation units, cultural items observed *in situ* were plotted and separately bagged, and the residue was sieved in a ⅛ inch wire mesh with the retained material subsequently sorted for cultural materials.

7. Five juxtaposed 1 × 1 m squares were excavated, forming a trench traversing from the back wall to beyond the dripline. Excavations proceeded to a maximum 80 cm below the present ground level, when bedrock was reached. Sediments were relatively homogeneous throughout, with sandstone rocks appearing towards the base.

8. Mike Smith undertook a single 1 × 1 m excavation towards the centre of the site, revealing three stratigraphic units. The lowermost layer 3 sits directly on bedrock, and consists of a sandy rock matrix similar to the lowermost units of Kweyunpe 1 and 2. The boundary with the overlying layer 2 – a fine pink sand – is well demarcated. Above layer 2 and grading with it is layer 1, a dark grey and brown to black sand.

9. Representing a level approximately half-way into layer 1.

5 Symbols of the Dreaming: Rock-Art as Representation

When Hans-Georg Gadamer coined the term 'preunderstanding', he had in mind a world rendered meaningful through *language*. It is, he argued, the interpretive act that enables the world to be understood, and interpretation is linguistically mediated. The 'subject always finds herself in a linguistically disclosed world' writes Hans Herbert Kögler (1999, p. 41) of Gadamer's work.

> Thus the world is the common ground, trodden by none and recognized by all, uniting all who talk to one another. All kinds of human community are kinds of linguistic community: even more, they form language. For language is by nature the language of conversation; it fully realizes itself only in the process of coming to an understanding. That is why it is not a mere means in that process. (Gadamer 1989, p. 446)

What Gadamer does not adequately address is the power of non-linguistic *representations* in the creation of a community of culture, and the role of (non-linguistic) symbols in constructing and understanding the world (see Kögler's excellent critique of this problem). I do not wish to engage here in a debate on whether or not language ultimately mediates the experience of all symbolic expression and understanding, for such a debate is irrelevant to this book. What I do wish to highlight is that 'the symbolic power of the object lies in the way humans are attracted to it' (Dant 1999, p. 118). We are seduced by objects, a seduction whose roots go beyond the material thing to its entanglement in a world of meaning and preunderstanding. In this sense we are all captive, although this is not to deny our engagement as active agents. The telephone rings and we reach for the receiver (or we resist, choosing not to, in which case our captivity is in the resistance), yielding to its structured and structuring force; the telephone calls us as much as the person on the other end calls us. I am in the living room and I sit, not on the floor but on a chair; the chair beckons, guiding my experience of sitting and subsequent expectations. The walls of my house demarcate my own, 'private' space, a place that extends in altered fashion to the edge of my property. By demarcating it signals, not just to me but also to my neighbour (the boundary's existence helping to define the very concept of neighbour) as to the passer-by. I do not just own, nor do I just call upon, the material world around me, for I, too, am immersed in the power of its constructiveness. This is a world not of material culture nor of 'cognitive' behaviour (in the sense of action as hegemonic revelation, ultimately arising from fully controlled, conscious awareness), but of material behaviour both engaged and engaging. Instead of our consciousness reaching out and grasping the material, objects themselves draw out from us a certain way of engaging with them. This is a world lush with meaningful cues, a world of preunderstanding continuously transcended and (re)structured in *différance*.

On 27 January 1968, Jacques Derrida[1] introduced *différance* in his famous address before the Société Française de Philosophie. The paper was published twice in that same year (Derrida 1968a, 1968b), and subsequently translated and republished in a string of compilations (e.g. Derrida 1973, 1982). Derrida's *différance* was coined to highlight the impossibility of fixing an understanding of what a person means when they say something in terms of a pre-existing structure of linguistic signs. In the French language, where the word was coined, *différence* and *différance* are distinguished in writing, but not in speech. *Différance* emerged as a gloss on the scission between writing and linguistic intention, for the written word escapes and is of a different order than momentary spoken language, and cannot then merely be an inscribed copy or record of it. Derrida coined the word *différance* at a time when the spoken word was much given prior philosophical status over the written word. His account of the priority of the spoken word was developed principally with respect to Edmund Husserl. He chose Husserl because the German was the latest and most sophisticated representative of the dominant European philosophical tradition, the one that had roots in rationalism. One consequence of a rationalist account of human consciousness is that people have thoughts, then try to express them in language and then run into difficulties. It was this notion that Derrida – like Ludwig Wittgenstein – refuted. Later, Derrida expanded his criticism of an uncritical privileging of speech to include Ferdinand de Saussure, Jean-Jacques Rousseau, Plato and others.

Derrida aimed to refocus attention to the sign's elusiveness – or, more to the point, to its embeddedness in a 'network of signs' and to its shifting nature. In speech, a word has meaning in relation to the spoken moment. But in the written language, its meaning shifts with the emergence of new signs and, therefore, new structures of meaning. Derrida was pointing out that meaning continuously shifts from sign to sign. New signs emerge in pre-existing systems of signs and meaning – Gadamer's preunderstanding, although Derrida never used this term – and thus gain meaning as a passing brush against that pre-existing context. In the process of their emergence, however, new signs – new cultural expressions – modify the way the world is understood, that

is, they modify preunderstanding itself. The system of meaning shifts, or, to use Derrida's more accurate and less formidable expression, the 'open network of signs' shifts, and therefore the sign's symbolic content is in a continuous process of becoming. A word or an image or item of material culture's meaningfulness continuously shifts in relation to the preunderstanding that shapes it (a preunderstanding dialectically shaped by an 'open network of signs', not all of which necessarily are manifest linguistically).

Derrida was mainly concerned with linguistic signs, but his concept can also be applied to the broader world of material and non-material expressions that operate in the construction and articulation of preunderstanding. Derrida notes that *différance* consumes and unifies two concepts, difference and deference. Difference concerns distinction, deference a temporal spacing or delaying (Derrida 1973, p. 129). In their existence and recognition, things exist as difference, and therefore help construct the order by which we know the world. They also imply a temporal sequence, for things exist only through a prior structural recognition. The letter 'a' in *différance* is a case in point: it exists only subsequent to the recognition of an alphabetical system; and in the coining of *différance*, the word and its associated meaning emerge after the prior existence of the *différence* that Derrida aimed to transcend. Therefore *différance*, writes Derrida (1973, p. 130), 'is not simply active . . .; it rather indicates the middle voice, it precedes and sets up the opposition between passivity and activity'. *Différance* takes place at the moment of utterance; it takes place in the passing of the sign. It divides and marks the moment, and meaning in the moment. What takes place in the present creates a boundary with the before by the very act of its animation. Things exist in the world not simply as identity, but as alterity in a structured world that is both emergent and temporal.

There is another component that is relevant to this discussion of objects and ideas, although it is not explored by Derrida through *différance*: the sign as deference, as to concede, comply or obey – what Derrida discusses as deference to authority and 'obedience to the law' in his essays 'The law of genre' and 'Before the law' (Derrida 1992). Although Derrida does not relate this notion to *différance*, in surpassing and re-orienting the sign's authority it is, paradoxically, one of its lasting properties.

Différance is a movement of structuring that reveals the truth of the experienced world, a meaningful truth constructed in engagement. *Différance* is silent in that it 'belongs neither to the voice nor to writing in the ordinary sense', taking place, Derrida notes, even now as the reader engages with this text. *Différance* moves and re-arranges; it is the structuring that takes place as words, symbols, actions present themselves, halting existential continuity and yielding a 'magnetic' force on the onlooker. The world is never again the same, for in *différance* it is continuously re-articulated (in both the linguistic and mechanical senses).[2]

Derrida draws our attention in *différance* to the way in which the things we make escape or go beyond our conscious plans and anticipations, and which therefore confront us, seemingly, with evidence of external agency. *Différance* takes place in the momentary passing of a thing, marking the structured truth of its existence in the process. This attitude toward presence comes from Martin Heidegger (1962) who distinguishes *Anwesen* from *Anwesenheit*. *Anwesenheit* marks a hardening of presence, which Heidegger detects in Plato, while *Anwesen* is a coming-into-presence.

This de-privileging of the punctual moment and the privileging of coming-into-being through the shifting position of signs in networks of signs has implications for an archaeology of meaning, for how we view the archaeological record and how we deal with change in a world that is always-already engaged. In this chapter I consider in this light rock-art as a form of material expression that participates in the division of space, and in the process in the social marking, masking and making of engaged but unfolding space. That is, in its appearance (both as 'visual' and as 'emergence') as set forms, colours and the like, rock-art arises as a mean(s) of place making in a world of structure continuously unfolding and refolding in *différance*.

Fixed in the landscape, rock-art is a highly visual, and relatively long-lasting social expression that marks the land. It makes demands on the onlooker's attention, but such demands can only be understood in relation to the shifting systems of meaning through which the art operates. In their relatively fixed emplacement, items of rock-art are spatial inscriptions, social signs *in* and *of* place. They divide the world in their symbolic marking, a marking whose meanings continuously unfold in relation to preunderstanding. Products of a socially structured, territorial world, both rock-art and place emerge as already political, as meaningfully engaged in a social world of decision-makers from the moment of their social production, a politic that is legitimated and confirmed in marking. In marking rock-art animates the truth of a place. When systems of place marking change, people escape or go beyond established spatial experiences in a process of *différance*, transforming preunderstanding in the process.

Because in its historical emergence rock-art sets up new relations of deference (as in compliance to new forces) between the onlooker and marked place, it sets up new structural relations between people and between people and place. Paradoxically, while the 'work' of deference (compliance) moves counter to that of 'production', *différance* sets up new preunderstandings, as contexts of production.

New rock-art practices, as forms of place marking, signal alterations of socio-geographical forces. The marking of place exists not only as an aesthetic exercise, but as social action that, through a structure of compliance, guides the actor to new spatial expectations. Place marking yields to relations between people and to relations between people and places. Dialectically, marks in place also make demands upon the onlooker's attention. Inscriptions thus participate in the operation of social relations of power. Because rock-art marks the land, it emblazons social relations onto the land. Rock-art materializes as inherently political, by practice if not by explicit intent. This, of course, opens various doorways into the archaeological record, in particular an opportunity to investigate territorial relations and relations of power in pre-History.

Marking place: rock-art, land and the Dreaming in Aboriginal Australia

In Australia the ability to mark the land, such as in the creation of rock-art or the construction of monuments (e.g. mounds, burial structures), was subject during recent times to Dreaming-mediated concepts that informed both place and symbol. Rock-art socializes the land through a symbolling process that attributes metaphysical meaning to place by externalizing the cultural self onto the landscape and by socially engaging place. It enables people to write, read and, through time, to negotiate the land's cultural meaningfulness. Rock-art in this way plays a role in the definition of territory and identity, for the artist paints themes in styles that portray the particular reality of her or his own preunderstanding.

Australian examples of links between artist, land and place mediated by the Dreaming abound in the ethnographic literature. For the arid zone, Paul Taçon (1994) writes that specific rock-art styles delimit land ownership and its relationship to particular ancestral Dreamings who give identity to the land. In Yarralin country, in semi-arid Australia, people talk of rock-art as a 'photo' that identifies the land with its Dreaming beings (Rose 1992; see also Lewis and Rose 1987). There is knowledge associated with this art; some of this knowledge is public and some is restricted, even highly secret. It is, however, always linked to the shape, to the history, to the people, to the spirits and/or to the law of the land, as given to local groups by the ancestral spirits in the Dreaming.

For Arnhem Land, Howard Morphy (1991) has noted that named moieties and clans own particular songs, ceremonies and artistic motifs (see also Taylor 1996). 'Paintings', he writes, 'are part of the ancestral . . . inheritance of clans. They are as much the property of clans as the land itself' (Morphy 1991, p. 57). The creation and use of art are circumscribed by strict social and political conventions that involve a consideration of kin links, territorial concerns, ritual roles and contexts of use and presentation (which are interrelated concerns) (see also Williams 1986). Similarly, in Wardaman country of the Northern Territory, paintings and engravings portray specific historical events and/or designate the identity of the local Dreaming spirits who give identity to place (e.g. David et al. 1994; Merlan 1989); I will return to the Wardaman example in some detail below. To the west of Wardaman country, in the Kimberley region of Western Australia, Bob Layton (1985, 1992) has shown how Wandjina and associated paintings are linked to local clans, landed groups descended from the Wandjina Dreaming beings. The late

David Mowaljarlai, a Ngarinyin elder from the Kimberley, noted that in his homeland rock-art is united with the land on which it occurs. Both the land and the rock-art are expressions of the Dreaming beings and events that shape the landscape, thereby giving it territorial order and meaning (Mowaljarlai and Malnic 1993). In southeast Cape York, Percy Trezise (1969, 1993) wrote of rock paintings that identify local ancestral beings and sorcery figures, both of which are grounded in local Dreaming beliefs.

In each case, the art documents local history and being, as represented by actual events between people and between people and metaphysical realities, each of which is grounded in the local landscape and in a particular kind of preunderstanding. In each case also, the art not only relates directly to the land on which it is created and to the spirit beings it portrays, but it is said by local, traditional landowners that the beings sit in the rock, having positioned themselves in the landscape during the Dreaming. That is, the 'art' is not art, but the spirit beings themselves, much as in Christian religion the Eucharist is said to be the 'body of Christ', not merely its representation. During ethnographic times, the only people who could 'create' the art were individuals officially sanctioned to do so by law, as given to local groups in the Dreaming. This right was defined by appropriate affiliation with local ancestors, the land and its Dreaming spirits, which together defined territorial integrity.[3]

During ethnographic times, rock-art in Australia was thus intimately linked with place, the Dreaming beings that gave the land its identity, and the people who were affiliated with the land and the Dreaming. It was a signpost to the land's identity and history, documenting very real metaphysical relationships. Rock-art was informed by the Dreaming, its conceptual categories, and its metaphorical relations. Once created, it confirmed and to some degree helped maintain (with or without noticeable modification) that Dreaming-based understanding.

Wardaman rock-art

Let us examine in some detail how the rock-art of one part of Aboriginal Australia – Wardaman country in the Northern Territory – is today informed by the Dreaming. We will then

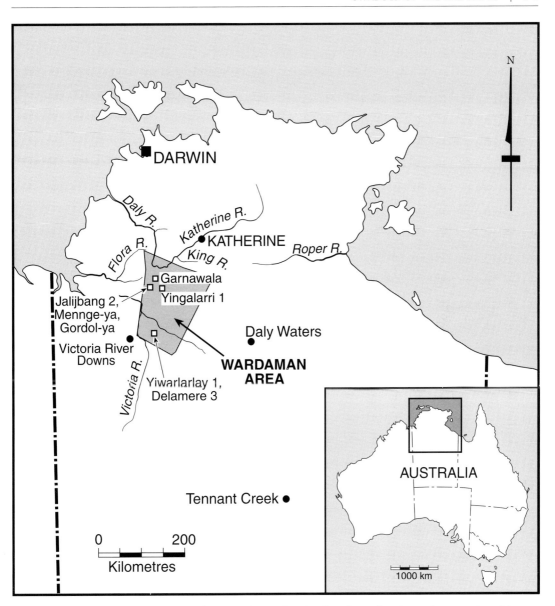

Figure 5.1 Wardaman country, Northern Territory, showing locations of rock-art sites mentioned in text (*Source*: Merlan 1989)

be in a position to trace back archaeologically the antiquity of these artistic practices (as symbols that reference recent Dreaming concepts), for this is one region where both the art's Dreaming significance and its archaeological manifestations have been studied in some detail.

Wardaman country is found some 70 km southwest of the modern town of Katherine in the Northern Territory. Covering a vast

expanse of land roughly quadrilateral in shape, it is delimited in the north by Scott Creek, Romula Knob in the southeast and the Victoria River crossing in the southwest (Figure 5.1). Wardaman country is surrounded by distinctive but related language groups and territories: Jaminjung to the west, Dagoman to the north, Yangman to the east, Mudburra to the south, Ngarinyman and Ngaliwurru to the southwest (Merlan 1994). Kin, exchange and other cultural relations were generally close between the Wardaman and members of many of these language groups during the early European contact period, especially with the west where a number of common cultural practices were observed (e.g. subincision rites and eight-class systems of kin affiliation).

Wardaman people generally recognize non-localized matri-totems (the *ngurlu*), assign sub-section partly, though not exclusively, through the mother, and practise a matri-focal system of parent–child relationship. There exists a matrifiliative complementary relationship to land, with patrifiliation being primary (Merlan, personal communication 1993). Francesca Merlan writes:

[Wardaman people] speak of different territorial sub-groupings, to which recruitment is normatively in the male line, as having different *madin* 'languages', or 'words'. Each such identifiable grouping is said to have minimally one, sometimes more, special words that are 'their' language. Typically, these are said to be either the sound made by, or the language spoken by, principal mythological figures saliently associated with given Wardaman sub-territories. For example, an important mythological association with the sub-country just west of Willeroo Station homestead running westerly to Garnawala (Mount Hogarth) is *gulirrida* 'peewees', which are abundantly represented in some of the spectacular rock paintings in this area. The 'language' or 'word' of the peewees, and therefore of the grouping of people patrifiliated to this area, is said to be *mamundajgani*, a form for which no etymology can be given. A few of the 'words' for particular sub-groupings may have etymologies in other languages of the Victoria River area. At least one is clearly onomatopoetic (e.g., standardization of a bird cry). (1994, p. 6)

During the recent past, Wardaman country was divided into eleven totemically based territorial estates, each of which recognized a cosmological identity with specific Dreaming beings, such as *gulirrida* – peewees – in the example above. In addition to the localized Dreamings of the various estates were also travelling beings that cut across patri-estates, such as *gorondolni* the Rainbow Serpent. Other Dreamings were restricted to individual locations only, such as *gandawag*, the Moon at Jalijbang. While the entire landscape thereby gained its identity and was made discontinuous by its affiliations with

disparate Dreaming beings and events, some of which identified patri-estates and others that were located on the land but did not signify patri-estates, the entire landscape was united into a cosmological whole by its common participation in a unified system of preunderstanding informed by the Dreaming. In this sense the way in which the various estates were divided and inter-linked at various levels reflects the pattern of Wardaman land tenure, land use and cosmology.

The Wardaman landscape thus consists of a complex patchwork of Dreamings criss-crossed by non-local, travelling ones, both of which give identity to the land and link Wardaman country with neighbouring lands. Individual places identified as of specific significance to Wardaman people take many forms, from features such as waterholes or hills to smaller objects such as rocks or prominent trees, including individual or complexes of rockshelters. Thus while rock-art tends to be found wherever there are rock outcrops and rockshelters, it is the entire landscape that is created by the Dreaming beings and that affirms and re-affirms the reality that is the Dreaming, not just the 'art' that strikingly and visually dominates many of the rock outcrops (David *et al.* 1994). The hills, creeks, rock outcrops and paintings *are* the Dreaming beings or events. In this sense Wardaman Dreaming – Wardaman Dreamtime – is not so much a period of time as the ongoing manifestation of the world's fecundity and presence.

Wardaman rock-art is produced in an existing system of social and territorial relations. It has, as social symbols, a place in the manifestation and maintenance of those relations. In particular, much of the rock-art of Wardaman country is created and interpreted narratively via reference to the totemic landscape. Two types of rock-art are identified today by Wardaman elders: 'art' that is a visual manifestation of the Dreaming beings themselves (*buwarraja*), and art created by people (*bulawula*). *Bulawula* rock-art concerns art that was undertaken during recent times by, usually, known individuals. It typically portrays postcontact events (e.g. droving scenes) or characters, such as individual station managers. Much *bulawula* art consists of European objects such as guns and pipes, but this is not always so. The historical status of *bulawula* art is not well understood, and it is uncertain whether or not such rock-art refers only to pictures that are assumed or known to have been created outside traditional practices since the advent of Europeans in the 1880s. Nevertheless, it always appears to be of recent character (i.e. it tends to have a fresh appearance; it relates narratively to the period of European contact, or to items of rock-art that traditional owners have no knowledge of and cannot easily position within their own Dreaming preunderstanding). *Bulawula* art is uncommon compared with the abundant *buwarraja* rock-art of Wardaman country.[4]

Irrespective of its European associations, my concerns in this chapter are not with *bulawula* art. It is, rather, with art that is recognized as *buwarraja* by the Wardaman elders. In *buwarraja* art the Dreaming beings placed themselves in the landscape during the creative events at the beginning of time. This understanding is well accommodated in Wardaman lexicon and grammar.

> The usual way of expressing in Wardaman the notion of placement in the landscape as 'dreaming' is by the combination of a verb particle, *barlb* or *barlb-(b)a*, and the inflecting auxiliary verb *we-*, which when used by itself has the full lexical meaning 'to fall' (also, secondarily, 'to be born').
>
> It is important to note that the combination *barlba we-* is not used exclusively with reference to becoming a painting or other aspect of 'rock art'. It is also the usual way of expressing the pan-Australian notion of metamorphosis into landscape or some aspect of the landscape. Thus, one may equally say:
>
> . . . 'the two Lightning Brothers turned into landscape'
>
> and
>
> . . . 'the King Brown (snake) turned into landscape'.
>
> The second refers to the metamorphosis of a legendary snake into a white gum tree near Willeroo Station homestead. In short, the means of expression provide no direct suggestion of a difference between features of the dreaming cosmology which (in our terms) are 'man-made' versus those which are 'natural'.
>
> . . . Nor is *barlb* restricted to meanings having to do with metamorphosis into landscape in general. If any primary or perhaps core sense may be derived from its various uses, this may be defined as bodily 'placement downwards' or 'inwards'.
>
> . . . Where . . . the subject noun is understood to be a dreaming figure, the appropriate interpretation of the particle is not the specific sense 'belly-down', but rather, as noted, apparently a much more general sense of location or placement downwards, inwards – perhaps, within the visible landscape. There is thus linguistic evidence here for a covert distinction between human and non-human subjectivity. (Merlan 1989, p. 16)

Thus *buwarraja* rock-art was never created by people, but is the Dreaming beings 'sitting' in the landscape.

People can nevertheless paint *buwarraja* figures as mediators of the Dreaming. Such an act should be undertaken by individuals of appropriate patrtifiliation to both place and totemic beings, although others may in some circumstances also undertake such a task (ibid., p. 17). Again, Wardaman language is imbued with the appropriate categoric expressions to articulate these links. Merlan (ibid.) thus noted that in Wardaman, the act of retouching or 'painting' Dreaming beings 'is commonly expressed as *wu-man marn+bu-* "to make good" (an *wu-* class thing, perhaps in reference to *wu-munburra* "rock")'.

Buwarraja rock-art is thus informed by a narrative tradition that articulates dimensions of Wardaman preunderstanding. In Merlan's (ibid., pp. 19 and 21) words, 'paintings and other figures are *buwarraja* if they are actively linked to contemporary mythological tradition', and '*buwarraja* is a basic categorical notion which underlies the encompassing narrative tradition'. *Buwarraja* rock-art include all the large images, the highly decorated figures of animal and human shape. They include also many abstract figures. In effect, the major images at most, if not all, sites are viewed by Wardaman elders today as Dreaming figures. It is only during the twentieth century that Wardaman artists stopped painting Dreaming motifs in the rockshelters, using the same conventions as evident in the earlier paintings.

These ethnographically documented features of Wardaman Dreaming enable us to trace archaeologically the antiquity of its visual symbolic expressions. If the rock-art symbolizes a particular Dreaming belief today, then the art's antiquity must necessarily give a maximum age for the artistic expression of that Dreaming belief within the considered site. To local Wardaman people, the *buwarraja* rock-art of their country is visual proof of the Dreaming itself. To archaeologists, such paintings were created some time in the past – they have a definable antiquity. Given their identity as signifiers and signified of the system of preunderstanding we know of ethnographically as the Dreaming, investigations of their antiquity may shed important light on the beginnings of the Dreaming as it is known today. In essence we are looking for temporal patterns, and I begin by asking whether or not the paintings that today express the identity of the land and the Dreaming were all initially undertaken within a relatively well-bounded and identifiable time frame. If this is the case, then it is possible that we are looking at the antiquity of the modern system of preunderstanding itself, although it could be said that we may still only be addressing the beginnings of the modern expression of a much older system. However, because the means of expressing a world-view is part of that very world-view, changes in expression or manifestation imply changes in the system of preunderstanding itself. The hegemonic character of a system cannot change without the system itself also changing.

The archaeology of *buwarraja* rock-art in Wardaman country

In 1988 Josephine Flood, then of the Australian Heritage Commission, began a long-term research project on the archaeology of rock-art in Wardaman country. With her co-researchers – Val Attenbrow, Bryce Barker, Jackie Collins, Robin Frost, Ben Gunn, Ian McNiven, Karen Saenz and myself – a series of painted rockshelters whose ethnographically known Dreaming stories were known were excavated. The aims of the excavations were to investigate the antiquity of occupation, and to attempt to recover clues, such as stratified and datable ochre fragments, as to the art's antiquity. As symbols of the Dreaming and (re)presentations of Dreaming beings and events, the antiquity of the *buwarraja* rock-art of Wardaman country has implications for the antiquity of the land's significance as an inscribed ethnographic Dreaming landscape.

The Lightning Brothers: Yiwarlarlay

D. S. Davidson (1936) was the first person to write of the rock-art of Wardaman country. His focus was a series of rock outcrops on Delamere Station, towards the south-centre of Wardaman territory. He was told of the Dreaming identity of two men that can be seen painted in one of the rockshelters known as Yiwarlarlay – Yagchadbulla and Tcabuinji (see Figure 2.2). They were the Lightning Brothers. Yagchadbulla was the youngest. Tall and handsome, he stood in stark contrast to his older brother, the not-so-well endowed Tcabuinji. Tcabuinji had a wife, Karnanda, who was also depicted on the rock wall.

A number of authors have written of the Dreaming story associated with the Lightning Brothers since Davidson. The first was Billy Harney Snr (1943), who described a dispute over Karnanda. During this dispute, the two brothers fought with weapons, the elder brother decapitating the younger with a boomerang (see also Arndt 1962, p. 165). Later commentators further wrote about the Lightning Brothers story, but until Wally Arndt's classic paper of 1962, all seem to have been based on Harney's earlier writings.

Wally Arndt (1962) recorded many details of the Lightning Brothers story from two old Wardaman men, one named Kulumput and the other who remains unnamed:

> Tcabuinji was an average-sized plain-looking married man who was annoyed by the attentions paid to his wife by a 'big young pretty fella', viz Yagchadbulla, who, as the painting shows, was the taller and more handsome person. Yagchadbulla was a tribal brother entitled to court the same woman as Tcabuinji. He was not a blood brother . . .
>
> The names of the characters were recorded in the field notes as Chabuin-ge, Yerkyerkbulla and Kaa-nan-da. They are obviously the same as those obtained by Davidson (1936).

Like Davidson, Arndt (1962) documented a fight between the two brothers, although he wrote that an axe, rather than a boomerang, was used. Arndt noted that thunder and lightning were created during the fight:

> Tcabuinji is depicted as the smaller and plainer of the two males, having no headdress and a relatively short penis. Yagdjadbula, on

the other hand, is much taller, with a longer penis and an elaborate headdress ... The informants also attached significance to the differences in the ankles, which Davidson (1936) does not show. It was explained that thunder was produced by the stamping which men do in warming up for a fight. Since Tjabuindji was the aggrieved one, and the more furious of the pair, he made most of the thunder and therefore must have had stronger ankles and feet. His ankles and feet are therefore heavier in shape and colouring. (1962, pp. 166–70)

Arndt also noted that the various colours used in the paintings had cultural significance. The black represented 'exceptional strength'. The ears needed to withstand the noise of thunder and the eyes lightning, and the arms needed to be strong; each was depicted in black. The backbone, loins and penis were painted in black, for 'both men must have had strong sexual impulses to stage such a furious fight over a woman' (ibid., p. 168); the heels and toes were also black, for it is

> well known that stamping in fighting or dancing routines produces an aching tiredness across the lower extremities of the tarsal bones or base of the toes. The two men did a lot of heavy stamping in producing thunder and must have been strong in this region.

Both Yagdjadbula and Tjabuindji are outlined in white and possess vertical red and yellow stripes said to represent the body markings of the goanna.

From 1989 to 1991 Josephine Flood, Ian McNiven, Robin Frost and I recorded further details of the Lightning Brothers story from the then-senior patrifiliated Wardaman owner of the site, the late Elsie Raymond, and from other related elders. The Dreaming story links the art at Yiwarlarlay with various features of the surrounding landscape. This is Elsie Raymond's version of events.

Yagjagbula and Jabirringi are brothers. Yagjagbula is the younger. He is tall and handsome, while his older brother is short and not so attractive. Both brothers are of the Jabijin sub-section. Yagjagbula has a wife, Gulliridan, and Jabirringi is married to Ganayanda (some people say that Jabirringi has been promised to Ganayanda, but that both brothers could potentially have married her given the correct sub-section affiliation). Each day one of the brothers goes hunting for food, bringing the day's catch back to camp where it is shared by all. One day it is Yagjagbula who hunts; the next it is Jabirringi.

One day Jabirringi returns from the hunt to hear Ganayanda whispering with Yagjagbula in a secluded break in the rock. Suspicious, he investigates to find them copulating. Jabirringi throws a spear at Yagjagbula, who evades it. A fight breaks out, with each brother taking his position on the plains at Yiwarlarlay (Figure 5.2). Spears and boomerangs are thrown, the fury of the fight producing lightning and thunder. The lightning strikes the sandstone outcrop at Yiwarlarlay and splits the rock in two (Figure 5.3). The Frogs come up from the south to watch the fight, clapping their thighs rhythmically (Figure 5.4). Wiyan, the Rain, was heading north to the Yingalarri waterhole, but gets distracted as it passes near Yiwarlarlay (at the same time, the Rainbow Serpent, Gorondolni, flashes at the Rain to warn it not to advance to Yingalarri). Wiyan metamorphoses into the Rain rock Ngalanjarri nearby. Eventually Yagjagbula hits Jabirringi across the forehead with his boomerang. Some say that Jabirringi's headdress is knocked off; others say that Jabirringi is decapitated. In either case, Yagjagbula wins the fight[5] (David et al. 1991).

The various versions of the Yiwarlarlay Lightning Brothers story generally corroborate each other, although there are minor differences in details. These differences are immaterial for our purposes, for like other Aboriginal Dreaming stories, it is the core themes that tend to be repeated in the telling; many of the finer details vary through time or between storytellers. Davidson's Karnanda, Yagchadbulla and Tcabuinji; Arndt's Kaa-nan-da, Yerkyerkbulla and Chabuin-ge; and Flood et al.'s Ganayanda, Yagjagbula and Jabirringi are the same Dreaming beings that today still live and can be seen on the rock wall at Yiwarlarlay.

Given that the Dreaming is symbolically represented in the Lightning Brothers rock-art at Yiwarlarlay, can we trace back in time the antiquity of the Lightning Brothers story, or at least its visual representation on the shelter walls?

Yiwarlarlay 1. We know that at least some parts of the two large anthropomorphs identified by Wardaman elders as the Lightning

Figure 5.2   Plains at Yiwarlarlay where the Lightning Brothers fought

Brothers at Yiwarlarlay date to the early parts of the twentieth century. When Davidson published his report of the site, only the upper portions of the two anthropomorphs were striped; the bottom half was only outlined. A few years after Davidson, Barrett and Croll (1943) published their own account of the paintings. Comparing their photograph of the site with Davidson's depictions, Arndt (1962, p. 165) concluded that paint had been added to the main figures since Davidson's visit. Arndt (ibid.) further noted Billy Harney's (1959) comment that he witnessed the paintings being retouched during the mid-twentieth century. By 1956, when Arndt visited the site, the paintings had been completed. Arndt's interviews with Wardaman elders reveal certain details of major interest for this work. He wrote:

> [Kulumput claimed that] the Lightning Brothers originally 'camped' on the Victoria River, where several neighbouring tribes were free to visit them. When the country and the people were divided between rival pastoral interests it was no longer practical for

the Wardaman people to visit the Lightning Place. The Wardaman elders at Delamere Station decided that the Lightning Brothers could 'camp' at the Rain Place near the homestead, so that they could be seen by the rising generation. A contemporary of Kulumput, Emu Jack, 'dreamed' (visualised) the design and did the painting. The task was delayed by station and tribal duties and was not finished until he was in bush-retirement prior to his death 'near the end of the Japanese war [the period of World War II, 1941–1945]'. (Arndt 1962, p. 169)

However, the question of the antiquity of the Lightning Brothers' first appearance on the rock wall at Yiwarlarlay remains to be answered. George Chaloupka (n.d.) has correctly observed that there is no direct evidence for the origins of the paintings themselves, as Davidson's, Barrett and Croll's, Harney's and Arndt's observations all relate to the enhancement of existing paintings. The original Lightning Brothers figures, it was argued, may have existed in outline for a considerable period of time (Chaloupka n.d.), and

Figure 5.3 Split rock outcrop at Yiwarlarlay, caused by the lightning created during the fight of the Lightning Brothers (*Source*: Ian McNiven)

until recently no evidence to the contrary was available.

Yiwarlarlay contains an isolated sandstone outcrop rising above the surrounding plains. Within the outcrop are three major rockshelters, two of which were test excavated by Ian McNiven and I in 1989. The main rockshelter (Yiwarlarlay 1) houses the Lightning Brothers, Ganayanda and other related Dreaming figures on the rock wall. The Lightning Brothers are impressive, polychrome anthropomorphs; Ganayanda is a small depiction to the side of Yagjagbula. At more than 4 m in height, Yagjagbula is one of the largest known anthropomorphs in Australia; Jabirringi is only slightly smaller. Together, these three paintings cover a significant portion of the rock wall surface in the main shelter at Yiwarlarlay. Because various parts of the rock wall (both painted and unpainted) are currently exfoliating – and this process of exfoliation may well have been taking place for a considerable time – the opportunity to excavate stratified evidence for the art's antiquity was considerable.

A series of six juxtaposed 50 x 50 cm squares positioned immediately beneath the Lightning Brothers were excavated. The excavation squares were located below a part of the wall containing Yagjagbula, under a section of the rock wall where rock cortex could be seen to have exfoliated away. It was hoped that through excavation sub-surface evidence for the origins of the paintings would be recovered.

Four major stratigraphic layers were identified. The basal layer 4 was deposited immediately above bedrock. It contained few stone artefacts, implying low intensities of site use. Importantly for our attempts to date the paintings, 36 unpainted pieces of exfoliated rock wall cortex were recovered from the main excavation square. No painted cortex fragments were found in this lowermost layer. Nor were any pieces of *in situ* ochre recovered. A radiocarbon date on charcoal shows that people first began to camp at the site around 700 calibrated years ago by extension of the depth-age curve.[6]

The beginning of layer 3 saw a major increase in deposition rates of cultural

Figure 5.4   The Frogs at Yiwarlarlay, visible as large boulders

materials such as flaked stone artefacts, food remains and charcoal from campfires. This is also the period when fragments of *in situ* earth pigments – red, yellow, white – first begin to appear. For the first time also, unpainted pieces of exfoliated rock cortex give way to painted fragments. This change from pigment-less to pigment-rich strata was dated to the last 200 years by radiocarbon dating. It also corresponds with the first appearance of European contact objects, such as glass and metal. David *et al.* (1990, p. 81) conclude that the occurrence of fragments of painted, exfoliated wall cortex, as well as of pieces of earth pigment only in deposits dating to the post-European contact period supports Arndt's (1962) earlier conclusion that the large, paired, striped anthropomorphs at Yiwarlarlay are of recent origin. Not only does the archaeological evidence suggest that the Lightning Brothers at Yiwarlarlay 1 date to the post-contact period, but also that all the other paintings linked to the Lightning Brothers Dreaming story in this part of the shelter date to this same period of time. There is no evidence here for any great

antiquity for the visual representations of the Lightning Brothers Dreaming story.

Delamere 3.   A second excavation was undertaken at Yiwarlarly, in a rockshelter on the other side of the large rock outcrop that shelters Yiwarlarlay 1 (Figure 5.5). The aim of this excavation was, in part, to test the Yiwarlarlay findings of a very recent antiquity for the paintings associated with the Lightning Brothers story. At Delamere three paintings were also found, one of which Kulumput informed Arndt (1962, p. 172) signified a baby Rainbow Serpent who 'came to "look" at Lightning from its home in a cave to the west where the "big" Rainbow Snake, called Kurakan, lives (as a huge wall painting)'.

Archaeological excavations at Delamere 3 were directed by Ian McNiven in 1989. Four 50 x 50 cm squares were dug near the painted rock surfaces.[7] McNiven *et al.* (1992, p. 71) noted that although cultural remains – charcoal and flaked stone artefacts in particular – were found to a depth of 34 cm below the ground surface, all pieces of earth pigment and

Figure 5.5   Delamere 3

fragments of exfoliated painted wall cortex, along with European contact items such as glass and metal, were recovered from the top 10 cm only. McNiven *et al.* thus concluded that 'while use of ochre in the shelter may extend back to 400 years, the bulk of cave painting (as indicated by exfoliated painted wall cortex) may have a very recent antiquity, dating to within the period of European contact' (ibid.) They continue:

> Despite differences in size, aspect and the nature of many painted and engraved motifs between Yiwarlarlay 1 and Delamere 3, the range and age of cultural remains excavated from both shelters are remarkably similar. Both shelters reveal relatively shallow deposits exhibiting stone artefacts . . . bones, freshwater mussel shell and ochre fragments dating to within the last 400 years. Of particular significance is the apparent synchronous introduction of major wall painting activities in both shelters around the time of European contact in the latter half of the last century . . .

Therefore, our current data indicate that Aboriginal use of Yiwarlarlay changed suddenly some 400 years ago, resulting in the discard of numerous stone artefacts, bones, shells and ochre fragments. At around the time of European contact in the latter half of the nineteenth century, however, Yiwarlarlay witnessed further dramatic changes in use and perception. A key feature of these changes was the manifestation of hundreds of painted images across the walls of shelters. (ibid., pp. 71–2).

Artistic symbols that reference aspects of the Lightning Brothers Dreaming story cannot be traced back beyond the nineteenth century CE at Yiwarlarlay.

The Rainbow Serpent–Two Sisters Story: Garnawala

While undertaking fieldwork near Port Keats during the early years of the twentieth century, W. E. H. Stanner (1961) recorded three versions of a Rainbow Serpent Dreaming story by members of various language groups to the west of Wardaman country. The first of these was told by a Marithiel man from the Daly River region:

> Lerwin, The Rainbow Serpent, had no wife. Amanggal, The Little Flying Fox, had two wives. Lerwin stole one of the women while Amanggal was looking for food. When he discovered the loss, Amanggal pursued Lerwin to a far country and slew him with a stone-tipped spear. Lerwin cried out in pain, jumped into deep water, and was transformed into a serpent. Amanggal flew into the sky. (Stanner 1961, p. 238)

The young man who recounted this story was not aware of its greater details: the story was fragmentary and little explanation was offered.

The second version was told by a Wagaman person. It, too, is sketchy:

> The main name of The Serpent was given to me as Djagwut, but the Wagaman appeared to distinguish two rainbows, one described as being 'high', one 'low'. I could not be sure if they were making a distinction between the main colour-bands of rainbows, and the spurious bows, or between primary and secondary rainbows. The 'high' (i.e. secondary) rainbow was described as the spit of Djagwut and the 'low' (i.e. primary) rainbow as the spit of Tjinimin. Djagwut was recognized as the source and protector of human life, and as the giver of spirit-children. He was supposed to persist in deep springs, rivers and billabongs, and to be especially dangerous to menstruating women, being able to smell them from afar. The Wagaman assigned Djagwut to the Tjimitj sub-section and Tjinimin to the Djangala sub-section, the two thus being in an affinal (wife's brother) relation. All I could recapture of the myth was that Tjinimin had two wives; that Djagwut stole both of them; that Tjinimin pursued and slew him with a stone-tipped spear while asleep, the spear striking him in the back. Djagwut cried out in pain, jumped into deep water, and was transformed into a serpent. Tjinimin flew into the sky. (Stanner 1961, p. 239)

The third is a Nangiomeri version:

> The Rainbow Serpent, Angamunggi, was described to me in terms of the familiar All-Father imagery: as the primeval father of men, the giver of life, the maker of spirit-children, and the guardian and protector of men . . . The Nangiomeri seemed to think of Angamunggi as a dualistic person. They suggested that he had a womb, that a son had died within it and that the 'low' or 'small' rainbow (Amebe) was also his son. He was assigned to the Tjanama sub-section, and Adirminmin (again described as The Little Flying Fox) was assigned to the Djangala sub-section, that is, to the correlative affinal sub-section of Tjanama . . .
>
> Adirminmin went about trying to find good stone for a spear. He went to many places. Finally he went to a spring at Kimul (on the Fitzmaurice River). There he went hunting for kangaroo. He was a Djangala man and took with him two Nangari women who had been given to him by Angamunggi. The two women went away and hid. Carrying a kangaroo, he caught up with them. They were on a high cliff and made a rope to lift him up. The rope broke and he fell down a long way, breaking his bones. The women went to bathe in the salt-water part of the river, and then ran away, with sexual intent, to Angamunggi. Adirminmin mended his broken bones, bathed in the salt-water, and set out to recapture the women. The tide kept on sweeping him back as he tried to cross the river. He went to try to find good stone for a spear. He tried several kinds of stone, but they were not sharp enough. Finally he found a sharp stone called *katamalga*, and put it on a spear-shaft. Then he chased and found the women. He said: 'Ah! Here you two are! I have to pick up my spear.' He sang the song that begins *Kawandi, kawandi*; then he danced by himself; and, after that, went to sleep. Wakening, he found Angamunggi, and threw the spear so that it pierced the Rainbow Serpent's backbone. (Stanner 1961, pp. 239–40)

A similar Dreaming story was recorded by Robin Frost and I in 1988–91 from Wardaman elders Elsie Raymond and Tarpot Ngamunagami at Garnawala, towards the northwestern corner of Wardaman country. The story tells of Two Sisters who are chased from Port Keats by Gorondolni, the Rainbow Serpent. In turn, they are chased by a Diver Duck and a Flying Fox, who are themselves followed by numerous animals – Kangaroos, Emus, Echidnas, Dingoes, etc. The Dreaming beings pass through Garnawala on their way southeast. The Rainbow Serpent arrives at a place near the Yingalarri waterhole, where he plays his didgeridoo. Dragging a spear along the ground between his toes, the Diver Duck approaches the Rainbow Serpent, who is not paying close attention to what is happening around him. Undetected by the Rainbow Serpent, the Diver Duck manages to get close and spear him (David *et al.* 1994, p. 247).

Garnawala 1. As these events unfold, the Dreaming beings at Garnawala watch. The elder beings, the Djangural, watch over the younger Yirmi-nyonong. The Djangural can still be seen today in one of the Garnawala rockshelters as large polychrome anthropomorphs towering above the smaller Yirmi-nyonong (Figure 5.6). The Yirmi-nyonong are represented on the shelter wall as a long line of matchstick figures, most of which have been repainted many times through the ages (six or more layers of paint can often be detected on an individual painting).

The rockshelter designated Garnawala 1 is where these Dreaming beings sit in the rock. The shelter is large. At some 32 m wide and 8 m deep it is one of the largest painted sites in Wardaman country. A series of nine juxtaposed 50 x 50 cm squares were excavated beneath the Djangural and Yirmi-nyonong, the sediments revealing large numbers of buried ochre pieces datable by stratigraphic association.

The Garnawala excavations revealed two major strata, an upper unit rich in cultural materials, and a lower unit with some, but few, cultural remains dating back to 5240 ± 70 years BP. The two strata are separated by a thick layer of sandstone, evidence of sheet roof-fall that took place between two radiocarbon dates of 939 ± 91 years BP and 860 ± 65 years BP (David *et al.* 1994). The implications are significant: the thickness and extent of the rocky layer imply that a large section of the rockshelter's ceiling, if not the entire surface itself, fell around 900 years BP, exposing the present, now richly decorated surface. The Dreaming paintings that today display the Rainbow Serpent–Two Sisters story cannot therefore be older than this. This is confirmed by the presence of hundreds of ochre pieces in the upper layer of the Garnawala deposits; the buried roof-fall shows no evidence of having been painted.[8]

In line with conclusions earlier reached by David *et al.* (1994), it is concluded that the ethnographically identified Dreaming paintings at Garnawala began to be painted after 900 years BP, in calibrated terms equivalent to some

time between 1000 and 800 years ago, despite the fact that people first started using the site much earlier.

Garnawala 2. Garnawala 2 is located a few tens of metres from Garnawala 1. It is the largest rockshelter yet recorded from Wardaman country (Figure 5.7). According to Wardaman elders Tarpot Ngamunagami and Elsie Raymond (personal communication, 1990), the numerous paintings represent Dreaming beings. These Dreaming beings include the Moon *gandawag*; Devil Dogs *wurrguru*; Emu *gumurrinji* (Figure 5.8), who went to the site of Nimji nearby from Buffalo Springs, only to return to Garnawala 2; Nail-tail Wallabies *galumanggan*; Echidnas *gawalyan*, Flying Foxes; Brolgas; Plain Kangaroos (Euro) *yunumburrgu*, who came from Port Keats; Eagles, who also came from Port Keats, chasing the Kangaroo and eating it at Garnawala 2; and Yirmi-nyonong from Port Keats. Few details are known of the story of Garnawala 2, although we know that many of the Dreaming beings associated with the Rainbow Serpent–Two Sisters story left the chase to 'stop' here. In addition to these Dreaming beings, Garnawala 2 also contains many post-contact *bulawula* (non-Dreaming) paintings that were said by Wardaman elders to have been painted in very recent times.

Fifteen juxtaposed 50 x 50 cm squares were excavated at Garnawala 2. Human occupation began some unknown time before a radiocarbon date of $10,256 \pm 92$ years BP, and continued into post-contact times. Intensities of occupation increased markedly after 3000 years BP (Clarkson and David 1995), with further changes in occupational trends occurring after the arrival of Europeans towards the end of the nineteenth and beginning of the twentieth centuries. Fragments of earth pigment were recovered in high numbers after 2920 ± 120 years BP, with a major increase around or shortly before the nineteenth century.

It is difficult to determine the age of Garnawala 2's rock paintings based on the excavated ochres. One reason is that the shelter is very large, and rock platforms are located in such inhibitive positions that the excavation squares could not be positioned beneath individual paintings or decorated wall surfaces. Another reason for the uncertainty is the presence of both *buwarraja* and *bulawula* – ethnographic Dreaming and (mainly post-contact?)

Figure 5.6 Djangural and Yirmi-nyonong at Garnawala: excavation in progress, 1990

Figure 5.7 Garnawala 2

non-Dreaming – paintings. Based on rates of recovery of stratified earth pigments from the excavations, I conclude at this stage that Garnawala's paintings are likely to date to the late Holocene, although it is uncertain whether this relates to the last 3000 years or to the last few hundred years only.

White Cockatoo Dreaming: Mengge-ya

In the area of Jalijbang, towards the western edge of Wardaman country, is a small rocky gorge (see Figure 5.9). Here can be found the rockshelter of Mennge-ya, 'at the White Cockatoo'. Two large polychrome anthropomorphs dominate the walls (see Figure 1.1). They are female White Cockatoos, wives of old man White Cockatoo who resides at Winybarr a few kilometres away. Elsie Raymond recounted the White Cockatoo story in June 1989:

> old man white cockatoo was there for them
>   at Winybarr
> they went walkabout from there to
>   Geberrung and what's it?
> Old Willeroo

> they pulled up kapok
> and in the afternoon the two went home to
>   Winybarr, they gave him food
> they went back to white cockatoo place
> they slept
> early they went from there
> they went in the morning
> they went to Old Willeroo
> they got kapok
> food
> they dug and in the afternoon went home
> all the time like that
> they went back to Winybarr and gave it to
>   the old man
> food
> they went from him to the white cockatoo
>   place
> to go in/under as dreaming
> they went in as dreaming.
>   (Merlan 1994, pp. 509–10)

The White Cockatoos of Mennge-ya gather the Native-Cotton (Kapok) to feed their husband, old man White Cockatoo, at Winybarr. They then return to Mennge-ya, the White Cockatoo place, where they sit in the rock as manifestations of the Dreaming.

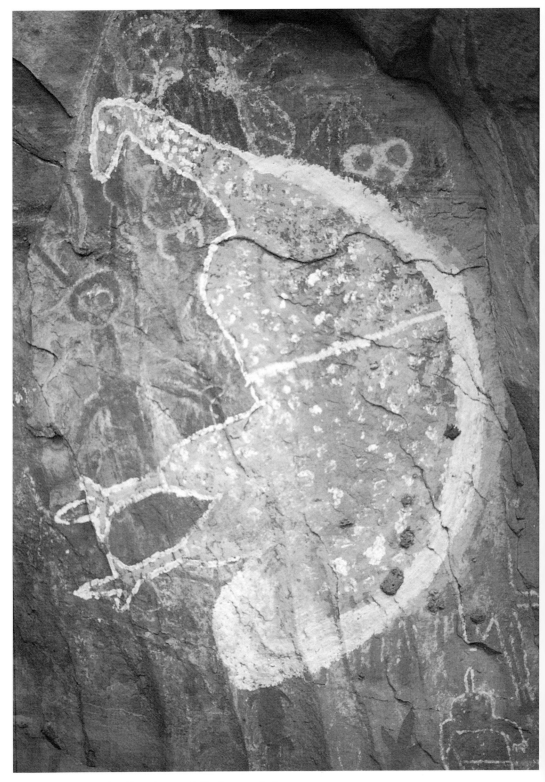

Figure 5.8 Dreaming Emu (*gumurrinji*), Garnawala 2

Figure 5.9 The small gorge at Jalijbang, seen from above

Mengge-ya was excavated in 1989 by Val Attenbrow and me (Attenbrow *et al.* 1995).[9] The two White Cockatoos are located near the ground level upwards to about 1.5 m above the shelter floor, on a small, localized vertical rock surface. Older, very faded paintings occur underneath and near the White Cockatoos; these are not known to be related to the White Cockatoo Dreaming story.

Six adjacent 50 x 50 cm squares were excavated immediately beneath the paintings. Cultural sediments began sometime shortly before a radiocarbon date of 2109±60 years BP. A major increase in deposition rates of cultural materials – flaked stone artefacts, bone (food remains), ochre and charcoal – took place around 2000 years BP (ibid.).

While the number of buried ochre pieces first increase with the acceleration of stone artefact deposition rates around 2000 years BP, that is, the evidence for painting activity increases along with other evidence for increased intensities of site use, the major increase in ochre deposition rates (including pieces of ochre with use-wear in the form of

striations and bevelling) does not take place until well after, around 1400 years BP (David *et al.* 1994, p. 247). These changes can be directly related to the now-visible rock paintings. David *et al.* (1994) have suggested that the earliest ochre pieces probably date the paintings underlying the White Cockatoos, given patterns of superimposition, degrees of fading, and colours used. The White Cockatoos themselves have been repainted many times since their initial creation. Their first painting corresponds to a second period of increase in ochre deposition rates, shortly after a radiocarbon determination of 380±60 years BP. This means that the first archaeological signs of the White Cockatoo paintings appear late in the second millennium CE.

Owl Dreaming: Gordol-ya

Gordol-ya, 'at the Owl', is the largest rockshelter of the sandstone outcrop known today as Jigaigarn by Wardaman elders. Located towards the western end of Wardaman country, it contains a culturally significant

Figure 5.10 The balancing rock at Jigaigarn, placed above the rockshelter by *gordol*, the Owl, in the Dreaming (*Source*: Jackie Collins)

landmark in the form of a balancing rock said to have been placed above the rockshelter by *gordol*, the Owl, in the Dreaming (Figure 5.10). Some 147 paintings decorate the shelter walls, including *gordol* (Figure 5.11). The paintings are dominated by a large red and yellow striped figure, identified by Wardaman elder Tarpot Ngamunagami (personal communication, 1991) as *gordol* (David *et al.* 1995). Little else is known of the site's Dreaming significance during recent times.

Gordol-ya was excavated in 1991 by Jackie Collins of the University of New England (see David *et al.* 1995 for a brief report). Sixteen 50 x 50 cm squares were dug below the decorated walls, spanning the back to the centre of the shelter. Human occupation began shortly before a radiocarbon date of 10,060 ± 110 years BP. However, few cultural materials were deposited until the late Holocene, when quantities of charcoal, mussel shell, flaked stone artefacts and animal bones increased greatly. Most of the fragments of stratified earth pigment came from a buried layer that began to

form shortly before 300 ± 50 years BP (David *et al.* 1995). David *et al.* (ibid., pp. 5–6) thus concluded that the Gordol-ya paintings date to the late Holocene, and probably only to the last few hundred years. While our understanding of the site's chronology remains coarse-grained, there is no evidence for the presence of the paintings recently associated with the Owl Dreaming story at Gordol-ya before the second half of the second millennium CE. As was the case at the other sites in Wardaman country, artistic expressions of the Dreaming known from ethnography at Gordol-ya emerge only during late Holocene times. These findings have major implications for the antiquity of the ethnographically documented Dreaming beliefs and expressions in this part of Australia, implications that I explore below.

Discussion

Symbols, as meaningful expressions of preunderstanding, help individuals know the world

Figure 5.11 *Gordol,* the Owl at Gordol-ya (*Source*: Jackie Collins)

as a realm of social and political order. In marking place with symbols, rock-art imbues space with meaningful, ontological structure; it writes the landscape with socially, culturally and politically ordered symbolism. Land becomes a canvas of cultural expression, cultural experience and knowledge. Material inscription transforms the land into a hand-crafted stage of and for human behaviour, an engaged landscape whose order is accessible for archaeological inquiry.

In much of Wardaman country during recent times, the Dreaming beings that inform artistic expression are often depicted as anthropomorphs. This is not surprising given the nature of Wardaman preunderstanding. Wardaman Dreaming concerns creation and transformation, an atemporal, even spatial, past where the world emerged in its present form. In Wardaman belief, people are intimately linked with all things. In the Dreaming, animals obtain their defining 'natural' characteristics as people obtain their defining 'cultural' traits through their links with particular

Dreaming ancestors. As a result of this, Wardaman Dreaming is often expressed allegorically, all things possessing recognizably human qualities. This is well exemplified by the Lightning Brothers who give what we would call 'natural' phenomena – lightning and thunder – a human, cultural dimension. This is metaphor at work – a dimension of symbolic behaviour I will explore in some detail in Chapter 9 – and it is in its particular representational and metaphoric construction that the Dreaming reveals itself as a way of looking at the world.

What we can access archaeologically are aspects of the dynamics of these ethnographically documented relations between people and their world through their symbolic representations. Symbols express a world order and help individuals and groups negotiate the world's meaningfulness. Changes in symbolic behaviour imply changes in the way we understand the world as a network of references.

In Wardaman country of recent times, the Dreaming defined how people categorized and ordered their known and experienced world.

This world was animated and populated by Dreaming beings, timeless essences that gave rise to all things. In signalling a Dreaming presence, the *buwarraja* rock paintings signal a particular preunderstanding that shapes social behaviour. In this rock-art symbolism can be found visual representations – visual *proof* – of the truth of the Dreaming. But as the antiquity of the *buwarraja* artistic representations akin to those of ethnographic times implies, such a truth appears to have a limited temporal depth. The commencement of intensified painting activity around 900–1400 years ago (with hints at Garnawala that the changes *may* have roots as far back as c. 2900 years BP), and its acceleration thereafter, implicates late Holocene transformations in the way belief systems were (re)presented. It is not just the aesthetic world that was altered, but the visual, symbolic manifestations of how that world was understood. After 900–1400 years ago emerged a new system of signs that divided the world symbolically, making new structural demands on the onlooker's attention. These signs differentiated the Wardaman landscape into a network of separate but ontologically linked, territorial spaces. The emerging rock-art conventions created new structures of difference and deference best understood through, and as, *différance*. The late Holocene antiquity of Wardaman visual symbols implies a late Holocene antiquity for the graphic presencing of the ethnographically known Wardaman Dreaming. The fact that Wardaman symbols associated with the ethnographic Dreaming cannot be securely traced further back in time implies an epochal reworking of the open network of signs, as system of meaning, 900–1400 years ago.

Notes

1. Gadamer and Derrida develop Heidegger's philosophy in slightly different ways. Gadamer makes more of the hermeneutic circle than Derrida does, although of course Derrida does not dispute that understanding occurs in a circular manner. For a discussion of the similarities and differences between Gadamer and Derrida, see Diane P. Michelfelder and Richard E. Palmer's (1989) *Dialogue and Deconstruction: The Gadamer–Derrida encounter*. Actually, this was rather more of a non-encounter than an encounter. The two met up again, more congenially, on Capri. See Derrida and Vattimo (1998) *Religion*. (Kevin Hant, personal communication 2001).

2. It is of interest that in words, symbols or actions, meanings are conjured. While such meanings are based in preunderstanding, they cannot simply be reduced to it, for they emerge in the passing of the sign in an open network of signs. Rather, preunderstanding and the passing of the sign intersect in *différance*, continuously readjusting preunderstanding in the process.

3. In Aboriginal ontology this does not signify a creation by the artist, but rather identifies her or him as the vehicle of a greater presence emplacing itself in the landscape.

4. Interestingly, it would appear that the motifs found in *bulawula* rock-art, and their degree of compositional complexity, can fairly easily be differentiated from *buwarraja* art. The former tends to be monochrome and relatively small, while the latter is often (but not in the majority of cases) polychrome and large. As already noted, Anglo-Australian contact subjects are often depicted in *bulawula* art, but almost never in *buwarraja* art. A detailed exploration of these themes would be warranted, but has not yet been attempted.

5. Wardaman elders recount how Jabirringi's headdress/head could be seen as a relatively small but conspicuous rock at Yiwarlarlay until recent times, when it was stolen by people of European decent.

6. The radiocarbon date obtained is 444 ± 87 years BP (NZA 860), with archaeological evidence of human occupation occurring slightly below this date.

7. Excavation at Delamere 3 proceeded to bedrock. As was the case at Yiwarlarlay 1, four major stratigraphic layers were identified. The lowermost layer 4 contained few cultural materials. Layers 1–3 were rich in cultural materials, and date approximately to the last 380 ± 60 years BP (Wk 1672).

8. This large shelter was not itself formed by the roof-fall that took place around 900 years BP. The site has existed as a very large shelter since at least 5200 years BP, which is when low intensity human occupation began.

9. The rockshelter is 12 m wide by 18 m deep.

6 The Present Past?

Every age must remember its history anew. Each generation must examine and think through again, from its own distinctive vantage point, the ideas that have shaped its understanding of the world.

(Tarnas 1991, p. xiv)

In the previous chapters I explored how, during recent times, Dreaming beliefs have affected the use of space, ritual performance and symbolic behaviour in three different parts of Australia. In each case indigenous ontology was seen to structure material behaviour in social participation and communication. In each case also the material manifestations of the Dreaming as we know it today could not be traced back in time beyond the late Holocene. There are some possible material traces of the Dreaming that we know from historical times going as far back as about 3000 years ago, but these are archaeologically problematic and remain uncertain. It is not until 700 to 1400 years ago that the Dreaming in Djungan, Arrernte and Wardaman country become archaeologically recognizable. This does not so much imply that the Dreaming itself, as indigenous cosmology, began during this period of time, but that its *modern* form did (when viewed from a Western historical perspective). No other reliable material evidence contradicting these temporal patterns is at hand. And, yet, the notion that the Dreaming that we know from ethnographic times is of very deep antiquity is well enshrined in popular imagination. We read of this in newspapers, magazines, travel books and novels, that is, in much of the popular literature on 'Australian Aborigines'. This has long been the case, and we need not go back to the sociological writings of James Frazer or Baldwin Spencer to find literary evidence for the notion in Western thought that Aboriginal world-views are most ancient. Let me cite a few examples of popular, non-anthropological writings from each decade of the second half of the twentieth century to illustrate the pervasive nature of such views. I will not here trace the historical contexts of each text cited, but merely point out the persistence of such notions in the popular literature. Later in this chapter I will explore further this common and public Western perception of the Dreaming and of Aboriginality by reference to other historical narratives, to show that long-standing dimensions of Western preunderstanding have themselves served to structure a modern understanding of the Dreaming and of Aboriginality.

Some popular writings on Aboriginal beliefs

In 1955, in *Dust for the Dancers* Beth Dean and Victor Carell (1955, p. ix) wrote of the 'age old beliefs and customs' of Australian Aborigines, paying particular attention to 'the traditional dances, songs and stories that have been handed down through untold generations as the tribes wandered on their long walkabouts over Australia'. In 1966, Roland Robinson (1966, pp. xi–xii) published a compendium of Dreaming stories entitled *Aboriginal Myths and Legends*, noting that the 'original traditions have been handed down for thousands of years. Some portions of their [Aboriginal people's] chants are so ancient as to have lost their meaning', alluding to more than 30,000 years of occupation as witness to the narrative tradition's great antiquity. Similarly, in their popular book *Dreamtime Heritage*, Melva Jean Roberts and Ainslie Roberts (1975, p. 11) present a way of life whose 'design was unchanged for thousands of years, until it was shattered, in the twinkling of an eye, by the invaders who forced the tribesmen to accept a new way of life'. The following year, Bobbie Hardy (1976, p. 1) wrote in *Lament for the Barkindji*:

> The Barkindji were traditionalists, for no unsettling influences from outside the familiar tribal world had penetrated the barrier of their isolation. Their lives were governed by ancient rules, obedience to which preserved in equilibrium both their lives and their environment.

This timeless equilibrium was not simply a characteristic of the ethnographically known Dreaming as a way of seeing the world, but one that imbued Aboriginality itself. This was the static constitution of a singular, unchanging culture whose present form could be traced deep into antiquity.

Such popular sentiments have carried into the 1980s and beyond. Richard Broome (1982 p. 21) wrote in *Aboriginal Australians* that, until the arrival of Europeans, Aboriginal people lived in a 'comfortable fashion of non-materialistic affluence', having 'survived for over 50,000 years with a Dreamtime philosophy that stressed continuity over change'. During the last decade of the twentieth century, Bill Edwards (1994, p. 65) similarly wrote of an implicit, deep-seated cultural continuity in 'Living the Dreaming':

> The roots of contemporary Aboriginal spirituality lie in a variety of traditions and experiences. First and foremost are the various stories, ceremonies, values and structures

which sustained Aboriginal peoples throughout their long period of relatively unchallenged occupation of the continent.

In a similar vein, Harvey Arden (1995, p. 3) wrote in his *Dreamkeepers* of the 'Aboriginal people of Australia, custodians of the oldest culture on earth, keepers of the Dreamtime'. And John Chambers (1999, p. 11) introduces the Dreaming in his book, *A Traveller's History of Australia*, with the words 'theirs is today the world's oldest continuous culture, with easily the world's oldest continuous religion'.

These examples of a widespread creed in the deep antiquity of modern indigenous world-views are but a small selection of a vast body of literature immersed in a Western preunderstanding that imbues Aboriginality with timelessness. Such preconceptions articulate a doctrine that has long remained unchallenged in popular thought.

Why is it that recently documented Aboriginal beliefs are considered in this way in popular culture, as at once old and timeless? One possible reason concerns the contents of the Dreaming stories themselves, which some claim to be evidence for things ancient. Hence Josephine Flood (1995, p. 10) has written: 'There are only two sources of knowledge about the really distant human past of Australia: archaeological evidence and Aboriginal oral traditions passed down as stories about the Dreamtime.' These oral traditions – the Dreaming stories – are often taken as evidence of a public consciousness that has remained essentially unchanged for tens of thousands of years. Examples include stories of boat peoples coming to Australia, supposedly documenting the Pleistocene origins of individual clans or language groups. Some stories tell of mountains of fire, interpreted as late Pleistocene or early Holocene volcanic eruptions by some researchers, and treated as evidence for the great antiquity of present-day stories. For example, Bob Dixon (1991, pp. 1, 41–4) recounts a Dreaming story that concerns the origins of Lake Eacham, a crater lake in north Queensland. The story was told by local Yidinyji elder Dick Moses in 1971 (another, similar story was recorded by Dyirbal elder George Watson in 1964, Dyirbal and Yidinyji countries are neighbours), and tells of darkening skies becoming increasingly yellow in colour.[1] Dixon (1991, pp. 41–2) interpreted this story as 'a plausible account of a volcanic eruption', the geological explanation for the lake's creation believed to have occurred some 13,000 years ago.

But two critical objections can be made for the historical and Dreaming implications of such stories. The first relates to the historical status of the stories themselves. There are thousands, and possibly tens of thousands, of Dreaming stories in Australia. Most, if not all, tell of a different time when the world was forming – a time when water was rock, when forest was desert, when the sky was black, when the world was somehow recognizable and yet different. This is the time of origins constructed in lore. Such tales of creation are found in all cultures, and are usually characterized by reference to a world that was different – if not somehow apposite – from the present (e.g. 'Genesis' of the Judaeo-Christian tradition).

Many (hi)stories, in any cultural tradition, are undoubtedly based on historical events, the knowledge of which has been modified through the ages. But to isolate a handful of cosmogonic stories from any culture as proof of folk memory because they remind the scientist of past geological events dating back 10,000 years or more is a dubious endeavour. It also belittles the ability of indigenous peoples to observe and interpret their own surroundings – to infer a prior molten state and even fiery origin for rocks (lava) with surficial flow marks, for example. This is not to say that there may not be some historical basis for some of the Dreaming stories, but determining what is historical from cosmogonic or heuristic reality is another matter.

The second line of objection is more critical for the viability of using such stories as evidence of the ethnographic Dreaming's deep antiquity. Irrespective of a story's historical merits, all reality was preunderstood to be of the Dreaming by Aboriginal people during recent times. Any past belief, whether or not viewed through the Dreaming, will have been continuously re-interpreted in light of the ontology of the time. In the recent past, all perceived past events, whether or not they represent folk memory, were communicated via a Dreaming-based ontology. All things belonged in the Dreaming. This does not mean that the Dreaming, as a belief system, is necessarily old, but that in *recent* times all things were

informed through it, as the contemporary system of preunderstanding. So while a particular story may relate to an historical event long past, the world-view through which such a past event is now understood and communicated cannot be dated by reference to the timing of that event.

Questioning the dominant paradigm

Given this, modern Dreaming stories cannot be used as evidence for the Dreaming's great antiquity, despite the possibility that a story's contents may represent traces of particular historical events passed down in folk memory. And the same could be said of any belief system that espouses views about the origins of the world, Christianity included. If such stories are held as evidence for the great antiquity of the Dreaming as a belief system – as evidence of a people who 'survived for over 50,000 years with a Dreamtime philosophy' – then the reason for such a perception of the ethnographic Dreaming's ancientness lies not in the stories themselves, but in a ready willingness to believe in its great age in the absence of any direct evidence that addresses its antiquity.

In Western scholarship the best evidence for the antiquity of ethnographically known world-views rests with the archaeology. Despite this, few archaeologists have ever researched the origins of specific Aboriginal stories, let alone of the belief systems themselves. The only archaeological attempt to date Dreaming beliefs yet to appear in the popular press was only reported in 1996 (see below), so it cannot account for earlier popular dispositions. A view of the ethnographic Dreaming's great antiquity is particularly striking when it is contrasted with the modern anthropological position that stresses its dynamism, its emergence in historical practice (e.g. Poirier 1993). In contrast to a lack of archaeological research, and in contrast also to the Dreaming of popular imagination, social anthropologists have long recognized the changing qualities of Dreaming beliefs. Their views, it is fair to say, are based on direct observations of Aboriginal lifeways in recent times and on the recognition that the documented Dreaming beliefs are about contemporary times. Anthropological writings relate to social practice and to social change as witnessed and measured in real-life temporal scales. Examples of the dynamism of Dreaming beliefs and practices abound in the professional literature of the past 50 years especially. For example, the linguist Patrick McConvell (1996) has modelled linguistic changes and changes in kinship systems across the western two-thirds of Australia during the late Holocene. He suggests on linguistic grounds that 'subsection forms of social categorisation' – the eight-class system – emerged in Australia only during the last 2000 years, significantly re-aligning social relationships in the process (McConvell 1996, p. 125). This has obvious implications for the antiquity of any Dreaming story that references the eight-class system. The Pama-Nyungan language system is also believed to have expanded across much of Australia only during the last 3000 years or so. This, too, has implications for the antiquity of Dreaming stories that deal with the origins of those language groups, as well as for the antiquity of the languages in which the narrative tradition operates. 'It is completely implausible', McConvell (ibid., p. 135) argues, 'to ascribe an age of say 10,000 years or more to the Western Desert language'.

Along similar lines, Sylvie Poirier (1993) has documented the recent creation and diffusion of new Dreaming rituals and dances among the Warlpiri of central Australia, a process of change that she argues testifies to a cultural dynamism that reveals intrinsic qualities of openness and flexibility. John Mulvaney (1975) has also reviewed the evidence for change in Dreaming performances, documenting the rapid spread of new Molonga rituals across Australia between 1893 and 1918. Walter E. Roth first documented the ritual in northwestern Queensland in 1893. Baldwin Spencer and Frank Gillen (1912) then documented it at Alice Springs in 1901. Molonga ceremonies were subsequently documented by Daisy Bates (1930) along the Nullarbor Plain in 1918. In only 25 years, the ritual had spread over a distance of more than 1600 km, stretching from near Australia's northern to its southern coastlines (Mulvaney 1975, pp. 90–2). Social change is implied here; a transformation of the way specific world-views were articulated and performed in ritual.

Howard Morphy (1998, p. 72) has also written of the Dreaming's inherent dynamism from an anthropological perspective, noting that it is an 'accommodation of change and process that has enabled Aboriginal religion to maintain its relevance in a rapidly changing world'. Like world-views elsewhere, through time what we now call the Dreaming changes. Similarly, Ronald and Catherine Berndt (1989, p. 408) have written of ethnographic Dreaming stories and the events they portray as continuously unfolding through the course of history: 'They were all in the process of "becoming", being transformed.' The Dreaming stories expressed the Dreaming's creative dynamism whose roots lay in worldly human life. It was not just the environment *around* the storyteller that was transformed in the Dreaming; perceptions of the world were themselves undergoing perpetual change. The Dreaming, as we know it from the ethnography and from indigenous voices, is the historical 'end product' of this process of change, and it continues to change as time goes by.

The dynamic nature of Dreaming beliefs has been recognized and widely reported by anthropologists and linguists since the 1960s at least. However, as presently evident in the myriad popular books and magazine entries on the subject, there is also a widespread public assumption that the Dreaming represents a primordial way of being, a world-view that is at once ancient and beyond time. Such a view is grounded in a hierarchical view of things traceable in European tradition at least as far back as Aristotle. Let us explore these historical roots, for as foundation they have significantly shaped our present attitudes towards the Dreaming which we know from ethnography. As Tim Murray (2002, pp. 237–8) has noted,

> Analysis of the disciplinary 'culture' of practitioners allows us to chart the ways in which social and cultural 'givens' (normative values) can be incorporated as privileged assumptions. . . . Exploring new histories of archaeology can help us understand how the edifice of modern archaeology – its agendas, concepts, categories, patterns of socialization, and institutions – became established, and the processes which have underwritten its transformations.

Such historical tracings reveal archaeology 'as a significant social and culture force [which] underscores the point that archaeology does not belong only to archaeologists' (Murray

2002, p. 238). In this context I note from the onset that the positioning of Aboriginal people in archaeological thought has parralles in various popular and academic movements such as eugenics, public policy, notions of health, geography, sociology and political economy amongst many (e.g. see Anderson 2002, McGregor 1997 and Wolfe 1999 for penetrating historiographies of eugenic and evolutionary anthropological thought). I focus here on the history of *archaeological* referencing, mainly in popularly accessible texts.

Much has been written about how the West has perceived other cultures through the ages (for a classic text from another part of the world, see Said's *Orientalism* of 1978; for how the 'edges' of the earth were perceived by the ancient Greeks and Romans, see Romm 1992). The dominant mid-nineteenth-century views are perhaps best exemplified by the works of the influential public commentators Thomas Huxley, Lewis Henry Morgan, Edward B. Tylor and Herbert Spencer, each of whom saw the world from social evolutionary perspectives. Each, in his own way, was concerned with identifying progressive stages in human development, positioning representatives of the West at the top of an evolutionary or developmental ladder that echoed the power relations of Western colonialism. Let us consider a few examples of such views from the 1860s to the middle of the twentieth century to illustrate the prevalence and pervasiveness of such notions in Western thought. My aim here is not to undertake a detailed historiography of the place of Australian Aborigines in the Western imagination, but, in the spirit of Johannes Fabian's (1983) critique of the temporalization of Otherness, to identify a few key and influential historical markers to illustrate the point that a willingness to view things Aboriginal as atemporal and ancient-in-design has long formed a cornerstone of Western thought.

'The common ancestor for all modern races'

The 1860s were in many respects foundational years in anthropology. When Charles Darwin undertook his voyages of exploration on the *Beagle* in 1831–6, the varied peoples of the globe were commonly perceived as descendants of the migratory tribes of Israel who long ago had colonized the farthest ends of the earth. The supposed savagery of some indigenous groups was seen not so much a result of evolutionary failures as a cultural and moral degeneration following centuries of isolation from Europe and the Mediterranean world, as the stronghold of civilization.

Yet while dominant at the turn of the nineteenth century, notions of degeneration and developmental stasis were never the only means of understanding cultural and biological difference. Following Darwin's publication in 1859 of *On the Origin of Species by Means of Natural Selection, or the Preservation of Favoured Races in the Struggle for Life*, the interpretative balance shifted as a new and popular mechanism became available to account for cultural and biological difference. The widespread embracement of natural selection, and more generally evolution, as a means of understanding geographical and temporal diversity meant that cultural and biological difference came to be seen not neatly as signs of a God-given order (as in the Great Chain of Being, see below), nor simply as the legacy of historical separations from a common ancestry. Rather, the recently discovered peoples at the 'uttermost parts of the earth' (Sollas 1911, p. 382) came to be seen as more or less isolated relics of Europe's own ancestral roots, having remained virtually unchanged since separation.

It thus soon became common to see indigenous peoples, in Tierra del Fuego, the Cape of Good Hope and Australia (including Tasmania) as the far corners of the earth in particular, as living representatives of Europe's (as the centre) own Stone Age. In 1863 and again in 1865, but four and six years respectively after the appearance of *On the Origin of Species*, three books thus came to influentially articulate such emerging views. In 1863 came Thomas Henry Huxley's – biologist, humanist, friend and popular champion of Charles Darwin – *Evidence as to Man's Place in Nature*. Huxley argued that the newly discovered Neanderthal possessed 'the most brutal of all known human skulls' (Huxley 1863, pp. 84, 87–8). Setting a precedent that many were later to follow, he compared the Neanderthal skull with those of Australian Aborigines, much assumed to be among the most ancient of living races. While important differences were noted between the two,

Huxley . . . indicated that similarities between (ancient) Neanderthal and (modern) Aboriginal skulls have more 'profound' meaning 'when it is recollected that the stone axe is as much the weapon and implement of the modern as the ancient savage; that the former turns the bones of the kangaroo and of the emu to the same account as the latter did the bones of the deer and the urus' (Lyell 1863, p. 89). (Hiscock and McNiven in press; see also David *et al.* in press)

Two years after *Evidence as to Man's Place in Nature* appeared Edward B. Tylor's *Researches into the Early History of Mankind*, and Sir John Lubbock's *Pre-Historic Times, as Illustrated by Ancient Remains, and the Manners and Customs of Modern Savages*. Lubbock was a close neighbour of Darwin, who praised the book in a letter to the author on 11 June 1865, its publication year (Bowler 1992, p. 724).

As the volume's title makes clear, Lubbock was more than ready to make direct links between the fossil record and living peoples. Having coined the terms Palaeolithic and Neolithic to refer to Europe's distant past, he also sought living examplars of this past in the geographically distant peoples at the ends of the earth. Like Tylor, Lubbock's presumption was that the globe was originally peopled by savages at an early stage of biological, moral and cultural evolution. Yet he also believed that 'Evidently . . . the lowest races of existing savages must, always assuming the common origin of the human race, be at least as far advanced as were our ancestors when they spread over the earth's surface' (Lubbock 1872, p. 587). Even so:

> It is too often supposed that the world was peopled by a series of 'migrations'. But migrations, properly so called, are compatible only with a comparatively high state of organization. Moreover, it has been observed that the geographical distribution of the various races of Man curiously coincides with that of other races of animals: and there can be no doubt that he originally crept over the earth's surface, little by little, year by year, just for instance as the weeds of Europe are now gradually but surely creeping over the surface of Australia. (Lubbock 1872, p. 587)

In some parts of the world, most notably Europe, cultural, spiritual, biological and intellectual developments eventually led to the emergence of high civilization. Elsewhere earlier evolutionary stages could still be found in the distant colonies. Lubbock was keen to dismiss the idea that living 'savages' were degenerate forms of earlier, more advanced peoples:

> If the Cape of Good Hope, Australia, New Zealand, etc., had ever been inhabited by a race of men more advanced than those whom we are in the habit of regarding as the aborigines, some evidence of this would surely have remained; and this not being the case, none of our travellers having observed any ruins, or other traces of a more advanced civilization, there does not appear to be any sufficient reason for supposing that these miserable beings are at all inferior to the ancestors from whom they are descended. (ibid., p. 429)

Australian Aborigines were more or less frozen in time, neither degenerate descendants of more advanced forms, nor more evolved than their (and once Europe's own) ancestors. 'Throughout the whole continent of Australia', concluded Lubbock (ibid., p. 438), 'the aborigines were remarkably similar in physical appearance, in character, and in general habits. They were, in some respects, scarcely, if at all, farther advanced than those of the Andaman Islands', living representatives of the Stone Age. As he made clear in the Preface of his subsequent *The Origin of Civilisation and the Primitive Condition of Man: Mental and Social Condition of Savages* of 1870:

> In my work on 'Prehistoric Times' I have devoted several chapters to the description of modern savages, because the weapons and implements now used by the lower races of men throw much light on the signification and use of those discovered in ancient tumuli, or in the drift gravels; and because a knowledge of modern savages and their modes of life enables us more accurately to picture, and more vividly to conceive, the manners and customs of our ancestors in bygone ages. (Lubbock 1882, p. v)

Lubbock's *Pre-Historic Times* has been heralded as perhaps the most important and influential archaeology book ever published. It is to archaeology what Lewis Henry Morgan's *Ancient Society* (1877) is to social anthropology. Morgan, too, advanced the notion that Australian Aborigines were among the lowest living representatives of humanity when he identified three developmental stages: Savagery, Barbarism and Civilization. His programme was clear:

> It can now be asserted upon convincing evidence that savagery preceded barbarism in all the tribes of mankind, as barbarism is known to have preceded civilization. The history of the human race is one in source, one in experience, and one in progress.
>
> It is both a natural and a proper desire to learn, if possible, how all these ages upon ages of past time have been expended by mankind; how savages, advancing by slow, almost imperceptible steps, attained the higher condition of barbarians; how barbarians, by similar progressive advancement, finally attained to civilization; and why other tribes and nations have been left behind in the race of progress – some in civilization, some in barbarism, and others in savagery. (Morgan 1964, p. 5)

Commenting on reports of contemporary Aboriginal customs, Morgan thus concluded that:

> Such pictures of human life enable us to understand the condition of savagery, the grade of its usages, the degree of material development, and the low level of the mental and moral life of the people. Australian humanity . . . stands on as low a plane as it has been known to touch on the earth. And yet the Australians possessed an area of continental dimensions, rich in minerals, not uncongenial in climate, and fairly supplied with the means of subsistence. Left to themselves they would probably have remained for thousands of years to come, not without any, but with such slight improvement as scarcely to lighten the dark shade of their savage state. (ibid., pp. 317–18)

'No exemplification of tribes of mankind in . . . [the earliest stage of human evolution] remained in the historic period' (ibid., p. 10), he noted. But Australian Aboriginal people were firmly situated into the 'Middle Status of Savagery' nonetheless, the earliest extant evolutionary representatives. 'The principal institutions of mankind originated in savagery, were developed in barbarism, and are maturing in civilization.' As savages, Australian Aborigines were not only supposedly ancient, but left behind as early representatives of Europe's own savage past.

In 1880, Lewis Henry Morgan thus prefaced Lorimer Fison and William Howitt's *Kami-laroi and Kurnai* – a book concerned with the cultural practices of living indigenous groups of southeastern Australia – with the words: 'the facts are so carefully and plainly presented that nothing seems left for me to do, except to call attention to the value of the materials contained in these memoirs, and to their bearing upon the *early history of mankind*' (Morgan 1880, p. 2, emphasis mine). Fison's own Preface introduces the book with the statement that 'The Australian classes [kinship divisions] are especially valuable . . . because they give us what seem to be the earliest stages of development' (Fison 1880, p. 23).

In 1899, the first Professor of Anthropology at Oxford University, Sir Edward B. Tylor (1899, pp. vii–ix), wrote with similar sentiment of the Tasmanian Aborigines in his Preface to the second edition of H. Ling Roth's (1899) *The Aborigines of Tasmania*:

> That these rude savages remained within the present century representatives of the immensely ancient Palaeolithic period, has become an admitted fact . . . Man of the Lower Stone Age ceases to be a creature of philosophic inference, but becomes a known reality.

Sir Arthur Keith, the great anatomist, palaeontologist and President of the Anthropological Institute, similarly wrote: 'The aboriginal race of Australia is the only race which, in my opinion, could serve as the common ancestor for all modern races' (cited in Simpson 1956, frontispiece). In 1901, (later Sir) Baldwin Spencer, the foundation Professor of Biology at Melbourne University, wrote a *Guide* for the stone artefacts then displayed in the National Museum of Victoria, noting that 'the objects are such as are at once typical of what are frequently spoken of as both Palaeolithic and Neolithic men', and concluded that 'Australian aborigines may be regarded as a relic of the early childhood of mankind left stranded in a part of the world where he has, without the impetus derived from competition, remained in a low condition of savagery' (Spencer 1901, p. 78).[2]

Around 1910[3] and building on Huxley's earlier claims, Joseph McCabe (n.d., p. 34) wrote in *Prehistoric Man* of a newly-discovered Middle Pleistocene lower jaw from Mauer (near Heidelberg, Germany) as being 'midway in profile between the jaw of the gorilla and that of an Australian native'. The use of modern Australian Aboriginal peoples as a reference is instructive of the preconceptions of the time: 'In the Neanderthal-Spy race these [skeletal] characters continue to be modified, and we approach the type of the living Australian native' (ibid., p. 36). But we need not read between the lines, for the preunderstanding that shaped contemporary Western concepts of Aboriginality are plainly outlined:

> Far away, on the frontiers of the inhabited earth we find representatives of the earliest human wanderers. The Tasmanians, driven by the oncoming Australians to the tip of their continent, and then cut off by the sea . . . represent the humanity of the earliest known days. The Australians, Papuans, and other tribes represent a next phase; and so on through the vast hierarchy of races . . . in a general way we can arrange these backward peoples in a cultural series which roughly represents the cultural development of humanity, and throws a useful light on the past. (ibid., p. 81)

It is in such a culture of understanding that William J. Sollas (1911, pp. 161–2), then Professor of Geology at Oxford University, wrote that:

> The Australians of all races make the nearest approach to the Mousterians [i.e. Neanderthals]. Many of the more brutal Australians, especially among those inhabiting the south of the continent [where European settlement was concentrated], present a depressed cranial vault with receding forehead and occiput, almost identical in profile with some forms of Neandertal skull . . . The Australians are a lower race than the Neandertal; at the same time, they are more closely allied to it than any other; and we may regard the Australian as a survival from Mousterian times.

Living Tasmanians represented an even earlier stage of human evolution:

> The Tasmanians . . . though recent, were at the same time a Palaeolithic or even, it has been asserted, an 'eolithic' race; and they thus afford us an opportunity of interpreting the past by the present – a saving procedure in a subject where fantasy is only too likely to play a leading part. (ibid., p. 70)

For Sollas, as for others of his time, 'the Australians, the Mousterians of the Antipodes'

(ibid., p. 170), and what were perceived to be the even more ancient Tasmanians represented equal or lower stages of evolution than the Neanderthals who were then believed to be the Middle Pleistocene representatives of modern Europeans. 'It would appear', he wrote in what must be one of the most cited passages in archaeological historiography:

> that the surviving races which represent the vanished Palaeolithic hunters have succeeded one another over Europe in the order of their intelligence: each has yielded in turn to a more highly developed and more highly gifted form of man. From what is now the focus of civilisation they have one by one been expelled and driven to the uttermost parts of the earth: the Mousterians survive in the remotely related Australians at the Antipodes, the Solutrians are represented by the Bushmen of the southern extremity of Africa, the Magdalenians by the Eskimo on the frozen margin of the North American continent and as well, perhaps, by the Red Indians. (ibid., pp. 382–3).

Such views continued to be propounded well into the twentieth century. In 1917 Henry Fairfield Osborn (1919, p. 234),[4] the President of the American Museum of Natural History, wrote that 'the low status of the Tasmanian [stone] implements can most correctly be described by the word Pre-Aurignacian, that is, of Mousterian or of an earlier stage'. Although Osborn argued that, biologically, evolutionary links between Neanderthals and Australian Aborigines could not be established, he continued to promulgate an understanding of modern-day Aboriginal people in terms of Europe's supposed Neanderthal past.

The tendency to discuss living Aboriginal peoples by reference to ancient hominids was commonplace towards the end of the nineteenth century and beginning of the twentieth, and says more about contemporaneous preconceptions than it does about evolutionary relationships. Professor G. F. Scott Elliott (1920) thus compared anatomical characteristics of 'the Australian' or 'Australian native' with those of 'Piltdown', 'Pithecanthropus', 'five gorillas', and 'six orang-utan' in the chapter of his *Prehistoric Man and His Story* entitled 'Missing Links'. No other modern peoples are there used as comparative examples. Elsewhere in the same book, the 'Australian aborigine' continues to be a favoured subject of comparison with various monkeys, apes and ancient hominid remains. They are positioned adjacent to – and often below – Neanderthals in comparative anatomical charts (with evolutionary overtones). The English (typically the 'Wiltshire Englishman Gros Propriétaire' [landed gentry] followed by the 'Wiltshire farmer') are unfailingly positioned at the top (e.g. Elliot 1920, p. 70). Not surprisingly in hindsight, we are told that 'it is not very easy to prove that increase of brain always accompanies increasing intelligence', but this statement is immediately followed with the rider 'but the table which follows shows that on the whole this seems to be the case'. The 'table that follows' indeed lists the now familiar order of things (beginning with the Wiltshire Englishman and ending with the Gorilla, with the 'Modern Australian aboriginal' four-fifths down the list).

In order to test the reliability of brain capacity as a measure of relative intelligence, Elliott (1920, p. 72) decided also to consider brain weight. 'Unfortunately', he wrote, 'the heaviest brain known, weighing 2,850 grammes, was that of an epileptic idiot'. Not to be outdone, with little discussion (and no added 'evidence') he immediately confirmed the 'truth' of his preconceptions: 'Still, the general results bear out exactly what has been suggested above' (ibid., p. 72).

Such approaches towards the relative social and evolutionary positioning of Aboriginal people were still alive and well into the 1930s. In 1936, R. R. Schmidt's (1934) *Der Geist der Vorzeit* was translated into English for the first time as *The Dawn of the Human Mind*, two years after it first appeared in German. Australian Aboriginal people are discussed only once in the book, and the tone is unmistakable:

> Its considerable capacity gives to the *Pithecanthropus* [*Homo erectus*] skull a decidedly human character. The cranial capacity, even of the largest anthropoids (which may weigh up to seven hundred-weight), is rarely more than 600 cubic centimeters. *Pithecanthropus*, however, had already brought this up to between 850 and 900 cubic centimeters. Among the lowest human races – the Veddas and the Australians – the lowest capacity descends to 930 c.cm.; while the large-skulled Neandertaler possessed a capacity of a least 1,230 c.cm. (Schmidt 1936, p. 41)

These examples of a repeated tendency to compare Australian Aboriginal biology and culture with those of monkeys, apes and ancient (pre-*Homo sapiens sapiens*) hominids could easily be dismissed as trivial ramblings, except that they much (and explicitly) represent the dominant sentiments of the mid-nineteenth to early-twentieth centuries, and continued to be voiced not so much prevalently as influentially into the 1930s. Living Australian Aboriginal people were openly discussed as a link in the developmental chain that joined modern Europeans with their past. Australian Aborigines were not simply an unchanging people in a faraway land, but a relic of Europe's own past, and in this capacity they were imbued with both great antiquity and timeless stasis.

It is but a short space of time from the early–mid twentieth century to our own era, a temporal space that continues to be possessed with vestiges of a Western construction of Aboriginality imbued with such sentiment. While notions that equate living peoples with stages of an evolutionary tree to some degree began to lose popular and scientific credence after the 1890s – not coincidently during a period of time when field and armchair (theoretical) anthropology were rapidly uniting and professionalizing – these assumptions were by no means thereafter discarded by even the most highly esteemed university professors. As the examples quoted above demonstrate, the deep-seated assumption that living or recently living Aboriginal peoples are essentially of great antiquity and ahistoricity remained popular well into the twentieth century. Indeed, I would argue that such assumptions remain with us today as the legacy of a Western preunderstanding that once viewed Aboriginal Australia as an unchanging people in an unchanging land (consider again the lack of scission between popular views of nineteenth-century and fifth-millennium BP 'Australian Aborigines').

Implications for archaeology

Such evolutionary notions explicitly reverberated in much of the scientific literature as recently as the middle of the twentieth century (despite a common assumption that such views were essentially defunct by the end of the nineteenth century). By 1962, Australian Aboriginal peoples were still considered simple, egalitarian and culturally undeveloped by many writers. Manning Clark's first volume of his encyclopaedic *A History of Australia*, widely acknowledged as one of the classic works of Australian history and still widely used today, introduced Australian history in the following way:

> Civilization did not begin in Australia until the last quarter of the eighteenth century . . . The early inhabitants of the continent created cultures but not civilizations . . . A distinction is made here between 'civilization' in the sense described in the Oxford English Dictionary, of a people brought out of a state of barbarism, and 'culture' in the sense defined in the Grosse Brockhaus as the sum of the efforts made by a community to satisfy and reconcile the basic human requirements of food, clothing, shelter, security, care of the weak and social cohesion by controlling its natural environment. (1962, p. 3)

Clark's views were popular in Australia through much of the 1960s and 1970s. A similar understanding was articulated by Professor J. B. Cleland (1966, p. 3), who prefaced *Aboriginal Man in South and Central Australia*[5] with the words: 'At the coming of the white man the Australian aboriginal was in equilibrium with other members of the fauna to which he belonged and fitted naturally and, on the whole, very successfully into his environment.'

Notions such as these were based on an assumption that change in Aboriginal Australia was slow, if present at all, and driven largely, if not entirely, by external forces. Charles Rowley (1986, p. 4) noted that 'for lack of historical background, the Aboriginal community is treated as a more or less static society' based on notions of intrinsic stability. Generally speaking, neither short-term processes of change nor long-term historical trends were even imagined to apply to Aboriginal Australia. But there were two exceptions. First, changes were generally acknowledged to have taken place when one people or culture replaced another (migration), as expressed by changes in, for example, stone artefact types within excavated archaeological sites (e.g. Birdsell 1967; Hale and Tindale 1930; Hossfeld 1966). Second, change was also acknowledged where external contacts, such as the arrival of Macassans during the last few hundred years,

produced cultural innovations (diffusion) (McCarthy 1943).

Such views dominated Australian archaeology through the first two-thirds of the twentieth century. Fred McCarthy (1964) questioned those who interpreted changes observed in the archaeological record in terms of migration, but he continued to propagate the idea that external influences were responsible for the main changes observed in the sites he investigated. He argued that in the Capertee Valley, New South Wales:

> the introduction . . . of the Bondi point, geometric microliths, elouera, gum hafting, the elaboration of the burin and later the introduction of the ground edge axe, and the working back of adzes into discarded slugs, indicates contact with an important stream of culture diffusion whose direction is not yet known . . . I prefer to regard these changes as being due to diffusion rather than to new waves of Aboriginal people. (McCarthy 1964, p. 239)

There was little acknowledgment that Aboriginal society had, or even could have, changed by the weight of internal forces.

Aboriginal people have long been seen as ahistorical, essentially static beings. Viewed in a synchronic framework and frozen in time, Aboriginal societies appeared to show little evidence of internal dynamism, especially when compared with other cultures. But to what degree were such notions a result of presumptions borne of colonial power relations, and to what degree were they based on 'evidence'? Peter Bowler (1992), Patrick Wolfe (1999) and Lynette Russell (in press) have written of how the social evolutionism of the mid-nineteenth century legitimated the colonial enterprise, pointing out that by considering living Aboriginal peoples as relics of Europe's ancestral past served to sever indigenous peoples not only from their own past, but from their worldly presence also. Lynette Russell and Ian McNiven (1998; McNiven and Russell 1997; Russell in press) likewise concluded that the claiming of the Aboriginal present as a European past enabled the invaders to legitimate the appropriation of indigenous lands; the low status of Aboriginal people 'endorsed the "inevitability" of European expansion into their territory' (Bowler 1992, p. 728). Nowhere is this more clearly stated than in Sollas's own *Ancient Hunters* of 1911:

> What part is to be assigned to justice in the government of human affairs? So far as the facts are clear they teach in no equivocal terms that there is no right which is not founded on might. Justice belongs to the strong, and has been meted out to each race according to its strength; each has received as much justice as it deserved. What perhaps is most impressive in each of the cases we have discussed is this, that the dispossession by a new-comer of a race already in occupation of the soil has marked an upward step in the intellectual progress of mankind. It is not priority of occupation, but the power to utilise, which establishes a claim to the land. (Sollas 1911, p. 383)

The colonial process was operationalized through ideologies of a past that implicated an invader evolved from, and therefore superseding, the invaded (and their lands). The living cultures encountered by explorers and 'ethnographers' were appropriated as living testimony to the West's own evolutionary history: across the seas, geographical distance from Europe signalled temporal distance from the civilized modern, until, on the other side of the world, 'in the pure state of nature' Australian Aborigines became living remnants of the West's own childhood. Australian Aboriginal people were unfailingly placed at the bottom of the evolutionary or developmental rung, a preconception that willingly saw a kinship between the biology, psychology, stone artefact types and technologies of living Australian Aboriginal peoples and those of the dawn or childhood of humanity as evidenced by the European Stone Ages (especially the Old and Middle Stone Ages). Such notions articulated a socially and spiritually hierarchical, Western preunderstanding that even by John Lubbock's time already had a long history in Western thought. The positioning of Aboriginal society as ancient with the land (but static and not necessarily of deep time), and as a living representation of Europe's own past articulated not so much an evolutionary principle as the way things were inherently ordered as historical geography. This was a preunderstanding that enabled the Western observer to locate him or herself near the apex of a world order. This existential nuance can be traced as a leg-

acy of earlier Western conceptions, popularly known as the Great Chain of Being (Lovejoy 1936).

The Great Chain of Being

Arthur Lovejoy has noted that:

> There are . . . implicit or incompletely explicit assumptions, or more or less unconscious mental habits, operating in the thought of an individual or a generation. It is the beliefs which are so much a matter of course that they are rather tacitly presupposed than formally expressed and argued for, the ways of thinking which seem so natural and inevitable that they are not scrutinized with the eye of logical self-consciousness, that often are most decisive of the character of a philosopher's doctrine, and still oftener of the dominant intellectual tendencies of an age. These implicit factors may be of various sorts. One sort is a disposition to think in terms of certain categories or of particular types of imagery . . .
>
> These endemic assumptions, these intellectual habits, are often of so general and so vague a sort that it is possible for them to influence the course of man's reflections on almost any subject. (1936, pp. 7–10)

Lovejoy was writing of the general process that Hans-Georg Gadamer was later to call preunderstanding, using the specific example of the Great Chain of Being.

The Great Chain of Being represents a 'complete rational intelligibility of the world' (Lovejoy 1936, p. 329). It formed both a subsumed framework in which the world order could be found, and a system of logic that explained God's superiority and independence. As Stephen Jay Gould (1986, p. 282) has noted, 'The chain is a static ordering of unchanging, created entities – a set of creatures placed by God in fixed positions of an ascending hierarchy representing neither time nor history, but the eternal order of things.' In its various expressions through the ages, the Chain presented white Europeans on top and others progressively down the order, the discovery of 'savages' in the far ends of the earth during the Enlightenment neatly accommodating such views.

The Great Chain of Being synthesized into

a unified world-view notions of nature, humanity and God. Peter Suber (1997) recounts the Chain's operative logic. First, he notes, can be found God, the perfect being who sits at the top of the hierarchy. In its entirety, the chain represents every possible level of perfection, from the most perfect at the top to the least perfect at the bottom – this logic is found, for instance, in Gottfried W. Leibniz (1953) and Benedict Spinoza (1991). It is in its completeness, in its inclusion of all stages of perfection, that reality manifests itself in the world. Without this complete representation, the God-created world would not be complete – it would not be perfect. This, argues Suber (1997), is why, in the Great Chain, God, in His perfection, creates an 'imperfect' world; hence, 'imperfect things are not evidence of the imperfection of creation' (ibid., clause 5; cf. Descartes 1958). At the bottom of the chain are those whose perfection has not been realized; all those above are imbued with various degrees of actualized perfection. 'In general', writes Suber (1997, clause 11), 'being or existence is a perfection; to be is more perfect than not to be. What has positive existence is good and was created by God; what is privation lacks being and goodness, and was not created at all.' If this is the case, then dependence is an imperfection, and whatever is found below the top of the chain (God) is dependent on God, while the 'being at the top of the chain is utterly independent or self-sufficient or absolute', in that it lacks privation (ibid., clause 16).

The Great Chain of Being is an expression of Judaeo-Christian thought that requires the Other to be both different and inferior to the informed Western being. The non-Christian Other is found at the lower rungs of the chain. The Great Chain of Being explains and legitimates the position of people in relation to everything else (e.g. humans are situated higher up the ladder than rocks), and it explains the relative position of individuals within society: peasants are lower than lords by virtue of their relative levels of privation, as ordained by divine emplacement. In the human ladder, at the top is God and the informed higher beings who sit next to God by virtue of their possession of the only Truth (Christians); below are the lost souls who long ago, near the beginning of time, lost their way in the Garden of Eden and have ever since been deprived of higher Truth. Nowhere are these unfortunate souls better represented than by Australian Aboriginal people, the Antipodean Other, the bottom of the evolutionary rung.

A people of the 'Antipodes'

The indigenous inhabitants of Australia have long been taken to represent a people at the world's geographical and conceptual ends. Two and a half thousand years ago, the philosopher and pure mathematician Pythagoras of Samos (c. 569–475 BCE) believed that the earth was a sphere at the centre of the universe. He held that the earth was geometrically ordered, its dynamics following laws based on the interaction of opposites (O'Connor and Robertson 1999). With balanced geometry in mind, Pythagoras coined the term 'Antipodes' to describe an imagined, inhabitable land on the opposite side of the northern hemisphere. Literally meaning 'having the feet opposite', the Antipodes accounted for people in the southern hemisphere, standing with the soles of their feet set in opposition to those of north.

From this comes the *Oxford English Dictionary*'s definition of Antipodes as 'places on the surfaces of the earth directly opposite to each other, or the place which is directly opposite to another; *esp.* the region directly opposite our own'. It notes that to be at Antipodes is to be 'in direct opposition', and that the Antipodean world is 'of or pertaining to the opposite side of the world; *esp.* Australasian'. The Antipodean world is a world of diametrical opposites. In this capacity the Antipodes readily accommodates an imaginary ancient people opposed to the European modern.

But the 'Antipodes' are more than the opposite side of the world, for as opposite, they imply an Other judged in relation to a Western centre, a Western norm. As the centre, the West is the standard against which all else is judged or ranked. The Other is always marginalized in its difference.

In their capacity as the Antipodean Other dwelling in an inaccessible, isolated land, Australian Aboriginal people have long been considered as historically arrested. They have been positioned in Western preunderstanding as a tragedy of geographical and spiritual isolation. Lynette Russell (in press) has thus discussed how Aboriginal Australians have long been portrayed as 'ancient, primitive and childlike' in both the written literature and in the visual arts. She relates Western notions of Aboriginality to Edward Said's (1978, p. 167) 'unimaginable antiquity' of the Other. In *Orientalism*, Said argued that the Western Other is constructed through stereotypes that not only highlight difference but that differentiate via a set of tropes (such as notions of timelessness) that serve to marginalize. Western scholarship on other cultures is based on a Western imperialism, and concepts such as the timelessness of the Dreaming are expressions of cultural politics.

It is in this implicit positioning of the Aboriginal Other in relation to a Western standard that the ethnographic Dreaming's assumed great antiquity can be found; it is a legacy of a long-standing Judaeo-Christian preunderstanding once explicitly informed by a Great Chain of Being that takes account of an Antipodean Other that is both geographically distant and temporally ancient. In such a view it is presumed that Aboriginal being is very old (or without time) and that it represents the West's own deep past. In the process, Aboriginal world-views (i.e. 'the Dreaming' of ethnographic times) are themselves preconceived as ancient and atemporal. This is a reference to a public imagination devoid of substance; a house of cards. There is a myopia in a hierarchical ladder of long standing, signalling a failure to look beyond. In this sense, it is not a post-modern world that we face, but a hegemonically constructed pre-modern Other. In the Other we continue to reproduce a colonial order, intruding, appropriating and suffusing equality and being. There is no post-colonial construction in the social world, only a change in approach to the colonial project.

But when we consider the historical character of Aboriginal world-views, the Dreaming does not lie down, reclining in the background, rearing its ancient head into the present, but rather stands as an emergent social product with a dynamic history of its own. We have seen in the previous three chapters evidence for the emergence of the Dreaming, as we know it today, late in Aboriginal history. The reason for the ethnographic Dreaming's ahistorical standing in popular imagination is, I would suggest, that our own preunderstanding is situated in our own ideological history. While some explicit notions have been broadly

dismissed during our unfolding intellectual history, for instance, the view that Australia's indigenous populations were an unchanging people in an unchanging land, others, such as the Dreaming's timelessness, have remained an ontological blind spot, continuing to hold root in our deeper social psyche. Indeed, I would suggest we have not truly left our own ontological roots, appropriately articulated in a Great Chain of Being.

In her recollections of life on Elsey cattle station in the Northern Territory, *We of the Never Never*, Aeneas Gunn (1908) wrote of a timeless, elusive land and of a timeless people. But it is not *we* of the 'never never' – of an existence out of time – that she was writing about, but *them*. This was life on the other side of the ontological frontier as much as it was life on the other side of the frontier of European settlement. The archaeological evidence presented in the previous chapters suggests that it is time we revisit these assumptions.

The Rainbow Serpent

In the previous three chapters, I presented archaeological evidence suggesting the Dreaming's dynamism and the relative recency of its ethnographically recognizable form. There is, however, one line of inquiry that we have not yet considered and that has been interpreted by some archaeologists as evidence for an antiquity of some 4000 to 6000 years for specific ethnographic Dreaming beliefs, although such an interpretation has been questioned by others (e.g. Davidson 1999). This is the evidence of the Rainbow Serpent, a Dreaming concept of varying signification that is today found across much of mainland Australia.

What has enabled an archaeological study of the Rainbow Serpent is its archaeological expression in rock-art symbolism. Paul Taçon, Meredith Wilson and Chris Chippindale (1996) have noted that the Rainbow Serpent is currently an important Dreaming being, especially in western Arnhem Land where it can be seen painted in many rockshelters. They examined 107 such paintings, exploring stylistic changes through space and time. Four rock-art styles were identified and chronologically arranged. The Rainbow Serpent paintings were positioned within this chronological framework. A

Figure 6.1   Dynamic period snake (*Source*: Paul Taçon)

single painting was identified as belonging to the earliest, so-called Dynamic style, tentatively dated to around 10,000 years BP (Figure 6.1). Some 61 paintings were attributed to the Yam style, believed to date from about 6000 to 4000 years BP (Figure 6.2); and 29 paintings to the Modern period (Figure 6.3), argued to date from 4000 years BP to the present. However, Taçon *et al.* (1996, p. 105) also note that the solitary Dynamic period Rainbow Serpent

> was included because of its unusual size in relation to nine male and female Dynamic human figures it is shown interacting with, and because of an unusual bulge on its neck. Unique in this style, and not necessarily a Rainbow Serpent, this figure does not share characteristics of other images but was suggested to be a Rainbow Serpent by Eric Brandl (1982: 16) because of the nature of the composition.

In other words, this unusual painting does not fit easily into the classificatory framework, and it is therefore tentatively placed in the earliest category, although it does not clearly depict a Rainbow Serpent form. It should therefore not

be taken as evidence for the presence of Rainbow Serpents during the Dynamic period of rock-art. Taçon *et al.* (1996) have largely dismissed this painting in their chronological investigations, a conclusion with which I concur.

The Rainbow Serpents of the subsequent Yam and Modern periods show some similarities and some differences. Rainbow Serpents are composite beings, incorporating elements of various creatures, usually interpreted by archaeologists as a kangaroo's head and a snake's body. In both periods they have somewhat elongated bodies, tails, and small, what would appear to be usually 'eared' heads (sometimes the top of the head possesses a feather-like protrusion). However, the Yam period Rainbow Serpents possess nodes or serrations along the neck, back of the spine, and sometimes along other parts of the body; the 'snake's body' resembles more a yam than a snake. Indeed, smaller, tuber-like protrusions usually emanate from the main body (see Figure 6.2). This does not happen among the Modern period paintings (see Figure 6.3), and indeed both the serrations and the yam-like

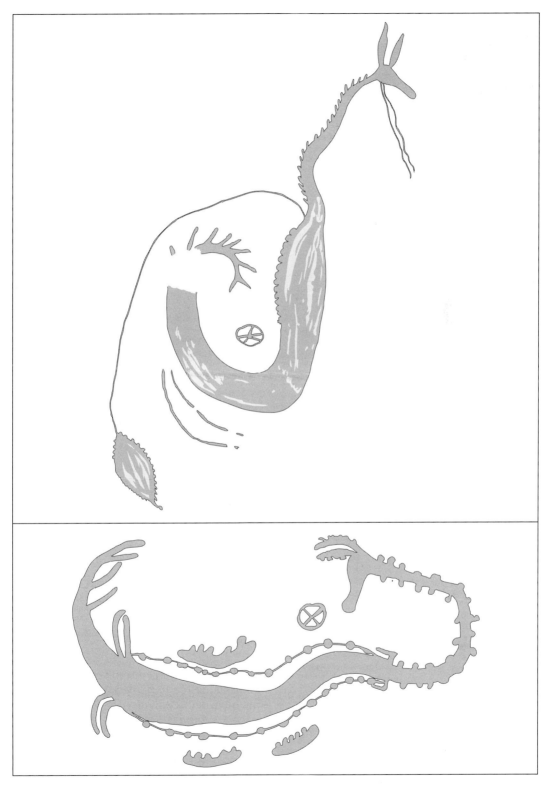

Figure 6.2 Yam period Rainbow Serpents, Arnhem Land (*Source*: Taçon *et al*. 1996, figs 3 and 17)

Figure 6.3   Modern period Rainbow Serpent, Arnhem Land (*Source*: Taçon *et al.* 1996, fig. 16)

appendages are defining characteristics of Yam period paintings. Tail and body shapes, and conventions of infilling and internal decoration can also be shown to have changed from the Yam to the Modern period. Taçon *et al.* (1996, p. 112) further conclude that morphological variation increases from the Yam to the Modern paintings.

There are two major limitations to Taçon *et al.*'s interpretations for an antiquity of up to 4000–6000 years BP for the Arnhem Land Rainbow Serpents and their associated narrative significance. The first concerns the antiquity of the art itself, but this is not critical to their general model. The second concerns the antiquity of the Dreaming belief associated with the depictions: the antiquity of the art's recent meanings.

Antiquity of the art

Taçon *et al.* (1996, p. 103) suggest that Rainbow Serpents 'are evidence of one of the oldest continuous religious traditions', although unlike the comparable sentiments noted earlier in this chapter, here it is based on evidence rather than on recourse to popular knowledge. Following the publication of Taçon *et al.*'s results in the scientific literature, newspapers around Australia crowed what had long been assumed while escaping modern scientific scaffold: 'Scientists find religion in ancient Aboriginal rock art' (*Sydney Morning Herald*, 26 October 1996), and 'Rock serpent may predate all religion' (*Canberra Times*, 30 October 1996). 'But just how much of the Rainbow Serpent religious complex can we safely say had its origins up to 6000 years ago and what changes have occurred over time?', asked Taçon *et al.* (1996, p. 103). These are key questions that need to be addressed.

First, let us, as far as we can, assess the antiquity of Arnhem Land's so-called Rainbow Serpent paintings. There have been various attempts to arrange the paintings of the region stylistically into chronological order, and to date each style to a particular period of time. The dating evidence has always been circumstantial: there are no reliable 'direct' dates for Arnhem Land's rock art except for nearly 150 relatively simple, morphologically speaking, beeswax figures dated to the past 4000 years, none of which include Rainbow Serpent depictions (Nelson *et al.* 1995; Christopher Chippin-

dale, pers. comm. 2001)). The general chronological models presented by various researchers are varied, although Taçon *et al.*'s (1996) chronology appears to take a reasonable position. Eric Brandl (1972, 1982) was the first to make systematic statements about the art's antiquity, having identified the earliest Rainbow Serpent paintings as belonging to a period of time when thylacines were also represented in the art (Figure 6.4). Thylacines have been extinct in mainland Australia since around 3500 years ago. The earliest Rainbow Serpent paintings of this style therefore date to an earlier time – unless the style continued after the demise of thylacines. George Chaloupka (1984) soon after attempted to refine Brandl's chronology, originally arguing that Yam figures belong to a period some time between 20,000 and 9000 years BP. Like Taçon *et al.*, Chaloupka argued that it is 'in the yam figures style that the Rainbow Snake is represented for the first time in the rock art of the region' (1993, p. 139). In his later work, such paintings are argued to be 'at least 8000 years old' (ibid., pp. 89, 139). Chaloupka's work was followed by that of Darrell Lewis (1988, pp. 86–95), who argued that the 'Hooked Stick' period of rock-art dates from 6000 to 9000 years ago. It is towards the end of this period that Rainbow Serpent paintings first appeared, rendering his chronology comparable to Taçon *et al.*'s later sequence. Ivan Haskovec (1992), however, later argued that the Yam style ended around 7000 years BP, further noting that the distinctive styles that have hitherto been identified for western Arnhem Land may have been erroneously sequenced. He tentatively suggests that different styles may be contemporaneous, placing in doubt the chronological logic that has hitherto framed the various models.

Nevertheless, by all accounts the paintings that morphologically resemble the ethnographically documented Rainbow Serpents, but that are painted in Yam style, are believed to date to some time between 3000 and 9000 years BP, Taçon *et al.*'s (1996) model being the most up-to-date and the most reliable chronologically. It is also the only one that takes into account the 'direct' AMS radiocarbon dates for the wax paintings. However, Yam period rock-art may also be older than this (it cannot have *begun* more recently given the presence of thylacines), as suggested by Chaloupka. But it

Figure 6.4 Thylacine, Arnhem Land (*Source*: Paul Taçon)

could have continued into more recent times (a possibility that remains untested). We must not forget that the various chronological models rely on indirect dating evidence of at times extremely poor reliability.

The paintings of Yam period 'Rainbow Serpents' can therefore only be usefully treated as likely pre-dating the 1400–600 years BP period for which archaeological evidence of the ethnographically known Dreaming beliefs first appears in other parts of Australia, as argued in this book. But how much older the Yam period paintings are remains a mystery, likely dating to sometime in the mid to late Holocene. It is in the original Dreaming significance (known from ethnography) of the early Arnhem Land 'Rainbow Serpent' paintings that greatest uncertainty exists.

Antiquity of the Dreaming beliefs

Taçon *et al.* (1996) note that the artistic conventions used to paint what have come to be called Rainbow Serpents changed from their earliest representation during the Yam period to their more recent forms during the Modern style. This is a Modern style dated to the last 4000 years or so, although again the evidence for its usage is poor. It does not contain any obvious depictions of extinct fauna, and is therefore a style that is likely to date to the period after the extinction of the thylacine (*c.* 3500 years BP). Furthermore, it represents the period from the beginning of the so-called X-ray art (Figure 6.5), and contains all of the artistic conventions used during ethnographic times, including X-ray art, which can be shown to evolve during the course of the late Holocene (cf. Taçon 1987). The Modern period is, therefore, the latest of western Arnhem Land's long sequence of rock-art styles. It is then that all of the Rainbow Serpents of a form akin to those of ethnographic times were painted.

If the Rainbow Serpent depictions of ethnographic times date to the Modern period of rock-art – that is, to the last 3500 to 4000 years only – what of the earlier forms? There are various possibilities. The first is that the Yam period Rainbow Serpents are not the Rainbow Serpents of recent narrative tradition at all,

Figure 6.5   X-ray art, Arnhem Land (*Source*: Paul Taçon)

say, mythic yam representations, but that their forms were appropriated later in the sequence when the ethnographically documented Dreaming beliefs emerged as a means of giving new meaning to the visible world (including the pre-existing paintings). We have no way of adequately assessing this possibility. The second possibility is that they are indeed Rainbow Serpents whose formal, but not significatory characteristics changed through time. The Yam period 'Rainbow Serpents' are positioned among a complex of artistic depictions unlike any found during ethnographic times. Depictions revolve around yam-like images; the entire iconography belongs to a unique artistic system that has no ethnographic parallel. We could say that the rock paintings of the Modern period, replete with X-ray depictions that 'see the inside' (Taylor 1996), have, as far as artistic conventions are concerned, moved away from the artistic canons of the Yam period. It is not just the Rainbow Serpents that are depicted differently during the Modern period, for what has changed is the entire system of reference and representation – the

'open network of signs' in which the 'Rainbow Serpents' were positioned and operated.

Under either of the above interpretations, rather than argue for continuity in meaning over the last 4000 to 6000 years, the 'Rainbow Serpent' iconography, as we could call it, despite a lack of knowledge as to the meaning(s) of the Yam period depictions, implies some degree of iconographic continuity that eventually led to the Dreaming-mediated Rainbow Serpents we have come to know from the ethnography. The 'Rainbow Serpent' findings reported by Taçon *et al.* (1996) are therefore important, for while they may not indicate any great antiquity for the Dreaming of ethnography itself, they do imply an *in situ* emergence of at least one of its art-depicted concepts, the Rainbow Serpent. Although iconographic conventions changed during the last 3500 to 4000 years, we can suggest that some aspects of the Dreaming that we know from the ethnography – in particular, the compound beings now known as Rainbow Serpents – had their roots in earlier local practices. The changes that took place in so-called

'Rainbow Serpent' iconography after 3500 to 4000 years ago involved changes not just in the 'Rainbow Serpent' depictions themselves, but in the entire artistic canon(s) that first informed all depictions during the Yam period. This was systemic change, in that artistic frameworks were transformed, probably beginning around (but possibly some time after) 3500 to 4000 years ago. In that the general network of visual signs changed significantly from Yam to later artistic periods, general artistic canons can be said to have also noticeably changed. It is not only ways of *depicting* the world that changed, but ways of *seeing*. Symbols represent worlds experienced, conceptualized and engaged. They naturalize social being – symbols are conventions of nature – in the sense that they represent (and in the process legitimate and reproduce) reality: symbols are at work in ontological and experiential engagement. By implication, the non-arbitrariness of the sign and the system of preunderstanding that informed the earliest 'Rainbow Serpent' paintings shifted; the images that we today identify as Yam period 'Rainbow Serpents' may or may not have shared common cosmological properties with later, ethnographically informed Rainbow Serpent depictions (i.e. relating to water, a serpent associated with the rainbow). But because their position changed in the 'open network of signs', Yam period 'Rainbow Serpents' cannot be said to be evidence of a 4000 to 6000 year antiquity for the ethnographically documented Rainbow Serpents, nor for the Dreaming world-views of ethnography itself.

Given these dating and interpretative problems, we still cannot add to the story revealed in Chapters 3–5 as far as the antiquity of the Dreaming we have come to know from the ethnography is concerned, although the evidence from Arnhem Land adds an important component in that it indicates its *in situ* emergence from older, different but historically ancestral *local* practices. This implies that social, cultural and psychological transformations took place during the late Holocene, in turn, implying changes in personal and social identity, a point I shall return to in Chapter 10. These transformations led to the local emergence of the Rainbow Serpent Dreaming beliefs that we know today. I will return to these points in the final chapter.

Conclusion

When the network of visual signs is identified to have systematically changed, expressions of preunderstanding are also implicated to have changed. On this basis, I suggest that what can be envisioned about the past may be usefully considered as a transformation in behaviour *as technology* (in the broadest sense of the word), in the present case, as it relates to the way the world has been constructed in place, performance and symbolism. But change is only one side of the coin. Martin Heidegger (e.g. 1962) suggested that with death comes the *end* of *Dasein*, the meaningful human being. Emmanuel Lévinas (e.g. 1987) responded with the view that death brings the *beginning* of being, for it is in the possibility of transcendence – of death – that being emerges. Further, we are born into a world already imbued with a meaningfulness derived from the actions of ancestral beings. It is this already-meaningfulness that, I suggest, the modern West has inherited in a conception of Aboriginality as timeless. I also suggest that the popular Western assumption of the Dreaming's simultaneous timelessness and deep antiquity lies somewhere beyond the realms of scientific or evidential reality. Nor is this assumption based on indigenous conceptions of time and creation. It is, rather, founded on underlying Western notions of how the world is ordered. It is based on our own Western preunderstanding as legacy of a past colonialism. I refer not to a Western preunderstanding that necessarily forces us to consciously treat Aboriginal ontology as primordial, child-like or 'inferior', but one that implicitly situates it as an expression of Otherness already loaded with Western notions of evolutionary and hierarchical difference. That is, I refer not to a difference of intent, but to one of ontological content.

To Australian Aboriginal peoples of recent times, the Dreaming was at once atemporal and very old because all reality was constructed around a Dreaming perspective. To non-indigenous Australians, the Dreaming is also atemporal and very old, but here the reason concerns how 'Aborigines' have been constructed in the Western imagination as the product of a colonial world order. When the historical roots of the ethnographically known

Dreaming are considered from a Western, scientific Western, scientific perspective, the Dreaming we have come to know emerges not as timeless, nor even as of great antiquity, but as an historical product that recently enabled Aboriginal people to make a very particular sense of their world.

Ian McNiven (1998) explores why indigenous writers such as Shawn Foley (1994), of the Badjtala people of Fraser Island (southeastern Queensland), fail to reference Western constructions of their past, noting that through dialogues of timelessness, Western social commentators have rendered Aboriginal people as ahistorical by transporting the ethnographic present deep into the past. This is Aboriginal history devoid of history, a past deferred to a timeless ethnographic present. Because of the historically embedded nature of knowledge (and of the sign), popular Western notions of the ethnographic Dreaming as ancient signal not so much a deep history as an entire world of preconceptions. It is not an Aboriginal past that we see in an assumed timeless Dreaming of ethnography, but an Other present. It is this process that imbues Western understandings of the Dreaming today with timelessness.

Notes

1. The full story is (Dixon 1991, p. 41):

These people, had their tribal marks cut, the initiated men.

Many (people) were sitting around in small and large huts. The old people are looking after (the initiands). A lot of people (the initiands and their minders) were sitting (there), and were left alone (by everyone else).

'I'm going out, to look for game. (And I'll) pick fruit' (the old man said).

'Sit behind! (If you) see lots of shadows anywhere, don't get up (to investigate them)! Sit down inside still!' (the old man tells the initiands before he goes out for food).

'I'll leave you. I'm going out for fruit, and for game.'

I went for a walk, went walkabout, looked for fruit. I looked for a place (to rest). (The narrator has here taken over the identity of the old man, guardian of the newly-initiated boys.)

It was getting dark at this place (i.e. at the place where the old man had reached on his walkabout). Why is (this place) getting dark?

'The people (newly-initiated boys) might be getting into trouble back there' (the old man thought to himself). (That is, the dark clouds that are now obscuring the sun may be due to the initiands having transgressed in some way.)

'Where did I leave (them)?' (he said, not being able to find his charges).

I went, went searching. I saw the camp.

(And I saw) a cloud high up (in the sky) getting yellower. (This indicated that there was trouble brewing.)

What's happened to my people (i.e. wards)? I left them alright, sitting down (in the camp). The people (my wards) might have got into trouble.

I stood, watching. (I'm) looking at the dark cloud up high, getting yellower.

I tried to go, to return. I went, went on all the way. (I) went and saw more easily from half-way.

'Hey, this camp is getting in trouble. This camp is getting in trouble? For what reason?'

I tried to go, to go and see what (was wrong). I went and saw the wind blowing strongly (like a whirlwind). A cold wind was rising up.

I saw (that and knew that) our people are in trouble.

By-and-by I saw the water (rushing up and engulfing everything).

The cassowary came running. The grey wallaby came running. The scrub-turkey, the pademelon, the dilly-bag and all the animals came running. The short-nose bandicoot and the black-nose wallaby came running. (All were running to escape the rushing waters; they were in fact partly blown by the wind.)

What's happened to our people?

(I) cut (the ground at) the camp, and hit (the ground all around the camp). (The old man did this to try to stop the wind and rain.)

(The old man spoke to the place:) 'What's wrong with you? (Literally: why are you getting too smart?) (This place) belongs to other people.'

(The old man) made deep cuts in the ground; threw fire; and cut the ground all around the camp; (he) cut (it, to try to stop the incursion of the waters).

The water came springing up; the water came out.

Lots of people were drowned in the water; we were covered by the water.

Our people had done wrong.

Then (a body) of water stood (there) up (in the tableland) – Lake Eacham. The people had drowned there.

(It came about) from the initiated men not having paid attention, none of them listened (to the old men, who told them, as initiands not to touch certain sacred things).

By-and-by the message was taken from there to the people (in other camps).

'The newly-initiated men were all covered by water; (they) sank down (and were drowned).'

2. See McNiven (in press) for further discussions of the history of displays in the National Museum of Victoria.

3. The book is not dated, but bibliographic entries end in 1909.

4. I could not get my hands on the first edition of this book, so I here cite from the second edition.

5. Quite appropriately given the thinking of the day, this book was published as a *Handbook of the Flora and Fauna of South Australia*.

Part II

Presenting the Past

7 Archaeological Trends in Australian Pre-History

So far I have approached the Aboriginal past from the present, tracing back in time the first archaeological traces of documented, ethnographic practices. I have noted that, during the early European contact period, the Dreaming of Aboriginal Australia did not represent a geographically homogeneous world-view, but rather a network of regional world-views. And just as the Dreaming varied across space, so too did it change through time, having emerged in its ethnographically recognizable forms in Arrernte, Djungan and Wardaman country, where it has been studied, only during the late Holocene. Let us now consider the historical contexts of the ethnographic Dreaming's late Holocene emergence by examining other archaeological trends from various parts of mainland Australia. To do this we will begin with the distant past and move forward in time, exploring transformations in various cultural practices through the course of pre-History. My aim is to contextualize the late Holocene emergence of the Dreaming, as we know it today, so as to better understand the historical conditions of its modern appearance.

This chapter is in many ways a general survey. It is not my intention to present a detailed overview of Australian pre-History. Rather, I concentrate on patterns of change and stability in a range of cultural practices, as evident in selected regional studies of eastern Australia.[1] The chapter is presented in three sections. The first is a detailed consideration of the archaeological record of one region, south-

east Cape York Peninsula. This is followed by a general survey of temporal trends for other parts of Australia. The third section critically discusses from the extant literature the dominant interpretations of published archaeological trends. I concentrate on the mid to late Holocene, for this is the period of time relevant to the emergence of the ethnographically known Dreaming, as discussed in the first Part of this book.

The archaeological records of most regions of Australia are patchy at best. Because of this, the present chapter focuses on those areas where research has been concentrated. Even here, however, much remains to be done. Rarely in Australia do we have a detailed understanding of settlement systems, technological practices, exchange relations, diet breadths, symbolic behaviour, seasonality of residential patterns, inter-regional relations or the like over broad spans of time. Nowhere have potential international relations been adequately explored, so that we have little understanding of whether *any* cultural changes ultimately resulted from internal or external causes (apart from the dingo, which must have come from elsewhere). This interpretative limitation is largely due to an on-going emphasis in Australian archaeology on establishing general regional occupational trends, a product of the relative youth of Australian pre-History as a discipline. In setting an archaeological context for the late Holocene emergence of the Dreaming, therefore, we will be restricted in most cases to general temporal trends. More detailed investigations of selected cultural themes and their social implications will be presented in Chapters 8 and 9.

Regional trends in Australian pre-History

Mainland Australia today covers an area of eight million square kilometres, the world's largest terrestrial island. During the last glacial maximum (22,000 to 17,000 years BP), when sea levels were at their lowest and the area of exposed land its greatest, Greater Australia[2] (also known as Sahul) was half as large again (Figure 7.1). As a vast insular landmass that extends from the tropics in the north to cold temperate latitudes in the south, the Australian landscape today, as in the past, is biogeographically and geologically diverse. So, too, has it long contained a varied human population. People first arrived on the continent some time before 40,000 years BP, with some researchers suggesting the first landings took place from southeast Asia between 53,000 and 60,000 years ago (e.g. Roberts *et al.* 1990). Every major habitat on the Australian main-

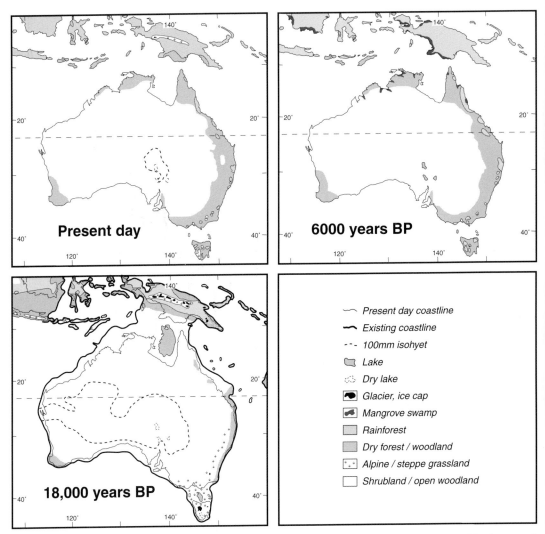

Figure 7.1   Australia's exposed lands at 18,000 years BP, 6000 years BP and present (*Source*: Kershaw *et al.* in press)

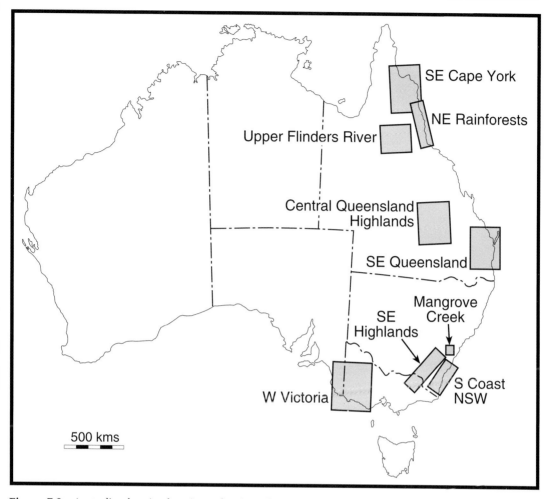

Figure 7.2   Australia, showing locations of regions discussed

land was occupied or used by at least 21,000 years BP, and probably much earlier. However, many of the cultural characteristics of the peoples concerned remain completely unknown, for little archaeological research has been undertaken and details are increasingly difficult to detect the further back we go in time.

In the following pages I review the archaeological evidence from various parts of the continent, beginning in the northeast of mainland Australia and moving southwards (Figure 7.2).

Southeast Cape York Peninsula

Cape York Peninsula is Australia's largest peninsula, the long finger of land in the northeastern corner that points northward to the island of New Guinea. During the early Holocene,

this was the last part of Australia to be attached to New Guinea as rising seas finally sundered the last of the land bridge to form what has come to be known as Torres Strait.

Some 800 km long, Cape York today contains a broad range of landforms, including low-lying sandy plains, plateaux, rugged hills and dissected gorges. The peninsula can be divided into three general longitudinal topographic, geological and biogeographic zones. Along the eastern seaboard is a narrow coastal plain that rarely exceeds 5 km in width, rapidly giving way to the mountains of the Great Dividing Range in the west. Along its lower western slopes, the Great Divide merges with the broad, expansive plains that stretch all the way to Cape York's west coast, up to 300 km away.

Modern vegetation communities are similarly varied, although generally speaking much of the peninsula is vegetated by *Eucalyptus*-dominated dry sclerophyll woodlands. The eastern coastal plains and sub-coastal highlands contain a narrow strip of thick, tropical rainforest that has expanded and contracted with fluctuating rainfall and sea levels (see Figure 7.1).

Some 50,000 years ago Cape York was attached to New Guinea to form the continent of Sahul, only to once again become severed by rising post-glacial seas about 8000 years BP. For the general region, long-term climatic and environmental trends based on ancient pollen and lake levels indicate that conditions were dry during the last glacial maximum, some parts of southeast Cape York then receiving about one-third of today's rainfall levels (currently 800–1100 mm per annum in most parts). Arid conditions prevailed until 14,000–13,000 years BP, when rainfall levels began to increase. However, climatic 'amelioration' may not have taken place until just prior to 10,000 years BP in the Atherton Tableland (southeastern corner of Cape York), where changes in precipitation were probably most extreme (Hiscock and Kershaw 1992).

The highest levels of precipitation and temperature occurred during the early Holocene after 10,000 years BP. During this time, and within the space of only about 2000 years, precipitation levels almost tripled in the most humid regions. They continued to climb during the mid-Holocene, when forests (and rainforest in Atherton) were most extensive, so that by 6500 to 5900 years BP they had more than quadrupled their terminal Pleistocene levels in the Atherton Tableland. Rainfall levels then decreased slightly after 3000 years BP, becoming driest between 2600 and 1400 years BP, with more open vegetation. However, rainfall never again reached the low levels that had prevailed during the end of the Pleistocene (Kershaw 1994; cf. David and Lourandos 1998).

Archaeological research

Archaeological research in the southeastern corner of Cape York began in the early 1960s.[3] Since then, more sites have been excavated in this region than in most other parts of Australia (see Figure 3.6). Some 42 caves and rockshelters have been excavated in southeast Cape York, with radiocarbon dates having been obtained from 38 (90 per cent) of these. In addition, ten shell mounds have also been radiocarbon-dated. These sites are found in six main regions: Princess Charlotte Bay and the Flinders Islands; the Koolburra Plateau; Laura; the Mitchell-Palmer limestone belt; Chillagoe and Ngarrabullgan. These regions represent a range of environmental conditions, including small continental islands and sandstone-rich coastlines (Princess Charlotte Bay and the Flinders Islands) (Figure 7.3), limestone karst outcrops on alluvial plains (Mitchell-Palmer and Chillagoe) (Figure 7.4), rugged, dissected sandstone ranges (Koolburra Plateau and Laura) (Figure 7.5), and a large conglomerate mesa surrounded by volcanic and metamorphic sediments (Ngarrabullgan) (see Chapter 3). With the exception of three rockshelters and the shell mounds from Princess Charlotte Bay and the Flinders Islands towards the extreme north of the study region, all of these sites are situated well inland (and mostly west of the Great Dividing Range), in environmental settings never directly affected by rising or falling sea levels.

Despite the largely autonomous undertakings of each research project, they have all shared one common concern: the search for long-term temporal trends. In practice this has meant the almost exclusive excavation of potentially *old* sites with deep or long sequences. As we shall see below, however, it is in the more recent phases of site sequences, around the time of the ethnographic Dreaming's archaeologically recognizable emergence, that the most pronounced cultural changes are evident.

The archaeological trends

Most researchers who have worked in Cape York have focused on qualitative changes in material behaviour (e.g. stone artefact types; food processing strategies), or quantitative changes in intensities of site and regional land use (as measured by, for example, deposition rates of artefacts or sedimentation rates). In the following pages I review these archaeological trends and consider them in terms of both change and continuity in past cultural behaviour across the peninsula.

Figure 7.3 Clack Island, off the coast of Princess Charlotte Bay (*Source*: Graeme Walsh)

Number of sites occupied through time

The oldest known human occupation in southeast Cape York dates to 35,460+750/-690 years BP at Ngarrabullgan Cave[4] (see also Chapter 3). Numerous other caves and rockshelters (e.g. Sandy Creek 1, Nonda Rock) contain Pleistocene occupation (some dating to 30,000 years BP or more), but the majority of sites date only to the Holocene (Table 7.1).

Of the 38 rockshelters from which radiocarbon dates have been obtained, 33 have basal or near-basal dates. From these, we can calculate changing occupational trends for the region as a whole by plotting the number of sites known to have been occupied through time[5] (Figure 7.6). Of course, such a curve concerns rockshelters and caves only, given the nature of the data, and other kinds of sites should also be considered if we wish to address overall regional occupational trends. But this limitation notwithstanding, the rockshelter curve is suggestive of changing numbers of occupied sites, giving one measure of changing intensities of regional occupation (see Bird and

Frankel (1991) for a regional Australian example where rockshelter trends mirror general occupational trends).

Over the long term, the temporal trends for southeast Cape York are clear. Most sites were inhabited after 4800 years BP, with accelerated increases in the numbers of occupied sites occurring through time. At no stage do early levels clearly exceed later ones, with major increases initially occurring after the last glacial maximum, followed by further increases during the mid to late Holocene. If the number of sites occupied during a given period of time are a reflection of both the frequency of visits and the length of stay at each site, then it appears that, during the Holocene, the onset of wet conditions was accompanied by major increases in intensities of regional occupation. The implication is that (1) more people were moving across the landscape, creating and using more sites in the process or (2) settlement systems changed as more or less stable populations moved residence more frequently. Furthermore, assuming the incidence of rockshelter use to be

Figure 7.4 Limestone outcrop, Mitchell-Palmer region

Figure 7.5 Dissected sandstone plateau, Laura (*Source*: Mike Morwood)

indicative of general regional trends, the numbers of occupied sites in southeast Cape York continued to rise through time. These increases in intensities of regional occupation indicate that socio-demographic conditions – population numbers and/or residential structures – were changing.

Rates of site establishment

Another way of looking at this same occupational data is by plotting the rate of establishment of *new* sites; that is, regional settlement trends may be glimpsed by tracking the number of sites initially settled through time. Rather than focusing on increases or decreases in the number of inhabited sites, rates of site establishment emphasize the emergence of new dwellings in regional landscapes. Changes in the numbers of newly established occupational sites relate to such things as changing settlement strategies, changing familiarity with local environments, and the establishment of new settlement locations in the face of changing demographic pressures. While rates of

initial site establishment reveal similar temporal trends to the occupational patterns apparent in the previous test (being based on the same data set), reframing the question by addressing site establishment rates rather than regional occupational intensities serves to reframe the way we look at the data and understand the patterns.

The Cape York trend indicates that after the early Holocene, many new sites were first occupied, indicating regional demographic transformations. This pattern is likely to have been caused by general rises in population numbers and densities across the regional landscape. These changes continued into the mid-Holocene, with a major increase in overall settlement numbers, shifts in the spatial distribution of occupation sites, or population displacement reaching a peak after *c.* 4800 years BP (Figure 7.7). Irrespective of ultimate causes, expansions into new residential locations and increasing intensities of regional land use are implicated. These changes are consistent with increasing demographic packing of southeast Cape York.

Table 7.1 The timing of earliest occupation, by site

Site	First evidence of human occupation, in uncalibrated radiocarbon years BP
Hand Shelter	667 ± 33
Fig Tree Shelter	1440 ± 60
Mordor Cave	1580 ± 70
Grass Tree Shelter (inner)	1610 ± 40
Lookout Shelter 1	1880 ± 100
Endaen Rockshelter	2370 ± 100
Courtyard Rock	2790 ± 80
Kookaburra Rock	2950 ± 80
Alkaline Hill Rockshelter	3440 ± 80
Painted Ell	3620 ± 70
Gorge Creek Shelter	3700 ± 60
Giant Horse Gallery	3750 ± 80
Pete's Chase	4040 ± 80
Bush Peg Shelter	4160 ± 60
Dragonfly Hollow	4430 ± 80
Walaemini Rockshelter	4760 ± 90
Initiation Cave	5290 ± 60
Platform Gallery	6120 ± 150
Echidna Shelter	7280 ± 130
Red Bluff Rockshelter	7530 ± 110
Grass Tree Shelter (outer)	7600 ± 60
Sandy Creek 2	7830 ± 80
Red Horse Rockshelter	8310 ± 120
Quinine Bush Shelter	8390 ± 60
Green Ant Rockshelter	8660 ± 340
Tunnel Shelter	10,120 ± 60
Magnificent Gallery	10,250 ± 90
Early Man Rockshelter	15,450 ± 1500
Yam Camp	~25,000
Nonda Rock	~26,200 ± 450
Hay Cave	29,700 ± 1050
Fern Cave	30,300 ± 800
Sandy Creek 1	31,900+700/-600
Ngarrabullgan Cave	35,460+750/-690

The frequency of radiocarbon dates as data on occupational trends

In 1987, John Rick described a new method for investigating long-term occupational trends within and between regions by plotting the frequencies of known radiocarbon dates through time. He suggested that within any particular geographic region, the number of radiocarbon dates obtained by archaeologists for any given period of time will be partly dependent on the *availability* of datable materials within a sedimentary sequence, and partly on the *selection* of appropriate samples

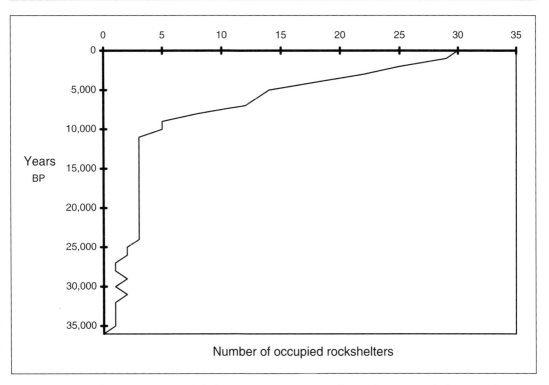

Figure 7.6 Number of occupied rockshelters in 1000-year intervals, southeast Cape York Peninsula

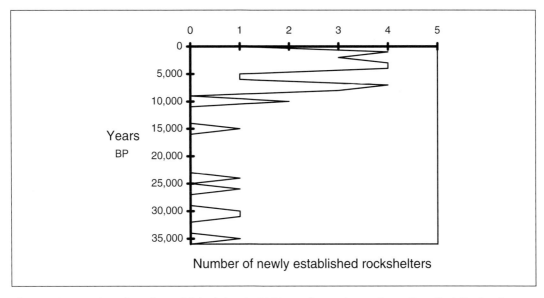

Figure 7.7 Number of newly established sites in 1000-year intervals, southeast Cape York Peninsula

for dating by researchers. He concluded that for any given region, the presence of high numbers of radiocarbon dates from a particular period of time may not be indicative of chang-ing occupational trends, but rather may simply indicate taphonomic biases in the sampling of charcoal for radiocarbon dating. These biases may skew frequencies of dated occupational

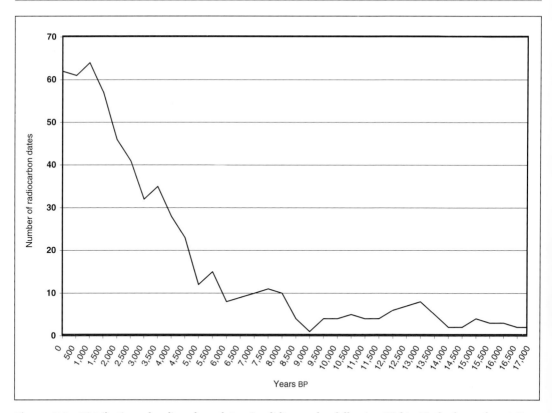

Figure 7.8 Distribution of radiocarbon dates, in sliding scales following Rick's Method, southeast Cape York Peninsula

events within a region towards one period of time or another. There is no simple relationship between amounts of charcoal in a site, numbers of radiocarbon dates acquired, and patterns of pre-Historic land use. Rather, the sum of radiocarbon dates obtained by archaeologists from a particular region will be a function of the creation, preservation, recovery and selection of charcoal and other organic materials from sediments.

Nevertheless, Rick also suggested that radiocarbon dates that relate to cultural strata 'represent human activity at a point in time' (1987, p. 55). Given large sample sizes based on the work of numerous researchers in a large number of sites, the relative frequencies of radiocarbon dates obtained through time in one or more regions will reveal useful information on long-term occupational trends for those regions. Such frequency curves, plotted against timelines, can enable us to ask the important question of 'why more archaeological radiocarbon dates exist for some time periods' than others (ibid., p. 56), and whether apparent trends indicate observable directions (not to be confused with predetermination) to changes in regional trends. The pattern or trend revealed by plotting the incidence of radiocarbon dates through time may point future enquiries in new directions, enabling previously unrecognized cultural trends to be identified and further explored.

Rick's method plots the frequency of radiocarbon dates for a given region in sliding intervals of time. In Figure 7.8 I have plotted the 242 reliable radiocarbon dates which have been obtained from southeast Cape York's rockshelters and caves.[6] These dates are depicted in 1000-year intervals measured in 500-year overlaps. The total number of radiocarbon dates represented at 7000 years BP, for example, consists of the sum of dates that fall between 6500 and 7500 years BP. At 7500 years BP, the number of radiocarbon dates number those that fall in the range 7000–8000 years BP, and so on. This scaling technique allows long-term temporal trends to emerge, while smoothing out short-term fluctuations. I have used 1000-year intervals measured every 500 years, rather than Rick's 600/200 years interval/measurement, so as to minimize the effects of random short-term variations, potentially influential on a curve with low numbers of dates.

The Cape York results are clear, showing a doubling in the incidence of radiocarbon dates with the onset of wet conditions around 8500 years BP, followed by a stabilization until 6000 to 5000 years BP when rates rapidly double again. After 5000 years BP, rates continue to slowly rise, doubling again by 4000 to 3500 years BP, with continued increases until 1500 to 1000 years BP when a peak is reached and numbers stabilize. The net effect is that there are 15 times as many radiocarbon dates at 1500 years BP than at 9000 years BP, with the greatest increase occurring between 6000 and 5000 and 1500 and 1000 years BP when a stable peak is reached. The sustained but punctuated nature of the trend during the mid to late Holocene, coupled with a lack of obvious sampling or preservation biases (except for a general *reluctance* by archaeologists to date recent, late Holocene deposits), implies that the radiocarbon curve has some affinity with long-term regional occupational trends. Given that almost all of the radiocarbon dates are on charcoal, and that most of the research programmes resulting in these dates specifically targeted potentially old sites or sites with long sequences, this pattern is cautiously interpreted as evidence for a rapid, incremental rise in occupational intensities of the regional landscape during the mid and late Holocene, reaching a peak around the time when the ethnographically known Dreaming first becomes visible archaeologically, between 1500 and 1000 years BP. Let us further explore this scenario by considering other indices of site and regional land use.

Deposition rates of cultural materials

As people occupy places, they leave behind material traces of their actions in the form of hearths, stone artefacts, food remains, and the like. The deposition rates of such cultural materials within sites have been studied and used by many Australian archaeologists as gross indicators of relative intensities of site

use, although it is also recognized that structural (qualitative) rather than quantitative socio-cultural changes may at times best explain such archaeological changes.

Results for southeast Cape York demonstrate that in the majority of cases, deposition rates of cultural materials, and especially stone artefacts and ochre, increase significantly during the mid to late Holocene. Some sites have more than one major peak in deposition rates, such as Red Bluff 1 between 4500 and 3700 years BP, and again between 2300 and 1200 years BP. Others, such as Sandy Creek 2, show erratic fluctuations, although even in these cases peak rates occur after 4000 years BP. In a few, rare instances, local peaks in deposition rates of cultural materials are present before the mid-Holocene, such as at Nonda Rock between c. 23,000 and 21,500 years BP, Fern Cave between 22,000 and 17,000 years BP, Mushroom Rock West between 9000 and 7700 years BP, and Red Horse between 7200 and 4700 years BP.

With these singular exceptions, the major peaks in deposition rates of stone artefacts always occur during the mid to late Holocene. These increases begin at various times between 5400 years BP (Ngarrabullgan Cave) and 1800 to 950 years BP (Early Man Rockshelter), with most taking place during the last 4000 years and involving a doubling or tripling of rates during the mid to late Holocene (David and Chant 1995) (Table 7.2, Figure 7.9).

There is no clear geographical patterning to such temporal trends, indicating that the changes rapidly took hold across the Cape. The mid to late Holocene increases in deposition rates are in most cases apparent in both organic (e.g. animal bones) and non-organic (e.g. stone artefacts) cultural remains. In some cases, particularly the limestone caves (e.g. Fern Cave, Hearth Cave, Mitchell River Cave), organic items such as bone continue below the lowermost cultural layers in the form of well-preserved owl deposits or the like. The overall trends cannot therefore readily be dismissed as a result of differential preservation.

What these increases mean is not easily determined, for they could relate to population increases or to qualitative changes in cultural behaviour independent of population increase. However, the fact that increases in deposition rates of stone artefacts, charcoal, food remains and ochre occurred

Table 7.2 The timing when deposition rates of stone artefacts begin to peak, by site

Site	Time when deposition rates of stone artefacts begin to increase significantly in sites where change is distinct, in uncalibrated radiocarbon years BP (only sites where occupation begins before the mid-Holocene are listed)
Magnificent Gallery	1200
Yam Camp	1250
Echidna Shelter	1400
Mushroom Rock	1500
Mushroom Rock East	1500
Early Man Rockshelter	some time between 1800–950
Green Ant Rockshelter	some time between 2200–1800
Grass Tree Shelter (outer)	2100
Red Bluff 1	2300
Hann River 1	2400
Echidna's Rest	3000
Hay Cave	3100
Nonda Rock	3400
Hearth Cave	3500
Tunnel Shelter	3700
Walkunder Arch Cave	3700
Mitchell River Cave	3800
Sandy Creek 2	4000
Sandy Creek 1	4000
Red Bluff 1	4500
Quinine Bush Shelter	4900
Ngarrabullgan Cave	5400
Red Horse	7200
Mushroom Rock West	9000
Sandy Creek 2	15,000
Fern Cave	22,000
Nonda Rock	~23,000

Note: some sites have more than one major peak

simultaneously within most sites cannot simply be dismissed as a taphonomic illusion. Nor can these widespread increases be explained as a product of alterations in stone artefact production systems. Every detailed technological study to have been undertaken for Cape York's stone artefacts with such questions in mind has failed to explain the apparent increases in late Holocene lithic deposition rates to changes in stone artefact reduction strategies alone.[7] Overall, increasing intensities of site and regional land use are implied, indicating changing relations between people and their experienced landscapes. Here again, then, demographic conditions are implicated to have changed after 4000–3500 years BP, typically indicating a doubling to tripling of intensities of site use if artefact deposition rates can be taken to reflect general occupational intensities.

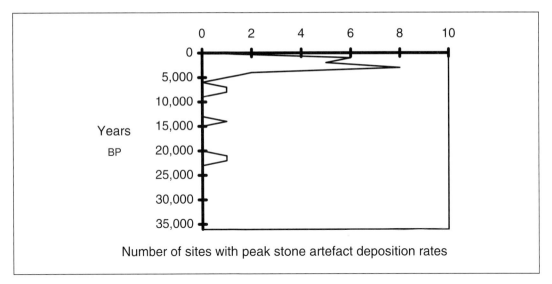

Figure 7.9 Number of sites with peak deposition rates of stone artefacts, in 1000-year intervals, southeast Cape York Peninsula

Sedimentation rates

Sediments are deposited under historically specific environmental conditions; changes in sedimentation rates within sites imply changes in depositional and/or erosional regimes. In general, other factors being equal, sedimentation rates in caves and rockshelters tend to increase with increasing intensities of human occupation. This correlation is largely the product of three factors: (1) the introduction of new raw materials (e.g. wood for fires) into a site; (2) the initiation or acceleration of cave wall disintegration as a result of human-induced microclimatic changes (e.g. fire-induced) and mechanical erosion (e.g. touching, trampling); and/or (3) the initiation or acceleration of slope instability and colluvial slope wash as a result of increased firing or clearing of the landscape. Sedimentation rates are therefore a potential tool for exploring changing relations between people and place.

Table 7.3 and Figure 7.10 present evidence for changing sedimentation rates within excavated sites in southeast Cape York. Major, 2.5- to 5.5-fold increases in sedimentation rates occurred in almost all the excavated sites during the mid to late Holocene, most sites hovering around a three-fold increase. That is, sediments accumulated consistently faster during the mid and late Holocene than earlier,

suggesting increasing intensities of site and regional land use. However, we must be cautious in interpretation as few detailed geomorphological studies have yet been undertaken. The results are nevertheless consistent with the findings of previous tests, changing sedimentation regimes apparently attesting to rising levels of regional land use during the mid and late Holocene, particularly after 3700 years BP.

Stone artefact types

Unlike many other parts of Australia, very few recognized stone artefact types have ever been excavated in southeast Cape York. The exceptions are edge-ground axes (present since the late Pleistocene[8]), seed-grinding stones and Burren adzes. Rare backed flakes are also found, but in very low numbers and in very few sites. When found, they are in mid to late Holocene contexts, the only exception being Walkunder Arch Cave where three flakes with backing were found in terminal Pleistocene deposits (Campbell 1982, 1984). Given this limited range of recognized formal types, few typological changes can be expected through time.

Burren adzes are stone tools that were once hafted onto wooden handles and used to shape wooden artefacts of various kinds (e.g. shields, wooden containers). They possess

Table 7.3 The timing of increasing sedimentation rates in sites where occupation first began before the mid-Holocene, by site

Site	Time when sedimentation rates begin to increase significantly (excluding sites first occupied during mid to late Holocene), in uncalibrated radiocarbon years BP
Mitchell River Cave	900–1100
Magnificent Gallery	<1000
Yam Camp	1000
Echidna Shelter	1200–5400
Grass Tree Shelter (outer)	2100
Echidna's Rest	3000
Hay Cave	3100
Hearth Cave	3500–4100
Walkunder Arch Cave	3700
Green Ant Rockshelter	4300–7600
Quinine Bush Shelter	4900
Tunnel Shelter	5400
Ngarrabullgan Cave	5400
Fern Cave	22,000
Nonda Rock	~23,000
Sandy Creek 1	continuously increasing (accelerating) rates since first occupation

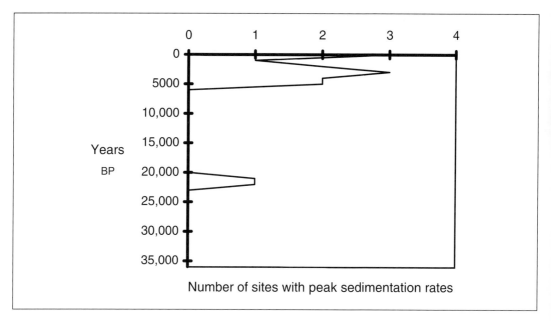

Figure 7.10 Number of sites with peak sedimentation rates, in 1000-year intervals, southeast Cape York Peninsula

Table 7.4   Antiquity of earliest Burren adzes, by site

Site	First appearance of Burren adzes, in uncalibrated radiocarbon years BP
Echidna's Rest	700
Yam Camp	1000
Hearth Cave	1100–700
Magnificent Gallery	1200
Red Horse Rockshelter	1400
Green Ant Rockshelter	1400–1200
Early Man Rockshelter	~1800
Sandy Creek 1	1900
Red Bluff Rockshelter	2100
Hann River 1	2400
Giant Horse Gallery	<3800
Mushroom Rock	4000
Sandy Creek 2	4000

characteristically convex ventral surfaces with modified edges occurring laterally to the striking platform. The used edges typically include deep and extensive step fracturing of a type consistent with the working of hard woods (Kamminga 1982). Edge angles are consistently 60–80°, with scalar retouch and intrusive step fracturing along a large portion of the margins. Burren adzes show clear signs of reduction through both use wear and retouch. They are repeatedly found across the peninsula after 4000 years BP (and especially after 2400 years BP), but clearly absent during earlier times (Table 7.4, Figure 7.11). They are, therefore, an exclusively late Holocene phenomenon that continued into ethnographic times.

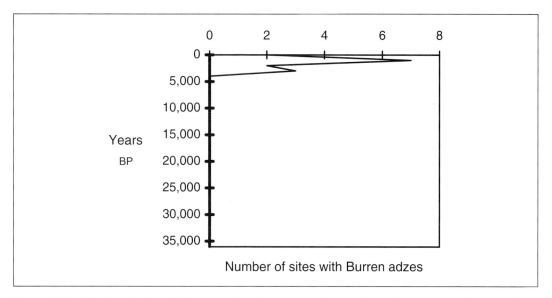

Figure 7.11   Number of sites with Burren adzes, in 1000-year intervals, southeast Cape York Peninsula

Table 7.5   First appearance of blades and microblades, by site

Site	Appearance of blades and microblades, in uncalibrated radiocarbon years BP
Yam Camp	1000
Sandy Creek 1	1900–1200
Mushroom Rock East	2100–1700
Red Bluff Rockshelter	2300
Hann River 1	2400
Giant Horse Gallery	<3800
Sandy Creek 2	3800
Early Man Rockshelter	5500–1000

Stone artefact technologies

Little research has yet been undertaken into stone tool production technologies. However, Andrée Rosenfeld *et al.* (1981) noted that there is a gradual increase in the use of chert, and a gradual decrease in the size of artefacts through time at Early Man Rockshelter, Laura. Similar observations were made by Josephine Flood and Nicky Horsfall (1986, p. 28) at Echidna Shelter (Koolburra Plateau), where 'chert replaced quartzite as the preferred raw material during the last millennium'. Richard Wright (1971) reported a decrease in the weight of stone artefacts at Mushroom Rock around 3000 years BP. Warwick Pearson (1989, pp. 97–8) also reported 'a general trend towards smaller artefact size in all raw materials' in the upper part of the Yam Camp sequence (dated to the last 1000 years).

While shifts in technological strategies are implied by changing raw materials and artefact sizes, the major technological change observed is the beginning of blade production during the late Holocene. At Early Man Rockshelter, this is suggested to have taken place with the first appearance of parallel-sided bladelets and a single prismatic core some time between 5500 and 1000 years BP, which together Rosenfeld *et al.* (1981, p. 22) argued was the nexus of a 'technological innovation'. Pearson (1989) found a similar trend at Yam Camp, where blades appeared in levels post-dating 1000 years BP. Mike Morwood (Morwood and Trezise 1989) also noted that microblades first appeared at Sandy Creek 1 in the upper grey layer, dated to some time after 1900 to 1200

years BP. However, evidence for blade production is not widespread nor intensive, being absent in most sites. Where they are present, blades and other evidence of blade production are not common, and are never systematically founded on prismatic core technologies.

Thus, while issues dealing with technological change have rarely been addressed and require more attention, normative changes have been documented on a number of fronts, including the selection of raw materials, mean artefact sizes, and the appearance of blade-based technologies during the late Holocene, particularly during the last 2400 years (Table 7.5, Figure 7.12).

Food processing strategies

In Australia generally, few stone artefacts can unambiguously be said to be directly related to food processing. Of these, an important and well-defined temporal trend has emerged. Demonstrated food processing stone artefacts are almost always limited to seed-grinding stones, which in Cape York have never been found in contexts older than 1900 years BP (at Sandy Creek 1; they also occur in the very upper, undated units of Giant Horse Gallery, a site whose base is dated to *c.* 3800 years BP) (Table 7.6). These dates correspond favourably with similar ages for the commencement of systematic seed grinding and for the processing of toxic plants elsewhere in central and eastern Australia (see Chapter 8). The implication is that major changes in diet breadths have taken place late in Cape York pre-History, changes that saw the exploitation of new staple plant

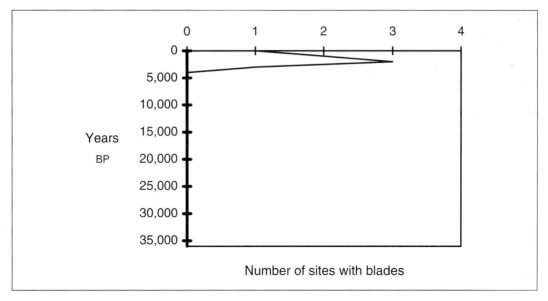

Figure 7.12 Number of sites with blades and microblades, in 1000-year intervals, southeast Cape York Peninsula

foods available in vast quantities in many parts of northeastern Australia. The ramifications of such a change are not exclusively 'economic' or demographic, but also imply changes in the way people interacted with and symbolized their immediate surroundings, transforming grasslands to harvestable fields, previously unused stone outcrops into sources of stone that could be worked into economically valuable (including tradeable) grinding stones. The changes imply, therefore, transformations as to how people visualized and signified their surroundings. These changes also have bearing on the scheduling of everyday life and seasonal cycles. There is an implication here for both a conceptualization of the landscape and for the use and management (labour) of the land – both instances of shifting relations between people and between people and their environ-

ments. I will explore these issues in some detail in the next chapter.

Open sites: mounds

At nearly 50 km across, Princess Charlotte Bay is a large bay (see Figure 3.6). It is here that the only detailed study of settlement patterns in southeast Cape York has taken place. Ten shell mounds represent the only open sites to have been radiocarbon-dated in southeast Cape York (Figure 7.13). Measuring up to 30 m in diameter and 5 m in height, the mounded middens consist almost entirely of a single species of shell, *Anadara granosa*, a species of cockle that can be found in mangrove beds nearby. Such shell mounds are common on the mid-Holocene chenier plains of the bay, and date to the last 2000–1700 years BP only.

Table 7.6 First appearance of specialized seed-grinding stones, by site

Site	First appearance of specialized seed-grinding grindstones, in uncalibrated radiocarbon years BP
Magnificent Gallery	1200
Sandy Creek 1	1900
Giant Horse Gallery	<3800

Figure 7.13   Shell mound, Princess Charlotte Bay (*Source*: John Grindrod)

Being more recent than the chenier plains themselves (formed 6000–4000 years BP), the mounds' formation can be attributed to the onset of new, centralized consumption bases across the bay. John Beaton has reported of the dated mounds:

> Three ¹⁴C dates for basal horizons of shell-mounds distributed on the chenier system suggest that earliest dates for the shellmounds will not much exceed 1700–1500 BP ... Seven other dates from basal horizons of other shellmounds also on the cheniers suggest that the period around 1200–800 years BP saw the production of more numerous (and larger) mounds. Five dates from the surfaces of shellmounds on all cheniers are all ca. 500–400 years BP, which I take to be the approximate period when large scale Anadara deposition ceased. (1985, pp. 8–9)

Mounds at Princess Charlotte Bay are at once evidence of novel foraging practices, disposal patterns and site selection. The systematic exploitation of mangrove beds (Figure 7.14), especially *A. granosa*, implies the beginnings of a new, specialized and focused subsistence

strategy 2000–1700 years BP. This subsistence strategy is unlikely to have had comparable historical precedents given that no earlier evidence for such a scale of focused activity has yet been obtained. While the presence of a marine-based economy during earlier times is evident from excavations at the rockshelter sites of Alkaline Hill, Endaen and Walaemini, in no case are intensities of shellfish exploitation comparable to those reached in the mound economies. While the exploitation of shellfish predates mound construction, the focused and intensive exploitation of *A. granosa* beds only reached its peak after the advent of mounded middens, less than 2000 years BP.

The northeast Australian rainforests

In the southeast corner of Cape York, and extending south for a further 200 km along the coastal plains and abutting eastern slopes of the ranges, are the tropical rainforests of northeast Australia. During ethnographic times, plant foods were known to have been particularly important in tropical rainforests

Figure 7.14 Mangroves, Princess Charlotte Bay (*Source*: John Grindrod)

and rainforest margins. Some of these plants, such as the black bean *Castanospermum australe* and the cycad *Cycas media* (Figure 7.15), are highly toxic in their raw states. Specialized leaching procedures were developed to enable the seeds or nuts to be eaten. Typically, the detoxification process involved a complex combination of roasting or steaming, grinding, mashing or slicing, submerging the mashed product in running water over a number of days, and final cooking in earth ovens. Because both the black bean and cycad are available in large quantities during various times of the year, relatively large aggregations of people could be supported over extended periods of time. The black bean and cycad could also be relied upon to feed domestic groups on a day-to-day basis, and supplement more highly ranked foods during lean years. Leaching technologies therefore have considerable importance for the support of large regional populations and seasonal aggregations over the long term, allowing new population thresholds and demographic structures to be established and maintained.

Archaeological investigations within the tropical rainforests of north Queensland have been limited, with the work of Nicky Horsfall (1987) representing the only substantial research. Horsfall's work at Jiyer Cave and the Mulgrave 2 site produced evidence of human occupation spanning the last 5100 years. Plant remains were an important component of the excavated deposits, with the first appearance of poisonous plant foods occurring during the last 1000 years at Jiyer Cave. Plant remains were present in the site's earlier phases; however, none were identified as toxic. Toxic plants first appeared at the Mulgrave 2 open site around 2000 years BP (Horsfall 1987, p. 263). Although these results are problematic in that organic materials within the deposits have been subject to considerable chemical breakdown, corroborative evidence was found in the stone tool assemblage. Stone artefacts known ethnographically to have been associated with the processing of poisonous plant foods were found only towards the top of the excavation at Jiyer Cave. Horsfall (ibid., pp. 266–7) thus concluded that the absence of specialized grindstones in the older deposits at Jiyer Cave,

Figure 7.15 *Cycas media* (*Source*: Mike Morwood)

Figure 7.16 Quippenburra Cave (*Source*: Mike Morwood)

and the occasional presence of 'expedient' grindstones may mean that intensive use of such plants is represented only in the uppermost deposits, probably within the last 1000 years ... the vertical distribution of stone artefacts possibly associated with complex processing appears to indicate that intensive use of toxic plants is relatively recent.

The beginnings of systematic processing of toxic plants in the northeastern rainforests were accompanied by a roughly contemporaneous increase in site and regional occupational intensities, as measured by noticeable increases in discard rates of other cultural materials after 850–650 years BP at Jiyer Cave, and after 1800–1000 years BP at Mulgrave 2. The likely implication is that the onset of systematic processing of high yielding toxic plants broadly coincided with major population increases and intensities of regional land use. The systematic production of toxic plant foods only during the last 1800 years (and particularly during the last 1000 years) in northeastern Australia's rainforests implies major alterations in diet breadths, a restructuring of

subsistence practices (including seasonal schedules), a major increase in the size of regional populations capable of being supported, and more generally alterations to systems of land use and perception.

The upper Flinders River region

Some 300 km south of Cape York is the watershed of the upper Flinders River and its tributaries. This area is drier and more hilly than much of Cape York, with the rainforest-clad peaks of the Great Divide located immediately to the east. To the west and south are extensive Mitchell Grass plains and brigalow woodlands, respectively.

In 1980 Mike Morwood (1990, 1992) began archaeological research in the upper Flinders River catchment. Extensive surveys and excavations at the rockshelter sites of Mickey Springs 31, 34, 38 and Quippenburra Cave were undertaken over a number of years (Figure 7.16), the major temporal trends revealing changes in lithic technology and artistic behaviour during the mid to late Holocene.

Two sites were particularly informative of long-term trends. At Mickey Springs 34, one of the largest sites excavated, a continuous 11,000-year cultural sequence was unearthed. Stone artefact deposition rates were found to increase slowly after 8000 years BP, in the form of 'trends rather than threshhold changes' (Morwood 1990, p. 19). This was followed around 3400 years BP by sharp increases in stone artefact deposition rates, the introduction of new artefact types, the appearance of large numbers of dense hearth deposits, and a broadening of the resource base (as evident especially by the commencement of systematic seed grinding). Morwood (ibid., p. 35) concluded that the 'development of a late Holocene committment to seed processing to meet both domestic and social demands upon the production system allowed occupation of previously marginal country' to take place after 3400 years BP. Population expansion into previously poorly frequented zones, as well as an intensification of occupation in already core lands are implied by these findings.

Concurrent with Morwood's demographic changes are major increases in the deposition rates of earth pigments (ochres), indicating changes in artistic activity at Mickey Springs 34. Changes in the spatial distribution of artefacts across the site were interpreted by the excavators as possible evidence for 'the establishment of more formalised patterns of site use and cleaning behaviour as occupation became more systematic and intensive' after 3400 years BP (ibid., p. 14). Mike Morwood concluded that:

> significant technological, economic and artistic change did not occur until 3360 BP. The range of new artefact types and technologies included backed blades, and adzes of both burren and tula type, edge-ground axes, and (probably) grindstones. From this time there were further increases in stone artefact and ochre discard rates, use of conservation strategies in knapping high-quality stone and rate of hearth manufacture.
>
> The evidence from Mickey Springs 31 shows that the nature and timing of this change is not site-specific. Here, 934 stone artefacts were recovered including three burren adze slugs, two tula adze slugs and two fragments of edge-ground axe, all of which came from post-5100 BP deposits. (ibid., p. 21)

At Quippenburra Cave, a 3300-year sequence revealed cultural materials comparable to those found after 3400 years BP at Mickey Springs 34. Morwood (ibid., p. 22) proposed that 'Overall, the evidence suggests use of the shelters by larger groups, for longer periods of time and for a wider range of activities over the past 3400 years.' These changes were associated with a 'late Holocene commitment to seed processing . . . [allowing] occupation of previously marginal country', and 'increases in local population and productivity' (ibid., p. 35).

Central Queensland Highlands

Some 800 km to the south of the Flinders River, and 400 km west of the coast, are the Central Queensland Highlands, a western extension of the Great Divide. Comprised of weathered sandstones rising up to 1000 m above sea level, the ranges are riddled with rugged plateaux, mesas and clifflines rich in archaeological sites.

It is from the site of Kenniff Cave in the Central Queensland Highlands that, in 1962, John Mulvaney (1984; Mulvaney and Joyce 1965) obtained the first Australian Pleistocene date for cultural deposits, thereby confirming that Aboriginal people had first settled the continent deep in antiquity. Since then, numerous other sites of similar or greater antiquity have been excavated from many other parts of Australia, but at 19,000 years BP Kenniff Cave remains the oldest known occupied site in this region.

Nine caves and rockshelters have been excavated and dated from the Central Queensland Highlands, mainly the product of research by Mulvaney (Kenniff Cave, The Tombs) and then-doctoral scholars John Beaton (Wanderer's Cave, Rainbow Cave, Cathedral Cave) and Mike Morwood (Native Well 1 and 2, Ken's Cave, Turtle Rock) (Beaton 1977; Morwood 1979, 1981; Mulvaney and Joyce 1965). A characteristic of all sites is their tendency to exhibit episodic, rather than gradual, change. The earliest stone artefact assemblages in the Central Queensland Highlands are represented by a predominance of amorphous flakes and core tools, and a very low proportion of blades. Around 5000 years BP new stone tool types were added to the existing artefact range, although the precise nature of technological and functional continuity between these two phases have never been adequately investigated (Mulvaney and Joyce 1965; Morwood 1979). Stone artefact deposition and sedimentation rates before 5000 years BP were slow, increasing noticeably thereafter.

The above general trends have been reported from all four excavated sites that span this period of time – Kenniff Cave, The Tombs, Native Well 1 and Native Well 2. Variation in the timing of changes between sites is minimal. Not one of the main site reports records a gradual change from the earlier to the later lithic assemblages, although it has been repeatedly noted that stone artefact types found during the earlier period continue into the later (e.g. Mulvaney and Joyce 1965).

The Central Queensland Highlands have a doubly significant place in Australian archaeology. Apart from being the source of Australia's first Pleistocene archaeological date, it is also from Kenniff Cave that the general type sequence was first described for Australian stone tools, when Mulvaney reported a series of lithic transformations beginning 5000 years BP (although influential but more regionally restricted lithic sequences had previously been proposed by Tindale, McCarthy and others). The two major stone artefact assemblages at Kenniff Cave have since been labelled the early 'Core Tool and Scraper Tradition' (Bowler et al. 1970) and the subsequent 'Small Tool Tradition' (Gould 1969) by later researchers, an influential schema that many have applied to other Australian sites. More recently, some have also suggested a third, late Holocene phase characterized by a decrease in the incidence of retouching and the loss of some types (including backed artefacts) beginning around 2000 years BP and variously named the 'Recent Tradition' by Mike Morwood (1981) and the 'Lesser Retouched Tradition' by John Campbell (1984). While the integrity and usefulness of lumping artefactual assemblages into 'traditions' have been questioned, the changing nature of artefact production during the mid-Holocene, and again during the late Holocene, has been confirmed many times for different parts of Australia (e.g. Flood and Horsfall 1986).

The so-called 'Small Tool Tradition' is represented in the Central Queensland Highlands by the appearance of a wide range of new tool types such as backed flakes, eloueras, unifacial points (including pirri points), ground-edge axes, and grinding stones (see Flood 1995;

Mulvaney and Kamminga 1999 for illustrations of these artefact types). There is a concomitant increase in artefact densities, a peak in ochre deposition rates, and the appearance of technological innovations based on systematic platform preparation. In spite of the initial appearance of some of these traits around 5000 years BP, they are most marked after 3500 years BP, during the period that Morwood (1979) calls the 'late' phase of the Small Tool Tradition. This is also the period when cycads begin to appear in the archaeological record, implying their systematic exploitation and the parallel appearance of complex leaching technologies (Beaton 1977).[9] The earliest evidence for cycads appeared in the deepest levels at Wanderer's Cave 4300 years BP, Rainbow Cave 3600 years BP, and Cathedral Cave 3500 years BP (Beaton 1977).[10] Given the total absence of cycads before 4300 years BP, Beaton (1977) concluded that cycad use, and the leaching technology necessary to render them edible, only had a late Holocene antiquity in the Central Queensland Highlands. After 2500 to 2000 years BP, major changes continued to take place throughout the region, with the disappearance of a number of stone artefact types (e.g. backed flakes) (the 'Lesser Retouched Tradition'), and a decrease in artefact discard and sedimentation rates.

Morwood (1979) also identified a three-phase sequence for the rock-art of the Central Queensland Highlands. The earliest phase consists of pecked animal and human tracks and non-figurative motifs such as circles, arcs, pits and sets of radiating lines. This phase of artistic production is superseded around 4200 years BP by a narrowing of the motif range, a decrease in composite designs, and the beginnings of pecked vulvae, which now account for 23 per cent of engravings. Stencilling, printing, painting and abrading also emerge as new artistic techniques. This phase continued until the arrival of Europeans during the nineteenth century, when grids predominate and various figurative designs such as lizards, tortoises and lizard-grid compositions make their appearance. It is during this time that white paintings and stencils also gain numerical significance.

During the course of the Central Queensland Highlands artistic history, major changes take place in the geographical patterning of techniques and motifs. Following Lesley

Maynard's (1976) prior study of Australian rock-art, Morwood (1979) noted that the earliest phase was geographically widespread, whereas the subsequent phases were restricted to the Central Queensland Highlands, indicating a regionalization of artistic conventions after 4200 years BP. To Morwood (1979), these changes indicated the emergence of new social, cultural and political boundaries – a restructuring of territorial networks – after 4200 years BP, a concept I shall revisit in some detail in Chapter 9.

Southeast Queensland

Coastal and subcoastal southeast Queensland, located 300 km southeast of the Central Queensland Highlands, has been the subject of intensive archaeological research by Jay Hall (1982) and his postgraduate research students (e.g. McNiven 1990; Neal and Stock 1986; Ulm and Hall 1996; Walters 1989) since the 1970s. Reliable radiocarbon dates have been obtained from 57 sites, with excavations undertaken in 53 shell middens, one burial ground and one open stone artefact scatter in coastal settings, and seven rockshelters and caves located between 40 and 160 km inland (Ulm and Hall 1996). The oldest of these sites is Wallen Wallen Creek, a coastal shell-bearing deposit dating back to 20,560±250 years BP (Neal and Stock 1986).

Most archaeological research in southeast Queensland has focused on changing intensities of regional occupation in the face of fluctuating sea levels. Jay Hall (most recently, Ulm and Hall 1996) in particular has suggested that human populations were tethered to resources of the sea, settlement patterns shifting with migrating coastlines. However, during the late Holocene, and particularly after 1200 years BP, site establishment rates, numbers of occupied sites and frequencies of available radiocarbon dates increase dramatically. 'Most significant', argue Sean Ulm and Jay Hall (1996, p. 54), 'is the apparent explosion of shellfish remains as evidenced by the dramatic increase in coastal shell middens' 1200 years BP, dating well after the period of sea level stabilization (6000 years BP). An expansion of human populations onto offshore islands is also apparent at that time.

In addition to increasing numbers of coastal shell middens during the late Holocene, Jay Hall and Peter Hiscock (1988) also noted that major increases in stone artefact discard rates took place in the subcoastal rockshelters, thereby indicating parallel regional occupational trends in coastal and subcoastal habitats. At Bushranger's Cave, Platypus, Maindenwell and Gatton rockshelters, Hiscock and Hall (1988) and Morwood (1986) reported initially low discard rates of cultural materials rapidly increasing after 4000–3000 years BP, followed by possible decreases during recent times. The number of known occupied rockshelters increases during the last 3000 years BP, with occupation in sites such as Bishop's Peak and Brooyar Rockshelter (Figure 7.17) commencing at that time (McNiven 1990).

Various interpretations have been proposed for these changes. In 1989, Ian Walters had suggested that increasing coastal occupation during the late Holocene was a result of the onset of a new settlement system focused on the coast and involving novel resource exploitation strategies based on intensive fishing technologies. Walters undertook detailed analyses of fish remains from Moreton Bay archaeological sites, concluding that intensive scale fishing only appeared after c. 2000 years BP, developing exponentially thereafter, some 4000 years after the stabilization of sea levels. He inferred a maximum age of 2000 years BP for the nearby stone fish trapping systems (Figure 7.18), concluding that human occupation became increasingly sedentary after this time, a sedentism resulting from the maintenance demands associated with the new fishing installations.

Mike Morwood (1986) similarly made much of fishing in his model of the evolution of social complexity in southeast Queensland. Morwood used ethnographic, historical and ecological details to explain the archaeological patterns. During ethnographic times, the seasonal migrations of large schools of mullet were targeted during winter by various peoples of southeast Queensland. During the summer, however, large gatherings from many Aboriginal countries were held further inland, supported by the fruiting bunya pines. Morwood suggested that population sizes rose and social systems became increasingly complex during the late Holocene as bunya pines and fish resources attained new geographical and seasonal configurations following the marine transgression, and marine fishery developed into specialized forms capable of

Figure 7.17 Brooyar rockshelter (*Source*: Ian McNiven)

Figure 7.18 Stone fish traps, Booral, southeast Queensland (*Source*: Ian McNiven)

high yields. What changed were not simply population numbers and resource targets, but the structure of land use and inter-regional interaction. The resulting bimodal distribution of resource abundances (i.e winter/coastal/fish vs summer/inland/bunya) promoted new population movements and systems of economic reciprocity incorporating the formalization of new inter-group aggregations and contexts of boundary (territory) crossing that these entailed.

Ian McNiven (1990) added important new qualitative details to these changes when he noted that after 2000 years BP the use of stone and shell resources became more regionalized across parts of southeast Queensland. This regionalization, he suggested, implied rising populations and the emergence of increasingly bounded social, economic and political blocs.

Southeast Queensland thus displays accelerated tempos of site formation and discard rates of cultural materials after 3000 years BP, with further sharp increases after 1200 years BP. These changes were associated with settlement expansions onto offshore islands, the establishment of new food procurement tech-niques (large, stone fish traps), and the exploi-tation and use of more noticeably localized shellfish and stone resources 3000 to 2000 years BP. Together, these strategic realignments imply quantitative and structural changes, including more people living closer together and local communities becoming increasingly differentiated and geographically formalized through time.

Mangrove Creek catchment

Some 600km to the south of southeast Queensland, 30 km inland of the modern city of Sydney and cutting through the Hawkes-bury Sandstone, is the upper catchment of Mangrove Creek. Rich in sandstone clifflines, the catchment was extensively surveyed by Val Attenbrow (1982, 1986) during the 1980s, when 31 habitation sites (most of which were rockshelters) were excavated to arrive at some understanding of regional trends in settlement locations, patterns of change and continuity in settlement concentrations over time, and lithic trends.

Two major periods of change were identified

among the stone artefact assemblages, the first dating to 5000–2800 years BP, and the second to 2800–1600 years BP. However, Attenbrow also found that typological phasing did not coincide with the timing of changes in stone artefact deposition and rockshelter establishment rates. Stone artefact deposition rates began to increase significantly after 3000 years BP, with major increases in rates of site establishment occurring after 2000 years BP. However, after *c.* 1600 years BP artefact discard rates noticeably *de*creased during the period when the greatest numbers of rockshelters were being occupied. To Attenbrow, these patterns indicated a complementarity that signalled shifting land use strategies rather than simply population increases. These patterns also implied that the observed cultural transformations were not a simple function of a singular change in stone artefact production strategies – petrological, technological or typological.

Southeastern Highlands

The mountainous high country of southeastern Australia, the southern section of the Great Dividing Range, is comprised of a series of distinct ranges and mountain peaks. Archaeological research within the highlands began in the 1960s and has proceeded spasmodically since then. In each case, general temporal trends are reminiscent of those of other regions to the north. Ian Johnson (1979) wrote of a conspicuous increase in intensities of site use after 4000–3000 years BP in the Blue Mountains. He interpreted this increase as being directly associated with the onset of the 'Small Tool Tradition', and due to a general demographic dynamism associated with late Holocene technological systems. Sandra Bowdler (1981) similarly generally noted that the southeastern highlands, a region that includes the Blue Mountains, began to be used systematically by Aboriginal people only during the last 5000 years, with further increases in intensities of regional land use during the last 3000 years, implying changing social geographies. She concluded that 'Aboriginal occupation of any intensity can only be dated to within the last 5000 years, concomitant with the inception of the Australian Small Tool tradition' (Bowdler 1981, p. 108). This period also witnessed the management of new resource bases in the high country, including the exploitation

of some toxic plants such as cycads, which require specialized and complex processing procedures similar to those already described for northeastern Australian rainforest toxic plants. Using ethnographic reports to generate her model, Bowdler (1981) concluded that the systematic use of the eastern highlands (southeast Queensland highlands, New England Tablelands, Blue Mountains and Southern Uplands) during the mid to late Holocene was associated with ceremonial activities made possible by the advent of new methods for managing and processing high yielding and dependable (staple) food resources (e.g. cycads, daisy yams and bogong moths), some of which are toxic in their raw states.

Sandra Bowdler's model received support in the mid-1980s when Josephine Flood and her colleagues (Flood *et al.* 1987) reported new archaeological findings from the Southern Uplands. Excavations at the Birrigai rockshelter yielded occupational deposits dating back to 21,000 years BP. For the first time, evidence of pre-late Holocene occupation had been found in the high country. The temporal trends at Birrigai were consistent with Bowdler's views, evidencing:

1 Extremely low sedimentation rates until 3000 years BP.
2 Higher sedimentation rates after 3000 years BP, most readily explicable by reference to rising occupational intensities within the site.
3 Accelerated charcoal concentrations after 3000 years BP until post-European contact times.
4 A pattern of artefact discard rates showing extremely low values until 3000 years BP, after which time rates increase four-fold and are then maintained until very recent times.
5 A major increase in the number of dated excavated shelters known to have been inhabited in the Uplands after 3000 years BP.
6 A dramatic rise in sedimentation rates over the last 500 years.

These trends were interpreted by Flood *et al.* (1987) to indicate growing occupational intensities after 3000 years BP, including increases in the use of individual sites such as Birrigai, expansions into previously marginal environments (the highlands), and a burgeoning establishment rate of new sites across the high country. Population increases and geographical expansions were both implicated.

The South Coast of NSW

Some 100 km to the east of the southeastern Highlands is the South Coast of New South Wales, where Phil Hughes and Ron Lampert (1982, p. 16) noted an 'obvious contrast' between the numbers of documented Pleistocene sites, on the one hand, and mid to late Holocene sites, on the other. They also identified a significant mid to late Holocene growth in stone artefact and sedimentation rates within sandstone rockshelters (Hughes 1977; for a differing view, see Hiscock 1986). They interpreted these archaeological trends as indicating gross increases in occupational intensities along the southeastern seaboard during the mid to late Holocene. Given that the investigated sites are located on stable landforms not subject to destruction by Holocene sea level fluctuations, the archaeological increases were taken by Hughes and Lampert (1982) to implicate demographic expansions which probably gained momentum during the course of the late Holocene. The approximate, but not exact, coincidence of numerical rises in the numbers of occupied sites, stone artefact and sedimentation rates, on the one hand, and of qualitative changes in artefact types and extractive technologies (including the beginnings of line fishing and backed artefacts), on the other, suggested to Hughes and Lampert that the changes were systemic, involving increases in intensities of use of individual sites and of the regional landscape in the Sydney Basin more generally. Their conclusions were supported by evidence for increased slope instability and by increases in numbers of charcoal particles in sediments from southern New South Wales valley systems, indicating an amplification of firing practices of the broader landscape around 4000 years BP (Hughes and Sullivan 1981). To Hughes and Lampert (1982), the implications were continued rises in absolute populations and intensities of regional land use during the second half of the Holocene.

However, these conclusions were questioned by Peter Hiscock (1989) who noted that while stone artefact and sedimentation rates could be shown to increase during the mid-Holocene, this was not the case for the last 2000–1500 years BP, when rates decreased at some sites. More recently, excavations by Phil Boot (1996a, 1996b) at nine rockshelters (the earliest dating back to 19,000 years BP) and three open stone artefact scatters have revealed broadly similar long-term trends to those earlier produced by Hughes and Lampert, with the last 2000 years producing mixed results: some sites evidence increased artefact deposition and sedimentation rates, others decreases. Thus, while increasing levels of regional land use and population growth may be implicated for the mid-Holocene, the situation for the late Holocene is not clear, some sites indicating a likely decrease in intensities of land use and others an increase. The overall indication is of major increases in levels of regional land use, settlement and population growth after 4000 years BP, followed by stabilizing long-term, or more fluctuating (and possibly decreasing) or geographically restructured short-term trends during the last 2000 years.

Western Victoria

Thirteen rockshelters and caves have been excavated in southeastern South Australia and western Victoria. A series of mounds, middens and a drainage ditch have also been excavated and radiocarbon dated. Despite this considerable attention, long cultural sequences have not easily been found. One of these is Bridgewater South Cave (Figure 7.19), an 11,400 years BP site containing generalized sediments with low-density cultural deposits in its lowest levels followed by finely stratified cultural deposits after 500 years BP. Bridgewater South Cave also witnessed a rise in the range of artefact types around 500 years BP, including a significant increase in proportions of modified flakes (tools). Increases in amounts of charcoal and faunal Minimum Numbers of Individuals also took place, along with a rise in stone artefact deposition rates. Additionally, a broadening of the resource base may be indicated by a more intensive use of marine resources after 500 years BP, although, as Harry Lourandos (1983, p. 84) has noted, this may 'merely document the site's proximity to the sea'. He concluded that the late Holocene witnessed a growth of human occupation at Bridgewater South Cave, noting that this was matched by a similar, although not exactly contemporaneous, late Holocene intensification in occupational intensities at the Seal Point midden site

Figure 7.19 Bridgewater South Cave (*Source*: courtesy of Aboriginal Affairs Victoria)

nearby. As these changes were associated with major increases in the numbers of rockshelters, earth mounds (Figure 7.20) and other site types used after 4000–2000 years BP, as well as with increases in intensities of individual site usage, Lourandos (1983) suggested that these patterns may signal the regional establishment of systematic, semi-sedentary occupation after 4000–2000 years BP. In formulating this conclusion, he noted that:

> while sites have been established since the terminal Pleistocene, or from around 12,500 years ago, most of these date from the last 4000–3000 years. During this final period sites appear to have been *increasingly* established, with the last 2000 years experiencing the most intensive phase. As well, an examination of the nature of these sites indicates that the most complex sites (in terms of size and economic aspects) were established late in the sequence. For example, all the earth mounds are less than 2500 years old together

with some of the larger shell middens and open sites. (ibid., p. 86).

The late Holocene antiquity of earth mounds in northern and western Victoria has been commented upon by numerous researchers, including Peter Coutts (e.g. 1982), Elizabeth Williams (1988), and Bill Downey and David Frankel (1992). Similarly, excavations by Harry Lourandos (1980a, 1980b) at Toolondo, where specialized water management networks were constructed to divert water flow from swamp systems to a maze of fish-trapping installations, revealed their probable late Holocene antiquity, although their dating is problematic and relies on a single radiocarbon date obtained from the base of silted ditches forming part of the Toolondo system – the radiocarbon determination is therefore likely a terminal date. Lourandos (1980a) concluded that the drainage of swampy ground through the construction of large artificial channels

Figure 7.20   Earth mound, southwestern Victoria (*Source*: courtesy of Aboriginal Affairs Victoria)

heralds a late Holocene amplification of a specialized fishing strategy that took advantage of the seasonal migratory runs of eels (*Anguilla australis occidentalis*). A late Holocene antiquity for the beginnings of systematic swamp management and occupation is supported by the ages of nearby earth mounds, known from nineteenth-century ethnographic records to have enabled the penetration of Aboriginal settlements into the wetlands (Coutts 1982; Williams 1988) (Figure 7.21).

These observations suggest that the changes which took place during the last 4000–2000 years BP in western Victoria may have been wide-ranging and multi-faceted. Such cultural changes were argued by Lourandos (1980a, 1983) to have involved increases in occupational intensities of individual sites and of the broader region, the commencement of artificial manipulation of resource zones (beyond firing), and an expansion of ecological niches. These changes, he suggested, signified an increase in degrees of energy harnessing during the late Holocene. It is this process of mid to late Holocene change that Lourandos (1983) has coined an 'intensi-

fication' of socio-economic practice for the later stages of Australian prehistory (see Bird and Frankel 1991; Frankel 1991 and Godfrey 1989 for critical comments).

Lourandos concluded that five major cultural transformations took place in western Victoria during the late Holocene:

1 An increase in the level of use of individual sites (measured by increased deposition rates of cultural materials within individual sites).
2 A rise in the establishment rate of new sites (measured by increases in the number of sites occupied within the region).
3 An intensification in the use of marginal environments (measured by the relatively recent beginnings for the systematic use of some environments, such as wetlands).
4 A diversification and increase in the complexity of resource management strategies (evident in the recent development of extensive water management installations targeting high fish yields).
5 The beginnings of intensive and extensive communication networks (including formalized trade relations), linking various parts of

Figure 7.21 Eel-fishing system, southwestern Victoria (*Source*: courtesy of Aboriginal Affairs Victoria)

mainland Australia into a complex set of alliance networks mediated via ritual and ceremonial activity.

Discussion

Australian archaeologists have interpreted the above long-term regional trends in a number of ways. Not all agree that they indicate cultural trends, some being of the view that they are no more than taphonomic illusions. I critically evaluate below these various interpretations.

Taphonomic biases

The most radical explanation for the apparent cultural changes were forwarded by Roger Cribb (1986) when he suggested that they may be no more than a taphonomic illusion. Noting that some landscapes are more apt to preserve cultural deposits than others, Cribb developed the concept of *archaeological catchments*, suggesting that archaeological materials located in some parts of Australia, and from certain periods of time, are more apt to have been preserved (and recovered by archaeologists) than those from other times and places. He argues that through the vagaries of time, compounded by the particularly dynamic nature of Pleistocene and early Holocene sedimentation, early archaeological deposits are unlikely to have survived or to be easily recoverable. Late Holocene cultural remains are therefore likely to have been over-represented archaeologically.

However, this explanation does not accommodate many of the apparent archaeological trends. While Cribb's conclusions may be valid for some periods of time, for some kinds of archaeological materials (e.g. stone arrangements; organic remains in sandy soils) and for some sites or regions, they do not explain the general trends observed across much of Australia. In many sites (e.g. Ngarrabullgan Cave, Nonda Rock, Hay Cave, Walkunder Arch Cave, to name but a few), *in situ* sediments spanning the late Pleistocene to the late Holocene have been recovered. In these sites the general archaeological trends presented above are much evident, despite the presence of pre-4000-year-old deposits. It cannot be said that relatively high deposition rates of cultural

materials after the mid-Holocene are a function of the degradation of earlier organic materials, for similarly high late Holocene and low earlier rates are also apparent in the durable stone artefacts. In some sites (in particular the limestone caves), cultural bone remains are also common in mid to late Holocene contexts, but less common in earlier deposits, despite the presence of non-cultural bone such as owl deposits and natural rodent deaths before the mid-Holocene. Furthermore, what appear generally to have changed during the mid to late Holocene are not only quantitative increases in deposition rates and in rates of site establishment and occupation, but also qualitative changes in stone artefact types and technologies, rock-art conventions, and site types. These cannot easily be dismissed as taphonomic illusions. The case against the taphonomic argument is well summed up by Phil Hughes and Ron Lampert (1982, p. 24) who note that 'there is no evidence for any environmental change that would have so greatly altered the decay rate of sites'. Hughes and Lampert were referring specifically to the south coast of New South Wales, but their observations have broader application.

Exponential trends

Caroline Bird and David Frankel (1991) also suggested that there were no sustained increases in intensities of site and regional land use during the late Holocene. Basing their arguments on the archaeological record of western Victoria and southeastern South Australia, they note that there are no systematic rises in numbers of occupied sites during the late Holocene. However, this conclusion does not match David Frankel's own observation that 'the lack of occupation in rockshelters between 7000 and 5000 years ago [i.e. increasing deposition rates of cultural materials after 5000 years ago] may ... be real', and that 'certainly the current evidence is unequivocal. Mounds are a recent phenomenon' (Frankel 1991, p. 146). Furthermore, I would suggest that occupational trends are likely to have been under-represented by Caroline Bird and David Frankel, who plotted on a curve the number of radiocarbon dates obtained from excavated sites in western Victoria and southeastern South Australia, rather than the number of sites known to have been occupied. As 'more than half the sites have only one date, three-quarters have one or two' (Frankel 1991, p. 146), and as most, if not all, of the archaeologists working in the region have radiocarbon-dated the earliest levels of occupation at the expense of more recent strata, the distribution of dates through time in this region will tend to under-emphasize later periods of occupation. This bias towards relatively early times is compounded by a tendency for archaeologists to excavate seemingly older sites, or sites with relatively long sequences. Small rockshelters showing little evidence of deep sediments greatly outnumber large or potentially deep sites in most parts of Australia, but are rarely excavated. When tested, they often prove to be recent in age and remain unpublished. Consequently, older deposits are over-emphasized in Bird and Frankel's (1991) quantifications. Despite this, significant increases in occupational intensities are clearly apparent for a number of site types not only in western Victoria and southeastern South Australia, but across mainland Australia in general. This trend is well demonstrated in Bird and Frankel's (1991) own published graphs.

Regional and site-specific changes: the problem of scale, time and temporal scaling

It is difficult to make general statements on the basis of a handful of sites. This problem was recognized by David Frankel (1991), who noted that the late Holocene changes apparent for western Victoria–southeastern South Australia may be site-specific rather than regional in character. The late Holocene increases may thus simply be a function of sampling, rather than a true reflection of widespread cultural or demographic change. However, the repeatedness of the trends across sites and regions does not sit well with this explanation.

The problem of temporal scale may also unduly skew the archaeological trends. Philip Gingerich (1983) has suggested that rates of change may be critically patterned by the temporal scales employed. Rates 'measured over different intervals of . . . time have been used', but 'perceived evolutionary rates are a function of the time interval over which they are measured, and temporal scaling is required before rates measured over different intervals of . . . time can be compared' (ibid., p. 159). This problem is relevant to the current concerns in that mid to late Holocene trends are largely calculated from radiocarbon dates obtained at intervals of a few hundred to two or three thousand years, whereas deposition rates for materials pre-dating the mid Holocene are often based on considerably longer time intervals, sometimes calculated from radiocarbon dates separated by more than 10,000 years. The routine calculation of diachronic trends by dividing observed quantifications by elapsed time does not remove the effect of time on the resulting rates, as rates are not independent of measurement interval. 'The greater the time separating similar initial and final states, the slower the inferred rate of change' (ibid., p. 159). That is, the greater the time interval in which a given change is investigated, the smaller the degree of change will be. This is partly because

> the shorter the interval of measurement, the more likely one is to observe high rates. The longer the interval, the more stasis and evolutionary reversals are likely to be averaged in the result. This effect . . . systematically damps the values of rates calculated over longer and longer intervals. (ibid., p. 160)

Peaks in deposition rates of cultural materials tend to have less influence in long time scales, rendering inappropriate comparisons of change in relatively recent prehistory (where time intervals of less than 3000 years are used to calculate deposition rates) with changes during earlier times (where time intervals of more than 10,000 years have sometimes been used).

Although the effects of time and temporal scaling cannot be ignored, the general archaeological trends presented in this book cannot be reduced to this phenomenon for two major reasons. First, the apparent diachronic trends involve significant changes in qualitative as well as in quantitative data. Changes in such things as artistic conventions or site types are not obtained by transforming quantitative data into calculated rates, but pertain to specific points in time. Hence mounds in northern Australia and in southeastern South Australia–western Victoria first appear in the archaeological record at various points in time, but always after 3000–2000 years BP. Second, the apparent mid to late Holocene increases in sedimentation and stone artefact deposition rates remain when they are calculated over similar intervals of time (e.g. at Ngarrabullgan

Cave, Nonda Rock and Tunnell Shelter). Significant archaeological transformations are apparent during the mid to late Holocene period independently of differences in the time intervals employed to investigate cultural trends.

Population increases

Other authors have accepted, and elaborated upon, the observation that the mid to late Holocene archaeological record is both quantitatively and qualitatively different from that of earlier times, but have differed in their explanatory frameworks (e.g. Beaton 1983, 1985; Lourandos 1983). Harry Lourandos's (1983, 1984) and John Beaton's (1983, 1990) views in particular are worth further discussion, for it is the Lourandos–Beaton debate that has been the most influential in explaining diachronic trends in Australian pre-History (Beaton 1983, 1985; Lourandos 1983, 1985).

John Beaton's position has changed through the course of the 1980s, beginning with an early conviction that the observed increases in deposition rates of cultural materials and the beginnings of toxic plant use after 4300 years BP in the Central Queensland Highlands imply alterations in social practice (Beaton 1977). Later, he argued that social explanations were not sufficient to explain the archaeological changes, suggesting instead that population increases, and population increases alone, were implicated (Beaton 1983). Beaton suggested that, given a founder population of limited size, a specific generation time, a constant survivorship rate, and regulated budding of social (and reproductive) groups, past Aboriginal population sizes increased following inherent biological rules. He argued that population expansions predetermined by intrinsic biological forces are sufficient to explain demographic patterns in human populations, and that such forces are only subject to environmental alterations (Beaton 1990). No acknowledgement is made that internal, socio-cultural practices act to interact with biological forces and serve to regulate population dynamics.

Beaton bases his model of past populations in Aboriginal Australia on the assumption that population sizes are dependent on intrinsic growth rates incapable of variation beyond the effects of external, environmental influences (Beaton 1990), suggesting that such a process

was outlined by Thomas Robert Malthus (1982 [1798]) towards the end of the eighteenth century. This is itself erroneous, for Malthus clearly acknowledged the role of social relations, power structures and ideological systems in regulating subsistence behaviour and population sizes ('the checks of vice', 'of misery' and 'of moral restraint' introduced in the first edition and further developed in the second edition of his *Essay on the Principle of Population*). Malthus well recognized the importance of social conditions to population dynamics; indeed, it is a centre-piece of his work. For example, he writes that 'in no state that we have known, has the power of population been left to exert itself with perfect freedom'; and 'left to exert itself unchecked, the increase of the human species would evidently be much greater than any increase that has been hitherto known' (Malthus 1982 [1798], p. 73).

Beaton's (1983) model of population dynamics in Aboriginal Australia as being a direct result of biological laws of incremental increase can be questioned on the grounds that:

1 The relationship between human population sizes and theoretical levels of 'maximum carrying capacity' has rarely, if ever, been adequately addressed (e.g. Anderson 1978), and the notion of simple biological forces regulating human populations in interaction with extrinsic environmental forces is unrealistic.

2 The distinction between a society's and an individual's needs and problems is fundamental to, but not considered in, Beaton's model. While an individual's needs may be fulfilled within the framework of an established order, if a society develops a need, the social order itself will be modified (Cowgill 1975).

3 The concepts of 'need' or 'stress' are distinct from that of economic demand. Social and individual 'stress' do not automatically create effective demand. Cowgill (1975) writes: 'Even if human population growth *were* difficult to regulate, it would not follow at all that stress is caused by overpopulation . . . [or that it] would be an effective incentive for responses of a developmental kind'.

4 Beaton's reliance on (1) a single, defined founder population; (2) a stable generation time; (3) a constant survivorship rate; (4)

regular budding of new residential groups; and (5) intrinsic growth rates to formulate his model of population dynamics for the duration of the Aboriginal past in Australia is unacceptable. As with Joseph Birdsell's (1957) prior employment of similar assumptions, none of these can be either practically or theoretically demonstrated. Irregularities (including punctuations) in social and economic practices are critical to population dynamics, including changes in population composition (e.g. age and sex structures, family and household sizes, regional structures), marriage and reproductive rules, and residence rules.

5 The archaeological record first and foremost indicates patterns of change and stability in human actions, not in population sizes. Changes in the archaeological record document changes in the things that people did (assuming adequate treatment of post-depositional factors). Population increases may (and indeed are likely to) be implicated by the mid to late Holocene archaeological records of much of Australia, but first and foremost changes in the material record imply quantitative and/or qualitative changes in decisions made and in their execution. They imply changes in the decision-making contexts in which social actions were undertaken.

Intensification

The popular use of the term 'intensification' in Australian pre-History dates to the 1980s. Although it was first employed by Sylvia Hallam (1977), John Beaton (1977) and Phil Hughes and Ron Lampert (1982) to loosely describe changes observed at a local scale, it was not until Harry Lourandos's work that it gained widespread attention. Lourandos interpreted the late Holocene archaeological changes in western Victoria and beyond as indicative of intensified susbsistence practices, including likely changes in production or productivity. Unlike Lewis Binford (1968, 1983), who had earlier argued that the general process of intensification involved an external (environmental) stimulus-response relationship directed towards solving subsistence needs, Lourandos followed Barbara Bender's suggestion that

Intensification may simply be about improving accessiblity, reducing travel time, or making returns more predictable. It need not be about food resources in particular, but about access to plants used for poison or for medicinal purposes or for cordage, or to animals for ritual, etc. (Bender 1979, pp. 205–6)

In this sense both Lourandos and Bender deviated from more traditional definitions of intensification that were directly concerned with the productive efficiency of food items (e.g. Binford 1968, 1983; Boserup 1965; Brookfield 1972; Smith and Young 1972).

Lourandos formulated his intensification model on two observations. The first was informed by an ethnographic record that documented large-scale ceremonial networks in western Victoria, including periodic congregations of many hundreds of people from allied land-owning and land-using groups. Such congregations required the use of large-scale energy harnessing technologies, such as the drainage (fishing) systems known from the site of Toolondo.

The second component of Lourandos's model was based on the archaeological observation that during the late Holocene many changes in land use, foraging strategies and settlement systems took place across western Victoria. He concluded that since there was no evidence for intensive fishing installations (and associated mounds) before this time, the social systems observed when Europeans first arrived were unlikely to have had any great antiquity. To Lourandos, intensification thus implied an increasing structural complexity of social strategies and increases in production and productivity. Large-scale gatherings created 'demands upon the economy and thus production' (Lourandos 1983, p. 81), and major increases in intensities of regional land use after 2000 years BP were taken to imply increased levels of production and productivity, socio-demographic alterations and probably also absolute population rises. Lourandos (ibid., pp. 87–8) concluded that:

1 Increasing occupation occurred throughout the late Holocene of what can be viewed as marginal resource zones (wetlands, peripheral rainforest areas and highlands).

2 Increasing complexity of site forms and their economies took place during this period of time. For example, base camps featuring a

wide range of semi-sedentary resource strategies were established in a number of areas – earth mounds in wetlands, open inland sites and coastal shell middens.

3 A trend could be detected from short-duration, perhaps seasonal usage of sites to long-duration, even annual usage. Individual sites were said to have been more intensively occupied through time.

4 These trends were in some ways associated with ceremonial events.

5 The complex semi-sedentary and resource-intensive settlement patterns observed from ethnohistorical sources from this region (Lourandos 1977, 1980a, 1980b) had all the above features and could be demonstrated archaeologically. Incentives for cultural change were seen to arise 'out of the nature of the social relations' (Lourandos 1983, p. 91), and were explained in structural terms: 'social relations primarily give rise to other cultural changes, such as economics, and thus must in some way precede them' (Lourandos 1984, p. 32). It was argued that these changes acted to amplify information exchange networks (e.g. congregations; ceremonial and large-scale, labour-intensive productive networks) and to increase productivity through increases in the complexity of forces of production (e.g. the appearance of complex eel-trapping systems in western Victoria) during the mid to late Holocene. For Lourandos, 'competitive relations between groups may have led to increases in production (including surpluses), and also to increases in environmental productivity' (1991, p. 149), thus generating a dynamic environment by which social, economic, ceremonial and political practices could further intensify. Consequently, the intensive and widespread (but often exclusive) alliance and ceremonial networks observed during ethnohistoric times were unlikely to have occurred before the mid to late Holocene.

Environmental causation and the onset of ENSO activity

Mike Rowland (1999; see Rowland 1983 for earlier views) has suggested that the widespread and multifarious cultural changes observed across Australia during the late Holocene indeed took place, but that they were ultimately caused by environmental changes stimulated by the onset of intensive El Niño-Southern Oscillation (ENSO) activity around 3500 years BP. The El Niño phenomenon brings periodic drought, at times of severe nature. ENSO is also associated with periodic floods, known as La Niña events. The severity of these events, and their relatively common frequency (each occurring in Australia on average once every three to seven years) likely impacted – as it continues to today – on social and cultural behaviour. They are particularly likely to have been critical to human behaviour in those regions of the arid zone where water availability was by then already a significant limiting factor. Although there are problems with Rowland's view that the onset of intensive ENSO activity during the late Holocene set in motion the major archaeological shifts documented above – the most critical of which are that (1) in many parts of Australia, increased ENSO activity has not been shown to have critically affected water or other resource availability at relevant scales; (2) we do not yet know with any great conviction whether or not heightened levels of ENSO activity took place at the same time or soon before the major archaeological changes (despite various lines of argument); and (3) even if contemporaneous, the causal links between environmental and cultural fluctuations are assumed rather than demonstrated – the arguments presented in this book are not so much concerned with the ultimate causes of cultural change as with the fact that major social and demographic shifts occurred during the mid to late Holocene. Whether or not ENSO activity is responsible, it remains that we cannot simply transfer recent ethnographic details of cultural practice onto the more distant Aboriginal past. It is therefore difficult at this stage to determine the role of ENSO fluctuations on long-term cultural change in Australia.

Increases, decreases and structural changes

Caroline Bird and David Frankel (1991) disagreed with Lourandos's interpretations of the apparent changes in the late Holocene record as reflecting increases in the size of settlements, duration of habitation within sites (increased sedentism) (but see Walters 1989), and a broadening and intensification of exchange networks. Bird and Frankel noted that the documented changes may signify changes in seasonality and structure of site use, and therefore changes in settlement systems, rather than increases in intensities of site use. As investigations of western Victorian prehistory have not furnished the data necessary to research questions relating to the *structure* of Aboriginal life in the past (including inter-regional networks), it has been argued that such issues could not be addressed from the archaeological record available.

Structural changes are not independent from the problem of *timing*. By this I refer to the apparent non-conformity in the timing of the mid to late Holocene changes documented from various parts of eastern Australia. Peter Hiscock (1986) has highlighted this problem when he noted that in the Hunter River Valley, the Sydney Basin, and parts of the Northern Territory, the most recent period (dated to the last *c.* 900 years in the Hunter River Valley) witnessed a *decrease* in stone artefact deposition rates.

In attempting to explain differences in the timing of changes between regions, Josephine Flood *et al.* argued that inter-regional, demographic networks may have changed, concluding that a 'late Holocene de-intensification of the type documented by Hiscock involved an *increased* use of marginal environments' during the late Holocene (Flood *et al.* 1987, p. 23), accompanied by a decrease in the use of former heartlands. A reorganization of people across the landscape may have taken place.

Ian Walters (1989) explored the above proposition by investigating occupational trends and the antiquity of complex fishery installations along the coastal and subcoastal zones of southeast Queensland. He concluded that the 'occupation of the marginal coastal Wallum of southeast Queensland intensified after mid Holocene times, and the marine fishery developed at an exponential rate after 2000 BP' (ibid., p. 221), but

the evidence . . . presented here does not fit the model proposed by Flood *et al.* (1987) for increased use of marginal environments and decreased use of favourable environments in late Holocene times. Though the present study supports their idea (and that of Hiscock 1986; Morwood 1986) of reorganization of people in the landscape, it finds no de-

intensification of a heartland accompanying the intensified use of a formerly marginal environment. It suggests that an intensified use of a marginal environment accompanied a steady if not intensified use of the formerly more favourable hinterland. (ibid., p. 222)

Conclusion

The Dreaming of Aboriginal Australia emerged in its ethnographically recognizable forms under historically dynamic social conditions, the nature of which can best be accessed through the archaeological record. But such traces can never reveal the full story, the full richness of the social states we are ultimately interested in, for they are mere footprints of complex social and cultural phenomena constituted of interacting sensual beings. Nevertheless, hints of past social, economic, territorial and demographic dynamics may be gained. Identifying the general shape of such dynamics, as socio-historical contexts for the emergence of the ethnographically known Dreaming, has been the aim of this chapter. More detailed probing of specific themes will be made in later chapters.

Most of the research projects undertaken in Australia have concentrated on the excavation and analysis of deposits that appeared to contain old or deep sequences prior to excavation. The Cape York case is a good example: John Beaton's work in Princess Charlotte Bay and the Flinders Island group involved excavations at the three rockshelters showing the greatest promise for deep sequences. His focus on the large, mounded middens commonly found on the chenier plains was geared to an investigation of their origins. In a similar vein, Josephine Flood's excavations in the Koolburra Plateau concentrated on the excavation of the deepest known archaeological deposits, while Andrée Rosenfeld's work at the Early Man Rockshelter followed from Percy Trezise's earlier conviction that this site was likely to be amongst the oldest known in the Laura region (hence the site's name).[11] Similarly, Mike Morwood's excavations at Laura entailed an investigation of what appeared to be the oldest sites, as informed by various archaeological clues such as the presence of ancient rock-art and potentially deep deposits, although his research aims were broad and also included a concern for the more recent past. At Yam Camp and Sandy Creek, patinated engravings reminiscent of those dated to pre-13,000 years BP at Early Man encouraged Morwood to excavate, with the promise of equally ancient deposits.

John Campbell's excavations at Walkunder Arch Cave (Figure 7.22) were part of a broader research project entitled 'North Queensland prehistory: a search for late Pleistocene and Holocene sequences' (Campbell 1984). Like most of the other projects undertaken in southeast Cape York, Campbell's project was not concerned specifically with recent sites, but with rockshelters possessing relatively deep sequences allowing the investigation of temporal trends over long periods of time. Potentially old sites were thus targeted. My own fieldwork in the Mitchell-Palmer and Chillagoe regions also focused on relatively deep sequences, so as to allow investigations of long temporal trends. Places such as Hearth Cave and Fern Cave were chosen for excavation to test the notion that patinated peckings of forms similar to those found at Early Man Rockshelter were likely to be of Pleistocene age across the Cape (see Chapter 9). Consequently, few of the research projects undertaken in southeast Cape York can be said to have set out to focus on relatively recent sites.[12] This is the case also for most of the other regions considered in this chapter. Rockshelters that appeared to be recent prior to excavation – such as sites possessing shallow sediments – have been almost entirely ignored, skewing results towards older deposits.

The focus on relatively early sites and/or deep deposits is a highly significant, although often ignored, aspect of Australian archaeological practice. Yet, in spite of this, *all* regional studies have revealed major increases in deposition rates of cultural materials and general sedimentation rates during the mid to late Holocene. From this alone, it can be concluded that major socio-demographic transformations were taking place during the same period of time that saw the emergence of the ethnographically known Dreaming practices investigated in this book.

The mid to late Holocene was thus a period of dynamism across mainland Australia. Documented changes included (1) significant increases in deposition rates of stone artefacts and food refuse; (2) the advent of new tool types (including fish hooks and grinding stones) and site types (e.g. shell and earth mounds); (3) the use of new plant foods (including systematic seed grinding in the arid zone and techniques for detoxifying poisonous plants in central and north Queensland); (4) demographic expansions onto previously unused offshore islands; and (5) probably also the beginnings of complex installations to increase productive yields in some parts of Australia (e.g. inland river eel-traps in western Victoria; coastal fish traps in southeast Queensland). In some areas (e.g. the Sydney Basin), there is evidence for significant increases in the frequency or intensity of firing of the landscape. Together, these innovations and amplifications of existing cultural practices imply an expansion of settlement into previously unused or little-used habitats, including (1) a more intensive use of marginal environments; (2) an 'intensification' of landscape management practices (e.g. burning); and (3) a broadening of resource bases during the mid to late Holocene. These changes imply population growth and geographical expansions, increases in intensities of site and regional land use, and increased levels of regional demographic packing across much of Australia.

Second, change was not uniform across the landscape, nor was it contemporaneous in all cultural dimensions. This begs the question of whether or not a single, systemic re-modelling of socio-economic networks is implicated, or whether the various, largely regional changes were in some cases independent of each other.

And third, an important aspect of change appears to have been a continuing increase in the use of some regional landscapes (e.g. western Victoria), and a possible decrease or stabilization in others (e.g. Central Queensland Highlands) during the last 2000 years or so. These geographically varied socio-demographic trends imply shifting demographic structures and settlement systems through time.

Two major questions remain largely unexplored, however, although they are embedded within many of the above observations and interpretations. The first of these relates to the role of staple foods in cultural change in late Holocene Australia, for population increases imply increases in food yields and likely also associated shifts in production systems. Such resource, technological and socio-structural changes need apply to the short term while

Figure 7.22 Walkunder Arch Cave, southeast Cape York Peninsula, excavation in progress, 1982

being effective over the long term if population trends are to be of long standing. We have already seen that technological innovations enabled the consumption of toxic plants late in Australia's pre-History. But high yielding toxic plants and leaching procedures were never available in all parts of Australia. Nor were they readily available year-round. So how were major population increases supported in regions devoid of such potential plant foods, and is there evidence for changing diet breadths coincident with other cultural changes in these regions? This issue forms the subject of the next chapter.

The second question concerns whether the major mid to late Holocene changes concern the beginnings of new settlement strategies set within established, regional social networks, or whether we are seeing a major restructuring of such networks through time. Did people just do more or less of the same within any given region, and begin to create new types of sites and collect and hunt more food during the mid and late Holocene, or was there a geographical and social reorganization of life, involving shifts in patterns of intra-regional and inter-regional relations? In short, did the documented changes in settlement systems also involve changes in territorial behaviour and in the structure of territorial networks, establishing novel socio-organizational and territorial contexts for the emergence of the Dreaming as we know it from ethnographic times? These questions form the subject of Chapter 9.

In this chapter I have attempted to review major archaeological changes that have been reported from selected parts of mainland Australia so as to situate the ethnographically known Dreaming's emergence in broader archaeological context. Similar archaeological trends have been written about by others for other parts of the continent, and I have not reviewed these here (cf. Flood 1995; Lourandos 1997; Mulvaney and Kamminga 1999). What I have tried to point out, rather than undertake detailed analyses of each regional data set, is that the mid to late Holocene witnessed widespread cultural transformations throughout much, if not all, of the Australian mainland and its offshore islands. This was a period of largely unprecedented rates of change, involving the appearance of new artefact forms, new manufacturing technologies, changing resource management strategies,

food processing procedures and settlement-subsistence systems. These alterations were not haphazard, but involved increases in the numbers of sites occupied and in deposition rates of cultural materials and sediments within sites, as well as a broadening of site types. Together, these innovations suggest a general, approximately three-fold increase in intensities of site and regional land use during the mid to late Holocene; a growth in the use of regional landscapes through time. This, then, is the major long-term cultural context that accompanied the emergence of ethnographically documented Dreaming practices maybe 3000 years BP, but largely during the last 1400 years.

Notes

1. This chapter does not review the archaeological records of the western half of the continent, nor those of the arid core. The general Holocene trends in those regions are, however, similar to those discussed here. See Chapter 8 for a discussion of arid and semi-arid Australia.

2. 'Greater Australia' is the term generally used for the lands exposed above sea levels during the last glacial maximum. It typically covers the present Australian mainland, its offshore islands (including Tasmania), New Guinea, and those parts of the Sahul shelf which became inundated by rising seas during postglacial times.

3. Some amateur explorations had taken place at Sandy Creek 1 and Platform Gallery during the 1960s (Morwood and Trezise 1989; Rosenfeld et al. 1981). However, professional excavations began in the early 1960s when Richard Wright (1971) excavated rockshelters near Laura, Chillagoe and Bare Hill (Davies Creek). Seven major research projects have since been initiated or completed, beginning with Andrée Rosenfeld's work at Laura in the mid-1970s, John Beaton's at Princess Charlotte Bay and the Flinders Islands in the late 1970s and early 1980s, John Campbell and Mireille Mardaga-Campbell's in the Chillagoe region in the early 1980s, Mike Morwood's at Laura between 1989 and 1994, and Harry Lourandos's and my own at Chillagoe, Ngarrabullgan and the Mitchell-Palmer region from the early 1980s onwards (Beaton 1985; Campbell 1982; Campbell and Mardaga-Campbell 1993; David and Chant 1995; Mardaga-Campbell 1986; Morwood 1995a,

1995b; Morwood and Dagg 1995; Morwood and Hobbs 1995; Morwood and Jung 1995; Morwood and L'Oste-Brown 1995a, 1995b, 1995c; Morwood *et al.* 1995; Rosenfeld *et al.* 1981).

Andrée Rosenfeld (Rosenfeld *et al.* 1981) excavated the Early Man Rockshelter near Laura in the mid-1970s.

John Campbell (1982; Campbell and Mardaga-Campbell 1993) began his on-going excavations at Walkunder Arch Cave, and Mireille Mardaga-Campbell (1986) her excavations at Pillar Cave (both near Chillagoe) in the early and mid-1980s, respectively.

Mike Morwood (1995a, 1995b; Morwood and Dagg 1995; Morwood and Hobbs 1995; Morwood and Jung 1995; Morwood and L'Oste-Brown 1995a, 1995b, 1995c; Morwood *et al.* 1995) excavated at Hann River 1, Sandy Creek 1 and 2, Magnificent Gallery, Giant Horse, Red Horse, Red Bluff 1, Yam Camp and Mushroom Rock from 1989 to 1994 (these sites are all in the Laura sandstones).

I began excavating at Fern Cave and Echidna's Rest (near Chillagoe) between 1985 and 1989 (David and Chant 1995); at Mitchell River Cave, Hearth Cave and Mordor Cave in the Mitchell-Palmer limestone belt between 1989 and 1991; and in a large series of sites at Ngarrabullgan after 1991. With Harry Lourandos, I began excavating at Hay Cave and Pete's Chase, in the Mitchell-Palmer limestone belt, in 1996. The data presented in this chapter are the product of these studies.

4. It was once thought that the earliest cultural levels at Ngarrabullgan Cave dated to > 37,170 years BP (David 1993). However, this conventional radiocarbon determination (originally run on a very small charcoal sample) has never been reproduced, despite dozens of subsequent AMS dates on single pieces of charcoal from the same and adjacent strata, and the employment of Bird *et al.*'s (1999) ABOX preparation technique (devised to eliminate or minimize the effects of contamination on radiocarbon results).

5. Only those sites whose basal occupation is known can be used, so as to ensure that apparent occupational trends are not affected by the absence of basal dates.

6. Each of these dates relates to cultural activity, and only excavated dates are here considered (i.e., the surface radiocarbon dates from Ngarrabullgan Cave, reported in Chapter 3, are not included). See David and Lourandos (1997, 1998) for discussions on how these dates were assessed.

7. New strategies to have been investigated include shifting raw material selection, the onset of heat treatment, changes in platform preparation, flaking precision and the incidence of longitudinal or transverse snapping, and the incidence of retouch (Holden 1999; Lamb 1993; L'Oste-Brown 1992). After accounting for technological change, late Holocene deposition rates have remained significantly higher than for earlier times.

8. Mike Morwood and Percy Trezise (1989) have claimed that edge-ground axes occurred during the Pleistocene across northern Australia, perhaps more than 30,000 years ago, but the evidence for this is poor. Nevertheless, edge-ground axes have been repeatedly reported in Pleistocene contexts (Morwood and Hobbs 1995; Rosenfeld *et al.* 1981).

9. Nevertheless, it is important to remember that Beaton (1977) did not excavate any site spanning both a pre-cycad and a cycad period, making it difficult to determine the precise antiquity of initial cycad use in the region.

10. No cycad remains were recovered from Mulvaney's (Mulvaney and Joyce 1965) or Morwood's (1979, 1981) excavations.

11. This was later confirmed when radiocarbon dates were obtained.

12. The singular exception is the Ngarrabullgan project reported in Chapter 3, where all rockshelters with surface cultural evidence and sediments were excavated.

8 Seeds of Change

The nineteenth-century Galician novelist Emilia de Pardo Bazán once wrote that 'Each historical epoque modifies the stove, and each group of people eats according to the dictates of their soul perhaps more so than with their stomach.'[1] Those words highlight the fact that the way we think about and use plants and animals is directly connected with the day-to-day workings of society.

Relationships between people and their surroundings (including plants and animals) in what have traditionally been termed hunter–gatherer and agricultural societies share fundamentally common properties. We have come to think of agricultural systems as mediated by processes of domestication or by processes of reproductive control ('culture'), while the plants used by hunter–gatherers are thought of as wild resources ('nature'). Qualitatively distinctive processes of people–plant–land interaction are called upon to explain the purported unique characteristics of hunter–gatherer and agricultural practices. But we can challenge such formulations, for in both so-called agricultural and hunter–gatherer systems the process of people–plant and people–land interaction is inherently domesticating, in that connections with plants are, in the words of Ross Hynes and Athol Chase (1982, p. 38), 'the outcome of strategies which include not only physical resource exploitation, but as well systems of locality and territoriality that recognize ties between particular individuals and groups and particular home environments'. Plants are experienced in life-spaces both ecological and psychological. It is not just plants or places that are domesticated as home environments; *people* are constructed as belonging, domestic subjects who dwell in a known world of socially ordered, and in this sense domesticated, objects. Through the movement of time, the experienced, domestic world is unceasingly re-domesticated.

Hynes and Chase (1982) coined the term *domus* to describe the geographically delimited space in which people operate on a daily basis. The *domus* consists of the hearth-centred life-space of daily activity; it is an area 'where selective environmental knowledge and resource strategies are applied at a specific time. We may consider each of these hearth-based parcels of knowledge, strategies and actions applied to each domus as a *domiculture*' (ibid., p. 38). The *domus* is smaller than Stanner's (1965b) range or estate – the total geographical landscapes used or owned, respectively, by Australian Aboriginal peoples in living out their lives. Like all residential spaces, the *domus* is socially constructed, social interaction resulting 'in a series of hearth-based areas of exploitation (domuses), each carrying with it a package of resource locations, restrictions upon open-ended exploitation (religious prohibitions, strategic planning for delayed harvesting, etc.), and localized technologies to fit particular domuses' (Chase 1989, p. 43).

All the plants within a *domus* are part of a

domicultural process in that they are socially engaged as embodied 'knowledge, strategies and actions'. Plants are meaningful in that they are known and have an origin. They are edible or not. They are 'wild' or they are managed. Plants are observed or ignored, burnt, uprooted, trampled, kicked, poisoned, cut, fertilized, manicured, picked, dried, hidden, sold, smoked, grafted or even painted. They may be worked or processed by women or by men, by children or by adults. Plants may be used for beads, thatching, fodder for horses, material for clothing, to communicate with the spirits, relax with strangers and friends, escape social pressures or as a source of human nutrition. Their value as a source of food relates to social context; plants are classified and positioned in a world of meaning and metaphor actively embedded in the everyday workings of society. In essence, relations between people and plants emerge in, and contribute to, social engagement and preunderstanding. A focus on Australian Aborigines as 'hunters and gatherers' reduces complex social strategies to narrow, economic categories, belittling in the process the complex relationships that exist between people and their meaningful, socially constructed worlds. It is thus inappropriate and inadequate to confine Australian Aboriginal gathering–hunting as an economic or social category 'ecologically passive in a supposedly "natural" landscape simply because they did not engage in a pattern of behaviour usually subsumed under the concept of agriculture' (Chase 1989, p. 42).

Material 'objects' such as food items are socially, ontologically and experientially ordered, and thus extensions of the subject self. The emergence of new food items or changing priorities in Aboriginal diets represents more than a change in nutritional habits. New foods signal a change in attitude towards a 'natural' world defined in culture. The advent of novel foods represents a new familiarity with the world, a changing relation of meaning between the agent subject and the meaningful object. New foods represent new relations of deference to how objects are to be engaged; they represent new social and cognitive schedules, redefining behavioural possibilities and expectations. In the words of Mihaly Csikszentmihalyi and Eugene Rochberg-Halton (1981, p. 17), items of food, like other objects, 'constitute an ecology of signs that reflects as well as *shapes* the pattern of the owner's self'.

A change in the material by definition signifies a change in one's place in the world, a change in relations between things. It represents a shift in social and personal identity, an identity that is by definition embedded in a world of relations between the subject and the object. As Tim Dant (1999, p. 14) has noted, material 'objects are physically formed within a culture but are also socially constructed in the ways that they are fitted into routine, everyday practices and ways of life. Culture is embedded and disembedded throughout the life of the object.' It is such a process of embeddedness that Ross Hynes and Athol Chase capture in the *domus* and in domiculture. Through the *domus*, as the space of everyday human action, relationships with things are operationalized and human identities take shape. In such relationships social engagement takes place, an engagement that locates people within the world, and that identifies the truth of the world.

These concerns have major implications for how we view patterns of change and continuity in Australian pre-History. In this chapter I explore some of these implications via a consideration of changing food habits and changing domicultural practices during the mid to late Holocene. I focus on the archaeology of one major food item and its related processing technology, specialized seed grinding. As already discussed in previous chapters, and in Chapter 4 in particular, Dreaming rituals in central Australia were fuelled during ethnographic times by the availability of plant staples – principally seed damper – enabling large gatherings of people to take place over extended periods of time. I now examine in greater detail the role of seed foods in social intercourse and the ideological systems in which such foods are based; that is, I examine the domicultural dimensions of seed use, the set of knowledge, strategies and actions that together transform raw seeds to an engaged source of staple foods depended upon by communities of people.

A number of questions direct this chapter. What is the place of seeds in maintaining ritual activity and in engendering and scheduling Aboriginal social life as we know it from the ethnographic record? How have seeds helped form the ethnographically known world of Aboriginal Australia? Can we date archaeologically the beginnings of systematic seed grinding in Australia, and if so, what are the implications of the emergence of the new dom-icultural habits for how Aboriginal people constructed their world in social and ecological relations?

Seeds as food

Dietary patterns have not remained unchanged during Australia's long occupation. Indeed, it is in plant foods that we find the greatest degree of dietary change in Australian pre-History. As will be apparent from the following discussions, these shifts have major implications for the long-term dynamics of social organization and human relations with place and its signification in Australia.

I limit my discussions in this chapter to the pre-History of seeds as staple food resources. Other plant products are also known to have served as important food staples in various parts of Australia, such as yams in the southeastern highlands (Bowdler 1981; Gott 1982) and in the southwest of Western Australia especially (Hallam 1975, 1989), toxic plants such as *Cycas media, Macrozamia moorei*, some species of *Pandanus* and various rainforest taxa in tropical and sub-tropical regions (Beaton 1982; Horsfall 1987), and during some seasons Bunya Pine in southeast Queensland (Sullivan 1977). I have already addressed the antiquity of use of some of these in the previous chapter, indicating a likely late Holocene origin for the specialized technologies associated with the processing of toxic plants in eastern Australia. Like these examples, grass seeds represent an abundant potential source of food.

Grass seeds as a source of food in ethnographic Australia

Once the appropriate technological knowledge was at hand, grass seeds opened a new world of possibilities with respect to relations between people and between people and land in Australia. However, I would argue that such technological knowledge is not what we should focus upon if we wish to explore the implications of seed grinding and the use of seeds as dietary staples for social landscapes. Rather, the emergence of seeds as a food resource signals the emergence of a new approach towards various plants as a resource

that fuels potentially large and long-lasting human congregations, plants as gendered objects whose knowledge, experience and engagement are intimately tied to preunderstanding. It is these relations that are ultimately at stake.

Grass seeds have a special place in the history of food in Australia. The small size of the grains means that they are only marginally viable in small quantities, but extremely important when high yields are found in fields. Grass seeds reproduce quickly, and as such represent an easily renewable and reliable food resource. And seed-bearing grasslands are abundant in many parts of arid to semi-arid central Australia, which can conveniently be defined as those parts of the continent that receive less than 250 mm and 500 mm mean annual rainfall, respectively.

During ethnographic times, plant seeds formed a critical food staple for all Aboriginal groups in central Australia. However, the range of species exploited varied from region to region. For the Great Sandy Desert of northwestern Australia, Scott Cane (1989) identified 42 species of edible seed-producing grasses, sedges, *Acacia, Eucalyptus*, succulents, herbs and shrubs. Each was exploited by local Aboriginal communities at various times of the year. Among the Martujarra of the Little Sandy Desert immediately to the south, 46 species of edible seeds have been recorded (Veth and Walsh 1988). Dick Kimber and Mike Smith (1987) similarly noted that seeds are a dominant source of plant food in all major ecological zones of Arrernte country of the Simpson Desert and surrounding lands, with 75 species known to be used. The greatest range is found in the spinifex sand plains, where 32 species are found, but seeds are also important along ephemeral watercourses, on spinifex hills, and in woodlands of various kinds (Kimber and Smith 1987, p. 227).[2] Jim O'Connell and Kristen Hawkes (1981) also found that 39 species of seed were used as a source of food by the Alyawarra of central Australia.

Seeds were predominantly an arid and semi-arid zone plant staple, although they were also used in more humid regions of Australia. In the wetter tropical landscapes of Arnhem Land to the north of central Australia, seeds and nuts were not as important, with only three species of seeds and five species of nuts identified by Jon Altman (1984) as used by the Gunwinggu. Of these, only two are taken in large numbers and ground into a paste from which bread is made, the seeds of the water lily *Nymphaea spp.*, and those of the bush rice *Oryza perennis*. Roots, tubers and corms (22 species) and fruit (39 species) of various kinds here generally take the place of seeds as the major plant staples (ibid.).[3]

The management and processing of plants for their seeds by various Aboriginal groups of central Australia are well known, the sequence of activities being more or less constant from place to place and from species to species (with some regional variations). Here I use Scott Cane's (1989) descriptions of Pintupi and Kukatja seed processing as a general guide so as to enter the social and experiential world of edible seed plants in central Australia.

Seeds from a wide range of plants – including grasses, sedges, bushes and trees – were eaten by the Pintupi and Kukatja. Among the sedges, *Fimbristylis oxystachya* was the most important, but two other species were also used. The most important grass was the native millet *Panicum australiense*, while fourteen other species, including *P. cymbiforme* and *Eragrostis tenellula*, were also highly regarded. Not every species grew in the same ecological zones, nor did they all grow at the same time of the year. Each of the 42 species of edible seeds required distinctive moisture conditions. Because rainfall was extremely variable from year to year, seasonality was not easily predicted. However, each of the various species could be found in seed more or less in sequence, and general seasonal patterns were mapped in social consciousness. During the wet season, typically around January, the seeds of the wild orange, *Capparis loranthifolia*, first became available. Then, as the land began to dry, three different species of spinifex, *Triodia spp.*, began to seed, soon followed by succulents of the *Portulaca* genus. Once this happened, between May and September most of the grass seeds began to ripen. From September into the early wet season, various plants went to seed, including species of *Stylobasium*, *Tecticornia*, *Acacia* and *Eucalyptus*. Thus edible seeds of one kind or another were available more or less year round, although some seasons were leaner than others. Nor were all species equally valued, whether for ease of collection or processing or palatability (Cane 1989, pp. 103–4).

Certain cultural practices also extended the natural availability of seeds. While seeds were not normally sowed, as they are in agriculture – sowing being a defining component of agriculture – their growth was sometimes promoted by anthropogenic practices such as firing of the landscape (O'Connell *et al.*'s (1983) 'low-cost cultivation'; Kimber's (1984) 'cultivation'; Rhys Jones' (1969) 'firestick farming'). Fires were often lit in patchwork pattern across the landscape to promote local growth of some grasses, although *Acacias* suffered adversely in the process.

Seeds may also have been retained or stored in one form or another. One intriguing example is of a symbiotic relationship between the plant-promoting 'firestick farming' practices and some species of ants that eat the eliaosome, or fatty attachments, of *Fimbristylis oxystachya* and *Panicum australiense* seeds. The seeds themselves could be found in piles near the entrance of ant nests, making for easy collection. Some seeds, *Acacia* and *Eucalyptus* in particular, were sometimes stored by Aboriginal groups for use during the hot season, while the seeds of at least three species of *Acacia* were kept for the wet season when food supplies were lean.

Most grass, sedge and shrub seed processing generally involved three major steps. *Eucalyptus* and *Acacia* seeds required only two. Other types of seeds were similarly processed, sometimes with the addition of species-specific steps. One example of the latter is the preparation of the seeds from the herbs *Chenopodium inflatum* and *C. rhadinostchyum*, whose strong aromatic perianth and ovary walls surrounding the seeds needed to be removed before further preparation could take place. This was achieved by laborious rubbing of the seeds (Cane 1989, pp. 103–10).

Grass, sedge and shrub seed processing was time-consuming. First came seed collection and dehusking. Seed collection was among the least demanding of the processing tasks, normally requiring the direct stripping of seeds from the stem into wooden containers. Seeds were dehusked by rubbing between the hands; as the seeds fell into the container, the lighter vegetable matter was blown away by the wind. In some rare cases, seeds could be directly collected from the entrance of ants' nests, as noted above. Cleaning via a process commonly known as yandying followed dehusking. This involved the rhythmic shaking and winnowing of the seeds and other remaining plant matter, grains of sand and small stones in shallow softwood dishes to separate the seeds from the unwanted matter (Figure 8.1). As can be expected, seeds collected from ants' nests possessed larger quantities of sand and stone than those collected directly from the stems. Consequently, the yandying process was more demanding, involving a greater amount of rocking of the dish than normal.

Once the seeds were separated from all contaminating matter, they could be ground (Figure 8.2). This was the most laborious stage of seed processing. Soaking in water for a few hours first softened some seeds, easing the grinding process. Most seeds were ground dry, water being added during grinding. Grinding involved a basal millstone and a smaller top muller. The millstone was set in the ground, a wooden dish positioned against one end to receive the ground paste. Small amounts of seed were placed on the grindstone, water slowly added as grinding proceeded. The ground paste was gradually built up in this way, and subsequently cooked into a damper in the ashes of an open fire.

Acacia and *Eucalyptus* seeds were collected directly from the plant. The hard *Acacia* seeds were generally soaked prior to grinding. The paste was made and cooked in a similar way to grass, sedge and shrub seeds (Cane 1989, pp. 104–10).

Scott Cane (ibid., pp. 104–10) has noted that 2 kg of grass or sedge seed and associated rubbish can typically be gathered in the space of an hour. This would represent approximately 1.5 kg of sand, stone and unwanted plant matter and 500 g of seed. The separation process – yandying – would take about 40 minutes. Grinding, the most laborious of the tasks, would take about 2.5 hours for 500 g of seed. These figures are general but give a good idea of the demands of seed processing. Cane (ibid., p. 107) concluded that a 1 kg seed damper required some five hours of handling time and returned approximately 350 kilocalories per hour of work.[4]

Seeds as social relations

Seed grinding articulates sentiment as much as bodily engagement. Many anthropologists have observed that the processing of grass seeds constituted one of the most unenvied tasks of food preparation in central Australia. Diane Bell (1987, p. 245) wrote that present-day Kaytej women 'recall that in their grandmothers' time much of the day was spent in preparing seeds for damper'; seed processing was one of the most demanding tasks of daily life. In the Great Sandy Desert, Scott Cane (1989, p. 118) noted that 'seed processing was a time-consuming and arduous task'. Among Aboriginal people of the eastern parts of the Western Desert, seed processing has been described by Annette Hamilton:

> The most striking aspect of grass-seed milling was the women's active dislike of this task. All other subsistence tasks they counted as a pleasure, but grinding grass-seed, with all its associated processes, was seen as arduous and, when important ceremonies were in progress, their product in the form of baked grass-seed cakes was appropriated largely by the men. (1980, p. 14)

The appropriation of women's products by men is a key point. Almost every aspect of production of ground-seed food was an exclusively women's task. The only exception was the production of the grinding stones themselves, which men often participated in:

> Grass-seed grinding was in the Western Desert wholly a woman's activity, and there is a cycle of women's songs and myths, centred on a particular species of grass-seed and located at a specific site, a granite hill on top of which are deep holes in the stone where the women trod the grain to separate the seed from the husks in the wind. (ibid.)

Diane Bell (1987) similarly wrote of seed processing as a women's role among the Kaytej, Mervyn Meggitt (1962) among the Warlpiri, and Fred Myers (1986) and Scott Cane (1989) among the Pintupi and Kukatja. The use of seeds as a staple cannot be disengaged from relations of power between genders. Ground-seed foods are gendered in their attainment, in their production and in their use, and in these capacities they are closely entwined with the sexual division of labour, gender roles in intra- and inter-group social relations, and territorial relationships with 'country'.

The gendered nature of seed processing and seed use in central Australia has been described by Annette Hamilton (1980) as an example of

Figure 8.1 Yandying (*Source*: Fiona Walsh)

Figure 8.2 Seed grinding (*Source*: Fiona Walsh)

a dual social system in operation. She suggests that one of the consequences of a strongly gendered division of labour in Aboriginal Australia is a strongly gendered relation of power, domination and subordination. Hamilton notes that the separation of the sexes in food production is one of the means by which more pervasive gender relations are established. In the Western Desert, many stone and wooden tools are produced along strongly gendered lines. The only exclusively female stone artefact is the milling stone and muller used for seed grinding (Hamilton 1980, p. 6). Women make and use other stone tools, but these are never exclusively female implements. Hamilton (ibid., p. 6) further notes that 'The separation of the sexes in the extractive base is seen clearly in the wooden implements, with the spear and spear-thrower being exclusively male objects, and the wooden dishes and digging stick being almost exclusively female.'

Wooden dishes served multiple purposes, including as containers to collect and winnow seeds and the water required for their grinding in the production of damper. The large milling stones and mullers used to grind seeds exclu-

sively belonged to women, being passed down from mother to daughter (ibid., p. 8). Hamilton further notes that transmission

> through the generations is affected by demographic accidents, such as the extinction of particular matrilines, in which case the grindstones will be appropriated by the nearest surviving matrilineal kinswoman and her uterine descendants. When a matriline grows too numerous to share effectively a single stone, pressure will be brought to bear on men of the local group to obtain a new one. (ibid., p. 8)

Because milling stones were rather large – they often weighed many kilograms – throughout central Australia they were stationed at sites where kin groups expected to return periodically (White and Peterson 1969). Such stones were repeatedly used from generation to generation, sustaining much wear and in the process requiring maintenance and ultimately disposal. In the milling process, one or more grooves were gradually worn through the stone. There came a time when the stone was too thin to continue use, and indeed milling stones often broke. Maintenance may require trimming, roughening of the grinding surface to increase the efficiency of grinding, or simply turning the stone around to convert the base into the working surface and vice versa.

The placement of milling stones at a site was an act of place marking, a process that Annette Hamilton suggested influenced social and territorial organization. Although not necessarily a favoured food item, seeds enabled the continued use of many of Australia's most arid regions. But seeds required heavy grinding stones, a scarce resource that could not readily be carried over the great distances covered in the annual cycle in central Australia. Because of this combination of factors, women's labour, as articulated in seed grinding, both constrained and guided residential patterns. Furthermore, as Hamilton (1980, p. 9) notes, 'men depended on the women's labour over their mills to finance certain of their own ceremonies', a process in continuous tension with 'the desire of men to create closed territories where they would live with their wives'. Hamilton continues:

> An obvious resolution of this dilemma is for groups of close 'brothers' to marry a group of sisters, living with them in the home area of the women's parents, until their deaths permitted the group to move back to the area which the men wish to identify as their own country. Indeed this accords well with the on-the-ground residential patterns of people at present living in the eastern Western Desert, where groups of sisters and their husbands are repeatedly found living in the same camp as the women's parents (cf. White 1977: 102). (ibid.)

Residential patterns are sensitive to the sexual division of labour, and in central Australia ground seeds, as a key source of food produced by women, were associated with matrilineally defined millstones that served to mark residential places to which people needed to periodically return for the production of seed foods. Both men and women were tethered, so to speak, to women's technologies, to the places where women's grinding tools were necessarily located and marked the land, and to their products. This socio-geographical calling was not limited to domestic day-to-day activities, for men's rituals were especially subject to women's labour and to the locations of matrilineally emplaced milling stones.

Women's seed technologies and the products of their labour were thus powerful forces in central Australian life. Seeds and seed production were not simply a question of food, but active influences on ritual and residential patterns and schedules. 'The organization of this aspect of women's labour around a single scarce resource (the grindstone and mill) acted as a kind of perpetual opposition to the men's desires to promote patrilocal residence', writes Hamilton (1980, p. 10), 'and augmented the ideological problems encountered by men in constituting patrilineal descent and patrilocal residence'. In this sense, systematic seed grinding had major effects on the psychological as well as social and territorial workings of Aboriginal groups across much of mainland Australia.

Rituals

I have already noted that meetings of large groups of people, including men's secret rituals, were sustained largely by women's food staples, in particular seed dampers. Fred Myers thus noted that among the Pintupi large congregations were held,

> including people from far away, near Lake Macdonald at seasons when *mungilpa* [seed plants] was available. Growing in large quantities near claypans filled with water, and abundant in August and September, this resource supported large populations, often gathered for ceremony. At such times, people with relatively distant ties might come to exploit the resource. (1986, p. 302)

So critical were seed foods that it was women who usually signalled the end of large-scale social events, where as many as 500 individuals would often congregate, when local seed resources became exhausted (for an example, see Chapter 4). Annette Hamilton has written:

> Major initiation and associated ceremonies occurred either at the hot times of the year when large numbers of people (and animals) fell back on the refuge waters, or at the end of autumn if rains had been good. This was also the period of major grass-seed availability (cf. Meggitt 1962: 49, O'Connell 1977: 269). In either case the pressure on the women's labour would be great. Tindale has noted that

'even the duration and scale of the most important of the men's initiation ceremonies are likely to be determined by the revolt of the women following the exhaustion of ready supplies of woman-gathered foods within a radius of three to four miles of the chosen place of meeting' (Tindale 1972: 245).

In conclusion, it would seem that women's labour was frequently absorbed in pursuits which required much energy for little yield to them, while the difference between subsistence needs and total output was appropriated by the men, who used this difference to carry out ceremonies excluding the women ... women's labour provided the economic basis for the men's ceremonial life, which in turn intensified the dominance of men in the culture. (Hamilton 1980, pp. 14–15)

In central Australia grass seeds were thus more than an important source of food, encapsulating an entire world of relations between men and women, a world of labour, sentiment, seasonal schedules, residential patterns and ritual practices. Rituals financed by seed grinding existed 'as an affirmation of the essentially separate status of women as a group' (ibid., p. 16). Through seed processing, women in a sense created the very possibility of large congregations around which men constructed their own ceremonies (women also have their own secret ceremonies). The ritual events known from the ethnography relied on a gendered separation of powers, and seed procurement and processing were an important component of that gendered structure.

In seed grinding, there is thus a separation of powers along gender lines that encroaches on sentiment and the rhythm of everyday life. In that men and women are not in total control of the products of their own labour, seed grinding and the production of ground-seed foods articulate specific forms of gender-based social tension and alienation. Men appropriate women's products to finance exclusive rituals, resulting in social contradiction. But in appropriating or being otherwise dependent on women's labour, men also become subject to the forces of women's production through ties of kinship, residence and seasonality, compounding into a complex and tangled web of social contradictions. The short-term and long-term demographic dynamics created by such contradictions are peculiar to seed grinding, and the historical emergence of seed grinding

thus has considerable significance for long-term social dynamics in Australian pre-History.

The archaeological record

In the spirit of the *domus*, it is apparent that changes in relations between people and seed plants imply more than changes in people–land relations, for sentiment and relationships between people are also at stake. This is because each specific relation between people and land or resource entails a specific pattern of social interaction, power relation and social scheduling.

Let us now examine the archaeological evidence from central Australia to determine the antiquity of seed grinding in relation to the socio-demographic trends discussed in the previous chapter. We will then be in a better position to assess broader cultural contexts for the late Holocene emergence of the Dreaming, as discussed in the first Part of this book.

Seed processing is visible archaeologically in two ways. First, the plants themselves can leave archaeological traces in the form of pollen, phytoliths, starch grains and other botanical materials. However, little archaeo-botanical research has ever been undertaken in Australia with the antiquity of seed processing in mind; such avenues of enquiry will therefore not be further considered here.

The second approach relates to the grinding stones. There is a considerable history of such research in Australia, culminating in Mike Smith's systematic analyses of the mid-1980s (e.g. Smith 1986a). Let us consider the defining attributes of seed grinding implements and review the archaeological literature with the above aims in mind.

Grinding stones

Australian grinding stones have been described in considerable detail by Mike Smith (1985, 1986a). Grinding stones are amongst the largest and heaviest of Australian stone tools, hence their relative permanence within occupation sites. As tools that people return to, grinding stones tend to be re-used over extended periods of time, resulting in recognizable wear patterns determined by function.

Not all grinding stones were used for seed grinding. Some were used for processing bush tobacco, ochre, tubers and even small animals. In the following section I will be restricting my discussion to specialized seed grinding implements that can securely be identified morphologically, for the motions of seed grinding require a relatively large surface area on the base stone, and over time result in the creation of relatively long and wide grooves.

Based on ethnographic observations, Smith (1986a) argued that specialized seed-grinding stones in central Australia are limited to millstones and mullers (Figure 8.3). Other types of grinding stones, such as the mortars and pes-tles that are sometimes used to pound the hard seeds of *Acacia spp.* before wet milling on mill-stones, are multipurpose implements; they are not restricted to seed processing. Consequently, it is the archaeology of millstones and mullers that we should focus upon in our investigation of the antiquity of specialized seed exploitation.

Smith defines millstones in the following way:

> These implements were used in the wet milling of seeds. Millstones ... are large

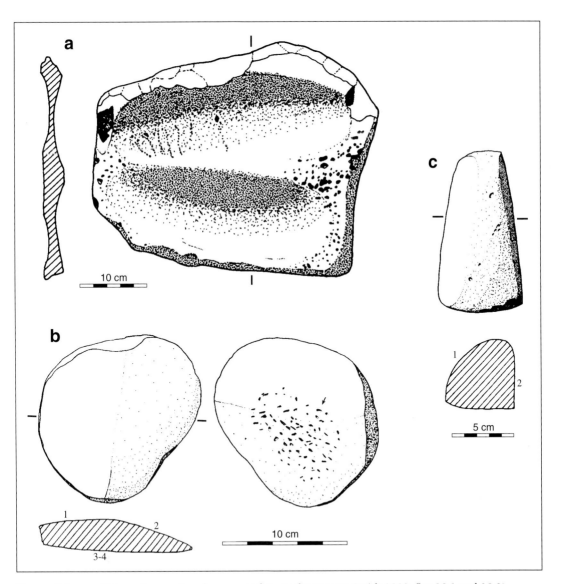

Figure 8.3 **a** millstone; **b**, **c** mullers from central Australia (*Source*: Smith 1989, figs 18.1 and 18.2)

flat-surfaced slabs with one or more long shallow grooves worn into the surface. A large surface area is necessary for the long grinding action with which these implements are used. The minimum length of groove for efficient grinding is probably around 300mm. Many millstones show evidence of careful manufacture. Often they have a trimmed margin, either flaked or hammerdressed. In some cases the faces have also been trimmed. The use-wear on millstones is distinctive. Usually it is in the form of a shallow, well-defined, ground groove about 100mm wide and 10–20mm deep. The ground surfaces are finely abraded and very smooth. A fine reflective polish, recently identified as a silica polish (cf. 'sickle gloss') . . . is commonly present on the ground surfaces. Millstones are rejuvenated when the surfaces become too smooth by using a topstone to lightly peck the surface forming a stipple-like pattern of small puncture marks. (1986a, pp. 32–3)

Mullers, the topstones used in conjunction with millstones, are considerably smaller. They tend to have a bevelled edge created by the angle the stone was held during the grinding process. Silica polish is sometimes visible (ibid., p. 33).

The sites

Eighteen rockshelters and five open sites possessing seed-grinding stones in stratified and reliably dated contexts have been excavated and published in Australia.[5] Let us briefly examine each to see what they tell us about the antiquity of seed grinding. The sites listed below are ordered geographically from north to south and west to east. A summary is provided in Table 8.1.

Garnawala 2

Garnawala 2 is a large rockshelter in Wardaman country, north of the Tanami Desert and located in semi-arid lands. A large, open excavation revealed tens of thousands of stone artefacts, occupation beginning some undetermined time below a radiocarbon date of $10,256 \pm 92$ years BP, continuing to the period of European contact (late nineteenth century). Numerous specialized seed-grinding stones occur on the present site surface (although these are not of the classic desert type), and

four fragments were excavated and reported from the deepest excavation square, the only one yet to have undergone systematic analysis. All of these occur above excavation unit 6, in association with items from the European contact period. Despite the presence of around 10,000 stone artefacts and peak artefact deposition rates below the lowermost fragments of grinding stone, no seed-grinding stones occur prior to the late nineteenth century (Clarkson and David 1995).

Delamere 3

Delamere 3, a rockshelter associated with the Lightning Brothers Dreaming site in Wardaman country (see Chapter 5), was first occupied around 380 ± 60 years BP. An unspecified number of fragments of grinding stones were recovered from the excavation (McNiven *et al.* 1992).

Lake Woods 1

Mike Smith undertook a series of test trenches in the strand-line of Lake Woods, in northern central Australia. Three fragments of grinding stones, including one specialized seed-grinding stone, were recovered from near the surface of Trench I10. Although the deposit remains undated, the presence of stone artefact types of known age (e.g. adzes, bifacial points) indicates a late Holocene antiquity (Smith 1986b).

Karlamilyi

Karlamilyi is a rockshelter located 2 km north of the Rudall River in the Little Sandy Desert. Human occupation began around 3180 ± 70 years BP, but grinding stones do not appear until around excavation unit 14, dated to shortly before a radiocarbon date of 1120 ± 50 years BP. The grinding stones consist of six fragments of millstones and mullers (Veth 1993).

Winakurijuna

Winakurijuna rockshelter is located in the McKay Range, Little Sandy Desert. It was first occupied 900 ± 70 years BP. Three fragments of grinding stone were excavated, the earliest coming from a stratum shortly above the

Table 8.1 Excavated seed-grinding stones from Australia, arranged geographically from north to south and west to east

Site	Antiquity of earliest occupation (radiocarbon years BP)	Number of seed-grinding stones or fragments	Date of earliest seed-grinding stone (radiocarbon years BP)	Reference
Garnawala 2	>10,256±92	4	European contact period	Clarkson 1994; Clarkson & David 1995
Delamere 3	380±60	?	<380±60	McNiven et al. 1992
Lake Woods 1	Mid to late Holocene?	1	late Holocene	Smith 1986b
Karlamilyi	3180±70	6	~1120±50	Veth 1993
Winakurijuna	900±70	3	900	Veth 1993
Puntutjarpa	10,170±230	5	6740±120–435±90 (3500? -000?)	Gould 1996; Smith 1986a
James Range East	>4640±260	33	700?	Smith 1986a
Kulpi Mara	29,510±230	'a small number'	<2500±60	Thorley 1998
Kweyunpe 1	265±75	12	265±75	Napton & Greathouse 1985
Kweyunpe 2	<320±55	3	<320±55	Napton & Greathouse 1985
Kweyunpe 6	2000	1	590±80	Smith 1988
Therreyererte	3000	54	570	Smith 1988
Urre	3600		980±80	Smith 1988
Keringke	920±130	6	<920±130	Smith 1988; Stockton 1971
Illarerri Kulpi Malu Tjukurr 17	5000?	1	<3000 (European contact period?)	Smith 1986c
Puritjarra	30,000	55*	<5860±150	Smith 1989
Hawker Lagoon	14,770±270	?	<5100±100 (possibly last few hundred years only)	Lampert & Hughes 1987, 1988
Native Well 1	13,000	3	4320±90–1270±70 (3000?)	Smith 1986a
Native Well 2	10,770±135	15*	<2200	Morwood 1981
Ken's Cave	>2000±80	2	2000±80–1380±70	Morwood 1981
Turtle Rock	2800±400	1	<2410±80	Morwood 1981
Graman 1		1	<3000	Smith 1986a
Graman 4		1	<3000	Smith 1986a

* Some of these grinding stones may not relate to seed grinding; as specialized seed-grinding stones were not differentiated from other grinding stones in the original reports, their exact numbers could not be ascertained.

radiocarbon date, and therefore dates to around 900 years BP (Veth 1993).

Puntutjarpa

Human occupation in the arid zone site of Puntutjarpa began around 10,170 ± 230 years BP (Gould 1996). In his re-analysis of the stratigraphic sequence, Mike Smith (1986a, pp. 33–4) noted that seed-grinding stone pieces are uncommon for the large excavation, numbering five in total. The lowermost grind-stone fragments came from a level above a radiocarbon date of 6740 ± 120 years BP but below a date of 435 ± 90 years BP. Intrapolation from the depth-age curve would give an age estimate of approximately 3500 years BP for the earliest grindstones. However, following Ian Johnson's (1979, pp. 131–4) re-analysis of Richard Gould's excavated stratigraphic sequence, Smith (1986a, p. 34) also noted that 'the maximum age of these implements could be as little as 1000 years BP'.

James Range East

Grindstones are considerably more abundant in the James Range East rockshelter than in many other excavated sites of the arid zone. Thirty-three seed-grinding stones were found. Human occupation probably began sometime before a radiocarbon date of 4640 ± 260 years BP, although chronostratigraphic problems make the timing of first occupation difficult to determine precisely (Gould 1980; Smith 1986c). Richard Gould (1980) and Mike Smith (1986c) noted that all of the millstone and muller fragments come from the Upper Unit, in layer F3, dating to the last 700 years BP.

Kulpi Mara

Kulpi Mara, a large rockshelter right at the heart of central Australia, contains a long cultural sequence spanning the period from 29,510 ± 230 years BP to the late Holocene. Cultural deposits dating to the Pleistocene period appear to be particularly rich immediately before and after the last glacial maximum (i.e. before and after 24,000 and 12,000 years BP, respectively). However, there are no traces of grinding stones during these times, the earliest fragments coming some undetermined time during the late Holocene, on the ground

surface and 'in the very upper levels of layer 1' (Thorley 1998, p. 40). Peter Thorley thus concludes:

> There is no evidence that seeds were relied on in any major way to offset shortages in other resources during the Pleistocene. In Kulpi Mara, grinding implements, though limited in number, are confined to the very uppermost levels of the deposit, above the age estimate of 2500 ± 60 years BP. (ibid., p. 43)

Kweyunpe 1

I have already discussed the archaeology of Kweyunpe 1, also known as Kuyunba 106, in Chapter 4 (along with Kweyunpe 2 and 6). To recall, this is a small rockshelter in the Pine Gap region near Alice Springs, central Australia. Human occupation began around 265 ± 75 years BP.

L. Kyle Napton and E. A. Greathouse (1985, pp. 98–9) reported excavating twelve fragments of grinding stone, most (eleven) of which were fragments of specialized seed milling stones. All came from excavation unit 5 or above, implying an antiquity of less than around 300 calibrated years ago for seed grinding at this site.

Kweyunpe 2

Excavations at Kweyunpe 2 (Kuyunba 107) revealed evidence of human occupation dating from 320 ± 55 years BP to ethnographic times (late nineteenth century). Here, too, a small number of grinding stones were found, including three basal stones and one muller. All belong to the European contact period, which began in this area around 1872 (Napton and Greathouse 1985).

Kweyunpe 6

Occupation at the small rockshelter known as Kweyunpe 6 began around 2000 years BP, although this is an estimate based on extrapolation from the depth-age curve whose lowest radiocarbon date is 590 ± 80 years BP. A single seed-grinding stone was recovered from excavation unit 4, located immediately above this radiocarbon date (Smith 1986c, 1988). The grinding stone is thus younger than this date.

Therreyererte

This is the famous Native Cat Dreaming site of central Australia, already considered in Chapter 4. Hundreds of seed-grinding stones are presently evident on the surface of this open site. A series of excavations revealed human occupation beginning around 3000 years BP, but it is not until approximately 570 years BP that the first seed-grinding stones appear. The Therreyererte excavations revealed a total of 54 grinding stones or grinding stone fragments (see Chapter 4; Smith 1988; Smith and Clark 1993).

Urre

This is an open site associated with Grass Seed rituals during ethnographic times, already discussed in Chapter 4. Human occupation at Urre began around 3600 years BP. Specialized seed-grinding stones are commonly found across the site's surface. They are only found in levels dating to after 980 ± 80 years BP (Smith 1988).

Keringke

Milling stones abound on the ground surface at Santa Teresa Mission, located some 70 km southeast of Alice Springs in central Australia; Eugene Stockton (1971) recorded more than 107 in various localities. Stockton excavated at the open site of Keringke (Stockton's Kurringa), revealing human occupation spanning the period from 920 ± 130 years BP to ethnographic times. Six milling stones were excavated, all restricted to the upper excavation units R4 and above. The grinding stones are therefore younger than the radiocarbon date (Stockton 1971; Smith 1988).

Illarerri Kulpi Malu Tjukurr 17

The central Australian rockshelter of Illarerri Kulpi Malu Tjukurr 17 was first occupied shortly before 3210 ± 90 years BP, probably around 5000 years BP by extrapolation of the depth-age curve (Smith 1986c). A single grinding stone was recovered from excavation unit 3 in the upper parts of the stratigraphic sequence. Given that the radiocarbon date was obtained from excavation units 22 and 23, located approximately 1.5 m below the grind-

ing stone, the latter is likely to be considerably younger than 3000 years BP, and may well date to the European contact period (Smith 1986c).

Puritjarra

Puritjarra represents the main site sequence from arid Australia. It possesses a near-continuous, stratified sequence dating back from around 30,000 years BP to 'modern' times (i.e. to the last 200 years). Stone artefacts are common during various phases of the Pleistocene, especially between 22,000 and 18,000 years BP, and between 13,000 and 12,000 years BP (Smith 1989). However, Smith noted:

> There are no grindstones of any description in the late Pleistocene assemblage, whereas 55 grindstones, including fragments of seed-grinding implements, were recovered from layer 1. This absence, despite the trenching of areas where we would expect large implements to be discarded, confirms an earlier inference that intensive use of seeds was not a feature of Pleistocene subsistence in the arid interior. (ibid., p. 99)

The age of the earliest grinding stones at Puritjarra have not yet been reported, but must date to sometime after 5860 ± 150 years BP, the age of the base of layer 1.

Hawker Lagoon

Hawker Lagoon is a small, ephemeral lake, a canegrass swamp 50 hectares in size. Located some 250 km south of Lake Eyre in the Flinders Ranges in South Australia, it contains a rich surface scatter of stone artefacts across much of the lunette and neighbouring dune field. Ron Lampert and Phil Hughes undertook excavations at the site, revealing a sequence of three stone artefact industries, each yet poorly dated. At the base, above the culturally sterile Unit 3, are core tools, cores and large flakes dated from around 14,770 ± 270 years BP (Unit 2B) (Lampert and Hughes 1988). Above this is a middle level containing a few small tools, the base of which is dated to 5100 ± 100 years BP. Above this is Unit 1A, 'a very rich small tool industry' in a 'top level which was laid down in the last few centuries' (Lampert and Hughes 1987, 1988).

Lampert and Hughes (1987, p. 32) reported

that seed-grinding stones can be found concentrated in small areas on the ground surface, in association with flaked artefacts of the so-called 'small tool industry'. Grinding stones are consistently associated with this industry, but whether Lampert and Hughes were referring to the middle or to the top small tool industry is ambiguous from their preliminary reports. It is therefore uncertain whether seed-grinding stones began to be deposited at Hawker Lagoon some time after around 5100 years BP – representing the age of the base of the middle industry – or only during the last few centuries (perhaps coincident with the arrival of Europeans).

Native Well 1

A number of rockshelters and caves have been excavated in the Central Queensland Highlands, a semi-arid region of eastern Australia. Human occupation at the rockshelter of Native Well 1 began shortly before 10,910 ± 140 years BP, probably around 13,000 years BP by extension of the depth-age curve (Morwood 1981). Although Morwood (1981) originally identified 102 'grinding stones', Smith's re-analysis showed that only three were seed-grinding implements, consisting of two mullers and a single millstone fragment (Smith 1986a, p. 35). The oldest of these came from a level located between radiocarbon dates of 4320 ± 90 and 1270 ± 70 years BP. Smith (1986a) suggested, based on intrapolation from the depth-age curve, that the earliest seed grinding stone dated to around 3000 years BP.

Native Well 2

The nearby site of Native Well 2 was first occupied around 10,770 ± 135 years BP. Morwood (1981) identified fifteen fragments of grinding stones, although their status as specialized seed-grinding stones is not noted. All came from excavation unit 6 and above, and therefore date to the last 2200 years BP.

Ken's Cave

Ken's Cave contained one grinding stone on its surface, and two fragments were excavated in excavation unit 4, between radiocarbon dates of 2000 ± 80 and 1380 ± 70 years BP. Human occupation began at Ken's Cave

shortly before 2000 ± 80 years BP (Morwood 1981).

Turtle Rock

Also located in the Central Queensland Highlands is Turtle Rock site. Human occupation at Turtle Rock began around 2800 ± 400 years BP; a single muller was excavated from the uppermost, undated excavation unit. This unit almost certainly dates to considerably less than 2410 ± 80 years BP by virtue of an underlying radiocarbon date (Morwood 1981).

Graman 1 and Graman 4

The semi-arid sites of Graman 1 and 4, from eastern Australia, have revealed numerous grinding stones. However, Mike Smith (1986a) could only positively identity a single specialized seed-grinding stone from Graman 1, many of the others representing axe grinding or expedient grinding stones of one kind or another. The single millstone came from the upper Layer 1, dated to the late Holocene. Similarly, Graman 4 nearby contained a single specialized seed-grinding tool, a fragment of a muller, from the top excavation unit of Layer 2.

It is difficult to determine the age of these seed-grinding stones, as the ages of the Graman sequences have long proven problematic. However, following his review of the Graman data, Smith (1986a, p. 35) concluded that the seed-grinding stones 'are from levels that probably post-date 3000 years BP'.

In addition to the above sites, where specialized seed-grinding stones were recovered in stratified contexts, a number of other dated rockshelters and open sites containing surface grinding stones have also been reported. In the Pilbara region (northwestern Australia) such sites include Newman Orebody Rockshelter (Site P0187) and a series of rockshelters along Packsaddle Ridge. At Newman Orebody Rockshelter, where occupation began around or before 20,740 ± 345 years BP (Maynard 1980; Brown 1987), the only evidence of seed grinding is in the form of a dolerite upper and base grinding stone on the ground surface (Brown 1987, p. 23). At Packsaddle Ridge P4623, where occupation began around 770 ± 50 years BP, nine grinding stones were found on the ground surface. At Packsaddle Ridge P4627 nearby, occupation began 2640 ± 130 years BP. Three grinding stones were here found on the surface. At Packsaddle Ridge P5315, a single grinding stone was also found on the ground surface. Occupation at this site began 8090 ± 80 years BP (Brown 1987). Interestingly, most of the stone artefacts at Packsaddle Ridge P5315 were found stratified in sediments older than 2440 ± 60 years BP. The complete absence of grinding stone fragments from the deposits, but their presence on the ground surface (undated, but of late Holocene age), is chronologically meaningful. In each of these sites, the surface grinding stones date to relatively recent, late Holocene times.

Other excavated sites with relatively extensive Pleistocene or early to mid-Holocene deposits have failed to reveal any evidence of specialized seed grinding. These include Newman Rockshelter in the Pilbara, where a near-basal date of 26,300 ± 500 years BP was obtained (Brown 1987), and the JSN location in the Strzelecki Desert, where sites dating back to 14,400 ± 200 years BP have been investigated (e.g. Smith *et al.* 1991). In contrast to the stone artefacts from the older excavated deposits, none of the seed-grinding stones recovered at the JSN site showed visible signs of great antiquity. Smith *et al.* (1991, p. 188) concluded that 'As none of the grindstones is heavily patinated or carbonate encrusted, there is nothing to suggest that they pre-date mid-late Holocene occupation of the site.'

It should also be noted that seed-grinding stones are absent from Kangaroo Island, situated some 14.5 km south of South Australia's shores. Kangaroo Island is approximately 145 km long by 60 km wide, consisting of Australia's second-largest continental island. The island was part of the mainland until separated by rising seas between 9500 and 9300 years BP. Sea levels stabilized to their present levels approximately 6000 years BP (Lampert 1981).

Despite specialist archaeological studies over many decades, not a single plant grinding stone of any kind has ever been found on Kangaroo Island, neither as a surface find among the rich open sites nor in the stratified deposits. This is the case also for other specialized stone tool types of the late Holocene, such as pirri points and backed flakes (although two adzes – highly portable items – described by the excavator as 'tula-like' occur at Rowell's Site, an open site with cultural deposits dated

to around 5300 years BP) (Lampert 1981, p. 122). Grinding stones were thus absent from both late Pleistocene and early to mid-Holocene deposits on the island, as evidenced by excavations at Seton's Shelter (16,110 ± 100 to 10,940 ± 60 years BP); Cape de Couedic Rockshelter (7450 ± 100 years BP); Pigs Water Hole (of unknown antiquity but probably dating from the terminal Pleistocene to early Holocene); Rainy Creek (7890 ± 170 years BP); Rowell's Site (5300 years BP); Sand Quarry (4310 ± 90 years BP); and Bales Bay (6230 ± 300 years BP) (Draper 1987; Lampert 1981).

All evidence for human presence on Kangaroo Island ceases by 4300 years BP, at a time when its geographical links with the mainland had already been severed for some 5000 years (Lampert 1981). This probably indicates the end (extinction) of long-standing resident populations on the island. Late Holocene grinding stones abound on the mainland; were systematic seed grinding to have originated prior to 9500 years BP, when Kangaroo Island was last attached to the mainland, seed-grinding stones would be expected on the island.

Given the above, coupled with the presence of grinding stones in many late Holocene deposits across arid and semi-arid Australia, I would suggest that lack of reliable evidence of specialized seed grinding in mid-Holocene and earlier deposits in all parts of Australia can be taken as evidence of absence.

Pleistocene seed grinding?

Claims for the presence of specialized seed grinding during the Pleistocene have nevertheless appeared in the literature from time to time. The first was published in 1974 by Harry Allen, who argued that seed-grinding stones could be found from 15,000 years BP onwards in open sites of the Murray–Darling basin. Allen suggested that as lake levels lowered and aquatic resources became less abundant during the terminal Pleistocene, local communities adapted to the new challenges through technological and dietary innovations focused on seed processing. Seed grinding represented a solution to decreasing resources in a previously rich landscape (Allen 1972, 1974). Support for his views was readily apparent by the presence of seed-grinding stones at seven exposed, surface sites on lunettes of the now-dry Willandra lakes and on nearby landforms. Each of these sites, along with the associated seed-grinding stones, was claimed to date to the post-glacial period beginning around 15,000 years BP.

However, each of Allen's sites is a surface exposure on a deflated surface. In some cases, no component of a site was directly dated, their antiquity assumed by virtue of the age of other exposed, dated sites nearby. In three sites, purported late Pleistocene seed-grinding stones were associated with backed artefacts and other well-known late Holocene stone artefact types, indicating the contaminated nature of the deflated deposits. None of the fragments of grinding stones came from *in situ* deposits dating to the Pleistocene (Balme 1991).

In 1990, Harry Allen revisited his earlier claims, rejecting them on the grounds that all evidence for Pleistocene grinding stones came from unreliable evidence in the form of undatable and likely contaminated deflated surfaces. With these problems in mind, Jane Balme re-surveyed many of the areas previously studied by Allen, observing many instances of active deflation. Grinding stones were frequently encountered, but 'No grindstone remnants have been found in situ, either in sediments of known age or within middens, so none can be dated with assurance' (Balme 1991, p. 6). In every case, grinding stones were found on deflated or otherwise disturbed sediments, along with archaeological materials known to belong to the late Holocene. The antiquity of the Murray–Darling grinding stones thus remain speculative, and chronological models rest more closely with ecologically adaptive preconceptions – expected 'optimal' or maximizing technological strategies that tracked environmental changes – than with direct temporal evidence. The purported Pleistocene antiquity of the Murray–Darling grinding stones has now been dismissed by most, if not all, archaeologists, including all of those who have undertaken primary fieldwork in the region and published on the subject.

Yet a single locale with reported Pleistocene seed-grinding stones is left: the central northern New South Wales spring site of Cuddie Springs. Little has so far been published of the geomorphological or taphonomic contexts of these finds. As few as 21, and possibly as many as 26, Pleistocene grinding stones have been claimed from this site. Based on a combination of the stones' morphologies and on the pres-

ence of certain classes of use wear and residue, at least five of the grinding stones are treated as plant-processing millstones or mullers by the excavators. All are claimed to be around 30,000 years old, and all of the claimed Pleistocene specialized seed-grinding stones illustrated are very small fragments, less than 7.2 cm maximum length (Fullagar and Field 1997, Figure 3b). However, only one of these specialized seed-grinding stones (artefact CS6034) was found below a chrono-stratigraphically critical 'deflation surface' (Stratigraphic Unit 5, Archaeological Level 4) that is overlain by mixed mid-Holocene and Pleistocene sediments (with another five grinding stones of one kind or another found below Stratigraphic Unit 5). This 'deflation surface' has been reported as a key to the interpretation of the site's stratigraphic integrity. Field and Dodson (1999, p. 284) report that the 'bone recovered from this unit was fragmented, and the degree of mineralisation varied considerably ... Since some of the bone was very dense and black, while other bone was brown in colour and friable, the bone assemblage may be mixed.' Consisting of an up to 5 cm thick mass of interlocked rocks and bones (including stone artefacts), Stratigraphic Unit 5 'marks the upper limit of the *in situ* megafauna deposits' (ibid., p. 283), and with this the upper limit of the *in situ* stratigraphy generally (see Photo 12 at http://artalpha.anu.edu.au/web/arc/resources/photos/cuddie/cuddie97.htm). Said to be continuous across the excavation squares, this 'deflation surface' is reported as a 'pavement of stone formed by the lag deposits [that] seals the overlying clays from the archaeology and faunal record below' (Field and Dodson 1999, p. 284), an 'archaeology and faunal record below' that threatens to revise our understanding of human–megafaunal relations as well as our understanding of the antiquity of systematic seed grinding in Australia. I ask, where do the Stratigraphic Unit 5 rocks come from in this stone-poor riverine plain? The modern lake floor itself consists of grey alluvial soils, and the surrounding plains of red soils. The other excavated strata below and above this unit are clayey (Stratigraphic Unit 4), clayey and silty (Stratigraphic Unit 6), clayey and sandy (Stratigraphic Unit 1), silty (Stratigraphic Unit 3) or gravely (Stratigraphic Unit 2). Field and Dodson write:

The low relief in the area around Cuddie Springs, the fine-grained sediments that comprise the deposit and the absence of any stone outcrops for at least 4 km supports the notion that the stone present in the archaeological levels must have been brought on site by people ... The closest and most accessible stones are silcrete cobbles from a gibber plain (a plain covered in cobber-sized stones) *c.* 4 km west of the site. (1999, pp. 291, 292–3)

How did the rocks come to be deposited in Stratigraphic Unit 5, and what is their source? Where have the sediments above the 'pavement' come from, given that between 1876 and 1933 more than 25 m³ (and possibly considerably more) of sediment had been dug up and accumulated just a few metres to the northwest of the archaeological excavation pits? This question is significant as it may shed critical light on the nature and antiquity of the 'pavement', and whether or not this 'pavement' has truly sealed the underlying sediments since the late Pleistocene (there is evidence of extant (but presumably dead) tree roots immediately below the 'pavement' (see Photo 14 at http://artalpha. anu.edu.au/web/ arc/resources/photos/cuddie/cuddie97.htm).

Geomorphological investigations are required to answer these questions. It must also be asked whether or not the pavement is anthropogenic, perhaps even constructed by farmers during the late nineteenth or early twentieth centuries to create a firm footing for people or cattle (a European well was dug in 1876 but 10 m from the excavation; did the rocks come from the well sediments, as one possibility, or were they brought in from the gibber plain 4 km away?). The pavement's possible post-European antiquity is only strengthened by the presence of cattle bone in the stratum immediately overlying it: 'Archaeological Level 5 is considered to be significantly disturbed as the bone from this level contains skeletal elements of both megafauna and modern cow' (Field and Dodson 1999, p. 295). It may be worth in this context to radiocarbon-date the cow bone to determine whether or not it is of the pre-bomb period (atmosphereic testing of nuclear weapons in the 1950s produced large increases in ¹⁴C values, detectable through radiocarbon dating). If the cow bone is of the pre-bomb period, then it would imply it was deposited not long after the diging of the palaeontological trenches nearby, the possible source of sediments overlying the 'pavement'. It would strengthen the argument that the 'pavement' was exposed as ground surface during the early European contact period (and therefore its potential as an anthropogenic construction). If the cow bone is of the post-bomb period, there would be greater likelihood that it has moved through a metre or so of sediment since original deposition, finally resting on top of the hard 'pavement'; arguments for the 'pavement' being a natural stratum would be strengthened. Tracing the extent of the pavement through excavation or other means, including an assessment of its relationship to the recent well, may be warranted to resolve such questions.

The stratigraphic integrity of underlying cultural sediments at Cuddie Springs is also problematic. First, the site is a ground-fed spring according to Flannery (1997), although this is not clear from the literature as it is also reported as an 'ephemeral freshwater lake' by the excavators (Fullagar and Field 1997, p. 300; also Field and Dodson 1999, p. 279). While Field suggests that the site is an ephemeral lake rather than a spring, the water table may intrude into the lowermost cultural sediments during periods of high rainfall (given the construction of a European well near the archaeological excavation). As a site that is periodically inundated, there is the very real problem of episodic sediment movement (in particular during the wet phase of the early Holocene), and doubts will remain of the stratigraphic integrity of sediments until geomorphological results appear in press.

In addition to the potential problem of sediment mixing from below through a fluctuating water table, there is also the question of sediment mixing from above as a result of surface inundation. Whether or not deposits become fluid or viscous when wet requires address. The presence of stratification within the deposits is not in itself sufficient to dispel these potential problems, for viscosity of the sediment matrix may affect the stratigraphic integrity of certain masses but not others. In particular, the question needs to be asked as to whether or not stone, bone, large pieces of charcoal and other relatively large items had a tendency to settle onto a firmer but mixed stratigraphic level during times of inundation when sediments were muddy, creating a contaminated deposit in the critical Stratigraphic Unit 6A (again, the origins and antiquity of the 'pavement' are critical here). Second, stone artefacts occur in direct chronological association with extinct Pleistocene fauna (particularly in Stratigraphic Unit 6B), including *Sthenurus*, *Diprotodon* and *Genyornis* that have elsewhere been shown to have become extinct by 46,000 years ago (although only *Sthenurus* is claimed to have been directly used by people at Cuddie Springs, as evidenced by a burnt femur) (Dodson *et al.* 1993; Field 1999). The giant flightless bird *Genyornis* in particular has recently been the subject of intensive study in the Lake Eyre basin to the west of Cuddie Springs, where its extinction has been dated to $50,000 \pm 5000$ years ago (Miller *et al.* 1999), at least 15,000 years before their apparent presence at Cuddie Springs. Significantly, Miller *et al.* found evidence of the still extant emu throughout the period 120,000 years ago to present, so here the extinction of *Genyornis* cannot be taken as a taphonomic bias. More recently, Roberts *et al.* (2001) dated materials associated with megafaunal remains from various sites across Australia, and failed to find reliable evidence of megafauna survival after 46,000 years ago (cf. Gillespie and David 2001). Furthermore, Field and Dodson (1999, pp. 294–5) note:

> The presence of a *Pallimnarchus* sp. tooth in AL2 [Stratigraphic Unit 6A, Archaeological Level 2] is considered intrusive and may have been derived from an exposure in another part of the site, for example well digging. The tooth is exfoliated and heavily mineralised and the preservation is not consistent with other bone and teeth from this level.

And again:

> The incidence of heavily mineralised bone is higher [in Stratigraphic Unit 6A = Archaeological Levels 2 and 3] than in AL1 [Stratigraphic Unit 6B] and increases again in AL4 [Stratigraphic Unit 5, the 'pavement']. It is not yet clear whether differences in mineralisation of bone represent differential preservation or the presence of intrusive material from other horizons. (ibid., p. 295)

In these critical units there is thus evidence of intrusions. Never before have such megafaunal remains been found in direct chronostratigraphic association with cultural materials in reliable stratigraphic contexts,[6] fuelling scepticism over the integrity of deposits. Indeed, all the megafaunal species represented at Cuddie Springs are commonly suspected of having become extinct more than 40,000 years BP, 8000 years or more before the apparent age of the deposits in which they are found. In this context, it must also be asked why so many stone artefacts (including grinding stones) are found in sediments suggesting past 'marshy conditions', and 'shallow, still freshwater environments' of the earliest 'cultural' levels (ibid., p. 285, and elsewhere). And if 'a substantial proportion' of the megafauna in the earliest 'cultural' sediments 'died *in situ*', why are there no articulated megafaunal bones in those strata?

There are other signs that there may be critical taphonomic problems at Cuddie Springs, not least from the distribution of radiocarbon dates. Of note are the ten AMS and conventional dates from the critical and supposedly more or less intact Stratigraphic Unit 6 below the 'pavement' (ibid., Table 3). From the lowest part of this layer, Stratigraphic Unit 6B (= Archaeological Level 1), come six radiocarbon dates averaging $30,720 \pm 160$ years BP. Stratigraphic Unit 6A (= Archaeological Levels 2 and 3) above has four dates averaging $29,553 \pm 170$ years BP (averages calculated on Calib 4.1). Despite this apparent near-contemporaneity, the faunal and stone artefact remains in the two strata show major differences. Of special concern is that the bone distribution implies a sequential stratigraphic structure, with an increasing incidence of modern fauna and decrease in megafauna in the upper Stratigraphic Unit 6A, despite the apparent near-contemporaneity of Units 6A and 6B as indicated by the radiocarbon dates:

> The bone assemblage from AL2 was more fragmented compared to AL1, as well as containing a higher percentage of extant species . . . The species composition of AL2 shows a greater number of animal species represented in the deposit compared to AL1, with four species of extinct fauna identified.

These are worrying signs: why is there a sequential change from much modern fauna and few megafauna in the upper cultural levels of Stratigraphic Unit 6, to increasing proportions of megafauna in the lower parts of this Unit, if these strata are near-contemporaneous?

Are we to believe that we are faced with *the* moment of extinction? More likely is the possibility that there has been some significant degree of mixing of likely pre-human megafaunal deposits with more recent cultural deposits. This is especially so given that Richard Gillespie failed to find any traces of collagen in the Cuddie Springs bones (except in the cow bone discussed above). Yet 'the sediments contain, in addition to the dated macro charcoal, well-preserved pollen and macro plant debris as well as identifiable organic residues on stone tools. This is in complete contrast to the very poorly-preserved skeletal remains, a disharmonious assemblage in my view' (Gillespie, AUSARCHserver, 16 June 2001). If such mixing has taken place, it becomes difficult to determine which artefacts relate to which periods of time within the cultural sequence, especially if the overlying strata contain very recent materials (including cattle bone).

Also of concern is the apparent association of Pleistocene dates and Tula adzes or Tula adze-like artefacts, a stone tool type shown by Peter Hiscock and Peter Veth (1991) to be restricted to the mid to late Holocene elsewhere in the arid zone. John Dodson *et al.* (1993, p. 97) have thus noted of Cuddie Springs: 'from sediments dated between 30,000 and 19,000 BP, grindstones, ochre fragments and woodworking tools with identical usewear and similar morphology to tula adzes (Kamminga 1982) were recovered'. Recently Richard Roberts *et al.* (2001a, 2001b) have reported on single grain optically stimulated luminescence (OSL) dates at Cuddie Springs, concluding that the sediments are considerably disturbed; indeed, it is difficult to understand how an unarticulated *Genyornis* femur could stand perfectly upright (Wroe and Field 2001, p. 25) without sedimentary movement playing a role.

The Cuddie Springs archaeological excavations were undertaken towards the low points of this basin depression. Yet higher up on the lake's edge is a highly deflated remnant lunette, almost entirely eroded away. Where have the lunette sediments gone? Have they washed downslope sometime in antiquity, resting among the upper levels of more ancient magafaunal-rich sediments? Did this ancient lunette contain abundant cultural materials from c. 30,000 years BP? Archaeological research in this part of the site may be war-ranted to help resolve these problems. At present, Cuddle Springs seems to offer more questions than answers.

While the Cuddie Springs sediments are reported to be stratified by the excavators, the absence of post-depositional movement of materials within and between layers must be demonstrated empirically via geomorphological studies before this otherwise important site that threatens a need to revise established wisdom on human–megafaunal relations as well as on the antiquity of seed grinding in Australia can be reliably accepted.

Discussion

Pawel Gorecki *et al.* (1997) have noted that seed grinding as a method of food preparation need not require the use of specialized seed-milling stones such as those observed during ethnographic times. Multi-purpose or expedient stones with only minor traces of seed grinding may have long been used prior to the advent of specialized seed-milling stones. What changed with the emergence of milling stones, they caution, may relate to patterns of discard, rationing or the like, rather than the emergence of seed grinding as such. Gorecki *et al.* also note that seed-grinding stones or their fragments are infrequent even in rich cultural deposits. Pleistocene deposits tend to contain few stone artefacts of any kind. Consequently, they argue, the absence of seed-grinding stones from Pleistocene deposits is not surprising and may imply sampling limitations rather than evidence of absence.

However, while these possibilities should be kept in mind, we should also note that after 40 years of research, it remains that reliable archaeological evidence for seed grinding does not appear in the Australian archaeological record until the late Holocene, despite the presence of some rich cultural deposits preceding the grinding stone-bearing strata (e.g. Garnawala 2, where approximately 10,000 stone artefacts were recovered in levels predating the grinding stones; Kulpi Mara). Grinding stone fragments are also found in poor cultural deposits dating to the late Holocene, but they are never found in similarly poor deposits of earlier times. Furthermore, while the probability of finding seed-grinding stones may be small at sites where total artefact numbers are low, I would expect to find some within a region where the sum total of excavated sites is relatively high. That not a single reliable late Pleistocene or early Holocene specialized seed-grinding stone has been recovered in the whole of Australia, including Kangaroo Island, cannot simply be attributed to sampling inadequacies.[7] The archaeologically observable milling stones of the late Holocene imply the beginnings of systematic seed grinding only after a maximum 3500 years BP (and possibly only after *c.* 1400 years BP in the arid zone) (see Smith 1986a for similar conclusions).

Conclusion

The seed grinding issue is important in the context of this book for a number of reasons. First, it is seeds that formed the major source of food during the large, periodic congregations that were held for the Dreaming rituals of central Australia in recent times. Second, seeds represent more than items of food; they are also a part of the perceived and signified world, and as seeds became a targeted food resource so, too, did the signified world change accordingly. And, third, in their social entanglement, seeds sentimentalize social being and *habitus*, as social action. What is at stake is not simply the material seed, but the way seeds were enmeshed in the social and ontological world.

Systematic seed grinding as evidenced by, and requiring, millstones was a key to social relations and land use in much of arid and semi-arid Australia during ethnographic times, ecologically acting to minimize risk in the peopling of the arid and semi-arid zones. Mike Smith (1986a) has elsewhere suggested that without systematic seed grinding, the intensities of human use of the arid zone documented by social anthropologists would simply not have been possible. As was seen in the previous chapter, the emergence of systematic seed grinding during the late Holocene was coincident in time with massive increases in intensities of regional and individual site use throughout much of Australia. Seeds formed part of a package of socio-cultural change that involved various economic dimensions and major demographic shifts.

The archaeological evidence presented in this chapter indicates that specialized seed grinding in arid and semi-arid Australia was restricted to the late Holocene period, possibly beginning as early as 3500–3000 years BP in the semi-arid zone, and probably only around 1400–1000 years BP in the arid zone. However, it was not until the last millennium that specialized seed grinding became widespread and intensive, continuing to gain momentum through time. Indeed, the largest numbers of seed-grinding stones found in excavated sites almost invariably come from deposits dating to the last 700 years.

These technological changes signal profound social and psychological transformations, involving relations between people and relations between people and the land in which they dwell.

> The things that we relate to have embodied within them the social relations that gave rise to them through their design, the work of producing them, their prior use, the intention to ·communicate through them and their place within an existing cultural system of objects . . . The things of the world are incorporated into social interaction and provide an embodiment of social structures reflecting back the nature and form of our social world. (Dant 1999, p. 2)

If this is so, then the emergence of specialized seed grinding signals a change in human *engagement* and sentiment, the process of meaningful participation in the world. The emergence of systematic seed grinding is 'not simply about consuming goods but about living with them, appropriating objects into our everyday lives' (ibid., p. 84); our being and understanding of the world are shaped through engagement.

In this chapter I have thus tried to show that the things we eat are not simply items of food, physical presences ripe for the picking. They are, in the words of Nicholas Thomas (1991), 'entangled objects', defined by and (re)defining preunderstanding in human engagement. The transformation of grasslands into food resource fields signals the emergence of novel relations between people and the world in which they live. In that seasonality is involved, systematic seed grinding entails particular temporal relations between people and between people and the land. Seasonality of ripeness affected the location of social groups, including residential units and the timing of gatherings. Seed availability – geographical distributions and seasonality – impinged upon residential patterns and demographic trends. Alliance patterns and power relations attuned to resource structures were influenced. Kinship relations were affected, for ethnographically grinding stones are shared and/or passed down matrilinealy, affecting food preparation and relationships between hearth groups. In that territorial rights are marked or emphasized by matrilinealy demarcated grinding stones, relations between people and place are affected by seed grinding. Through place marking, territorial hegemony and rights to place are enhanced and may even be manipulated. Also affected was an ability to support large congregations, during ethnographic times critical to the performance of sacred Dreaming rituals. In that seed staples fuelled such congregations, we could say that seeds were not simply gathered by people, but that seeds gathered the people. During such rituals initiations were performed, marriages were arranged and disputes were settled. Seeds impacted on trade relations, in that seed foods enabled large gatherings to take place, and in that new, valuable items in the form of milling stones, whose natural availability was in many regions highly restricted, were traded. The heaviness of such tools, and the large distances they required to be transported from source to homeland, resulted in their highly valued status as trade items in some parts of the continent. Ecologically, seed grinding also enabled people to inhabit otherwise inhospitable places where staple resources were limited or where ecological risk was high; seed grinding served as a major risk-minimizing strategy in an otherwise poor or highly unpredictable limiting environment. As a highly gendered task, seed grinding signalled the presence of particular gender (power) relations. Such gender relations cut across many, if not all, of the points listed above. And not least, in the labour of seed food production, as in its consumption and in the new behavioural possibilities that it created, sentiments were shaped, a dimension rarely glanced at in traditional archaeological discourse yet critical to the construction of social being and identity.

If we thus see the way that people familiarize themselves with their surroundings and work out strategies of dwelling as a process of meaningful social engagement, then the emergence of systematic seed grinding represents a new form of landscape construction. The transformation of previously unused ('wild') and otherwise signified materials into consumable, managed products has deep and wide-ranging psychological and social as well as culinary implications. This is a transformation of the domestic mind and of the social world. What changed with the emergence of systematic seed grinding during the late Holocene was the *domus*, the experienced landscape that incorporated the entire network of social relations and relations to place, and the framework of understanding, sentiment and experience through which personal and social identity are built. The emergence of grass seeds as a source of staple food affected dietary habits, together with an understanding and experience of the world in social practice. It signalled the emergence of new environmental knowledge, social strategies and actions. What came about were new domicultural relations and practices. The beginning of seed grinding at a definable point in antiquity motioned the emergence of new ways of being, new systems of social relations and personal identity, and in the process new preunderstandings. The newly positioned grass seeds represent, literally, seeds of change. It is in this that emerges the significance of systematic seed grinding in Aboriginal Australia during the late Holocene, heralding a transformation in the construction of self and identity, concepts that I will revisit in greater detail in Chapter 10.

Notes

1. The original Spanish reads: 'Cada epoca de la historia modifica el fogón, y cada pueblo come segun su alma antes tal vez que con su estómago.' I thank Nick Dolby (Monash University) for making me aware of this quote.
2. See also Diane Bell (1987), Mervyn Meggitt (1962) and Fred Myers (1986) for comparable observations among the Kaytej, Warlpiri and Pintupi, respectively.
3. See Jones and Meehan (1989) for similar observations among the Gidgingali of Arnhem Land; see also Veth and Walsh (1988) for discussion of the importance of tubers in arid zone diets.
4. Douglas Edwards, Jim O'Connell and Melissa Heck recalculated Scott Cane's rates by eliminating resting and eating times, concluding that return rates were between 300 and 1100 kcal/hr (Edwards and O'Connell 1995). These

results are slightly lower than estimates made by Jim O'Connell and Kristen Hawkes (1981) for the Alyawarra, where on average *c.* 500 to 3600 kilocalories of ground seeds were produced per hour of processing.

5. A number of excavated sites report the presence of ground stone artefacts, but it is not specified whether these are edge-ground tools, such as axes, or grinding stones of one kind or another. Examples are Rainbow Cave, Cathedral Cave and Wanderer's Cave, late Holocene rockshelters in the Central Queensland Highlands (Beaton 1977). The uncertainty of the nature of such grinding stones is well illustrated by the original site report for Cathedral Cave (ibid., p. 115), which notes the incidence of ochre stains on many ground stone fragments. No mention is made of specialized seed-grinding stones. These sites could therefore not be considered in this chapter.

    Mulvaney and Joyce (1965, p. 192) also report from Kenniff Cave that 'Four stream-abraded, rounded, weathered, basalt pebbles were excavated, all of which bore distinct traces of grinding wear. Their rather granular and pitted composition would have made them most suitable grindstones.' These descriptions do not read like specialized seed-grinding stones. Furthermore, the thick excavation units used, common to the times, make their antiquity difficult to determine. Their uncertain stature as specialized seed-grinding stones and antiquity are therefore not further considered here.

6. What were once thought to be *in situ* associations between megafaunal remains and stone artefacts dating to 26,000 years BP at the Victorian site of Lancefield have recently been reinterpreted as a redeposited (i.e. mixed) deposit. The megafauna have been suggested to predate the stone artefacts by at least 14,000 years (e.g. van Huet 1999).

7. I would also suggest that even if some degree of seed grinding occurred prior to the late Holocene, that seed processing was undertaken via a different technology – such as expedient rather than specialized seed-grinding implements – the absence of specialized milling stones and associated mullers would imply a categorically different degree of seed processing and the various social processes associated with it (as discussed above) to those documented in Australia during ethnographic times. Not that this would be likely, for seed grinding by nature produces grinding surfaces recognizable archaeologically. Systematic seed grinding simply requires a systematic technology. And yet were this to be the case, even expedient seed grinding would hardly be possible in areas where stone slabs are not available, as is the case in much of central Australia; grinding stones of one kind or another have to be present for their use to be possible. They should, that is, be found in archaeological contexts if they ever existed.

    Whether or not some form of seed grinding was known prior to the late Holocene is largely immaterial to the arguments presented in this chapter, for the case being made is for the emergence of ethnographically documented relations between people, land and resources during the late Holocene, relations that require *systematic* seed grinding and the marking of place with milling stones.

9 Regionalization

Symbols present a world socially constructed in preunderstanding by *re*presenting it as a system of normative categories. In this capacity symbols help individuals and groups order the world in which they live. In signalling conceptual categories, symbols help individuals understand the world as a realm of socially ordered knowledge and experiences. This knowing is attained through a process of referencing: symbols presence the world as a network of references. Because landscapes are understood through symbolic representations including, but not limited to, language, and because representations are by definition metaphoric (in that they identify one thing in terms of another), understanding takes place through a process of metaphoric inter-referencing. Preunderstanding is the truth that is constructed in a total system of metaphoric relations.

These general comments have major implications for how we view and interpret material culture, including rock-art. Let me begin by elaborating on the concept of metaphor as reference before venturing into the world of archaeologically observable symbols. This will enable us to look at Australian rock-art in a way that sheds new light on the antiquity of the ethnographically known Dreaming's symbolic expressions, and through time the dynamics of indigenous preunderstanding(s).

Metaphor as reference

In their appropriately titled book *Metaphors We Live By*, George Lakoff and Mark Johnson (1980) write that the world we experience and know is socially and meaningfully constructed through metaphors, that is, the world is understood by relating one thing to another in a total referential system.

Because all things are experienced in time, our initial experience and knowledge of things take place in an already-present preunderstanding, and are therefore processed and positioned in an existing referential system already imbued with meaning. From their initial conceptualization, all things emerge as already positioned in a referential frame that nevertheless continually shifts through engagement.

The concepts we call upon when we give meaning to things are founded on preunderstanding. When one value-laden object or concept is called upon to understand another – or more correctly, when one *representation* of an object or concept is called upon to understand another – reference is made to a socially and historically positioned system of meanings that links one thing to another. The known world is negotiated and confirmed in the process. We have already considered examples of this process of referencing and confirmation in Chapter 1, when discussing how a group of Pintupi men gave meaning to previously unknown buried sediments, and how Wardaman elders who came across new cave paintings eventually identified them as Dreaming White Cockatoos. In a similar vein, Western constructions of Aboriginality have also emerged from contemporary systems of meaning that call upon already loaded concepts for understanding. It is in this sense that popular Western constructions of Aboriginality often revolve around assumptions of timelessness that differ from the assumptions of timelessness that inform indigenous understandings of the Dreaming (see Chapters 1 and 6).

Inter-referencing is a property of cognitive thinking that lies at the very core of how we understand and communicate the world (see also my discussion of Derrida's *différance* and the open network of signs in Chapter 5). Let us consider some examples that show how our most basic concepts are metaphorically imbued, for it is not just material objects that are understood through referential links, but the very notions that enable us to perceive those objects. I take my examples from Lakoff and Johnson (1980).

Let us begin with a definition: 'The essence of metaphor is understanding and experiencing one kind of thing in terms of another' (Lakoff and Johnson 1980, p. 5). Consider for example the statement 'argument is war' (in the sense that arguments create tension). We relate one category (argument) to another (war), reflecting metaphorical relations that go deeper than the juxtaposition of labels (ibid., p. 4):

Your claims are *indefensible*.
He *attacked every weak point* in my argument.
His criticisms were *right on target*.
I *demolished* his argument.
I've never *won* an argument with him.
You disagree? Okay, *shoot*!
If you use that *strategy*, he'll *wipe you out*.
He *shot down* all of my arguments.

As Lakoff and Johnson (ibid., p. 5) have noted, 'We talk about arguments that way because we conceive of them that way – and we act according to the way we conceive of things.' The metaphoric effect is not an event but a conceptual process. To highlight the point: my own description of preunderstanding as socially produced talks of *constructing* a reality, of *building* a metaphoric world. I write of social and experiential reality as an additive process (rather than, say, something that is spiritually set for all time – while allowing for change – as in the notions that nuance and inform *Aboriginal* constructions of the Dreaming), consisting of a pre-existing, historical *foundation built upon* through engagement. It is not just in communication – linguistic, artistic or otherwise – that these metaphors are called upon,

but in the very rhythm of my own cultural preunderstanding.

A concept need not engage just a single metaphor. Indeed it cannot be limited in this way, for so-called 'disparate' concepts are linked in a net of metaphorical connections that constitutes the matrix of preunderstanding. We employ the notion of, and sometimes we think of, argument as war. This is not to say that the only idea or understanding we reference argument to is war: we sometimes also metaphorically say that 'arguments are building blocks'. At other times, two metaphors may be inter-related, the two stemming from a single referential notion: 'argument is war' and 'argument hurts' both identify and relate the dangers of argument to other dangerous things or to their properties. But not every referential notion will be internally coherent: we sometimes think of argument as dangerous, and at other times as a vehicle to understanding. A concept's metaphorical load is in this sense multivalent. This multivalency reflects the web of truths – sensual, emotional, intellectual – that frames preunderstanding.

There will always be historical reasons why a particular group of people, or context of talk or understanding, employs a particular metaphor. This is simply to say that things arise from historical circumstances. We cannot simply assume that a particular metaphor will directly reflect the 'natural' properties of things, independent of their human conception. Such a view of theorizing about metaphors and the categories with which we think has been labelled by Lakoff (1987) the 'classical view' of scientific logic. An example of this approach would be to treat the metaphor 'argument is war' as a natural condition of argument, for both argument and war are imbued with conflict. However, this would be to miss the cultural point, for what is at stake is how argument and war are each understood and valued within a given social system or context. The classical view assumes that categories directly reflect the 'natural' properties of objects. What such a view silences is that people give meaning to the world through concepts that have emerged from their own social-historical experiences. The meaning of a particular thing is not isolated from broader cultural contexts – the open network of signs. Such a view does not suit my purposes at all, for what I am interested in is precisely how people have socially constructed their worlds through a system of culturally meaningful references, and how these constructions have changed through time. It is the dynamics of a particular, historically positioned preunderstanding expressed in referential symbols and their metaphoric load that I wish to investigate.

What is important for this chapter is therefore not why a particular conceptual category or metaphor was first used by a given individual or group of people. Nor am I concerned here with why a particular representation was retained or rejected by the community at large. Rather, I am interested in how the experienced and known world has been variously referenced via a system of symbols through time. The system of symbolic references used is what is at stake. I am interested in how experience and knowledge of the world have been categorized, and how those symbolic categories have been inter-referenced through meaningful associations.

The Dreaming production of rock-art in Aboriginal Australia

Symbols imply reference, and reference implies metaphor. Metaphor is not simply how we think about the world. It is praxis, in that it orients the knowing subject in the world. Metaphors are imbued with a 'gravitational energy' (Gerhart and Russell 1984), an ontological directionality that aligns disparate concepts, rendering them known and experienced in their linkages. This applies equally to non-linguistic symbolic (including rock-art) as to linguistic expressions. Through time, changes in the way particular images have been referenced in rock-art imply changes in the metaphoric load of the concepts behind representations, and thus imply changes in preunderstanding. The antiquity of the Dreaming as we know it today can thus be investigated by tracking back in time its graphic representations, as conceptual categories referenced in a web of metaphoric relations.

Throughout mainland Australia, the world and all those who dwell in it were ordered during recent times in the Dreaming's totemic landscape. Dreaming affiliations employ concepts and symbols that enable people to relate to others and to the land. We have already seen many examples of this in previous chapters.

Take for example the Arrernte Native Cat Dreaming story discussed in Chapter 4. Totemic affiliations structure the fecund powers of the Dreaming, and totemically ordered human existence is an effect of that fecundity. Dreaming-mediated categories, such as Native Cat or Kangaroo totems, relate people, land and all things in a particular world order. Symbolic expressions, whether expressed in rock-art, dance or ritual seclusion, are representations of that order.

Rock-art thus involves a marking of the land by people who do more than wander around a politically neutral, open landscape. As Conkey (1990, p. 15) notes in relation to art styles, what artistic practices 'can tell us about is not culture or groups per se, but the contexts in which group or other social/cultural phenomena are mobilized as process'. Preunderstanding acts to structure and regulate symbolic behaviour by reference to meaningful conceptual categories. It is towards such concerns that I now turn by considering the pre-Historic rock-art of one part of Australia, southeast Cape York Peninsula.

Cape York rock-art

The archaeology of Cape York has already been discussed in previous chapters (in particular Chapter 7). It is along the Great Dividing Range that rock outcrops are commonly found, many of which are decorated with rock-art. Most of Cape York's known rock-art comes from the Koolburra Plateau, Laura and Ngarrabullgan (sandstone), and the Mitchell-Palmer and Chillagoe-Mungana-Rookwood (limestone) regions. Some granite outcrops are also known to contain paintings, stencils and prints, but rock-art here is never as common as it is in the sandstone and limestone outcrops (Figure 9.1).

Due to the limited distribution of rock outcrops suitable for marking, rock-art is found only in very restricted parts of Cape York. The southeastern corner of the Cape, however, has long been recognized as one of the world's great rock-art regions, early coined 'Quinkan Country' by rock-art enthusiasts, after the local Quinkan spirits documented from local indigenous groups (Trezise 1969). However, as we shall see below, this broad-brush characterization does not accurately tag the region's rock-art, for the ethnographically recorded Quinkan

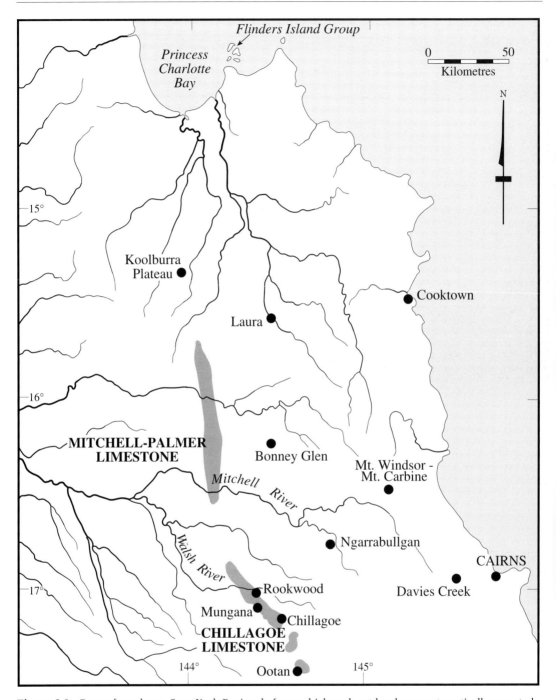

Figure 9.1 Parts of southeast Cape York Peninsula from which rock-art has been systematically reported

images likely only emerged during the late Holocene, part of a package of cultural innovations that changed the shape of Cape York's pre-History. Further, Quinkan rock-art is geographically restricted, being only found along the Laura sandstones, stylistically one of many more or less distinctive and discrete bodies of art to emerge in Cape York during the late Holocene.

Systematic recordings have been made in

Figure 9.2 Patinated peckings from People's Palace, Mitchell-Palmer limestone zone

Cape York of 10,746 rock pictures from 398 sites, representing nineteen geographically distinct regions (see Figure 9.1). It is from these recordings that the art's spatial and temporal patterning can be explored.

Spatial and temporal trends

The rock-art of Cape York has traditionally been divided into three broad techniques by archaeologists, stencils/prints, engravings and paintings. Stencils/prints[1] and paintings are geographically widespread, occurring in all regions where systematic surveys have been undertaken. Engravings tend to be restricted to limestone and sandstone country; harder granites or basalts have yielded only one known example of an engraving (David and Wilson 1998).

Peckings

Most of Cape York's engravings are pecked, although abrasions and poundings are also found. Heavily patinated peckings occur in all regions where engravings have been recorded: the Koolburra Plateau, Laura, the Mitchell-Palmer (Figure 9.2) and Chillagoe-Mungana-Rookwood regions. Patinated peckings include mazes (Figure 9.3), pits (sometimes singly, sometimes in rows or sets), radiating lines (star-shapes), circles and their variants, single or sets of lines and structurally simple linear, non-figurative designs. In the Koolburra Plateau, Mitchell-Palmer and Chillagoe-Mungana-Rookwood regions, macropod and bird tracks are also present. These patinated engravings have been suggested to possess considerable antiquity by all researchers who have come across them during the course of their research in Cape York, from Percy Trezise in the 1960s (e.g. 1969, 1971), to Andrée Rosenfeld (Rosenfeld *et al.* 1981) who was able to convincingly argue for their minimum age of 13,000 years BP at the Early Man site, to Josephine Flood (1987) who argued for a minimum age of 7280 ± 130 years BP in the Koolburra Plateau (based on associations with occupied deposits). At Sandy Creek 1 near Laura, a pecked sandstone fragment was

Figure 9.3   Heavily patinated pecked maze from the Pleistocene site of Sandy Creek 1 (*Source*: Josephine Flood)

found buried beneath sediments dated to 12,620 ± 370 years BP (Morwood *et al.* 1995, pp. 78–9). Other buried peckings have been found beneath sediments at Green Ant Shelter (Koolburra Plateau) (> 1570 ± 60 years BP); Sandy Creek 1 (> 1890 ± 70 years BP); and Yam Camp (Laura) (> 950 ± 50 years BP) (Flood 1987; Morwood and Dagg 1995; Morwood *et al.* 1995). At Magnificent Gallery, Noelene Cole *et al.* (1995, p. 154) have argued for their maximum antiquity shortly before 10,250 ± 90 years BP by association with the commencement of human occupation. At Chillagoe, David Chant and I also suggested their Pleistocene antiquity by association with dated occupation at Fern Cave (beginning 30,300 ± 800 years BP) (Figure 9.4) and Walkunder Arch Cave (beginning by at least 15,950 ± 770 years BP) (Campbell and Mardaga-Campbell 1993; David and Chant 1995).

Cole *et al.* (1995) and John Campbell and Mireille Mardaga-Campbell (1993) have also obtained minimum AMS radiocarbon determinations for oxalates captured in stratified, laminated cortex found immediately over peckings. At Walkunder Arch Cave near Chillagoe, Campbell and Mardaga-Campbell (1993, p. 59) reported a single radiocarbon date of 7085 ± 135 years BP for oxalates over a patinated, pecked star-shape, indicating its minimum age. At Sandy Creek 1, a minimum date of 2810 ± 150 years BP has been obtained for accumulated crust deposits over a linear non-figurative pecking, but we are not told whether or not this picture is patinated (Cole *et al.* 1995, pp. 155–6). At the Deighton Lady rockshelter, a reworked pecked maze, parts of which are heavily patinated and others fresh and unpatinated, has been dated to more than 2784 ± 85 years BP. However, Cole *et al.* (1995, p. 156) warn that this radiocarbon date probably represents 'the most recent refurbishing of much older engravings'. At the Kennedy River site, a lightly pecked bird track with unreported degrees of patination has been dated to over 1210 ± 245 years BP (Cole *et al.* 1995, p. 156). And in Quinkan B6 Rockshelter, a set of radiating lines was similarly dated to > 2850 ± 115 years BP (Cole *et al.* 1995, p. 156). The level of patination on this picture was not reported.

The patinated, non-figurative peckings of Cape York thus appear to have some considerable antiquity, at least in some cases going back to Pleistocene times. Unfortunately, all of the radiocarbon determinations dating cortex development in direct association with peckings are *minimal* dates, so it is not possible to argue with any conviction the spread of time involved in their creation.

However, there are also data to suggest that peckings are not restricted to Pleistocene or early Holocene times. In addition to the patinated engravings, there are also what appear to be more recent, unpatinated peckings in some regions, particularly at Laura and the Koolburra Plateau (Figure 9.5). In the Koolburra Plateau, Josephine Flood (1987) has reported two cases of unpatinated over patinated peckings. Noelene Cole *et al.* (1995, p. 156) have argued that the pecking from Deighton Lady reported above was last reworked around 2784 ± 85 years BP, even though the original pecking is probably much older than this, while the figurative peckings (including a dingo) at the Amphitheatre Site must date to less than 4000–3500 years BP (time of arrival of dogs in Australia). A very few unpatinated peckings have also been found in the Mitchell-Palmer limestone zone (from the People's Palace site only). These unpatinated peckings include both figurative and non-figurative forms reminiscent of the late Holocene paintings (see below). A small number of what appear to be very recent, unpatinated, shallow pounded pits have also been recorded from the Chillagoe-Mungana-Rookwood regions further to the south (David and David 1988).

In sum, we can say that patinated peckings throughout Cape York tend to be very old, dating to the early Holocene and/or late Pleistocene. At Laura they are in some cases older than 13,000 years BP. In the Koolburra Plateau, patinated peckings are believed to be more than 7300 years BP by association with occupied deposits. Motif forms consist of patinated pits, circles and their variants, mazes, star-shapes, single and multiple lines, and simple linear motifs. In the Koolburra Plateau, Laura, and in some very rare cases in the Mitchell-Palmer area, peckings were also undertaken during more recent, mid to late Holocene times, by then including both non-figurative and figurative designs (including dogs and anthropomorphs). We do not know whether this indicates a continuity of tradition, or whether pecking activity stopped, perhaps around the early Holocene, to resume again

Figure 9.4 Heavily patinated pecked bird track shape from the Pleistocene site of Fern Cave

Figure 9.5 Unpatinated peckings beneath paintings at Green Ant rockshelter, Koolburra Plateau (*Source*: Josephine Flood)

during the mid or late Holocene (see Cole *et al.* 1995; Flood 1987; Rosenfeld *et al.* 1981 for further details).

Paintings

Unlike the early peckings, Cape York's paintings are geographically highly regionalized. This is so of motif forms and of design linearity, use of infilling and of internal decorations. To a lesser extent, regionalism is also apparent in the use of specific colours (see David and Chant 1995, for multivariate statistical analyses).

The regional character of paintings is most apparent in the geographical distribution of motif forms. This regionalism occurs at two geographic scales. At its broadest scale, the rock paintings to the north of the Walsh-Mitchell Rivers are predominantly figurative in form. This is so of all regions studied: the Mitchell River, Palmer River, Bonney Glen Station, Jowalbinna, Laura River, Jackass Station, Davies Creek (Bare Hill), Mt Windsor/Mt Car-

bine, Koolburra Plateau, Jane Table Hill, Clack Island, Cliff Island, Bathurst Range and the Flinders Island group. In each region, figurative pictures account for at least 65 per cent of the art, and in all but one case for over 76 per cent. To the immediate south, however, motifs take on a different character. This shift in predominant motif form takes place over a short distance, occurring near the Mitchell or Walsh Rivers; there is no evidence of gradual change as one approaches these rivers. In contrast to the situation in the north, at Ngarrabullgan, Rookwood, Mungana, Chillagoe and Ootan figurative pictures never account for more than 9 per cent of paintings (David and Chant 1995). Such geographical patterning is clearly distinctive from that characterizing the old (patinated) peckings, where uniformity in motif forms is found across a broad geographical expanse.

The paintings are further geographically fragmented when specific motifs are considered. In the Koolburra Plateau echidna–human shapes are common, accounting for 28

Figure 9.6 Human-echidna therianthropes, Koolburra Plateau (*Source*: Josephine Flood)

per cent of paintings – more than one in four (Figure 9.6). Such motifs are *never* found elsewhere. In the contiguous regions of Jane Table Hill, Clack Island, Cliff Island, Bathurst Range and the Flinders Island group, moth/butterfly designs and zoomorphs with crescent heads always account for at least 43 per cent of paintings/drawings, and in most of these areas they account for more than 50 per cent; again, these are never found elsewhere (Figure 9.7). In the Laura region to the south, zoomorphs (of a broad range of taxa) predominate, including many in bichrome (Figure 9.8). Further to the south, in what is today Gugu Yalanji Aboriginal country, anthropomorphs predominate. These are usually monochrome infilled designs, rarely showing any signs of internal decoration. This predominance of anthropomorphs is found in all areas where rock-art surveys have been undertaken in Gugu Yalanji country: Bonney Glen Station, Mitchell River (Figures 9.9–9.10), Palmer River and Mt Windsor/Mt Carbine (Figure 9.11). In all cases anthropomorphs account for over 62 per cent of paintings. In no other region are such high

proportions found (anthropomorphs elsewhere always account for less than 22 per cent of paintings). Furthermore, in all parts of Gugu Yalanji country anthropomorphs are commonly (but not predominantly) painted upside-down. This is not the case elsewhere, although the occasional upside-down anthropomorph can occur anywhere. Last but not least, at Davies Creek anthropomorphs with up-bent arms and down-bent legs are common, again an endemic feature of the local paintings (Clegg 1978; David and Chant 1995).

To the south of the Mitchell and Walsh Rivers, paintings are predominantly non-figurative motifs dominated by extended linear designs and geometric shapes. Many of these are reminiscent of the older, Pleistocene to early–mid Holocene patinated peckings: lines, spots, star-shapes, circles and their variants, simple linear designs (such peckings continue into the late Holocene in some regions) (Figures 9.12–9.14).

In short, many of the painted motifs of Cape York are geographically restricted. There is also a regionalism by colour, with no part of

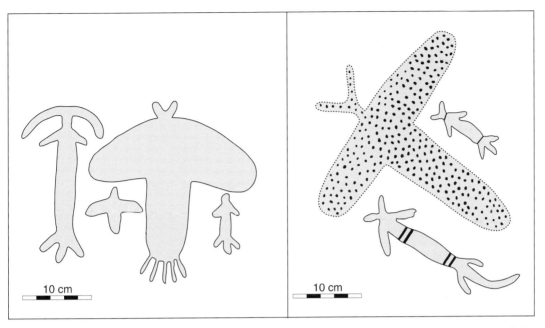

Figure 9.7 Moth-butterfly designs and zoomorphs with crescent heads, Princess Charlotte Bay and the Flinders Islands (*Source*: Graeme Walsh)

Figure 9.8 Flying foxes, Jackass Station

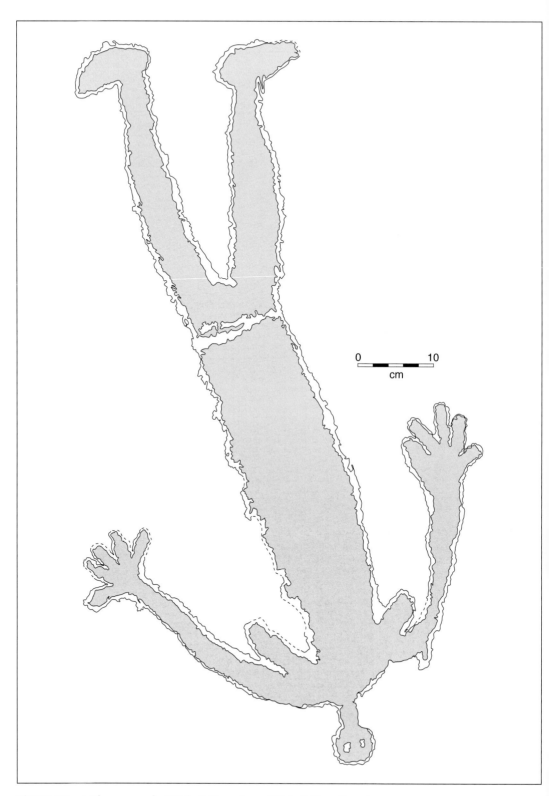

Figure 9.9 Anthropomorph, Mitchell River Cave, Mitchell River limestones

Figure 9.10 Anthropomorphs, Mitchell River limestones

Figure 9.11 Anthropomorphs, Mt Windsor/Mt Carbine (*Source*: M. David 1990, fig. 13)

the northern region possessing more than 13 per cent, and all parts of the south possessing more than 27 per cent white paintings. This has been suggested elsewhere (David and Chant 1995) not to be a simple reflection of the geological availability of white or other pigments, for white, red and yellow earth pigments are naturally available in many parts of Cape York. Rather, the distribution of paintings indicates geographical variation in the cultural choice and use of colours across space.

The age of paintings

There are a number of ways in which the absolute or relative age of Cape York's cave paintings have been estimated. Each approach, of its own, does not say much about the antiquity of the paintings as a whole. But together they offer considerable circumstantial evidence for their predominantly late Holocene antiquity.

Animals of known antiquity. In most parts of Cape York where figurative art is found, paintings of animals of known antiquity are depicted. Such animals fall into three categories. First, none of the paintings have been identified as of extinct animals – such as thylacines or megafauna – by any of the archaeologists who have worked in the region,

Figure 9.12   Radiating lines, Chillagoe region

Figure 9.13 Non-figurative designs, Walkunder Galleries, Chillagoe region

implying that the paintings date to a time after their extinction (given the overwhelmingly figurative nature of the northern paintings). Megafauna almost certainly became extinct during the late Pleistocene (almost certainly before 30,000, and probably before 40,000 years BP); an absence of such Pleistocene fauna in the art likely means that the figurative depictions are younger than 40–30,000 years BP. Thylacines, however, became extinct much later, during the mid-Holocene, probably around the time dingoes arrived. A total absence of thylacines in the art implies that figurative traditions largely, if not entirely, date to the last 4000–3500 years (contrast with the paintings in Arnhem Land 1100 km to the northwest, where thylacines are commonly painted in some of the older styles), although using absence of evidence as evidence of absence has of course to be treated cautiously.

Second, there is the presence of dogs in the paintings (Figure 9.15). Dogs never occur among the patinated peckings in caves or rockshelters. However, the finding of a pecked dingo in an open setting at the Amphitheatre Site near Laura (Cole and Trezise 1992), in the same style as the dingo paintings in the caves, is evidence that certain peckings, including some of figurative form, were undertaken during the mid to late Holocene, overlapping with the period of figurative paintings.

In some areas, such as the Mitchell River and Bonney Glen Station, paintings of dogs are relatively common. In many sites, including those of Laura, they are often incorporated within larger painted panels. In some rockshelters, such as Magnificent Gallery and Death Adder near Laura, large numbers of figurative paintings such as anthropomorphs, echidnas, lizards/crocodiles and flying foxes superimpose paintings of dogs (Cole *et al.* 1995, Figures 13.4a and 13.4c). The implication is that it is not only the individual dog paintings that must be less than 4000–3500 years old, but also the broader panels of which they are a part.

Third, animals (and items of material culture) imported into Australia from Europe occur in some regions, including Laura (e.g. pigs, horses, letters of the alphabet, anthropomorphs in European clothing) (Figures 9.16–9.17), the

Figure 9.14 Non-figurative designs, Ngarrabullgan

Mitchell–Palmer (pig) (Figure 9.18), Bonney Glen Station (horse) and Princess Charlotte Bay and the Flinders Island group (e.g. ships) (Figure 9.19), indicating continuity of tradition into very recent times. This does not mean that most of the individual paintings found in Cape York need date to the last 200 years, but that the painting traditions which included these pictures continued until this time.

In situ *earth pigments.* Thirty-two painted caves and rockshelters have been excavated and radiocarbon dated in Cape York. In 26 of these, stratified pieces of ochre were found in the ground (Table 9.1). In some sites, pigments are found from earliest times. One example is Sandy Creek 1, where two use-worn fragments of ochre were found in levels dated to around 32,000 years BP (Morwood *et al.* 1995). The precise timing of peak ochre deposition rates, and by implication peak ochre use, varies site by site. In some sites there is more than one peak. In every painted site excavated, however, peak rates are evident sometime during the last 3500 years, especially during the last

2000 years (David and Chant 1995; David and Lourandos 1998). At Ngarrabullgan Cave, a paint palette – a flat-surfaced rock with a dense splatter of yellow ochre – was also found just above a charcoal date of 3990 ± 70 years BP (Figure 9.20). In many sites, ochre is found only in mid to late Holocene levels (e.g. Mordor Cave, Lookout Shelter, Painted Ell, Initiation Cave, Kookaburra Rock, Dragonfly Hollow, Mitchell River Cave, Giant Horse Gallery, Ngarrabullgan Cave) (Figure 9.21). This is despite the fact that approximately half the excavated sites also possess earlier cultural deposits, often extending into the Pleistocene (Cole *et al.* 1995; David and Chant 1995; David and Lourandos 1997, 1998, in press; Morwood and Hobbs 1995). It is such observations that have led Josephine Flood (1987, p. 117) to suggest for a 'flowering of the Koolburra stencil and painting art' after 2500 years BP.

Superimpositions. Patterns of superimposition consistently show paintings over patinated peckings, but never the reverse. At Jowalbinna near Laura, Cole *et al.* (1995, p. 149) report 'at

Figure 9.15 Painted dogs, Mordor Cave, Mitchell-Palmer region

least 15 examples . . . in which paintings occur over engravings', but 'no cases . . . in which deeply pecked engravings overlie paintings'. For the Koolburra Plateau, Josephine Flood and Nicky Horsfall (1986, p. 26) report that 'all the rock paintings at Green Ant Shelter seem fresh and overlie the engravings'. Flood (1987, pp. 95–6) further notes that while paintings have been seen to occur over peckings, no examples of engravings over pigment art have been recorded. In the Mitchell-Palmer region, David Chant and I (David and Chant 1995, p. 465) report that 'the only cases of paintings and [patinated] peckings occurring in superimposition are at Hearth Cave, where paintings are repeatedly placed over peckings'.

There are no obvious patterns of superimposition among the paintings of Ootan, Chillagoe, Mungana and Rookwood (David and David 1988). Cole *et al.* (1995, p. 149) also note for the Laura paintings that 'analysis of superimpositions in the Jowalbinna data . . . shows no correlation between attributes such as motif, form, dimensions and position in the sequence'. I likewise have seen no clear-cut

motif changes through time for the Mitchell-Palmer region via superimpositions, although there are some indications that an earlier, non-figurative painting tradition may once have existed (sample size is too small for the trend to be definitive). This possible earlier non-figurative tradition is quite distinct from the predominantly figurative traditions that today characterize these regions. Similarly at Jowalbinna Cole *et al.* (1995, p. 149) note that 'stylistically different paintings covered by mineral deposits have been recorded at Red Lady, Echidna People, Magnificent Gallery, and Kennedy River'. Unfortunately, we are not told what these 'stylistically different paintings' look like. The fact that human occupation at Magnificent Gallery is known to have begun sometime before $10,250 \pm 90$ years BP (Morwood and Jung 1995) here allows for a considerable period of time for artistic change. In the Mitchell-Palmer region, the only cases of superimposition involving non-figurative and figurative paintings have the former underlying the latter. In one site, barred, irregular ovals are superimposed by a painted anthro-

Figure 9.16 Painted letters, Jackass Station, Laura

Figure 9.17   Painted horse, Giant Horse, Laura

pomorph typical of the paintings of the region. The underlying non-figurative paintings are, like the Magnificent Gallery old paintings, covered by mineral crusts, lending further support for their greater antiquity than the superimposing figurative paintings.

Fragile pigments.   In many parts of Cape York, fragile pigments have been used for painting. This is the case especially of brown mud and white clays (in particular kaolinite). In all regions to the south of the Mitchell and Walsh Rivers, white is very common, as I have already noted accounting for more than one-quarter of the paintings. That this pigment has survived suggests a relatively young age for much of the art of these regions. While less common to the north, fragile white kaolinite and brown mud pigments also account for many paintings – around one in ten – executed in similar artistic conventions as the paintings found in other colours. Again, the implication is that the painting traditions of each region have an antiquity that continues late into history (contrast this situation, for example, with the oldest paintings of Arnhem Land and the

Kimberley to the west, where white pigments are almost entirely absent).

Pigments in microstratified rock cortex.   Since the early 1990s, a number of researchers have attempted to better understand the antiquity of Cape York's rock-art by obtaining AMS determinations on carbon-bearing compounds closely associated with pigment art. One method, developed by Alan Watchman (e.g. 1993; Watchman *et al.* 2000), aims to reveal the presence of ancient pigments now buried above and/or beneath laminae within the rock cortex, and to extract datable materials by laser-ablating adjacent carbon-bearing layers for AMS dating. Such methods of micro-excavation have enabled the acquisition of sequences of dates, giving minimum and/or maximum ages for artistic events. In perhaps the best example of this technique, a sequence of ten radiocarbon determinations was obtained from a 2.1 mm-thick gypsum-oxalate crust from Walkunder Arch Cave. All dates were in sequence, the oldest ($29,700 \pm 500$ years BP) near the base of the crust and the youngest (3340 ± 60 years BP) near the present

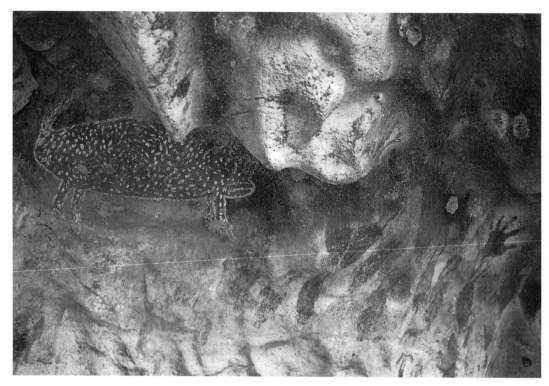

Figure 9.18   Painted pig, Mordor Cave, Mitchell-Palmer region

wall surface (Campbell *et al.* 1996). These internally consistent results offer confidence in the individual dates as well as in the technique as a whole. However, since the pigments have only been revealed in cross-section, we do not know if they relate to paintings or stencils or to some other form of pigment art. We do not know the shapes of the motifs, nor the source of the carbon. This method is therefore considered still experimental.

So far such dating of rock-art has been applied to two regions only, Laura and Chillagoe. At Laura, Alan Watchman found traces of pigment in rock cortex from a number of sites. At Sandy Creek 2, AMS determinations indicate the presence of haematite 24,600 ± 220, 16–15,000, and 6655 ± 80 years BP (Cole *et al.* 1995, p. 156). At Sandy Creek 1, laminae possessing traces of red pigment have been dated to shortly before 2810 ± 150 years BP, while a layer of yellow pigment was dated to greater than 2850 ± 115 years BP at the Quinkan B6 rockshelter (Cole *et al.* 1995, p. 156).

At Walkunder Arch Cave (Chillagoe), red haematite dating to 28,100 ± 400,

16,100 ± 130, and 6790 ± 70 years BP, yellow goethite (25,800 ± 280 and 22,800 ± 210 years BP), and one layer of white clay (age not reported) embedded in laminated rock cortex have been published (Campbell and Mardaga-Campbell 1993; Campbell *et al.* 1996; Watchman and Campbell 1996; Watchman and Hatte 1996, pp. 90–1). These have been interpreted as pigment art. For another part of the cave, Campbell *et al.* (1996, p. 233) report a maximum AMS date of 9470 ± 120 years BP 'for a painting [read pigment art] which has been obscured by crustal growth' (see also Watchman and Hatte 1996). The pigment art (painting, stencil or print) must be younger than this. These results strongly imply that the creation of pigment art was undertaken before 3500 years BP. They are an important line of evidence to the emerging chronology of Cape York's rock-art, indicating that the marking of place through pigment art (of undetermined technique and of unknown forms) did not suddenly begin during the mid to late Holocene, but has a much older antiquity.

Figure 9.19   Painted ship, Flinders Islands (*Source*: Graeme Walsh)

Direct AMS dates on paintings.   Since the early 1990s, direct AMS dates on paintings have become available for the Laura, Mitchell-Palmer, Chillagoe-Mungana-Rookwood and Ootan regions. At Yam Camp, Laura, Alan Watchman and Noelene Cole (1993) reported radiocarbon dates of 725±115 and 730±75 years BP on plant fibres (probably brush filaments) incorporated within the earth pigments of two adjacent painted anthropomorphs.

Thirty-seven rock-art sites have been recorded from the Mitchell-Palmer region. Systematic recordings have revealed 1093 items of rock-art, most of which are paintings. Nine of these have been radiocarbon-dated. All dated paintings were undertaken in charcoal, most in parts of caves well protected from the elements. At Hay Cave, where archaeological excavations have shown human occupation beginning around 30,000 years BP and continuing until the European contact period, four radiocarbon dates were obtained from two separate painted panels. One panel is located along the cave's back wall in a protected part of the site, in semi-dark conditions on the wall

of a large limestone pillar. Here can be found a small number of abstract paintings. A set of radiating lines, 30 cm long, was sampled for dating, revealing an AMS determination of 1010±60 years BP. Some 8 m to the west, on a separate, overhanging ceiling about 3 m above a boulder scree deposit, a series of thin linear, black infilled anthropomorphs, many with inverted V-shaped heads, can be found. Averaging around 30 cm in length, each of these paintings possesses similar characteristics. They are positioned close to each other and spatially isolated from most of the other art in the cave, the entire group appearing to represent a single artistic event. Three of these paintings were sampled, revealing AMS dates of 1480±50, 1570±110 and 1700±90 years BP. The dates overlap at two standard deviations, confirming their likely contemporaneity and with this the reliability of their radiocarbon ages.

A few tens of metres from Hay Cave can be found Painted Shelter, a small rockshelter under an overhanging limestone boulder, where the limestone outcrops meet the plains.

Table 9.1   The timing of increasing deposition rates of ochre, by site

Site	Dates when deposition rates of ochre begin to increase within excavated rock-art sites, in uncalibrated radiocarbon years BP
Hand Shelter	650
Mitchell River Cave	1100–900
Magnificent Gallery	1200
Yam Camp	1250
Mordor Cave	1500
Early Man Rockshelter	~1800
Sandy Creek 1	1900–1200
Lookout Shelter 1	1900
Green Ant Rockshelter	2200–1800
Grass Tree Shelter	2100
Red Bluff Rockshelter	3000
Echidna's Rest	3000
Kookaburra Rock	~3000
Hay Cave	3100
Nonda Rock	3400
Hearth Cave	3500
Painted Ell	3600
Gorge Creek Shelter	3700
Tunnell Shelter	3700
Giant Horse Gallery	<3800
Pete's Chase	4000
Dragonfly Hollow	<4400
Initiation Cave	<5300
Ngarrabullgan Cave	5400
Magnificent Gallery	10,000
Fern Cave	22,000

Three paintings are found under the overhang. One of these, a series of thin black lines underlying an orange, horizontal anthropomorph, was AMS dated to 2420±130 years BP. The anthropomorph is therefore more recent than this date (Figure 9.22).

At Pete's Chase, a limestone cave perched high above the surrounding plains a few kilometres to the north of Hay Cave, paintings occur both near the cave entrance and on its internal walls. A 15-cm-high, black infilled anthropomorph on the back wall of the cave was sampled for AMS dating. A radiocarbon date of 310±70 years BP was obtained. The painting overlies a red outlined, tan infilled anthropomorph, and underlies a brown infilled anthropomorph. The brown anthropomorph is therefore younger than about 300 years BP, and the red outlined anthropomorph older. Some 5 m to the south, a black infilled anthropomorph also occurs. It dates to 2090±100 years BP.

Two AMS dates have been obtained from Alcove Cave, also in the Mitchell-Palmer region. This is a medium-sized limestone cave near the ground level of the surrounding plain. A well-protected painted alcove occurs within the cave, some 2 m above the ground level. Within the alcove can be found a larger panel

Figure 9.20   Paint palette, Ngarrabullgan Cave
Note: Scale in mm

of long, linear anthropomorphs with slanted heads or headdresses, mostly painted in red ochre but including two charcoal examples. The two charcoal anthropomorphs were each AMS dated as 'modern' (i.e. < 200 years BP). It is likely that the entire panel dates to around the period of European contact.

Finally, there are also now available numerous dates from charcoal paintings in the Chillagoe, Mungana, Rookwood (limestone) regions and nearby Ootan (granite), located in the non-figurative artistic zone to the south of the Walsh River. The AMS dated paintings include seventeen that came from the limestone outcrops, and one from a granite boulder near Ootan. These paintings include examples of each of the major motif categories: star-shapes, grids and barred enclosed designs, geometric shapes and other simple linear forms. They come from six sites. In some cases, the sampled paintings occur beneath other (undated) paintings, in which case they give a maximum date for the overlying art. Two paintings lying in superimposition are also

each dated. The overlying is younger than the underlying painting, in line with expectations.

The oldest AMS date for these paintings and drawings is 3350 ± 350 years BP, with most dates younger than 2000 years BP (David *et al.* 1999). There are no apparent changes in motif shapes through time: the entire set of motifs appears to pertain to the entire period of time covered by the paintings. This is not surprising, as previous analyses of superimpositions had revealed no significant patterns for this region (David and David 1988).

Discussion

Rock painting activity in Cape York Peninsula dates largely to the last 3500 years BP, and especially to the last 2000 years BP, although older pigment art clearly also took place, as indicated by Alan Watchman's research on microstratified rock cortex. One implication of this contrast between late regional painting traditions and earlier homogeneous peckings (and possibly paintings) is that artistic regionalization in Cape York is relatively recent, not exceeding 3500 years BP and coming into full force especially during the last 2000 years. It is, therefore, not just the art that is being dated, but also the changing geographical structure of the archaeological record.

Before discussing further the implications of such artistic regionalization for the way groups of people increasingly called upon regionally distinctive symbolic references to understand and mark the world, for landscape construction, and for social and territorial behaviour during the late Holocene, let us further explore some of the symbolic dimensions of these changing artistic patterns. In particular, I wish to focus on how animals were referenced across space in the late Holocene paintings. For as we shall see, people did not just suddenly begin to paint in different 'styles' after 3500–2000 years BP. What took place involved also the referential signs through which peoples marked, understood, experienced and deferred to their worlds.

The key here is the concept of *reference*, or, more correctly, the way the world is ordered in a chain of inter-connected signifiers. This process involves the construction and relation of categories in a metaphorical system of meanings. It is when the sign is called upon to

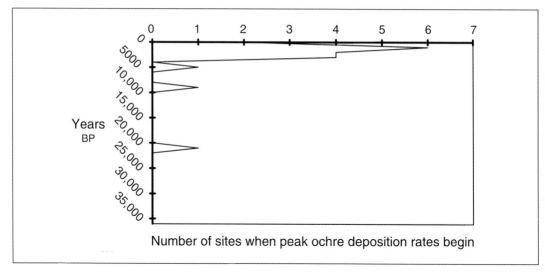

Figure 9.21 Number of sites when peak ochre deposition rates begin, in 1000-year intervals

express the way things are that its referential load is identified. And because categories operate in a world of values, the referential points are themselves value-laden. By exploring the world of references, we position ourselves such that we can explore world orders and systems of signification and, in the process, dimensions of meaning in particular modes of preunderstanding. The animals depicted in Cape York's late Holocene cave paintings are evidence for the emergence of newly regionalized referential systems.

Figure 9.22 Black lines underneath a yellow anthropomorph. The black lines in rectangular boxes were AMS dated

Let us first begin with the animals found in nature. Cape York possesses no large animals of any kind by world standards: the largest are the macropodoids (kangaroos, wallabies and bettongs), the flightless emu (up to 2 m tall) and the cassowary (up to 1.8 m tall). The macropodoids are very common throughout the mainland, varying in numbers through the year and from year to year. Numerous species are known for the late Holocene: eastern grey kangaroo, *Macropus giganteus* (4–66 kg body weight); common wallaroo, *Macropus robustus* (25–47 kg); antilopine wallaroo, *Macropus antilopinus* (16–49 kg); swamp wallaby, *Wallabia bicolor* (13–17 kg); agile wallaby, *Macropus agilis* (9–27 kg); northern nailtail wallaby, *Onychogalea unguifera* (6–8 kg); spotted-tailed quoll, *Dasyurus maculatus* (4–7 kg); rock wallabies, *Petrogale godmani* and *P. mareeba* (4–5 kg); pademelon, *Thylogale stigmatica* (4–5 kg); spectacled hare-wallaby, *Lagorchestes conspicillatus* (2–5 kg); rufous bettong, *Aepyprymnus rufescens* (3–4 kg); and northern bettong, *Bettongia tropica* (1 kg). There are also other small mammals: northern brown bandicoot, *Isoodon macrourus* (1–3 kg); common brushtail possum, *Trichosurus vulpecula* (1–5 kg); common ringtail possum, *Pseudocheirus peregrinus* (1 kg); northern quoll, *Dasyurus hallucatus* (1 kg); the monotreme short-beaked echidna, *Tachyglossus aculeatus*, also known as the spiny anteater (2–7 kg); and the sub-kilogram striped possum, *Dactylopsila trivirgata*; sugar glider, *Petaurus breviceps*; feathertail glider, *Acrobates pygmaeus*; long-tailed pygmy possum, *Cercartetus caudatus*; red-cheeked dunnart, *Sminthopsis virginiae*; kultarr, *Antechinomys laniger*; common planigale, *Planigale maculata*; and fourteen species of rodents (rats and mice). A broad range of bats and flying foxes are also present, all weighing less than 1 kg (see entries in Strahan 1995). In addition to these mammals, Cape York also has, since its arrival probably from southeast Asia 4000–3500 years BP, the Australian dog *Canis lupus dingo* (9–24 kg) (David in press).

The non-mammalian vertebrate fauna include many species of snakes, lizards (some of which can measure up to 2 m in length), turtles, fish, and well over 150 species of birds. Along the coastal fringes and northern and eastern waterways, saltwater crocodiles are found, as is the freshwater crocodile in many rivers (Cogger 1996).

The vertebrate fauna of Cape York are of seven general body shapes. It is these body shapes that feature in the generalized figurative paintings of Cape York, and representatives of each faunal category are found in nature, in large numbers, in all regions:

1 Macropodoids, with long legs/feet and very small arms/hands.
2 Mammalian quadrupeds other than macropodoids, with four limbs of roughly equal length.
3 Bipedal birds.
4 Lizards and crocodiles, with long tails and relatively short limbs.
5 Echidna and turtles, with protruding heads and opposing short tails, roundish bodies and short lateral extensions for arms and legs.
6 Snakes.
7 Fish.

Let us consider the animals that were part of the diet, so as to better understand the significance of the faunal range in the paintings. Identifiable animal bones have been found from five of the regions from which rock-art is here considered: Princess Charlotte Bay and the Flinders Island group (three sites), Laura (seven sites), Mitchell and Palmer rivers (one site), Ngarrabullgan (one site), and Rookwood-Mungana-Chillagoe (three sites). Of the faunal remains attributed to cultural activity, and excluding the (semi-domestic) dog, a narrow range of species has been identified. In all regions, the range and order of predominance of eaten fauna are similar: *Petrogale* predominates, followed by other macropodoids, bandicoots, possums and snakes. Macropodoids account for about half the Minimum Number of Individuals recovered from every region. It is remarkable indeed that in each of the fifteen excavated sites, not a single exception to the rule has emerged, implying widespread dietary habits and food technological bases (see David in press for further details of diet breadths from individual sites).

This region-wide similarity does not, however, extend to the animals depicted in the art. The faunal paintings from the nineteen regions of Cape York to have been reported are highly regionalized. In the north, the five analytical regions that together comprise Princess Charlotte Bay and the Flinders Island group – Clack

Island, Cliff Island, Flinders Islands, Bathurst Head, Jane Table Hill – contain 1246 paintings of animals (Grahame Walsh, pers. comm. 1996); 223 – 18 per cent – are of marine fauna. Many are invertebrates – squid, octopus and crustacean. Curiously, another 74 per cent are of moths and butterflies or zoomorphs with crescent heads that closely resemble moths and butterflies.

In archaeological contexts, few of these would be recoverable food items if eaten. We cannot, therefore, neatly compare and contrast animals consumed for food with those depicted in the rock-art. Of the vertebrates, 303 sting-rays, dugongs/sharks, fish/eels, turtles, birds, crocodiles/lizards, snakes and dogs are represented in the art. Marine items predominate. Sea turtles and dugongs/sharks are the most common, together accounting for 57 per cent of vertebrate fauna in the art. Turtles and dugongs were also recovered among the excavated food remains. Macropodoids are totally absent from the art. Yet they appear in *every* excavation, and they predominate as vertebrate food items in all sites. While the animals commonly frequented in the marine environment are represented in the art, the terrestrial fauna are not. Nor does the art accurately reflect diet breadths.

In the Koolburra Plateau to the south, the range of painted fauna is small (Flood 1987): only 56 paintings of animals in total, excluding the echidna–human therianthropes. Of these, crocodiles are the most common, followed by turtles, lizards, fish and snakes. A total absence of mammals implies that it is improbable that the painted animals are subsistence-related. If we include the echidna-human therianthropes, the pattern becomes even more curious, for now 126 of 182 animal paintings (69 per cent) relate to echidnas (monotreme mammals). In the Koolburra Plateau, again, we fail to see the macropodoids that are among the largest and most readily visible animals in the landscape, as well as the most common vertebrate food items everywhere across southeast Cape York.

At Laura to the south there are 730 animal paintings, excluding the rare introduced animals such as horses and thirteen sets of invertebrates (bees) (Cole 1992; Cole and David 1992; David and Chant 1995; David and Cole 1990; Maynard 1976; see David and Lourandos 1998 for a compilation of data). The most com-

mon animals are flying foxes and fish, followed by birds and macropodoids. Flying foxes and birds contribute only 4 per cent of the excavated (eaten) fauna; fish are totally absent. Macropodoids are numerically important, accounting for 52 per cent of food items. Other marsupials – possums, bandicoots and *Petaurus* – together account for nearly a quarter (23 per cent) of food items. They make up < 1 per cent of the art. There is a clear difference between the faunal range as represented in the food remains, and that represented in the paintings.

In the Palmer and Mitchell Rivers to the south, the 75 paintings again include a relatively broad range of animal taxa (a painting of the introduced pig is excluded). As is the case at Laura to the immediate north, flying foxes predominate, accounting for 44 per cent of the painted animals. Dogs are also numerically important (31 per cent), with birds (Figure 9.23), eel/fish and turtles coming next. No marsupials of any kind are represented, including macropodoids, despite their predominance as a meat food (David and Chant 1995).

At Ngarrabullgan to the south, two animals – a crocodile and a snake – occur. In the Rookwood-Mungana-Chillagoe regions nearby, five animals are found, two snakes, two echidnas and one turtle. Again, the marsupials fail to be depicted, including the ubiquitous food item, *Petrogale*.

In rock-art, animals across Cape York were thus conceived and employed differentially across space, testimony to the presence of regionalized referential frames across the Cape. The late Holocene rock-art of Cape York can thus be read as a statement of the structured division of socially engaged, marked and signified space. In the increasing regionalism of post-3500 years BP times, space became newly differentiated. The rock-art can be seen as a mark of regional difference and symbolic structure. What we find in Cape York is not a widespread and static socio-spatial system, but instead a dynamic and emerging set of geographically distinctive networks of place marking. During the late Pleistocene and early Holocene, the landscape was inscribed with geographically relatively homogeneous artistic symbols, becoming increasingly regionalized after 3500 years BP. This process of regionalization continued with increasing momentum through the course of the late Holocene, the intensity and nature of painting activity begin-

Figure 9.23   Bird, Mitchell-Palmer region

ning to approximate the ethnographic situation around 2000 years BP.

Regionalization in Cape York thus concerned more than motif forms or colours or techniques. More fundamentally, it involved also the emergence of geographically singular animal motifs, symbols that were meaningful in geographically distinctive chains of signification. Such animals emerged as meaningful not simply as animals in 'nature' or as food items, but as components in regionalized networks of reference that served to order social space and meaning in the world.

A picture sets up 'the formal properties of disjunction, rupture, difference and deferral of meaning before the content itself becomes visible' (Elkins 1998, p. 19). This is the inherent power of things, an empowerment realized not through the function of an object's end product, but in its very coming into being. Pictures, like words but not because of words, help individuals construct and experience the world as social and ontological structuration, a structuration to which experience is deferred ('the act of making a mark divides', notes Elkins (ibid., p. 25)). The emergence in Cape York of regionalized artistic traditions, including regionalized faunal referential systems, signals a radical restructuring of the chain of signifiers

in which rock-art operated, a new division of knowledge and experience. These late Holocene changes represent the emergence of new, regionalized systems of difference and deference; a reworking of the open network of signs and a transformation in the overall system of preunderstanding, as the historical framework of referenced understanding. These are transformations of a major structural kind. What took place during the late Holocene was a regionalization of compliance to (marked) place and preunderstanding.

These changes in networks of signs through which meaning is attained, symbolized and communicated imply that the signification of artistic and other cultural practices across Cape York also shifted. The ethnographically recognized network of references that informed the art came into being through the course of the late Holocene, rather than having remained virtually unchanged over the many millennia of Aboriginal occupation on the peninsula.

Note

1. I will not further discuss stencils here for they are largely restricted to hand stencils, occurring in all regions and through the entire artistic sequence.

10 Conclusion

The real voyage of discovery consists not in seeking new landscapes but in having new eyes.[1]

In this book I have tried to tease out two intersecting threads of the Australian Aboriginal past. The first strand concerns the past as seen from a scientific perspective; in particular it concerns the history of the Dreaming, as indigenous ontology known from ethnography. Here Aboriginal history is revealed as dynamic, social history knowable through archaeological discourse. The second strand concerns Western historical practice as a hermeneutic project rich – or poor, depending on how one wants to look at it – in Western preconceptions. I now conclude by re-weaving these two strands into a new fabric of understanding about the dynamics of social being in the Australian Aboriginal past. I go beyond artefacts as facts about objects, and archaeological writing as a disengaged, objective enterprise. In its stead, I build a pre-History of social alterity, identity, and preunderstanding hermeneutically built in the consciousness of the writer, as engaged social commentator.

History as the testimony of (non)experience

Maurice Blanchot (1994), the French writer and critic, recounts a story about 'a young man' in occupied France towards the end of World War II. The year is 1944, and the enemy[2] are set on a last-ditch murder spree across the countryside, randomly executing young men from farming households. At Blanchot's château, everyone is told to file outside, and the young man is singled out for the firing squad. Alone and facing a line of armed soldiers, he encounters the moment of his death.

With the gunmen ready, the Lieutenant in charge is about to give the order to fire when a commotion breaks out nearby. The Lieutenant leaves his post to investigate, giving the opportunity for one of the soldiers to tell the young man to flee, and he escapes.

Blanchot was writing about himself (Jacques Derrida (1994) confirms this through the publication of extracts of a personal letter he was sent by Blanchot). *The Instant of My Death* recounts the experience of his own death unexperienced. Blanchot's written work is authoritative of the instant of his death, and yet it cannot be said to mark a knowledge of the moment of a death that never happened. This is an authority derived not from the experience of the moment of death, but from an experience that *approaches* the instant of death. *The Instant of My Death* does not reveal history as authority about the experienced, for Blanchot never truly experienced his death, but history as authorship. Blanchot's own authorship of the instant of his death is a moment of literary interpretation and commitment, and says as much about his approach towards something he has not experienced as about the event (of death) itself.

So, too, with the writing of a past unexperienced. This is at least doubly so when writing about the history of others, from other cultures. My own writings about Aboriginal history can never testify to the meaning of Aboriginality, nor indeed can it ever be a testimony of *Aboriginal* history. It can only ever be a statement of *approach*, from my own contemporary Western viewpoint. It is a commitment to the scientific project, and to Western preunderstanding in dialogue with novel experiences. Western understandings about Aboriginal history will always be imbued with Western preconceptions, necessitating a reflexivity that will continually call for a revisiting of knowledge. This is the hermeneutic impasse so much discussed by critical theorists (e.g. see papers in Wachterhauser 1986b). But for some, Paul Ricoeur (e.g. 1981) in particular, an 'hermeneutic detour' may be taken to access meaning in what can never be truly experienced. This detour is based on the notion that the symbols of preunderstanding carry messages accessible through philosophical enquiry. Accordingly, I have attempted to approach the history of Aboriginal religion and preunderstanding through material signs of relations to place, ritual and reference. But these remain approaches, never truly crossing the barrier of ontological and experiential Otherness and difference. A non-indigenous history of the Aboriginal past will always remain an approach to that past as a commitment of Western preunderstanding in dialogue with the symbolic traces of that Other's past.

The Dreaming in pre-history

Having focused on the Dreaming of ethnography as a way of addressing the historical nature of Aboriginal being, I have noted that when examined from a scientific perspective, the material traces of the past do not concur with popular preconceptions of Aboriginality. Let me now conclude by reviewing the archaeological evidence for the antiquity of the Dreaming as we know it from ethnography in different parts of Australia.

When Europeans first began to document Aboriginal world-views, the Dreaming was found to inscribe indigenous constructions of place with preunderstanding. By place I do not mean simply a detached stage upon which human praxis can be played out – places are not simply 'out there' as the where of human action. Place is, rather, the landscape of engagement, sentient and sentimentally constructed by interacting human beings. It is always-already here, meaningfully constituted in preunderstanding. Such meaningfulness is imbued with a culturally distinctive spatial and temporal logic that marks all practice, knowledge and experience.

To Aboriginal people, the Dreaming – and life itself – are in this sense at once beyond time and continuous yet transformative, always presencing the past, the present and the future. The world is given its social and sensual topography in the Dreaming as originary time; the present continues to be informed by the laws of the Dreaming; and Dreaming forces guide life into the future. In that all things are understood to operate in the Dreaming, all engagement implicates its truth: as Henri Lefebvre (1991) has noted there is a *truth of space* rather than a true space, and that truth is generated in human engagement and preunderstanding. Truth of space emerges at the moment of emplacement, and one's presence in place confirms the truth of that same knowable space. Therefore, we can think of place as pre-ontological, yet structured and knowable only through the social shaping that is preunderstanding (in our case, the Dreaming).

The Dreaming as social emplacement

Aboriginal relations to place, ritual and symbolism during ethnographic times were informed by the Dreaming, sometimes explicitly, sometimes implicitly. Because each of these realms of cultural conduct is shaped by preunderstanding, and the experience of place comes even before a conscious and reflective awareness of spatial order (and of possible alternative knowings of place), praxis can be said to inscribe the land not only with ontological, but also with pre-ontological experiential order. This creates the possibility of an archaeology of the Dreaming of ethnography, as a set of world-views rich in meaning and that shapes engagement and experience.

In Aboriginal Australia of recent times the Dreaming was the scene for the creation of the world and what locates human experience in meaningful space. It gave rise to place, orienting people in a familiar world. The Dreaming shaped Aboriginal understanding and the human experience of place, giving substance to place. Such a shaping directed not only one's conscious understanding of the world but also, of greater immediacy for the purposes of this book, everyday bodily engagement in a socially constructed world.

As preunderstanding, the Dreaming thus positioned people in meaningful space, and both people and place were brought into existence through the intimacy of worldly engagement. What can and cannot, what should and should not, what does and does not happen in space are each experienced by the truth of place confirmed in social engagement. I am not talking here of a truth epistemologically constructed in conscious, self-reflective preunderstanding – this would amount to no more than one's *understanding* of a particular preunderstanding, not of preunderstanding itself – but rather of ontological and experiential presence (pre-sense) operationalised in *habitus*. This is what I mean when I write of place as already-meaningful and sentient. People are born into places experienced *as* reality. People are emplaced, in that we are in-place, and places are abiding truths. Throughout Aboriginal Australia during ethnographic times, these abiding truths concern the Dreaming of the various Aboriginal cultural groups.

And yet places, and therefore the preunderstanding that informs place, are not fixed. They continuously come about – in the dual sense that they *arrive*, while they remain *approximate*, in a constant state of flux, renegotiated in time through the interplay of memory and life's experiences and discoveries. Ngarrabullgan is one such example that presents us with a rare opportunity to investigate archaeologically the temporal dynamics of cultural space. In the sense that the mountain is given meaning by the Dreaming, its use is patterned by a Dreaming preunderstanding.

The truth of Ngarrabullgan was, during recent times, its totemic *Mirki* emplacement in the Dreaming, home of the dangerous spirit-being *Eekoo*. The mountain was naturalized as Ngarrabullgan in its Dreaming conception. This meaningful constitution led to particular attitudes towards the mountain, including its avoidance in the presence of powerful spirits.

Ngarrabullgan's unambiguous status as a Dreaming mountain replete with spirit-beings has given rise to a distinctive archaeological record. But this is not an archaeological signature that can be shown to have great antiquity. Following an examination of the timing of site abandonment, systemic changes were shown to have taken place in people's relations with the mountain around the fourteenth century. Before 600–700 years ago, Aboriginal people routinely occupied rockshelters on and around the mountain. Thereafter, relations between people and place changed to the extent that sites became systematically abandoned. By 600 years ago, Ngarrabullgan was accessed infrequently. This is in marked contrast to the situation in surrounding areas, where occupation continued until the arrival of Europeans late in the nineteenth century.

If identity is grounded in spatial relations, that is, if 'the construction of the subject [is] a matter of self-interpretation in the context of experienced space' (Thomas 1993b, p. 93), then a shift in the way people identified in place occurred at Ngarrabullgan 600 to 700 years ago via their changing engagement with and experience of their surroundings. After 600–700 years ago, there was a systemic shift in the way people related to their physical world, as is attested by a systematic abandonment of rockshelters on the mountain. The changes in the mountain's conception and use imply alterations in geographical patterns of social engagement and territoriality (as space already-owned through engagement). The Dreaming, as we know it today, informed Ngarrabullgan's significance during the last 600–700 years. But changing patterns of land use imply that before that time space was differently signified in human consciousness.

The Dreaming as social performance

As is the case with the social construction of place, so too does ritual present us with an archaeological opportunity to investigate the antiquity of particular forms of *habitus* and preunderstanding as structured social phenomena. Ritual represents a codification of relationships between people and the world in which they live. It formalizes relations between social actors and their environs, meaningfully binding and celebrating the socialness of things in the face of ontological chaos.

In ritual the social construction of preunderstanding is performed and reproduced. In the sense that it recognizes, formalizes, codifies and performs a world-view, ritual confirms and re-activates people's place in the world. As the codified performance of preunderstanding, ritual's archaeological manifestations can be used to address the antiquity of the Dreaming we know from ethnography. The archaeology of such performances of the recent Dreaming was considered in Chapter 4 by pondering various Arrernte and related central Australian rituals. In each case, the archaeological evidence implied an antiquity of less than 1400 years for the rituals. As was the case at Ngarrabullgan, archaeological evidence for the Dreaming of recent times could not be traced beyond that time.

The Dreaming as reference

As the world of the Dreaming is performed, so too is it ordered in a network of visual representations. Symbols re-present the world as categories that gain meaning through their immersion in established relations between things. Such relations are expressed in symbolic references. Through symbols, people mark social relationships and associations with the land. Symbolic order inscribes and naturalizes social relations onto the land, making particular demands upon people's attention and understanding of the landscape in the process.

Rock-art participates in this process, both in societies with and in societies without written language. As marks of emplacement – of being-in-place – rock pictures mark territory, as socially ordered space. Rock-art is a form of territorial engineering, of inscribing political, ontological and experiential order onto the land.

By considering Wardaman rock-art as metaphor and reference, I have thus presented archaeological evidence for the antiquity of a network of signs – a system of visual markers of meaning – that contributes to the Dreaming's communication as a source of social and territorial order. In Wardaman country I could not trace back the rock-art that was recently practised as part of a Dreaming ontology to

more than 1400 years ago, although there are some hints that may trace recent artistic expressions back to around 3500–3000 years BP in other parts of Australia (Arnhem Land, Cape York). Here too, then, archaeological evidence for the Dreaming as we know it today appears rather late in pre-History. Despite the heterogeneity of cultural practice across the continent today, and the likelihood that things did not change everywhere at the same time, the evidence for the antiquity of the ethnographically known Dreaming's spatial structure, ritualism and symbolism is broadly consistent and coherent across those parts of the continent where it has been investigated.

Contexts of change

The Dreamings of Aboriginal Australia, as recognizable from the ethnographic record, thus appear archaeologically not out of time, but as having emerged at recognizable occasions in the past (likely gradually unfolding 3500–1400 BP). As discussed in Chapters 7–9, this emergence came during a period of heightened cultural dynamism across much of Australia, a period of epochal transformations. During the late Holocene, after 4800 years BP and accelerating through time, intensities of site and regional occupation began to increase noticeably so that by 3500 years BP they had amplified about three-fold since the mid-Holocene. These increases involved a marked proliferation in the number of occupied rockshelters and in establishment rates of newly occupied sites across regional landscapes. They also involved rises in frequencies of re-occupation, and/or duration of visitation, of individual sites as measured by rates of deposition of cultural materials and sediments within sites. Together, these heightened levels of land use most likely signal rises in absolute populations, and in regional population densities beginning around 5000 years BP and increasing with time, with peak levels reached after 2000 years BP. There is no evidence for complementary shifts in levels of land use across the landscape, similar increases being evident in all parts of the mainland where such investigations have been undertaken. Many offshore islands across northern Australia were also first occupied only after 3000 years BP (O'Connor 1992), indicating an expansion of populations into previously unused or poorly used areas. These increases can therefore be said to have been geographically widespread and systematic, affecting most, if not all, parts of Australia (with the exception of some southern islands such as Tasmania and Kangaroo Island).

Along with these increasing populations and levels of land use came numerous qualitative changes in cultural and social practice. For example, new stone tool types began to be manufactured and used in many parts of the mainland, including Burren adzes in Cape York after 4000 years BP (and particularly after 2400 years BP) and Tula adzes in the arid and semi-arid zone some time during the mid to late Holocene.[3] In some regions, stone artefact technologies began to change, as evidenced by the emergence of blades, a systematic reduction in artefact sizes, and a shift in raw material preferences in Cape York after 1900 years BP. Around 3000 years BP in semi-arid Australia, and possibly as late as 1400 years BP in the more arid core of the continent, seeds began to be collected systematically in large quantities and processed on specialized grinding stones. The emergence of systematic seed grinding at this time implies also the emergence of new gender relations, new systems of territorial marking through matrilineally emplaced millstones, and an increasing potential for supporting large congregations. The implication is that new possibilities emerged for inscribing regional landscapes with social order and performance, including probable shifts towards heightened levels of matrilineal control over territoriality and land use in those regions where women's labour necessitated the marking of place with more or less immobile tools that remained under the ownership and/or control of women. In such regions, both men's and women's social performances became geographically and socially tethered, so to speak, to women's labour, and in so doing became subject to new systems of territorial emplacement and marking. These changes signal shifts in gender-based power relations (and means of affirming those relations through place marking), and social being became subject to new sentiments and social contradictions.

Around 4200 to 2000 years BP, poisonous nuts also began to be leached of their toxins and used as staple foods in environments ranging from rainforests to dry sclerophyll woodlands. Together, the emergence of systematic seed grinding and the processing of toxic plants

for food in a range of environments 4200 to 2000 years BP imply the commencement of heightened levels of staple plant production and the capacity to support greater populations, findings consistent with other archaeological traces for increasing human populations at this time. In some regions, these increases in population and degrees of regional land use were accompanied by the emergence of new centres of cultural activity, such as shell mounds at Princess Charlotte Bay and earth mounds in various parts of Victoria 3000–2000 years BP. The Princess Charlotte Bay mounds in particular traditionally have been considered as evidence for novel sites of domestic refuse, but equally could now be seen as new residential foci and centres of social activity at scales with no comparable historical precedents. As with seed grinding and toxic plant foods, such innovations imply new forms of geographical signification and landscape marking (directly associated with mangroves and wetlands), seasonal schedules, and social expectation focused on community endeavours of unprecedented magnitude.

With rapidly rising human populations between 4000 and 2000 years BP also came socio-structural changes, best evident in a rise of regionalism in rock-art symbolism. The emergence of geographically shorter-spaced artistic conventions after 3500 years BP, most marked after 2000 years BP, implicates social fragmentation and an increasingly localized social inscription of place. Place became more demarcated through symbols that were founded upon and drew attention to indigenous world views and socio-territorial affiliations akin to those of the Dreaming during ethnographic times.

If the dating of these various cultural transformations is accurate, then it would appear that regional populations may have been rising since the early to mid Holocene, at a time when mean annual rainfall levels in some regions were quadruple those of the terminal Pleistocene and natural levels of bioproduction were at their peak. As climates moderated during the mid to late Holocene human populations continued to rise, probably a result of critical demographic (quantitative and structural) alterations already set in motion during the previous period, leading to enhanced structural changes, in particular social fragmentation and a regionalization of artistic practices

3500 years BP. It is this cultural and demographic dynamism that serves as a backdrop for the emergence 3500–1400 years BP of the Dreaming that we have come to know from ethnographic sources, a process of change that continued through time.

Together, the archaeologically identifiable cultural trends and innovations imply that the late Holocene was a period of heightened social, demographic and ontological dynamism (irrespective of what was going on previously). Population increases are implicated, along with shifts in territorial organization and the emergence of increasingly short-spaced territorial and/or land using groups. In *différance*, the world was experienced as new systems of difference and deference, the products of social activity calling upon the onlooker in novel ways. In that people began to mark place and social emplacement in categorically new ways, new demands were made upon the attention of individuals. Such shifts in attention were effected not only by innovations in place marking, but also by new stone tool types, plant foods, central places, trade items and congregations, and ecological relations. Novel social demarcations and corporate groups began to emerge, and with these changes came transformations in collective and personal identity. The implication is that the late Holocene witnessed radical changes in means of understanding the landscape, and therefore radical changes in landscape recognition. The new demands are testimony to new understandings of the world, and with this are implied shifts in preunderstanding.

It is in such contexts that the Dreaming, as we know it today, emerged. As the framework through which reality was understood, the Dreaming of recent times arose historically as preunderstanding rich in social and territorial order. It appeared, I suggest, as the logic behind a new territorial understanding. During the late Holocene the Dreaming began to take a form akin to that presently recognizable from ethnography. It arose as an ontological means of organizing people on the ground and socially in the face of rising populations and social fragmentation. The Dreaming that we have come to know confirmed the truth of changing cultural, demographic and ecological conditions, and of a world rich in social meaning, metaphorical structure and emplacement. By giving cosmogonic sense to emplaced existence, the Dreaming's modern forms linked people to place in the face of a social world undergoing rapid change. The Dreaming that we know from ethnographic times arose historically through a shifting, open network of signs – and as the system of meaning – by which people began to know their newly engaged landscapes. It emerged in the face of changing constructions of alterity and Otherness, being and identity born of sociodemographic dynamism and *différance*.

In the cultural and demographic changes that begin to show in the archaeological record especially after 4000–3500 years BP, we thus see new ways of engaging with the world, including Others. It was not just the stone tools, the rock-art or the sites that changed, but the way people engaged with their surroundings and with each other, and by implication how they perceived themselves in the world. The truth of the world was newly demarcated through symbols, rituals and conceptions of place. It was reshaped at an accelerating rate, including qualitative changes in tools of social and spatial production, and quantitative increases in overall populations, population densities, and intensities of site and regional land use. The system of references by which people knew their world also changed. The world was remarked, and therefore remade. These changes imply changing social constructions of difference.

As noted in Chapter 5, the world is experienced as systems of alterity that attract. Cultural innovations reshape the world of difference and deference (both as temporal spacing and as ceding), re-marking reality and calling upon the subject in new ways. The work of innovation is not so much the newly created thing, as how it creates new scissions, how it newly engages the subject in a world of Otherness. Innovation (through *différance*) causes a divergence in social expectation, preunderstanding and *habitus*, a decentring from the prior known, the prior norm, towards new alterities and therefore constructions of self. Life's rhythms are renegotiated, orderly interests are re-worked, and what makes us feel at-home is reconstituted. In that the world is reframed in, and as, new systems of alterity, new constructions of Otherness also imply new constructions of self. Such social and personal transformations are each implied by the cultural changes of the late Holocene in Aboriginal Australia. It is not just the stone tools, population structures, settlement types, dietary habits and the like that are implied to have changed, but experienced difference, identity and being. Let me conclude these observations of why the late Holocene archaeological changes noted in this book imply transformations in social and personal identity by making brief reference to the work of Martin Heidegger.[4]

Heidegger (1889–1976) was a German philosopher whose early work was strongly influenced by the existentialist Søren Kierkegaard. He was subsequently taken by an encounter with Friedrich Nietzsche, and there is a Wilhelm Dilthey influence in some of his writings. He was also much affected by the phenomenonology of his master Edmund Husserl. However, he influenced existentialist thought at least as much as he was influenced by the early existentialists. Working with Husserl, Heidegger was expected to follow in his footsteps, but in 1927 published his masterwork *Being and Time* (*Sein und Zeit*). Unlike his neo-Kantian contemporaries who were more concerned with questions of epistemology, Heidegger was more interested in questions of ontology. In *Being and Time* he thus addressed issues that had been much avoided by continental philosophers of the time (because of their apparent simplicity, or closeness of everyday being), in particular how it is for a person to *be*. Heidegger's own writings eventually were to be reframed as an exploration on the meaning of being. Later he began to focus more on the historicity of being.

Heidegger argued that people do not exist in isolation from their environments. People are always situated, and being is always an expression of this embeddedness. Being can therefore be thought of more appropriately as a presence constructed through engagement in the world, rather than as an essence. The distinction between subject and object is here lacking, for object versus subject denies the constructivity of each in the other. To transcend these inadequacies, Heidegger uses the German term *Dasein* (being-there), and coined the word-phrase being-in-the-world. *Dasein* does not refer to an essential human being, but to a pre-ontological, experiential bodily presence in the world that nevertheless always-already knows itself ontologically. *Dasein* is therefore constructed as human presence emplaced in the particularities of the social and contextual situation of the time. Being is thus emergent in relation to the everyday practices in which it is embedded; it is, in Heidegger's words, *An-wesen* – the letting come forth into presence (presencing) – and *physis* (emerging-into-presence).

So rather than timeless essence, being can be thought of as temporally emergent in relation to the world in which it dwells. This is a world inscribed with art, with monuments – a scarification of the earth that reveals the world as socially and experientially engaged. This world is always ready-to-hand, in the sense that the things around us are already rich in meaning – what Gadamer would later call preunderstanding. A chair is already-here as notion of sitting, and *Dasein* emerges in this constructed world as already-engaged. But this ready-to-handness relates not to *concerns* over the use of a thing – a chair – for such concerns *reveal* the thing in an open network of signs. This revelation of what lies before us announces the world with which we engage. In doing so, such revelations call upon the possibility of alternative significations, and in the process break the hegemonic power of the object to make demands on our attention. Human dwelling is thus a situation in which people are *thrown into the world*; people are never quite apart from things, always defined in relation to them. The way we do things defines our being, and the way we do things is constructed in the here and now of dwelling, as worldly engagement. Because of this, being and identity are continuously reshaped in relation to the changing world. Presence is therefore already-here, as pre-sense, an already-here that is at once worldly and emergent. *Dasein*'s presence reveals its own identity as being-in-the-world.

We cannot therefore keep restricting explanations or understandings of Aboriginal being by reference to 'ecological' relations, or the Aboriginal past as symptomatic responses to environmental change or external influences, or of egalitarian, 'economic' practices geared to meeting subsistence needs. Such approaches appear oblivious to the experiential, sensual, social and political dimensions of Aboriginal existence. Landscapes are rich in meaning, sentiment and social enterprise. They are institutionally constituted as at once sentient and societal, unceasingly emerging in relations of social and political power.

I am not, of course, the first to point out the dynamic nature of pre-Historic Aboriginal society, despite a general tendency to approach the Aboriginal past as ontological stasis. Many of the innovations I have listed above have long been reported in the archaeological literature (the most influential being Harry Lourandos (1983, 1997) and John Beaton (1983)).

But in this book I have attempted to approach the Aboriginal past in a different way, as one rich in social knowledge, sentiment and experience, aspects of which are accessible through archaeological and philosophical enquiry. Yet any approach towards such a past will necessarily be effected through the analyst's own preunderstanding, rendering as always the historian of the past also a social commentator of the present. This hermeneutic impasse calls for a self-reflectivity that traces historically the writer's own culture of interpretation.

The main message of this book is thus: both Aboriginal people and Westerners see the Dreaming as atemporal, but the notions of time that imbue each are based on different (pre)conceptions. Western notions of Aboriginality are imbued with a timelessness paradoxically long founded on progressive/degenerative (and since the mid-nineteenth century at least, evolutionary) thinking, unlike the Aboriginal notions of cosmogonic timelessness that imbue the ethnographically known Dreaming. Concepts are always interpreted in relation to existing world-views: there is an intertextuality that defines an understanding of things in relation to an open network of signs. The Dreaming in the West can only be understood in relation to Western ontologies, irrespective of how close or distant these may be to Aboriginal ontologies, and irrespective also of how these Western ontologies come to change through dialogue with novel experiences. In popular Western thought, we have in-stilled Aboriginality – and the Dreaming – with a temporality that is the mark of our own notions of an hierarchical and evolutionary past. Such a situation has been deeply stamped in the Western social psyche as a circumstance of our own historical positioning, a positioning that has to date received too little critical attention. And yet when we examine the archaeological manifestations of the Dreaming of ethnographic times, it reveals itself not as unchanging or even of deep

antiquity, but as dynamic and emergent cultural practice.

How we have come to locate the antiquity of the Dreaming and Aboriginality in Western world-view is more a reflection of our own prejudices than it is of indigenous notions of being and time. As argued in Chapter 6, for the West to conceive of Aboriginality thematically around timeless and static cultural products such as stone tools, didgeridoos, cave paintings or the Dreaming is to conceive of Aboriginal people as living remnants of a timeless past, an ancestral precondition of our own presence. Even though we have by now long explicitly rejected the notion that the living peoples of the world represent different stages of human evolution, the idea that Aboriginal peoples are somehow ancient, living remnants of a deep ancestral past still figures prominently in our social psyches. Into the twenty-first century the official Web page of the Northern Territory Tourist Commission, the government body that promotes tourism in this north-central part of Australia, notes that:

> The Northern Territory is home to an ancient culture in an even more ancient landscape. The breathtaking landforms of the Northern Territory were formed hundreds of millions of years ago; and they have given rise to a culture that, according to some estimates, is 60 000 years old (to put that into perspective, the time of the Pharaohs in Egypt was around 4000 years ago). That makes Australian Aboriginal culture the oldest living culture in the world.

We are invited to go (as the Commission's television advertisement says, 'you'll never never know, if you never never go') to this 'destination' of ancestral Otherness, a place we can visit *as* a past where the modern can never truly arrive. This is a strange state of affairs: because Aboriginal peoples have a local ancestry that can be traced to ancient times, they are deemed to represent 'the oldest living culture in the world'. There is no reference in the Commission's statement about the historical nature of Aboriginal culture, of its dynamism, of its historical transformations. Instead, much as Lieutenant James Cook had pronounced more than 200 years ago, 'we see this country in the pure state of nature'. This is reference to an Aboriginal presence fixed as part of the land. This is doubly curious, for it is precisely

Aboriginal rights to lands that have long been resisted or denied by the West, until the 1990s explicitly in Australian law through the notion of *terra nullius*. By affirming continuity of culture, rather than of emplacement and ownership of place, we affirm Aboriginality's originary signification while at the same time denying Aboriginal rights to place. Representation is always political, irrespective of explicit intent.

Such Western constructions of Aboriginality as the traditional, ancient and unchanging Other remain deep, pervading ontological undercurrents that are a legacy of what were once more prominent views. These are Western preconceptions harboured about the (ab)original Other that betray the apparent and often stated political neutrality of our conscious thoughts.

And so it is that the deep antiquity of *the* Aboriginal Australia known from ethnography has reigned supreme in Western preunderstanding, masking our ability to address Aboriginal social life as driven by institutional, political, judicial, sentimental, religious and intellectual (ontological and epistemological) forces. The very existence of Aboriginal nationhood is denied (explicitly in many legal rulings). It is this inadequacy of approach to the Aboriginal past and present that I have tried to address in this book by exploring one of our deepest preconceptions about the ancientness of modern Aboriginal culture, belief and practice as temporal absence.

An archaeology of preunderstanding can never simply be about recovering the Other, always entwined with the self as centre and as preconception. The challenge, as Ian McNiven (1998, p. 47) has aptly put it, is that writing about the history of others 'is more than a clash of belief systems – it is a clash of powers to control constructions of identity'. For this reason, like Blanchot's experience of the instant of his death unreached, we can only aim to unfold the authorship of authority, rather than seal the authority of authorship.

Western understandings of other peoples will always be imbued with Western preunderstandings. The West cannot simply take one concept, for example, an Aboriginal notion of the Dreaming's atemporality, and understand it outside other Western notions, other Western frames of reference, while claiming to have entered Aboriginal world-views. But we can remember ourselves as authors prejudiced by our own preunderstandings in dialogue with other ways of being. It is by reflecting upon our ontological centredness *as alterity*, an alterity informed in a community of other Others, that we may reflect upon the 'truth' of our own preconceptions and preunderstanding as dynamic structures of *différance*, alterity and identity.

Notes

1. I was made aware of this saying by Dr David Bush of the Center for Historic and Military Archeology, Heidelberg College, Ohio. Its origins are unknown.
2. Blanchot initially thought the militia men involved were Germans, but there is some uncertainty of their identity as Germans or Russians.
3. The timing of the first Tula adzes in the arid zone is uncertain. Peter Hiscock and Peter Veth (1991) have shown that they date to the last 6000–5000 years BP at the most, but there are some problems in dating. Ian Johnson (1979) suggested that sediments believed to date to 6000 years BP, and that contain Tula adzes in the arid zone, may in fact date to only 1000 years BP.
4. I have here begun by discussing concepts of alterity and otherness to point out that changes in identity and being are implicated by the late Holocene archaeological trends. However, I have in a way reversed philosophical history, for Martin Heidegger's work on being came first, and then came discussions of alterity, in particular Emmanuel Lévinas's reactions against Heidegger's prioritization of being over otherness.

References

Adorno, T. W. 1996. *Negative Dialectics*. London: Routledge.

Allen, H. 1972. Where the crow flies backwards: man and land in the Darling Basin. Unpublished PhD thesis, Australian National University, Canberra.

Allen, H. 1974. The Bagundji of the Darling Basin: cereal gatherers in an uncertain environment. *World Archaeology* 5: 309–22.

Allen, H. 1990. Environmental history in south-western New South Wales during the Pleistocene. In C. Gamble and O. Soffer (eds), *The World at 18,000 BP: Low Latitudes* Vol. 2, pp. 296–321. London: Unwin Hyman.

Altman, J. 1984. The dietary utilisation of flora and fauna by contemporary hunter-gatherers at Momega Outstation, north-central Arnhem Land. *Australian Aboriginal Studies* (1): 35–46.

Anderson, A. 1978. The role of a competition model in the archaeological explanation of economic change. In D. Green, C. Haselgrove and M. Spriggs (eds), *Social Organisation and Settlement*, pp. 31–46. Oxford: British Archaeological Reports.

Anderson, W. 2002. *The Cultivation of Whiteness: Science, Health and Racial Density in Australia*. Carlton South: Melbourne University Press.

Arden, H. 1995. *Dreamkeepers: A Spirit-journey into Aboriginal Australia*. New York: Harper Perennial.

Aristotle 1983. *Aristotle's Physics*. Oxford: Oxford University Press.

Arndt, W. 1962. The interpretation of the Delamere Lightning paintings and rock engravings. *Oceania* 32: 163–77.

Attenbrow, V. 1982. The archaeology of Upper Mangrove Creek catchment: research in progress. In S. Bowdler (ed.), *Coastal Archaeology in Eastern Australia*, pp. 67–79. Canberra: Australian National University.

Attenbrow, V. 1986. Temporal change and regional variation in the archaeological record in eastern Australia. Paper presented at the World Archaeological Congress, Southampton.

Attenbrow, V., David, B. and Flood, J. 1995. Mennge-ya 1 and the origins of points: new insights into the appearance of points in the semi-arid zone of the Northern Territory. *Archaeology in Oceania* 30 (3): 105–20.

Attwood, B. 1989. *The Making of the Aborigines*. Sydney: Allen and Unwin.

Balme, J. 1991. The antiquity of grinding stones in semi-arid western New South Wales. *Australian Archaeology* 32: 3–9.

Barfield, T. 1997. *The Dictionary of Anthropology*. Oxford: Blackwell.

Barrett, C. and Croll, R. H. 1943. *The Art of the Australian Aboriginal*. Melbourne: The Bread and Cheese Club.

Barthes, R. 1979. *The Eiffel Tower and Other Mythologies*. New York: Hill and Wang.

Bates, D. 1930. Great aboriginal trade route. *Australasian*, 1 November: 4.

Beaton, J. 1977. Dangerous harvest: investigations in the late prehistoric occupation of upland southeast central Queensland. Unpublished PhD thesis, Australian National University, Canberra.

Beaton, J. 1982. Fire and water: aspects of Australian Aboriginal management of cycads. *Archaeology in Oceania* 17: 59–67.

Beaton, J. 1983. Does intensification account for changes in the Australian Holocene archaeological record? *Archaeology in Oceania* 18: 94–7.

Beaton, J. 1985. Evidence for a coastal occupation time-lag at Princess Charlotte Bay (North Queensland) and implications for coastal colonisation and population growth theories for Aboriginal Australia. *Archaeology in Oceania* 20: 1–20.

Beaton, J. 1990. The importance of past population for prehistory. In B. Meehan and N. White (eds), *Hunter-Gatherer Demography: Past and Present*, pp. 23–40. Sydney: Oceania Monograph, University of Sydney.

Bell, D. 1987. Gathered from Kaytej women. In D. J. Mulvaney and J. P. White (eds), *Australians to 1788*, pp. 239–51. Broadway: Fairfax, Syme and Weldon Associates.

Bender, B. 1979. Gatherer-hunter to farmer: a social perspective. *World Archaeology* 10 (2): 204–22.

Benterrak, K., Muecke, S., Roe, P., Keogh, R., (Nangan), B. Joe and Lohe, E. M. 1984. *Reading the Country: Introduction to Nomadology.* Fremantle: Fremantle Arts Centre Press.

Berndt R. M. 1998 [1979]. A profile of good and bad in Australian Aboriginal religion. In M. Charlesworth (ed.), *Religious Business: Essays on Australian Aboriginal Spirituality*, pp. 24–45. Cambridge: Cambridge University Press.

Berndt, R. M. and Berndt, C. H. 1989. *The Speaking Land: Myth and Story in Aboriginal Australia.* Ringwood: Penguin.

Binford, L. R. 1968. Post-Pleistocene adaptations. In S. R. Binford and L. R. Binford (eds), *New Perspectives in Archaeology*, pp. 313–41. Chicago: Aldine.

Binford, L. R. 1982. The archaeology of place. *Journal of Anthropological Archaeology* 1: 5–31.

Binford, L. R. 1983. *In Pursuit of the Past: Decoding the Archaeological Record.* New York: Thames and Hudson.

Bird, C. F. M. and Frankel, D. 1991. Chronology and explanation in western Victoria and southeast South Australia. *Archaeology in Oceania* 26 (1): 1–16.

Bird, M. I., Ayliffe, L. K., Fifield, L. K., Turney, C. S. M., Cresswell, R. G., Barrows, T. T. and David, B. 1999. Radiocarbon dating of 'old' charcoal using a wet oxidation, stepped-combustion procedure. *Radiocarbon* 41 (2): 127–40.

Birdsell, J. B. 1957. Some population problems involving Pleistocene man. *Cold Spring Harbor Symposium on Qualitative Biology* 22: 47–69.

Birdsell, J. B. 1967. Preliminary data on the trihybrid origin of the Australian Aborigines. *Archaeology and Physical Anthropology in Oceania* 2: 100–55.

Blanchot, M. 1994. The instant of my death. In M. Blanchot and J. Derrida, *The Instant of My Death and Demeure: Fiction and Testimony*, pp. 1–11. Stanford, CA: Stanford University Press.

Boast, R. 1997. A small company of actors: a critique of style. *Journal of Material Culture* 2 (2): 173–98.

Bonnemaison, J. 1995. Le territoire, nouveau paradigme de la géographie humaine? In J. Bonnemaison, L. Cambrézy and L. Quinty-Bourgeois (eds), *Actes du Colloque: le territoire, lien ou frontière?* CD-Rom, ORSTOM, Paris.

Boot, P. 1996a. Aspects of prehistoric change in the South Coast hinterland of New South Wales. In S. Ulm, I. Lilley and A. Ross (eds), *Australian Archaeology '95: Proceedings of the 1995 Australian Archaeological Association Annual Conference*, pp. 63–79. Tempus 6, St Lucia: Anthropology Museum, University of Queensland.

Boot, P. 1996b. Pleistocene sites in the South Coast hinterland of New South Wales. In S. Ulm, I. Lilley and A. Ross (eds), *Australian Archaeology '95: Proceedings of the 1995 Australian Archaeological Association Annual Conference*, pp. 275–88. Tempus 6, St Lucia: Anthropology Museum, University of Queensland.

Boserup, E. 1965. *The Conditions of Agricultural Growth.* Chicago: Aldine.

Botton de, A. (ed.) 1999. *The Essential Plato.* New York: Book-of-the-Month Club.

Bourdieu, P. 1977. *Outline of a Theory of Practice.* Cambridge: Cambridge University Press.

Bourdieu, P. 1980. *The Logic of Practice.* Stanford, CA: Standford University Press.

Bowdler, S. 1981. Hunters in the highlands: Aboriginal adaptations in the Eastern Australian Uplands. *Archaeology in Oceania* 16 (2): 99–111.

Bowler, J. M., Jones, R., Allen H. and Thorne, A. G. 1970. Pleistocene human remains from Australia: a living site and human cremation from Lake Mungo, western New South Wales. *World Archaeology* 2: 39–60.

Bowler, P. J. 1992. From 'savage' to 'primitive': Victorian evolutionism and the interpretation of marginalized peoples. *Antiquity* 66: 721–9.

Brandl, E. 1972. Thylacine designs in Arnhem

Land rock paintings. *Archaeology and Physical Anthropology in Oceania* 7: 24–30.

Brandl, E. 1982. *Australian Aboriginal Paintings in Western and Central Arnhem Land*. Canberra: AIAS.

Brookfield, H. C. 1972. Intensification and disintensification in Pacific agriculture: a theoretical approach. *Pacific Viewpoint* 13: 30–48.

Broome, R. 1982. *Aboriginal Australians*. St Leonards: Allen and Unwin.

Brown, S. 1987. *Toward a Prehistory of the Hamersley Plateau, Northwest Australia*. Occasional Papers in Prehistory 6. Canberra: Australian National University.

Butler, D. 1998. Environmental change in the Quaternary. In B. David (ed.), *Ngarrabullgan: Geographical Investigations in Djungan Country, Cape York Peninsula*. Monash Publications in Geography and Environmental Science 51, pp. 78–97. Clayton: Department of Geography and Environmental Science, Monash University.

Campbell, J. B. 1982. New radiocarbon results for north Queensland prehistory. *Australian Archaeology* 14: 62–6.

Campbell, J. B. 1984. Extending the archaeological frontier: a review of work on the prehistory of north Queensland. *Queensland Archaeological Research* 1: 173–84.

Campbell, J. B., Cole, N., Hatte, E., Tuniz, C. and Watchman, A. 1996. Dating of rock surface accretions with Aboriginal paintings and engravings in north Queensland. In S. Ulm, I. Lilley and A. Ross (eds), *Australian Archaeology '95: Proceedings of the 1995 Australian Archaeological Association Annual Conference*, pp. 231–9. Tempus 6, St Lucia: Anthropology Museum, University of Queensland.

Campbell, J. B. and Mardaga-Campbell, M. 1993. From macro- to nano-stratigraphy: linking vertical and horizontal dating of archaeological deposits with the direct dating of rock art at 'The Walkunders', Chillagoe (north Queensland, Australia). In J. Steinbring, A. Watchman, P. Faulstich and P. Taçon (eds), *Time and Space: Dating and Spatial Considerations in Rock Art Research*, pp. 57–63. Melbourne: Australian Rock Art Research Association.

Cane, S. 1989. Australian Aboriginal seed grinding and its archaeological record: a case study from the Western Desert. In D. R. Harris and G. C. Hillman (eds), *Foraging and Farming: The Evolution of Plant Exploitation*, pp. 99–119. London: Unwin Hyman.

Caputo, J. D. 1986. Hermeneutics as the recovery of man. In B. R. Wachterhauser (ed.), *Hermeneutics and Modern Philosophy*, pp. 416–45. Albany, NY: State University of New York Press.

Caruana, W. 1993. *Aboriginal Art*. London: Thames and Hudson.

Casey, E. 1998. *The Fate of Place: A Philosophical History*. Berkeley, CA: University of California Press.

Chaloupka, G. no date. Endangered site: a famous example. Report to the Australian Heritage Commission, Canberra.

Chaloupka, G. 1984. *From Palaeoart to Casual Paintings: The Chronological Sequence of Arnhem Land Plateau Rock Art*. Monograph Series 1, Darwin: Northern Territory Museum of Arts and Sciences.

Chaloupka, G. 1993. *Journey in Time: The World's Longest Continuing Art Tradition*. Chatswood: Reed.

Chambers, J. 1999. *A Traveller's History of Australia*. Gloucestershire: The Windrush Press.

Chase, A. 1989. Domestication and domiculture in northern Australia: a social perspective. In D. R. Harris and G. C. Hillman (eds), *Foraging and Farming: The Evolution of Plant Exploitation*, pp. 42–54. London: Unwin Hyman.

Clark, C. M. H. 1962. *A History of Australia*, Volume 1: *From Earliest Times to the Age of Macquarie*. Parkville: Melbourne University Press.

Clarkson, C. 1994. A technological investigation into the beginnings of blade production at Garnawala 2, Northern Territory. Unpublished BA Honours thesis, University of Queensland, St Lucia.

Clarkson, C. and David, B. 1995. The antiquity of blades and points revisited: investigating the emergence of systematic blade production south of Arnhem Land, Australia. *The Artefact* 18: 22–44.

Clegg, J. 1978. Mathesis words, Mathesis pictures. Unpublished MA Honours thesis, University of Sydney, Sydney.

Cleland, J. B. 1966. Preface. In B. C. Cotton (ed.), *Aboriginal Man in South and Central Australia*, pp. 7–8. Adelaide: Government Printer.

Cogger, H. G. 1996. *Reptiles and Amphibians of Australia*. Port Melbourne: Reed Books.

Cole, N. 1992. 'Human' motifs in the rock paintings of Jowalbinna, Laura. In J. McDonald and I. P. Haskovec (eds), *State of the Art: Regional Rock Art Studies in Australia and Melanesia*. pp. 164–73. Melbourne: Australian Rock Art Research Association.

Cole, N. and David, B. 1992. 'Curious Drawings' at Cape York: a summary of rock art investigation in the Cape York Peninsula region since the 1820s and a comparison of some regional traditions. *Rock Art Research* 9 (1): 3–26.

Cole, N. and Trezise, P. 1992. Laura engravings: a preliminary report on the Amphitheatre site. In J. McDonald and I. P. Haskovec (eds), *State of the Art: Regional Rock Art Studies in Australia and Melanesia*, pp. 83–8. Melbourne: Australian Rock Art Research Association.

Cole, N., Watchman, A. and Morwood, M. 1995. Chronology of Laura rock art. In M. Morwood and D. Hobbs (eds), *Quinkan Prehistory: The Archaeology of Aboriginal Art in SE Cape York Peninsula, Australia Tempus 3*, pp. 147–59. Brisbane: University of Queensland.

Conkey, M. W. 1990. Experimenting with style in archaeology: some historical and theoretical issues. In M. W. Conkey and C. A. Hastorf (eds), *The Uses of Style in Archaeology*, pp. 5–17. Cambridge: Cambridge University Press.

Cook, J. 1968. *Captain Cook's Journal*. Adelaide: Libraries Board of South Australia.

Coutts, P. J. F. 1982. Victoria Archaeological Survey activities report 1979–80. *Records of the Victorian Archaeological Survey* 13: 1–28.

Cowgill, G. L. 1975. On causes and consequences of ancient and modern population changes. *American Anthropologist* 77: 505–25.

Cribb, R. L. D. 1986. When the tide came in: Pleistocene-Holocene sea levels, archaeological catchments and population change in northern Australia. Paper presented at the World Archaeological Congress, Southampton.

Csikszentmihalyi, M. and Rochberg-Halton, E. 1981. *The Meaning of Things: Domestic Symbols and the Self*. Cambridge: Cambridge University Press.

Dant, T. 1999. *Material Culture in the Social World*. Buckingham: Open University Press.

Darwin, C. 1859. *On the Origin of Species by Means of Natural Selection, or the Preservation of Favoured Races in the Struggle for Life*. London: John Murray.

David, B. 1990. Echidna's Rest, Chillagoe: a site report. *Queensland Archaeological Research* 7: 73–94

David, B. 1993. Nurrabullgin Cave: preliminary results from a pre-37,000 year old rockshelter, north Queensland. *Archaeology in Oceania* 28 (1): 50–4.

David, B. 1998. Cultural landscapes: the rock art. In B. David (ed.), *Ngarrabullgan: Geographical Investigations in Djungan Country, Cape York Peninsula*. Monash Publications in Geography and Environmental Science 51, pp. 143–56. Clayton: Department of Geography and Environmental Science, Monash University.

David, B. in press. The emergence of late Holocene symbolism in NE Australia. In C. Chippindale and G. Nash (eds), *The Landscapes of Rock-Art*. Cambridge: Cambridge University Press.

David, B., Armitage, R. A., Hyman, M., Rowe, M. and Lawson, E. 1999. How old is north Queensland's rock-art? A review of the evidence, with new AMS determinations. *Archaeology in Oceania* 34 (3): 103–20.

David, B. and Chant, D. 1995. *Rock Art and Regionalisation in North Queensland Prehistory. Memoirs of the Queensland Museum* 37(2). South Brisbane: Queensland Museum.

David, B. and Cole, N. 1990. Rock art and interregional interaction in northeastern Australian prehistory. *Antiquity* 64: 788–806.

David, B., Collins, J., Barker, B., Flood, J. and Gunn, R. 1995. Archaeological research in Wardaman country, Northern Territory: the Lightning Brothers Project 1990–91 field seasons. *Australian Archaeology* 41: 1–8.

David, B. and David, M. 1988. Rock pictures of the Chillagoe-Mungana limestone belt, north Queensland. *Rock Art Research* 5 (2): 147–56.

David, B., Langton, M. and McNiven, I. In press. Re-inventing the wheel: indigenous peoples and the master race in Philip Ruddock's 'wheel' comments. *Philosophy, Activism, Nature.*

David, B. and Lourandos, H. 1997. 37,000 years and more in tropical Australia: investigating long-term archaeological trends in Cape York Peninsula. *Proceedings of the Prehistoric Society* 63: 1–23.

David, B. and Lourandos, H. 1998. Rock art and socio-demography in northeastern Australian prehistory. *World Archaeology* 30 (2): 193–219.

David, B., McNiven, I., Attenbrow, V., Flood, J. and Collins, J. 1994. Of Lightning Brothers and White Cockatoos: dating the antiquity of signifying systems in the Northern Territory, Australia. *Antiquity* 68: 241–51.

David, B., McNiven, I., Bekessy, L., Bultitude, R., Clarkson, C., Lawson, E., Murray C. and Tuniz, C. 1998. More than 37,000 years of human occupation. In B. David (ed.), *Ngarrabullgan: Geographical Investigations in Djungan Country, Cape York Peninsula*. Monash Publications in Geography and Environmental Science 51, pp. 157–78. Melbourne: Monash University.

David, B., McNiven I. and Flood, J. 1991. Archaeological excavations at Yiwarlarlay 1: site report. *Memoirs of the Queensland Museum* 30 (3): 373–80.

David, B., McNiven, I., Flood, J. and Frost, R. 1990. Yiwarlarlay 1: archaeological excavations at the Lightning Brothers site, Delamere station, Northern Territory. *Archaeology in Oceania* 25 (2): 79–84.

David, B. and Wilson, M. 1998. *Jawiyabba (2 Brother Mountain): Cultural Site Mapping in Gugu Yalanji Country, July 1998.* Report to the North Queensland Land Council Aboriginal Corporation, Cairns.

David, B. and Wilson, M. 1999. Re-reading the landscape: place and identity in NE Australia during the late Holocene. *Cambridge Archaeological Journal* 9 (2): 163–88.

Davidson, D. S. 1936. *Aboriginal Australian and Tasmanian Rock Carvings and Paintings.* Memoirs of the American Philosophical Society 5, Philadelphia: The American Philosophical Society.

Davidson, I. 1999. Symbols by nature: animal frequencies in the upper Palaeolithic of western Europe and the nature of symbolic representation. *Archaeology in Oceania* 34: 121–31.

Davis, S. L. and Prescott, J. R. V. 1992. *Aboriginal Frontiers and Boundaries in Australia.* Melbourne: Melbourne University Press.

Dean, B. and Carell, V. 1955. *Dust for the Dancers.* Sydney: Ure Smith.

Derrida, J. 1968a. Différance. *Bulletin de la Société Française de Philosophie* 62 (3): 73–101.

Derrida, J. 1968b. La Différance. In P. Sollers (ed.), *Théorie d'Ensemble*, pp. 41–66. Paris: Éditions du Seuil.

Derrida, J. 1973. *Speech and Phenomena and Other Essays on Husserl's Theory of Signs.* Evanston, ILL: Northwestern University Press.

Derrida, J. 1982. *Margins of Philosophy.* New York: Harvester Wheatsheaf.

Derrida, J. 1992. *Acts of Literature.* New York: Routledge.

Derrida, J. 1994. Demeure: fiction and testimony. In M. Blanchot and J. Derrida, *The Instant of My Death and Demeure: Fiction and Testimony,* pp. 13–108. Stanford, CA: Stanford University Press.

Derrida, J. and Vattimo, G. (eds) 1998. *Religion.* Stanford, CA: Stanford University Press.

Descartes, R. 1958. *Philosophical Writings.* New York: Modern Library.

Dixon, R. M. W. 1991. *Words of Our Country: Stories, Place Names and Vocabulary in Yidiny, the Aboriginal Language of the Cairns-Yarrabah Region.* St Lucia: University of Queensland Press.

Docker, J. 1991. *The Nervous Nineties: Australian Cultural Life in the 1890s.* Melbourne: Oxford University Press.

Dodson, J. R., Fullagar, R., Furby, J. and Prosser, I. 1993. Humans and megafauna in a late Pleistocene environment from Cuddie Springs, northwestern New South Wales. *Archaeology in Oceania* 28: 93–9.

Draper, N. 1987. Context for the Kartan: a preliminary report on excavations at Cape du Couedic rockshelter, Kangaroo Island. *Archaeology in Oceania* 22 (1): 1–8.

Downey, B. and Frankel, D. 1992. Radiocarbon and thermoluminescence dating of a central Murray mound. *The Artefact* 15: 31–5.

Edwards, B. 1994. Living the Dreaming. In C. Bourke, E. Bourke and B. Edwards (eds), *Aboriginal Australia,* pp. 65–84. St Lucia: University of Queensland Press.

Edwards, D. and O'Connell, J. F. 1995. Broad spectrum diets in arid Australia. *Antiquity* 69 (Special Number 265): 769–83.

Ehrman, B. D. 2000. *The New Testament: A Historical Introduction to the Early Christian Writings.* Oxford: Oxford University Press.

Elkin, A. P. 1964. *Australian Aborigines: How to Understand Them.* 4th edition. Sydney: Angus and Robertson.

Elkins, J. 1998. *On Pictures and the Words That Fail Them.* Cambridge: Cambridge University Press.

Elliott, G. F. S. 1920. *Prehistoric Man and His Story.* London: Seeley, Service and Co. Ltd.

Fabian, J. 1983. *Time and the Other: How Anthropology Makes Its Object.* New York: Columbia University Press.

Field, J. 1999. The role of taphonomy in the identification of site function at Cuddie Springs. In M.-J. Mountain and D. Bowdery (eds), *Taphonomy: The Analysis of Processes from Phytoliths to Megafauna,* pp. 51–4. Research Papers in Archaeology and Natural History 30. Canberra: Australian National University.

Field, J. and Dodson, J. 1999. Late Pleistocene megafauna and archaeology from Cuddie Springs, South-eastern Australia. *Proceedings of the Prehistoric Society* 65: 275–301.

Fison, L. 1880. Kamilaroi marriage, descent, and relationship. In L. Fison and A. W. Howitt, *Kamilaroi and Kurnai,* pp. 21–96. Melbourne: George Robertson.

Fitzpatrick, B. 1946. *The Australian People 1788–1945.* Melbourne: Melbourne University Press.

Flannery, T. 1997. *The Future Eaters.* Port Melbourne: Reed Books.

Flood, J. 1987. Rock art of the Koolburra Plateau, north Queensland. *Rock Art Research* 4 (2): 91–126.

Flood, J. 1995. *Archaeology of the Dreamtime: The Story of Prehistoric Australia and Its People.* Sydney: Angus and Robertson.

Flood, J., David, B., Magee, J. and English, B. 1987. Birrigai: a Pleistocene site in the south-eastern highlands. *Archaeology in Oceania* 22: 9–26.

Flood, J. and Horsfall, N. 1986. Excavation of Green Ant and Echidna Shelter, Cape York Peninsula. *Queensland Archaeological Research* 3: 4–64.

Foley, S. 1994. *The Badtjala People.* Hervey Bay: Thoorgine Educational and Cultural Centre Aboriginal Corporation Inc.

Fortes, M. 1967. Totem and taboo. *Proceedings of the Royal Anthropological Institute* 1966: 5–22.

Foucault, M. 1977a. *Discipline and Punish: The Birth of the Prison.* New York: Vintage.

Foucault, M. 1997b. Sex, power, and the politics of identity. In P. Rabinow (ed.), *Michel Foucault: Ethics, Subjectivity and Truth,* pp. 163–73. New York: The New Press.

Foucault, M. 1997c. The ethics of the concern for Self as a practice of freedom. In P. Rabinow (ed.), *Michel Foucault: Ethics, Subjectivity and Truth,* pp. 281–301. New York: The New Press.

Frankel, D. 1991. *Remains to Be Seen: Archaeological Insights into Australian Prehistory.* Melbourne: Longman Cheshire.

Frazer, J. 1933. *The Golden Bough* (abridged edition). London: Macmillan.

Frazer, J. 1938. Preface. In B. Spender and F. Gillen, *The Native Tribes of Central Australia.* London: Macmillan.

Fullagar, R. and Field, J. 1997. Pleistocene seed-grinding implements from the Australian arid zone. *Antiquity* 71: 300–7.

Gadamer, H.-G. 1975. *Truth and Method.* New York: Seabury.

Gadamer, H.-G. 1985. *Philosophical Apprenticeships.* Cambridge, MA: Massachussetts Institute of Technology Press.

Gadamer, H.-G. 1988. The problem of historical consciousness. In P. Rabinow and W. M. Sullivan (eds), *Interpretive Social Science: A Second Look.* Berkeley, CA: University of California Press.

Gadamer, H.-G. 1989. *Truth and Method.* New York: Crossroad.

Gamble, C. 1992. Archaeology, history and the uttermost ends of the earth – Tasmania, Tierra del Fuego and the Cape. *Antiquity* 66: 712–20.

Gerhart, M. and Russell, A. 1984. *Metaphoric Process: The Creation of Scientific and Religious Understanding.* Forth Worth, TX: Texas Christian University Press.

Giddens, A. 1995. *A Contemporary Critique of Historical Materialism.* London: Macmillan.

Gillespie, R. and David, B. 2001. The importance, or impotence, of Cuddie Springs. *Australasian Science* 22(9): 42–3.

Gingerich, P. D. 1983. Rates of evolution: effects of time and temporal scaling. *Science* 222: 159–61.

Godfrey, M. C. S. 1989. Shell midden chronology in southwestern Victoria: reflections of change in prehistoric population and subsistence? *Archaeology in Oceania* 24: 65–79.

Goffman, E. 1959. *The Presentation of Self in Everyday Life.* New York: Doubleday.

Gorecki, P., Grant, M., O'Connor, S. and Veth, P. 1997. The morphology, function and antiquity of Australian grinding implements. *Archaeology in Oceania* 32 (2): 141–50.

Gott, B. 1982. Ecology of root use by the Aborigines of southern Australia. *Archaeology in Oceania* 17: 59–67.

Gould, R. A. 1969. Puntutjarpa Rockshelter: a reply to Messrs. Glover and Lampert. *Archaeology and Physical Anthropology in Oceania* 4: 229–37.

Gould, R. A. 1980. James Range East Rockshelter, Northern Territory, Australia: a summary of the 1973 and 1974 investigations. *Asian Perspectives* 21: 86–126.

Gould, R. A. 1996. Faunal reduction at Puntutjarpa rockshelter, Warburton Ranges, Western Australia. *Archaeology in Oceania* 31 (2): 72–86.

Gould, S. J. 1986. Bound by the Great Chain. In S. J. Gould, *The Flamingo's Smile: Reflections in Natural History,* pp. 281–90. Harmondsworth: Pelican.

Grange, J. 1985. Place, body and situation. In D. Seamon and R. Mugerauer (eds), *Dwelling, Place and Environment: Towards a Phenomenology of Person and World,* pp. 71–84. Dordrecht: Martinus Nijhoff Publishers.

Griffiths, T. 1996a. The social and intellectual context of the 1890s. In S. R. Morton and D. J. Mulvaney (eds), *Exploring Central Australia: Society, the Environment and the 1894 Horn Expedition,* pp. 13–18. Chipping Norton: Surrey Beatty and Sons.

Griffiths, T. 1996b. *Hunters and Collectors: The*

Antiquarian Imagination in Australia. Cambridge: Cambridge University Press.

Gunn, A. 1996 [1908]. *We of the Never Never*. Sydney: Angus and Robertson.

Hale, H. and Tindale, N. B. 1930. Notes on some human remains in the Lower Murray Valley, South Australia. *Records of the South Australian Museum* 4: 145–218.

Hall, J. 1982. Sitting on the crop of the bay: an historical and archaeological sketch of Aboriginal settlement and subsistence in Moreton Bay, Southeast Queensland. In S. Bowdler (ed.) *Coastal Archaeology in Eastern Australia*, pp. 79–95. Occasional Papers in Prehistory 11, Department of Prehistory, Research School of Pacific Studies, Canberra: Australian National University.

Hall, J. and Hiscock, P. 1988. The Moreton Region Archaeological Project (MRAP) – Stage 2: an outline of objectives and methods. *Queensland Archaeological Research* 5: 4–24.

Hallam, S. 1975. *Fire and Hearth: A Study of Aboriginal Usage and European Usurpation in Southwestern Australia*. Canberra: Australian Institute of Aboriginal Studies.

Hallam, S. 1977. Topographic archaeology and artifactual evidence. In R. V. S. Wright (ed.), *Stone Tools as Cultural Markers: Change, Evolution and Complexity*, pp. 169–77. Canberra: Australian Institute of Aboriginal Studies.

Hallam, S. 1989. Plant usage and management in southwest Australian Aboriginal societies. In D. R. Harris and G. C. Hillman (eds), *Foraging and Farming: The Evolution of Plant Exploitation*, pp. 136–51. London: Unwin Hyman.

Hamilton, A. 1980. Dual social systems: technology, labour and women's secret rites in the eastern Western Desert of Australia. *Oceania* 51: 4–19.

Hardy, B. 1976. *Lament for the Barkindji*. Sydney: Alpha Books.

Harney, W. E. 1943. *Taboo*. Sydney: Australasian Publishing Co.

Harney, W. E. 1959. *Tales from the Aborigines*. London: Robert Hale Ltd.

Haskovec, I. 1992. Mt. Gilruth revisited. *Archaeology in Oceania* 27 (2): 61–74.

Heidegger, M. 1962. *Being and Time*. New York: Harper and Row.

Hiscock, P. 1986. Technological change in the Hunter River valley and the interpretation of late Holocene change in Australia. *Archaeology in Oceania* 21 (1): 40–50.

Hiscock, P. 1989. Prehistoric settlement patterns and artefact manufacture at Lawn Hill, north-west Queensland. Unpublished PhD thesis, University of Queensland, St Lucia.

Hiscock, P. and Hall, J. 1988. Technological change at Bushranger's Cave (LA:A11), southeast Queensland. *Queensland Archaeological Research* 5: 90–112.

Hiscock, P. and Kershaw, P. 1992. Palaeoenvironments and prehistory of Australia's tropical Top End. In J. Dodson (ed.), *The Naïve Lands: Prehistory and Environmental Change in Australia and the Southwest Pacific*, pp. 43–75. Melbourne: Longman Cheshire.

Hiscock, P. and McNiven, I. In press. *Peopling of Ancient Australia*. Sydney: Allen & Unwin.

Hiscock, P. and Veth, P. M. 1991. Change in the Australian desert culture: a reanalysis of tulas from Puntutjarpa Rockshelter. *World Archaeology* 22 (3): 332–45.

Holden, A. 1999. A technological analysis of the lithic assemblage from Hay Cave, SE Cape York Peninsula: considering diachronic variations in patterns of 'intensity of site use'. Unpublished BA Honours thesis, University of Queensland, St Lucia.

Horsfall, N. 1987. Living in rainforest: the prehistoric occupation of north Queensland's humid tropics. Unpublished PhD thesis, James Cook University, Townsville.

Hossfeld, P. S. 1966. Antiquity of man in Australia. In B. C. Cotton (ed.), *Aboriginal Man in South and Central Australia*, pp. 59–96. Adelaide: Government Printer.

Hughes, P. J. 1977. A geomorphological interpretation of selected archaeological sites in southern coastal New South Wales. Unpublished PhD thesis, University of Sydney, Sydney.

Hughes, P. J. and Lampert, R. 1982. Prehistoric population change in southern coastal New South Wales. In S. Bowdler (ed.), *Coastal Archaeology in Eastern Australia*, pp. 16–28. Canberra: Australian National University.

Hughes, P. J. and Sullivan, M. E. 1981. Aboriginal burning and late Holocene geomorphic events in eastern NSW. *Search* 12: 277–8.

Huxley, T. H. 1863, *Evidence as to Man's Place in Nature*. London: Norgate.

Hynes R. A. and Chase, A. 1982. Plants, sites and domiculture: Aboriginal influence upon plant communities in Cape York Peninsula. *Archaeology in Oceania* 17: 38–50.

Johnson, I. 1979. The getting of data. Unpublished PhD thesis, Australian National University, Canberra.

Jones, P. 1996. The Horn Expedition's place among nineteenth-century inland expeditions. In S. R. Morton and D. J. Mulvaney (eds), *Exploring Central Australia: Society, the Environment and the 1894 Horn Expedition*, pp. 19–28. Chipping Norton: Surrey Beatty and Sons.

Jones, R. 1969 Fire-stick farming. *Australian Natural History* 16: 224–8.

Jones, R. and Meehan, B. 1989. Plant foods of the Gidjingali: ethnographic and archaeological perspectives from northern Australia on tuber and seed exploitation. In D. R. Harris and G. C. Hillman (eds), *Foraging and Farming: The Evolution of Plant Exploitation*, pp. 120–35. London: Unwin Hyman.

Kamminga, J. 1982. *Over the Edge*. St Lucia: Anthropology Museum, University of Queensland.

Keesing, R. 1991. Experiments in thinking about ritual. *Canberra Anthropology* 14 (2): 60–74.

Kershaw, A. P. 1994. Pleistocene vegetation of the humid tropics of northeastern Queensland, Australia. *Palaeogeography, Palaeoclimatology, Palaeoecology* 109: 399–412.

Kimber, R. G. 1984. Resource use and management in central Australia. *Australian Aboriginal Studies* 2: 12–23.

Kimber, R. G. and Smith, M. A. 1987. An Aranda ceremony. In D. J. Mulvaney and J. P. White (eds), *Australians to 1788*, pp. 221–37. Broadway: Fairfax, Syme and Weldon Associates.

Kügler, H. H. 1999. *The Power of Dialogue: Critical Hermeneutics after Gadamer and Foucault*. Cambridge, MA: The MIT Press.

Lakoff, G. 1987. *Women, Fire, and Dangerous Things: What Categories Reveal about the Mind*. Chicago: University of Chicago Press.

Lakoff, G. and Johnson, M. 1980. *Metaphors We Live By*. Chicago: University of Chicago Press.

Lamb, L. 1993. Fern Cave: a technological investigation of increased stone artefact deposition rates. Unpublished BA Honours thesis, University of Queensland, St Lucia.

Lampert, R. 1981. *The Great Kartan Mystery*. Terra Australis 5, Canberra: Australian National University.

Lampert, R. J. and Hughes, P. J. 1987. The Flinders Ranges: a Pleistocene outpost in the arid zone? *Records of the South Australian Museum* 20: 29–34.

Lampert, R. J. and Hughes, P. J. 1988. Early human occupation of the Flinders Range. *Records of the South Australian Museum* 22 (1): 139–68.

Langton, M. in Press. The edge of the sacred, the edge of death: sensual inscriptions. In B. David and M. Wilson (eds), *Inscribed Land-scapes: Marking and Making Place*. Honolulu: University of Hawaii Press.

Layton, R. 1985. The cultural context of hunter-gatherer rock art. *Man* (n.s.) 20: 434–53.

Layton, R. 1992. *Australian Rock Art: A New Synthesis*. Cambridge: Cambridge University Press.

Lefebvre, H. 1991. *The Production of Space*. Oxford: Blackwell.

Leibniz, G. W. 1953. *Discourse on Metaphysics*. New York: Barnes and Noble.

Lévinas, E. 1987. *Collected Philosophical Papers*. Dordrecht: Nijhoff.

Lewis, D. 1988. *The Rock Paintings of Arnhem Land, Australia: Social, Ecological and Material Culture in the Post-glacial Period*. Oxford: BAR International Series 415.

Lewis, D. and Rose, D. B. 1987. *The Shape of the Dreaming: The Cultural Significance of Victoria River Rock Art*. Canberra: Aboriginal Studies Press.

Lourandos, H. 1977. Aboriginal spatial organization and population: southwestern Victoria reconsidered. *Archaeology and Physical Anthropology in Oceania* 12: 202–25.

Lourandos, H. 1980a. Forces of change: Aboriginal technology and population in southwestern Victoria. Unpublished PhD thesis, University of Sydney, Sydney.

Lourandos, H. 1980b. Change or stability? Hydraulics, hunter-gatherers and population in temperate Australia. *World Archaeology* 11: 245–66.

Lourandos, H. 1983. Intensification: a late Pleistocene–Holocene archaeological sequence from southwestern Victoria. *Archaeology in Oceania* 18: 81–94.

Lourandos, H. 1984. Changing perspectives in Australian prehistory: a reply to Beaton. *Archaeology in Oceania* 19: 29–33.

Lourandos, H. 1985. Intensification and Australian pre-history. In T. D. Price and J. A. Brown (eds), *Prehistoric Hunter-Gatherers: The Emergence of Cultural Complexity*, pp. 385–423. Orlando, FL: Academic Press.

Lourandos, H. 1991. Palaeopolitics: resource intensification in Aboriginal Australia. In T. Ingold, D. Riches and J. Woodburn (eds), *Hunters and Gatherers: History, Evolution and Social Change*, pp. 148–60. New York: Berg.

Lourandos, H. 1997. *A Continent of Hunter-Gatherers*. Cambridge: Cambridge University Press.

Lovejoy, A. O. 1936. *The Great Chain of Being*. Cambridge, MA: Harvard University Press.

Lubbock, J. 1872. *Pre-Historic Times, as Illustrated*

by Ancient Remains, and the Manners and Customs of Modern Savages. 2nd edition. New York: D. Appleton and Company.

Lubbock, J. 1882. *The Origin of Civilisation and the Primitive Condition of Man: Mental and Social Conditions of Savages.* 4th edition. New York: D. Appleton and Company.

Lyon, D. 1994. *The Electronic Eye: The Rise of Surveillance Society.* Minneapolis: University of Minnesota Press.

Maddock, K. 1982. *The Australian Aborigines: A Portrait of Their Society.* Ringwood: Penguin.

Malthus, T. 1982 [1798]. *An Essay on the Principle of Population.* Harmondsworth: Penguin.

Mardaga-Campbell, M. 1986. Prehistoric living-floors and evidence for them in north Queensland rockshelters. *Australian Archaeology* 23: 42–61.

Mathews, R. H. 1898. Group divisions and initiation ceremonies of the Barkungee tribes. *Journal and Proceedings of the Royal Society of New South Wales* 32: 250–5.

Mathews, R. H. 1899. Divisions of some Aboriginal tribes, Queensland. *Journal and Proceedings of the Royal Society of New South Wales* 33: 108–14.

Maynard, L. 1976. An archaeological approach to the study of Australian rock art. Unpublished MA thesis, University of Sydney, Sydney.

Maynard, L. 1980. A Pleistocene date from an occupation deposit in the Pilbara region, Western Australia. *Australian Archaeology* 10: 3–8.

McCabe, J. no date. *Prehistoric Man.* London: Milner and Co. Ltd.

McCarthy, F. 1943. An analysis of the knapped implements from eight *elouera* industry stations on the south coast of New South Wales. *Records of the Australian Museum* 21 (3): 127–53.

McCarthy, F. 1964. The archaeology of the Capertee Valley, New South Wales. *Records of the Australian Museum* 26 (6): 197–246.

McConvell, P. 1996. Backtracking to Babel: the chronology of Pama-Nyungan expansion in Australia. *Archaeology in Oceania* 31 (3): 125–44.

McGregor, R. 1997. *Imagined Destinies: Aboriginal Australians and the Doomed Race Theory, 1880–1939.* Carlton: Melbourne University Press.

McNiven, I. 1990. Prehistoric Aboriginal settlement and subsistence in the Cooloola region, coastal southeast Queensland. Unpublished PhD thesis, University of Queensland, St Lucia.

McNiven, I. 1998. Shipwreck saga as archaeological text: reconstructing Fraser Island's Aboriginal past. In I. McNiven, L. Russell and K. Schaffer (eds), *Constructions of Colonialism: Perspectives on Eliza Fraser's Shipwreck,* pp. 37–50. London: Leicester University Press.

McNiven, I. in press. Australian archaeology at the Museum of Victoria. In C. Rasmussen (ed.), *A History of the Museum of Victoria.* Melbourne: Museum Victoria.

McNiven, I., David, B. and Flood, J. 1992. Delamere 3: further excavations at Yiwarlarlay (Lightning Brothers site), Northern Territory. *Australian Aboriginal Studies* 1992 (1): 67–73.

McNiven, I. and Russell, L. 1997. 'Strange paintings' and 'mystery races': Kimberley rock-art, diffusionism and colonialist constructions of Australia's Aboriginal past. *Antiquity* 71: 801–9.

Meggitt, M. J. 1962 *Desert People.* Sydney: Angus and Robertson.

Merlan, F. 1989. The interpretive framework of Wardaman rock art: a preliminary report. *Australian Aboriginal Studies* 2: 14–24.

Merlan, F. 1994. *A Grammar of Wardaman.* Berlin: Mouton de Gruyter.

Michelfelder, D. and Palmer, R. E. (eds). 1989. *Dialogue and Deconstruction: The Gadamer-Derrida Encounter.* Albany, NY: State University of New York Press.

Miller, G. H., Magee, J. W., Johnson, B. J., Fogel, M. L., Spooner, N. A., McCulloch, M. T. and Ayliffe, L. K. 1999. Pleistocene extinction of *Genyornis newtoni*: human impact on Australian Megafauna. *Science* 283: 205–8.

Moizo, B. 1998. Rôles et usages contemporains d'un objet culturel aborigène: le *Churinga*. In D. Guillaud, M. Seysset and A. Walter (eds), *Le Voyage inachevé – à Joël Bonnemaison,* pp. 669–674. Paris: ORSTOM.

Morgan, L. H. 1880. Prefatory note. In L. Fison and A. W. Howitt, *Kamilaroi and Kurnai,* pp. 2–20. Melbourne: George Robertson.

Morgan, L. H. 1964. *Ancient Society.* Cambridge, MA: The Belknap Press of Havard University Press.

Morphy, H. 1991. *Ancestral Connections: Art and an Aboriginal System of Knowledge.* Chicago: University of Chicago Press.

Morphy, H. 1996a. More than mere facts: repositioning Spencer and Gillen in the history of anthropology. In S. R. Morton and D. J. Mulvaney (eds), *Exploring Central Australia: Society, the Environment and the 1894 Horn*

Expedition, pp. 135–48. Chipping Norton: Surrey Beatty and Sons.

Morphy, H. 1996b. Empiricism to metaphysics: in defence of the concept of the Dreamtime. In T. Bonyhady and T. Griffiths (eds), *Prehistory to Politics: John Mulvaney, the Humanities and the Public Intellectual*, pp. 163–89. Melbourne: Melbourne University Press.

Morphy, H. 1998. *Aboriginal Art*. London: Phaidon.

Morwood, M. 1979. Art and stone: a prehistory of central western Queensland. Unpublished PhD thesis, Australian National University, Canberra.

Morwood, M. 1981. Archaeology of the Central Queensland Highlands: the stone component. *Archaeology in Oceania* 16 (1): 1–52.

Morwood, M. 1986. The archaeology of art: excavations at Maidenwell and Gatton shelters, southeast Queensland. *Queensland Archaeological Research* 3: 88–132.

Morwood, M. 1990. The prehistory of Aboriginal land use on the upper Flinders River, North Queensland Highlands. *Queensland Archaeological Research* 7: 3–40.

Morwood, M. 1992. Changing art in a changing landscape: a case study from the upper Flinders region of the North Queensland Highland. In J. McDonald and I. Haskovec (eds), *State of the Art: Regional Rock Art Studies in Australia and Melanesia*, pp. 60–70. Melbourne: Australian Rock Art Research Association.

Morwood, M. 1995a. Excavations at Giant Horse. In M. Morwood and D. R. Hobbs (eds), *Quinkan Prehistory: The Archaeology of Aboriginal Art in SE Cape York Peninsula, Australia. Tempus 3*, pp. 101–6. St Lucia: Anthropology Museum, University of Queensland.

Morwood, M. 1995b. Excavations at Red Bluff 1. In M. Morwood and D. R. Hobbs (eds), *Quinkan Prehistory: The Archaeology of Aboriginal Art in SE Cape York Peninsula, Australia. Tempus 3*, pp. 127–32. St Lucia: Anthropology Museum, University of Queensland.

Morwood, M. and Dagg, L. 1995. Excavations at Yam Camp. In M. Morwood and D. R. Hobbs (eds), *Quinkan Prehistory: The Archaeology of Aboriginal Art in SE Cape York Peninsula, Australia*, pp. 107–15. *Tempus 3*. St Lucia: Anthropology Museum, University of Queensland.

Morwood, M. and Hobbs, D. R. (eds) 1995. *Quinkan Prehistory: The Archaeology of Aboriginal Art in SE Cape York Peninsula, Australia. Tempus 3.* St Lucia: Anthropology Museum, University of Queensland.

Morwood, M., Hobbs, D. R. and Price, D. M. 1995. Excavations at Sandy Creek 1 and 2. In M. Morwood and D. R. Hobbs (eds), *Quinkan Prehistory: The Archaeology of Aboriginal Art in SE Cape York Peninsula, Australia. Tempus 3*, pp. 71–91. St Lucia: Anthropology Museum, University of Queensland.

Morwood, M. and Jung, S. 1995. Excavations at Magnificent Gallery. In M. Morwood and D. R. Hobbs (eds), *Quinkan Prehistory: The Archaeology of Aboriginal Art in SE Cape York Peninsula, Australia. Tempus 3*, pp. 93–100. St Lucia: Anthropology Museum, University of Queensland.

Morwood, M. and L'Oste-Brown, S. 1995a. Excavations at Hann River 1, central Cape York Peninsula. *Australian Archaeology* 40: 21–8.

Morwood, M. and L'Oste-Brown, S. 1995b. Excavations at Red Horse. In M. Morwood and D. R. Hobbs (eds), *Quinkan Prehistory: The Archaeology of Aboriginal Art in SE Cape York Peninsula, Australia. Tempus 3*, pp. 116–25. St Lucia: Anthropology Museum, University of Queensland.

Morwood, M. and L'Oste-Brown, S. 1995c. Chronological changes in stone artefact technology. In M. Morwood and D. R. Hobbs (eds), *Quinkan Prehistory: The Archaeology of Aboriginal Art in SE Cape York Peninsula, Australia. Tempus 3*, pp. 161–77. St Lucia: Anthropology Museum, University of Queensland.

Morwood, M. and Trezise, P. 1989. Edge-ground axes in Pleistocene Greater Australia: new evidence from southeast Cape York Peninsula. *Queensland Archaeological Research* 6: 77–90.

Mowaljarlai, D. and Malnic, J. 1993. *Yorro Yorro*. Broome: Magabala Books.

Muecke, S. 1992. *Textual Spaces: Aboriginality and Cultural Studies*. Kensington: University of NSW Press.

Mueller-Vollmer, K. (ed.) 1985. *The Hermeneutics Reader*. New York: Continuum.

Mulvaney, D. J. 1975. 'The chain of connection': the material evidence. In N. Peterson (ed.), *Tribes and Boundaries in Australia*, pp. 72–94. Canberra: AIAS.

Mulvaney, D. J. 1984. Foreword: archaeology in Queensland. *Queensland Archaeological Research* 1: 4–7.

Mulvaney, D. J. 1996. 'A splendid lot of fellows': achievements and consequences of the Horn Expedition. In S. R. Morton and D. J. Mulvaney (eds), *Exploring Central Australia: Society,* the Environment and the 1894 Horn Expedition, pp. 3–12. Chipping Norton: Surrey Beatty and Sons.

Mulvaney, D. J. and Joyce, E. B. 1965. Archaeological and geomorphological investigations on Mt. Moffat Station, Queensland, Australia. *Proceedings of the Prehistoric Society* 31: 147–212.

Mulvaney, D. J. and Kamminga, J. 1999. *Prehistory of Australia*. St Leonards: Allen and Unwin.

Murray, T. 2002. Epilogue: why the history of archaeology matters. *Antiquity* 76: 234–8.

Myers, F. 1986. *Pintupi Country, Pintupi Self: Sentiment, Place, and Politics among Western Desert Aborigines*. Canberra: Australian Institute of Aboriginal Studies.

Napton, L. K. and Greathouse, E. A. 1985. Archaeological investigations at Pine Gap (Kuyunba), Northern Territory. *Australian Archaeology* 20: 90–108.

Neal, R. and Stock, E. 1986. Pleistocene occupation in the southeast Queensland coast region. *Nature* 323: 618–21.

Nelson, E., Chaloupka, G., Chippindale, C., Alderson, M. S. and Southon, J. 1995. Radiocarbon dates for beeswax figures in the prehistoric rock art of northern Australia. *Archaeometry* 37 (1): 151–6.

O'Connell, J. F. 1977. Aspects of variation in central Australian lithic assemblages. In R. V. S. Wright (ed.), *Stone Tools as Cultural Markers*, pp. 267–81. Canberra: Australian Institute of Aboriginal Studies.

O'Connell, J. F. and Hawkes, K. 1981. Alyawara plant use and optimal foraging theory. In B. Winterhalder and E. A. Smith (eds), *Hunter-gatherer Foraging Strategies: Ethnographic and Archaeological Analyses*, pp. 99–125. Chicago: University of Chicago Press.

O'Connell, J. F., Latz, P. K. and Barrett, P. 1983. Traditional and modern plant use among the Alyawara of central Australia. *Economic Botany* 37: 80–109.

O'Connor, S. 1992. The timing and nature of prehistoric island use in northern Australia. *Archaeology in Oceania* 27 (2): 49–60.

O'Connor, S., Veth, P. and Hubbard, N. 1993. Changing interpretations of postglacial human subsistence and demography in Sahul. In M. A. Smith, M. Spriggs and B. Fankhauser (eds), *Sahul in Review*, pp. 95–105. Department of Prehistory, Research School of Pacific Studies, Canberra: Australian National University.

O'Connor, J. J. and Robertson, E. F. 1999.

Pythagoras of Samos. World Wide Web: http://www-history.mcs.st-and.ac.uk/history/Mathematicians/Pythagoras.html

Osborn, H. F. 1919. *Men of the Old Stone Age: Their Environment, Life and Art*. New York: Charles Scribner's Sons.

L'Oste-Brown, S. 1992. Getting organised: causes of stone artefact variability in southeast Cape York Peninsula. Unpublished BA Honours thesis, University of New England, Armidale.

Pearson, W. 1989. A technological analysis of stone artefacts from Yam Camp surface scatter and rockshelter, southeast Cape York. *Queensland Archaeological Research* 6: 91–102.

Peterson, N. 1972. Totemism yesterday: sentiment and local organization among the Australian Aborigines. *Man* 7: 12–32.

Poirier, S. 1993. 'Nomadic' rituals: networks of ritual exchange between women of the Australian Western Desert. *Man* (ns) 27: 757–76.

Relph, E. 1976. *Place and Placelessness*. London: Pion Limited.

Richards, F. 1926. Customs and language of the western Hodgkinson Aboriginals. *Memoirs of the Queensland Museum* 8 (3): 249–65.

Rick, J. W. 1987. Dates as data: an examination of the Peruvian Preceramic radiocarbon record. *American Antiquity* 52: 55–73.

Ricoeur. P. 1981. *Hermeneutics and the Human Sciences*. Cambridge: Cambridge University Press.

Roberts, M. J. and Roberts, A. 1975. *Dreamtime Heritage*. Adelaide; Rigby.

Roberts, R. G., Flannery, T. F., Ayliffe, L. K., Yoshida, H., Olley, J., Prideaux, G., Laslett, G., Baynes, A., Smith, M., Jones, R. and Smith, B. 2001a. New ages for the last Australian megafauna: continent-wide extinction about 46,000 years ago. *Science* 292: 1888–92.

Roberts, R. G., Flannery, T. F., Ayliffe, L. K., Yoshida, H., Olley, J., Prideaux, G., Laslett, G., Baynes, A., Smith, M., Jones, R. and Smith, B. 2001b. The last Australian megafauna. *Australasian Science* 22 (9): 40–1.

Roberts, R. G., Jones, R. and Smith, M. 1990. Thermoluminescence dating of a 50,000-year-old human occupation site in northern Australia. *Nature* 345: 153–6.

Robinson, R. 1966. *Aboriginal Myths and Legends*. Melbourne: Sun Books.

Róheim, G. 1945. *The Eternal Ones of the Dream*. New York: International University Press.

Romm, J. S. 1992. *The Edges of the Earth in Ancient Thought, Geography, Exploration, and Fiction*. Princeton: Princeton University Press.

Rose, D. B. 1992. *Dingo Makes Us Human*. Cambridge: Cambridge University Press.

Rosenfeld, A., Horton, D. and Winter, J. 1981. *Early Man in North Queensland. Terra Australis 6*. Canberra: Department of Prehistory, Research School of Pacific Studies, Australian National University.

Roth, H. L. 1899. *The Aborigines of Tasmania*. Halifax: F. King and Sons.

Roth, W. E. 1897. *Ethnological Studies among the North-West-Central Queensland Aborigines*. Brisbane: Government Printer.

Roth, W. E. 1903. *Superstition, Magic, and Medicine. North Queensland Ethnography Bulletin* 5. Government Printer, Brisbane.

Roth, W. E. 1910. North Queensland Ethnography 18: Social and individual nomenclature. *Records of the Australian Museum* 8 (1): 79–106.

Rowland, M. J. 1983. Aborigines and environment in Holocene Australia: changing paradigms. *Australian Aboriginal Studies* (2): 62–77.

Rowland, M. J. 1999. Holocene environmental variability: have its impacts been underestimated in Australian pre-History? *The Artefact* 22: 11–48.

Rowley, C. D. 1986. *The Destruction of Aboriginal Society*. Ringwood: Penguin.

Russell, L. in press. *Savage Imaginings: Historical and Contemporary Constructions of Aboriginalities*. Melbourne: Australian Scholarly Publications.

Russell L. and McNiven, I. 1998. Monumental colonialism: megaliths and the appropriation of Australia's Aboriginal past. *Journal of Material Culture* 3 (3): 283–301.

Said, E. 1978. *Orientalism*. New York: Pantheon.

Schechner, R. 1987. Victor Turner's last adventure. In V. Turner, *The Anthropology of Performance*, pp. 7–20. New York: PAJ Publications.

Schmidt, R. R. 1936. *The Dawn of the Human Mind*. London: Sidgwick and Jackson Ltd.

Sharp, R. L. 1939. Tribes and totemism in northeast Australia. *Oceania* 9: 254–75, 439–61.

Simpson, C. 1956. *Adam in Ochre: Inside Aboriginal Australia*. Sydney: Angus and Robertson.

Smith, M. A. 1985. A morphological comparison of central Australian seed-grinding implements and Australian Pleistocene-age grindstones. *The Beagle* 2 (1): 23–38.

Smith, M. A. 1986a. The antiquity of seedgrinding in arid Australia. *Archaeology in Oceania* 21: 29–39.

Smith, M. A. 1986b. An investigation of possible Pleistocene occupation at Lake Woods, Northern Territory. *Australian Archaeology* 22: 60–74.

Smith, M. A. 1986c. A revised chronology for Intirtekwerle (James Range East) Rockshelter, Central Australia. *The Beagle* 3: 123–30.

Smith, M. A. 1988 The pattern and timing of prehistoric settlement in central Australia. Unpublished PhD thesis, University of New England, Armidale.

Smith, M. A. 1989 Seed gathering in inland Australia: current evidence from seed-grinders on the antiquity of the ethnohistorical pattern of exploitation. In D. R. Harris and G. C. Hillman (eds), *Foraging and Farming: The Evolution of Plant Exploitation*, pp. 305–17. London: Unwin Hyman.

Smith, M. A. 1993. Biogeography, human ecology and prehistory in the sandridge deserts. *Australian Archaeology* 37: 35–50.

Smith, M. A. 1996. Prehistory and human ecology in central Australia: an archaeological perspective. In S. R. Morton and D. J. Mulvaney (eds), *Exploring Central Australia: Society, the Environment and the 1894 Horn Expedition*, pp. 61–73. Chipping Norton: Surrey Beatty and Sons.

Smith, M. A. and P. M. Clark. 1993. Radiocarbon dates for prehistoric occupation of the Simpson Desert. *Records of the South Australian Museum* 26 (2): 121–7.

Smith, M. A., Frankhauser, B. and Jercher, M. 1998. The changing provenance of red ochre at Puritjarra rock shelter, central Australia: late Pleistocene to present. *Proceedings of the Prehistoric Society* 64: 275–92.

Smith, M. A., Williams, E. and Wasson, R. J. 1991. The archaeology of the JSN site: some implications for the dynamics of human occupation in the Strzelecki desert during the late Pleistocene. *Records of the South Australian Museum* 25 (2): 175–92.

Smith, P. 1999. The elementary forms of place and their transformations: a Durkheimian model. *Qualitative Sociology* 22 (1): 13–36.

Smith, P. E. L. and Young, Jnr, T. C. 1972. The evolution of early agriculture and culture in greater Mesopotamia: a trial model. In B. Spooner (ed.), *Population Growth: Anthropological Implications*, pp. 1–59. Cambridge, MA: Massachussets Institute of Technology.

Sollas, W. J. 1911. *Ancient Hunters and Their Modern Representatives*. New York: The Macmillan Company.

Spencer, B. 1896. Through Larapinta Land: A Narrative of the Horn Expedition to Central Australia. In B. Spencer (ed.), *Report on the Work of the Horn Scientific Expedition to Central*

Australia, Part 1, pp. 1–136. Melbourne: Melville, Mullin and Slade.

Spencer, B. 1901. *Guide to the Australian Ethnological Collection in the National Museum of Victoria*. Melbourne: Government Printer.

Spencer, B. and Gillen, F. 1899. *The Native Tribes of Central Australia*. London: Macmillan.

Spencer, B. and Gillen, F. 1912. *Across Australia*. London: Macmillan.

Spencer, B. and Gillen., F. 1927. *The Arunta: A Study of a Stone Age People*. London: Macmillan.

Spinoza, B. 1991. *The Ethics: The Road to Inner Freedom*. New York: Citadel Press.

Stanford, M. 1998. *An Introduction to the Philosophy of History*. Oxford: Blackwell.

Stanner, W. E. H. 1961. On aboriginal religion IV: the design-plan of a rite-less myth. *Oceania* 31 (4): 233–58.

Stanner, W. E. H. 1963. On Aboriginal religion. *Oceania* 34 (1): 56–8.

Stanner, W. E. H. 1965a. Religion, totemism, symbolism. In R. M. Berndt and C. H. Berndt (eds), *Aboriginal Man in Australia*, pp. 207–37. Sydney: Angus and Robertson.

Stanner, W. E. H. 1965b. Aboriginal territorial organization: estate, range, domain and regime. *Oceania* 36: 1–26.

Stanner, W. E. H. 1987 [1956]. The Dreaming. In W. H. Edwards (ed.), *Traditional Aboriginal Society: A Reader*, pp. 225–36. South Yarra: Macmillan.

Stanner, W. E. H. 1989. *On Aboriginal Religion*. Oceania Monograph 36, Sydney: University of Sydney.

Stanner, W. E. H. 1998 [1976]. Some aspects of Aboriginal religion. In M. Charlesworth (ed.), *Religious Business: Essays on Australian Aboriginal Spirituality*, pp. 1–23. Cambridge: Cambridge University Press.

Stewart, P. J. 1994. Dreamings. In D. Horton (ed.), *The Encyclopaedia of Aboriginal Australia*, pp. 305–6. Canberra: Aboriginal Studies Press.

Stockton, E. D. 1971 Investigations at Santa Teresa, Central Australia. *Archaeology and Physical Anthropology in Oceania* 6: 44–61.

Strahan, R. (ed.) 1995. *The Mammals of Australia*. Port Melbourne: Reed Books.

Strang, V. 1997. *Uncommon Ground: Cultural Landscapes and Environmental Values*. Oxford: Berg.

Strehlow, T. G. H. 1971. *Songs of Central Australia*. Sydney: Angus and Robertson.

Stuiver, M. and Kra, R. S. (eds), 1986. Calibration issue: Proceedings of the 12th International ^{14}C Conference, *Radiocarbon* 28 (2B): 805–1030.

Suber, P. 1997. *The Great Chain of Being*. World Wide Web: http://www.earlham.edu/~peters/courses/re/chain.htm

Sullivan, H. 1977. Aboriginal gatherings in south-east Queensland. Unpublished BA Honours thesis, Australian National University, Canberra.

Sutton, P. 1991. Language in Aboriginal Australia: social dialects in a geographical idiom. In S. Romaine (ed.), *Language in Australia*, pp. 49–66. Cambridge: Cambridge University Press.

Swain, T. 1985. *Interpreting Aboriginal Religion: An Historical Account*. Bedford Park: Australian Association for the Study of Religions.

Swain, T. 1993. *A Place for Strangers: Towards a History of Australian Aboriginal Being*. Cambridge: Cambridge University Press.

Taçon, P. 1987. Internal-external: a re-evaluation of the X-ray concept in Western Arnhem Land rock art. *Rock Art Research* 4: 36–50.

Taçon, P. 1994. Socialising landscape: the long-term implications of signs, symbols and marks on the land. *Archaeology in Oceania* 29: 117–29.

Taçon, P. and Chippindale, C. 1998. An archaeology of rock-art through informed methods and formal methods. In C. Chippindale and P. S. C. Taçon (eds), *The Archaeology of Rock-Art*, pp. 1–10. Cambridge: Cambridge University Press.

Taçon, P., Wilson, M. and Chippindale, C. 1996. Birth of the Rainbow Serpent in Arnhem Land rock art and oral history. *Archaeology in Oceania* 31 (3): 103–24.

Tarnas, R. 1991. *The Passion of the Western Mind: Understanding the Ideas That Have Shaped Our World View*. New York: Ballantine Books.

Taylor, L. 1996. *Seeing the Inside: Bark Painting in Western Arnhem Land*. Oxford: Clarendon Press.

Thomas, J. 1993a. The politics of vision and the archaeologies of landscape. In B. Bender (ed.), *Landscape: Politics and Perspectives*, pp. 19–48. Oxford: Berg.

Thomas, J. 1993b. The hermeneutics of megalithic space. In C. Tilley (ed.), *Interpretative Archaeology*, pp. 73–97. Oxford: Berg.

Thomas, N. 1991. *Entangled Objects*. Cambridge: Cambridge University Press.

Thorley, P. B. 1998. Pleistocene settlement in the Australian arid zone: occupation of an inland riverine landscape in the central Australian ranges. *Antiquity* 72: 34–45.

Tilley, C. 1993. Art, architecture, landscape (Neolithic Sweden). In B. Bender (ed.), *Landscape: Politics and Perspectives*, pp. 49–84. Oxford:Berg.

Tindale, N. B. 1972. The Pitjandjara. In G. Bicchieri (ed.), *Hunters and Gatherers Today*, pp. 217–68. New York: Holt, Rinehart and Winston.

Tindale, N. B. 1974. *Aboriginal Tribes of Australia*. Berkeley, CA: University of California.

Trezise, P. 1969. *Quinkan Country*. Sydney: Reed.

Trezise, P. 1971. *Rock Art of Southeast Cape York*. Canberra: Australian Institute of Aboriginal Studies.

Trezise, P. 1993. *Dream Road: A Journey of Discovery*. St Leonards: Allen and Unwin.

Tunbridge, D. 1988. *Flinders Ranges Dreaming*. Canberra: Aboriginal Studies Press.

Turner, V. 1987. *The Anthropology of Performance*, pp. 7–20. New York: PAJ Publications.

Tylor, E. B. 1899. Preface. In H. L. Roth, *The Aborigines of Tasmania*, pp. v–ix. Halifax: F. King and Sons.

Ulm, S. and Hall, J. 1996. Radiocarbon and cultural chronologies in Southeast Queensland prehistory. *Tempus* 6: 45–62.

van Huet, S. 1999. The taphonomy of the Lancefield swamp megafaunal accumulation, Lancefield, Victoria. *Records of the Western Australian Museum* Supplement 57: 331–40.

Veit, W. F. 1991. In search of Carl Strehlow: Lutheran missionary and Australian anthropologist. In D. Walker and J. Tampke (eds), *From Berlin to the Burdekin: The German Contribution to the Development of Australian Science, Exploration and the Arts*, pp. 108–34. Kensington: New South Wales University Press.

Veit, W. F. 1994. Carl Strehlow, ethnologist: the Arunta and Aranda tribes in Australian ethnology. In T. R. Finlayson and G. L. McMullen (eds), *The Australian Experience of Germany*, pp. 77–100. Australian Association of von Humboldt Fellows, Adelaide: The Flinders University of South Australia.

Veit, W. F. 2001. Baldwin W. Spencer und Carl Strehlow, ein Anthropologe und ein Missionär in Zentral-Australien. In T. Keller and F. Raphaël (eds), *Interculturalité, couples, mise en scène: langue – littérature – société: biographies au pluriel*, pp. 15–34. Strasbourg: Presses Universitaires de Strasbourg.

Veth, P. M. 1993. *Islands in the Interior: The Dynamics of Prehistoric Adaptations within the Arid Zone of Australia*. International Monographs in Prehistory Archaeological Series 3. Ann Arbor, MI: University of Michigan Press.

Veth, P. M. and Walsh, F. J. 1988. The concept of 'staple' plant foods in the Western Desert region of Western Australia. *Australian Aboriginal Studies* (2): 19–25.

Vogel, J. C., Fuls, A., Visser, E. and Becker, B. 1993. Pretoria calibration curve for short-lived samples 1930–3350 BC. *Radiocarbon* 35: 73–85.

Wachterhauser, B. R. 1986a. Introduction: history and language in understanding. In B. R. Wachterhauser (ed.), *Hermeneutics and Modern Philosophy*, pp. 5–61. Albany, NY: State University of New York Press.

Wachterhauser, B. R. (ed.) 1986b. *Hermeneutics and Modern Philosophy*. Albany, NY: State University of New York Press.

Wagner, R. 1975. *The Invention of Culture*. Englewood Cliffs, NJ: Prentice-Hall.

Walsh, M. 1991. Overview of indigenous languages of Australia. In S. Romaine (ed.), *Language in Australia*, pp. 27–48. Cambridge: Cambridge University Press.

Walters, I. 1989. Intensified fishery production at Moreton Bay, southeast Queensland, in the late Holocene. *Antiquity* 63: 215–24.

Ward, G. K. and Wilson, S. R. 1978. Procedures for comparing and combining radiocarbon age determinations: a critique. *Archaeometry* 20: 19–31.

Warner, W. L. 1958. *A Black Civilization: A Social Study of an Australian Tribe*. New York: Harper.

Watchman, A. 1993. Evidence of a 25,000-year-old pictograph in northern Australia. *Geoarchaeology* 8: 465–73.

Watchman, A. and Campbell, J. 1996. Microstratigraphic analyses of laminated oxalate crusts in northern Australia. *Proceedings, 22nd International Symposium, The Oxalate Films in the Conservation of Works of Art*, pp. 409–422. Milan, March 1996.

Watchman, A. and Cole, N. 1993. Accelerator radiocarbon dating of plant-fibre binders in rock paintings from northeastern Australia. *Antiquity* 67: 355–8.

Watchman, A., David, B., McNiven, I. and Flood, J. 2000. Micro-archaeology of engraved and painted rock surface crusts at Yiwarlarlay (the Lightning Brothers site), Northern Territory, Australia. *Journal of Archaeological Science* 27: 315–25.

Watchman, A. and Hatte, E. 1996. A nano approach to the study of rock art: 'The Walkunders', Chillagoe, north Queensland, Australia. *Rock Art Research* 12 (2): 85–92.

Weber, M. 1958. *The Protestant Ethic and the Spirit of Capitalism*. New York: Scribner.

Weiner, J. F. 1991. *The Empty Place: Poetry, Space, and Being among the Foi of Papua New Guinea.* Bloomington, IN: Indiana University Press.

Weiner, J. F. 1995 *The Lost Drum: The Myth of Sexuality in Papua New Guinea and Beyond.* Madison, WI: University of Wisconsin Press.

White, C. and Peterson, N. 1969. Ethnographic interpretation of the prehistory of western Arnhem Land. *Southwestern Journal of Anthropology* 25: 45–67.

White, I. M. 1977. From camp to village: some problems of adaptation. In R. M. Berndt (ed.), *Aborigines and Change: Australia in the Seventies,* pp. 100–5. Canberra: Australian Institute of Aboriginal Studies.

Williams, E. 1988. *Complex Hunter-Gatherers: A Late Holocene Example from Temperate Australia.* Oxford: British Archaeological Reports. International Series 423.

Williams, N. 1986. *The Yolngu and Their Land.* Canberra: Australian Institute of Aboriginal Studies.

Wilson, S. R. and Ward, G. K. 1981. Evaluation and clustering of radiocarbon age determination: procedures and paradigms. *Archaeometry* 23: 19–39.

Wolf, E. R. 1997. *Europe and the People Without History.* Berkeley, CA: University of California Press.

Wolfe, P. 1991. On being woken up: the Dreamtime in anthropology and in Australian settler culture. *Comparative Studies in Society and History* 33: 197–224.

Wolfe, P. 1999. *Settler Colonialism and the Transformation of Anthropology: The Politics and Poetics of an Ethnographic Event.* London: Cassell.

Wright, R. V. S. 1971. Prehistory in the Cape York Peninsula. In D. J. Mulvaney and J. Golson (eds), *Aboriginal Man and Environment in Australia,* pp. 133–40. Canberra: Australian National University Press.

Wroe, S. and Field, J. 2001. Mystery of megafaunal extinctions remains. *Australasian Science* 22(8): 21–5.

Yengoyan, A. 1976. Structure, event and ecology in Aboriginal Australia: a comparative viewpoint. In N. Peterson (ed.), *Tribes and Boundaries in Australia,* pp. 121–32. Canberra: Australian Institute of Aboriginal Studies.

Index